Foundations of ITIL® V3

Licensed Product

Colophon

Title:	Foundations of ITIL® V3
Authors:	Jan van Bon (Managing Editor)
	Arjen de Jong (co-author, Inform-IT)
	Axel Kolthof (co-author, Inform-IT)
	Mike Pieper (co-author, Inform-IT)
	Ruby Tjassing (co-author, Inform-IT)
	Annelies van der Veen (co-author, Inform-IT)
	Tieneke Verheijen (co-author, Inform-IT)
Copy editor	Jayne Wilkinson, Van Haren Publishing
Publisher:	Van Haren Publishing, Zaltbommel, www.vanharen.net
Design & layout	CO2 Premedia bv, Amersfoort - NL
ISBN:	978 90 8753 057 0
Edition:	First edition, first impression, September 2007
	First edition, third impression with minor amendments, May 2008
	First edition, fourth impression, March 2009
	First edition, fifth impression with minor amendments, June 2010

Foreword

It is with great pride that I present this rigorous update of "Foundations of ITIL® V3". With the long-awaited update of ITIL®, launched in June 2007, this ITIL Foundations guide had to be completely reconfigured to suit its objective: provide an easy introduction to the broad library of ITIL core books, to support the understanding and the further distribution of ITIL as an industry standard. In addition we managed to be the first in the market, to provide this service to our members.

The main focus of this guide is on the Service Lifecycle, as defined by ITIL. The information on this lifecycle was taken from the extensive documentation of the core books, and was concentrated in Part 1. Separately, the information on all the processes and functions that were also described in the core books, was concentrated in Part 2 of this book. This approach enables readers to get a firm grasp of the lifecycle's structure, while also having all information on functions and processes at their disposal.

The book was produced with a broad team of expert editors, expert authors and expert reviewers who all contributed to a comprehensive text, and a lot of effort was spent on the development and review of the manuscript.

For several years, "Foundations of ITIL® V3" has been a core element in the important series of ITSM guides and we expect this new edition will continue to hold that position.

Jan van Bon
Managing Editor

Acknowledgements

This publication is the result of the cooperation of many experts from the field, in many different countries, representing users, providers, government, trainers, examiners, and itSMF chapters. It was based on an itSMF publication in the Netherlands, developed as an introduction to IT Service Management, first published in April 1999. The book was originally initiated by Georges Kemmerling (Quint Wellington Redwood), and built by a Dutch itSMF project team, under the guidance of chief editor Jan van Bon. Since 1999, this project team of reviewers and co-authors has extended and improved the book, in a series of new editions, expressing the developments in the field of IT Service Management.

In May 2002 the first translation was published, in English. This first global edition was soon followed by a second, improved version, audited by selected itSMF members, cooperating in the itSMF International Publications Committee (IPESC), each representing an itSMF chapter. In addition to that, the global edition was reviewed by several experts from vendor and user organizations, and by representatives of the OGC. This resulted in the very first internationally endorsed itSMF publication, supported by the entire itSMF community, and accepted as a high quality introduction to ITIL® and IT Service Management. The book provided excellent services as an aid in understanding the published best practices in the field of IT Service Management, concentrated in and around ITIL publications, in many countries.

Since 2002, several other translations appeared. Each of these translations was developed and audited by a team of experts in the targeted language region, if possible under the guidance of an itSMF chapter. In all cases, a terminology translation table was determined, before translating the text. Translations were delivered in English, German, French, Spanish, Russian, Chinese, Japanese, Italian, Korean, Brazilian-Portuguese, Arabic, and Danish.

In 2004, this title was split into two separate publications: one covering the broad field of IT Service Management (this was the "Introduction" title), the other concentrating on the core of that field as it was scoped for the basic level of understanding of ITIL (this was the "Foundation" title).

A team of expert authors and editors who work for itSMF produced the updated text (see the Colophon). As with many of our publications a broad Review Team was composed, representing experts from various disciplines, covering user organizations, training organizations, consultancy organizations, global leaders in the IT service industry, and individual experts. All of these experts were deeply involved with ITIL in their daily practice. Most of them had already been involved in the review of one or more of the core ITIL books, or were directly involved in the ITIL Refresh project. A third publication, a pocket guide on relevant IT Management frameworks was also derived from this large manuscript. This way, the reviewers in fact reviewed three publications in one manuscript.

The reviewers that reviewed the entire manuscript, thus covering this Foundations level introduction to ITIL, are the following:
- John van Beem, ISES International, Netherlands
- Aad Brinkman, Apreton, Netherlands
- Peter Brooks, PHMB Consulting, itSMF South Africa
- Rob van der Burg, Microsoft, Netherlands
- Judith Cremers, Getronics PinkRoccade Educational Services, Netherlands
- Robert Falkowitz, Concentric Circle Consulting, itSMF Switzerland
- Rosario Fondacaro, Quint Wellington Redwood, Italy
- Peter van Gijn, LogicaCMG, Netherlands
- Jan Heunks, ICT Partners, Netherlands
- Linh Ho, Compuware Corporation, USA
- Ton van der Hoogen, ToTZ Diensten, Netherlands
- Kevin Holland, NHS, UK
- Matiss Horodishtiano, Amdocs, itSMF Israel
- Wim Hoving, BHVB, Netherlands
- Brian Johnson, CA, USA
- Georges Kemmerling, Quint Wellington Redwood, Netherlands
- Kirstie Magowan, itSMF New Zealand
- Steve Mann, OpSys - SM2, itSMF Belgium
- Reiko Morita, Ability InterBusiness Solutions, Inc., Japan
- Jürgen Müller, Marval Benelux, Netherlands
- Ingrid Ouwerkerk, Getronics PinkRoccade Educational Services, Netherlands
- Ton Sleutjes, CapGemini, Netherlands
- Maxime Sottini, Innovative Consulting, itSMF Italy
- Takashi Yagi, Hitachi Ltd., itSMF Japan

Their contributions are highly appreciated and, due to their detailed review, have improved the quality of the book significantly.

Contents

Colophon..IV

Foreword V

Acknowledgements..VI

1   **Introduction**..1
     1.1   Background 1
     1.2   Why this book...2
     1.3   Organizations 2
     1.4   Differences with previous editions...4
     1.5   Structure of the book 4
     1.6   How to use this book..5

PART 1 THE ITIL SERVICE LIFECYCLE

2   **Introduction to the Service Lifecycle** 9
     2.1   Introduction to ITIL 9
     2.2   IT governance..10
     2.3   Organizational maturity 11
     2.4   Benefits and risks of ITSM frameworks 13
     2.5   Service Lifecycle: concept and overview 14

3   **Lifecycle Phase: Service Strategy** 21
     3.1   Introduction 21
     3.2   Basic concepts...24
     3.3   Processes and other activities 31
     3.4   Organization 44
     3.5   Methods, techniques and tools..51
     3.6   Implementation..56

4   **Lifecycle Phase: Service Design**..69
     4.1   Introduction 69
     4.2   Basic concepts...74
     4.3   Processes and other activities 77
     4.4   Organization 85
     4.5   Methods, techniques and tools..87
     4.6   Implementation..89

5   **Lifecycle Phase: Service Transition** 93
     5.1   Introduction 93
     5.2   Basic concepts...95
     5.3   Processes and other activities 96
     5.4   Organization 100

5.5 Methods, technology and tools 105
5.6 Implementation.. 105

6 Lifecycle Phase: Service Operation 109
6.1 Introduction 109
6.2 Basic concepts... 110
6.3 Processes and other activities.. 113
6.4 Organization 121
6.5 Methods, techniques and tools... 134
6.6 Implementation.. 135

7 Lifecycle Phase: Continual Service Improvement..................... 139
7.1 Introduction 139
7.2 Basic concepts... 140
7.3 Processes and other activities.. 146
7.4 Organization 148
7.5 Methods, techniques and tools... 152
7.6 Implementation.. 159

PART 2 FUNCTIONS AND PROCESSES

8 Introduction to Functions and Processes 171
8.1 Introduction 171
8.2 Management of processes 172
8.3 Teams, roles and positions in ITSM 175
8.4 Tools used in ITSM 176
8.5 Communication in IT service organizations.. 176
8.6 Culture 177
8.7 Processes, projects, programs and portfolios 177
8.8 Functions and processes in the lifecycle phases 179

9 Functions and Processes in Service Strategy 181
9.1 Financial Management 181
9.2 Service Portfolio Management (SPM) 187
9.3 Demand Management... 190

10 Functions and Processes in Service Design............................. 193
10.1 Service Catalogue Management.. 193
10.2 Service Level Management.. 197
10.3 Capacity Management 201
10.4 Availability Management 207
10.5 IT Service Continuity Management.. 215
10.6 Information Security Management 220
10.7 Supplier Management... 225

11 Functions and Processes in Service Transition..**229**
11.1 Transition Planning and Support...229
11.2 Change Management...233
11.3 Service Asset and Configuration Management 242
11.4 Release and Deployment Management..252
11.5 Service Validation and Testing...260
11.6 Evaluation 266
11.7 Knowledge Management 269

12 Functions and Processes in Service Operation.......................................**273**
12.1 Event Management 273
12.2 Incident Management 278
12.3 Request Fulfilment...284
12.4 Problem Management...287
12.5 Access Management...294
12.6 Monitoring and Control 297
12.7 IT Operations...302
12.8 Service Desk 304

13 Functions and Processes in Continual Service Improvement................**309**
13.1 CSI Improvement Process 309
13.2 Service Reporting...319

References 323
Glossary 325
Index...359

Chapter 1
Introduction

1.1   Background

Developments in IT have had a tremendous effect on the business market during the last decade. Since the appearance of extremely powerful hardware, highly versatile software and super-fast networks, all connected to each other worldwide, organizations have been able to develop their information-dependent products and services to a greater extent, and to bring them to the market much faster. These developments have marked the transition of the industrial age into the **information age**. In the information age, everything has become faster and more dynamic, and everything is connected.

Traditional hierarchical organizations often have difficulties in responding to this rapidly changing market, and this has led to current trends for organizations to become flatter and more flexible. The focus has shifted from vertical silos to horizontal **processes**, and decision-making powers are increasingly bestowed on the employees. It is against this background that the work processes of IT service management have arisen.

An important advantage of process-oriented organizations is that processes can be designed to support a **customer-oriented approach**. This has made the alignment between the IT organization (responsible for supplying information) and the customer (responsible for using these information systems in their business) increasingly significant. Over the last couple of years, this trend has attracted attention under the title of **Business-IT Alignment (BITA)**.

As organizations gained more experience with the **process-oriented approach** of IT service management, it became clear that the process must be managed coherently. Furthermore, it was obvious that the introduction of a process-oriented work method meant a big change for the primarily line and project-oriented organizations. Culture and change management proved to be crucial elements for a successful organizational design.

Another important lesson learned was that the IT organization must not lose itself in a process culture. Just like the one-sided project-oriented organization, a one-sided process-oriented organization was not the optimum type of business. Balance was, as always, the magic word. In addition, it became clear that the customer-oriented approach required that an **end-to-end** and **user-centric** approach must be followed: it was of no help to the user to know that 'the server was still in operation' if the information system was not available at the user's workplace. IT services must be viewed in a larger context. The need for the recognition of the **Service Lifecycle**, and the management of IT services in light of that lifecycle, became a concern.

Due to the fast growing dependency of business upon information, the quality of information services in companies is being increasingly subjected to stricter **internal and external requirements**. The role of **standards** is getting more and more important, and **frameworks** of 'best practices' help with the development of a management system to meet these requirements. Organizations that are not in control of their processes, will not be able to realize great results on the level of the Service Lifecycle and the end-to-end-management of those services. Organizations that do not have their internal organization in order, will also not achieve great results. For these reasons, all these aspects are handled alongside each other in the course of this book.

1.2   Why this book

This book offers detailed information for those who are responsible for strategic information issues, as well as for the (much larger) group who are responsible for setting up and executing the delivery of the information systems. This is supported by both the description of the Service Lifecycle, as documented in ITIL version 3, and by the description of the processes that are associated with it. The ITIL core books are very extensive, and can be used for a thorough study of contemporary best practices. This Foundations book provides the reader with an easy-to-read comprehensive introduction to the broad library of ITIL core books, to support the understanding and the further distribution of ITIL as an industry standard. Once this understanding of the structure of ITIL has been gained, the reader can use the core books for a more detailed understanding and guidance for their daily practice.

1.3   Organizations

Several organizations are involved in the maintenance of ITIL as a description of the 'best practice' in the IT service management field.

OGC

Initially ITIL was a product of the CCTA, a UK Government Organization. On 1 April 2001 the CCTA was incorporated into the OGC, which thus became the new owner of ITIL. The aim of the OGC is to help its clients (within the UK Government) with the modernization of their procurement activities and the improvement of their services, by, among other things, making the best possible use of IT: "OGC aims to modernize procurement in government, and deliver substantial value for money improvements". The OGC promotes the use of 'best practices' in numerous areas, such as project management, program management, procurement, risk management and IT service management. For this reason the OGC itself has published several series of books (Libraries) which have been written by (international) experts from different companies and organizations.

itSMF

The target group for this publication is anyone who is involved or interested in IT service management. A professional organization, working on the development of the IT service management field, has been created especially for this target group.

In 1991 the Information Technology Service Management Forum (itSMF), originally known as the Information Technology Infrastructure Management Forum (ITIMF), was set up as a UK association. In 1994, a sister-association was established in the Netherlands, following the UK example.

Since then, independent itSMF organizations have been set up in more than forty countries, spread across the globe, and the number of "chapters" continues to grow. All itSMF organizations operate under the umbrella organization, itSMF International (itSMF-I).

itSMF is aimed at the entire professional area of IT service management. It promotes the exchange of information and experiences that IT organizations can use to improve their service provision. itSMF is also involved in the use and quality of the various standards and methods that are important in the field. One of these standards is ITIL. itSMF International has an agreement with OGC and APM Group on the promotion of the use of ITIL.

> *The **IT Service Management Forum (itSMF)** is a global, independent, internationally recognized not-for-profit organization dedicated to IT Service Management. itSMF is wholly owned and principally run by its membership. It consists of a growing number of national chapters, each with a large degree of autonomy, but adhering to a common code of conduct*
> *The itSMF is a major influence on, and contributor to, industry best practices and standards worldwide, working in partnership with a wide, international range of governmental and standards bodies.*
> *itSMF International is the controlling body of the itSMF national chapters and sets policies and provides direction for furthering the overall objectives of itSMF, for the adoption of IT Service Management (ITSM) best practice and for ensuring adherence to itSMF policies and standards.*

This Foundations book is a publication of itSMF International, published in the ITSM Library series. The book fits in well with the mission of itSMF International:

> *The **mission of itSMF International** is to support the development of **IT Service Management (ITSM)** through strategic direction, coordination of effort and the sourcing of expertise and financial support with strategic partners.*

This mission can be translated into the following publishing activities:

> ***itSMF Publishing activities:***
> *- publishing supporting material on accepted best practice*
> *- publishing material that represents 'new thought' in the ITSM field*
> *- ensuring that, through all activities, including the publication of relevant material, itSMF assists organizations in the implementation of solutions that will deliver real value to them*

By publishing this detailed introduction to the field of IT service management, based on ITIL, itSMF International offers a valuable contribution to the development of the subject.

APM Group

In 2006, OGC contracted the management of ITIL rights, the certification of ITIL exams and accreditation of training organizations to the APM Group (APMG), a commercial organization. APMG defines the certification and accreditation for the ITIL exams, and published the new certification system (see 2.1: ITIL exams).

Examination institutes

The Dutch foundation Examen Instituut voor Informatica (EXIN) and the English Information Systems Examination Board (ISEB, part of the BCS: the British Computer Society) cooperated in the development and provision of certification for IT service management. For many years they were the only bodies that provided ITIL exams. With the contracting of APMG by OGC, the responsibility for ITIL exams is now with APMG. To support the world-wide delivery of these ITIL exams, APMG has accredited a number of examination institutes: CSME, DANSK IT, DF Certifiering AB, EXIN, ISEB, Loyalist Certification Services and TÜV SÜD Akademie. See www.itil-officialsite.com for recent information.

1.4   Differences with previous editions

The "Foundations of ITIL® V3 " book has played a key role in the distribution of ideas on IT service management and ITIL for years. The title has been translated into thirteen languages and is recognized as the most practical introduction to the leading 'best practices' in this field. Earlier editions of the Foundations book focused on the content of three books from the ITIL series (version 2): Service Support, Service Delivery and Security Management, and placed them in a broader context of quality management.

The main difference between ITIL version 2 and 3 lies in the service lifecycle, introduced in version 3. Where the Foundations scope of version 2 focused on single practices, clustered in Delivery, Support and Security Management, the scope in version 3 takes the entire Service Lifecycle into account.

As a result of continuous development of best practices, various terms have disappeared between the introduction of ITIL version 2 and 3, and a large number of new terms have been added to version 3. As many of these concepts are part of the scope of an IT service management training or exam, they have been included in the relevant descriptions. For a definitive list of concepts, readers should refer to the various training and exam programs.

1.5   Structure of the book

This book starts with an introduction on the backgrounds and general principles of IT service management and the context for ITIL (**Chapter 1**). It describes the parties involved in the development of best practices and standards for IT service management, and the basic premises and standards that are used.

The body of the book is set up in two large Parts: **Part 1** deals with the Service Lifecycle, **Part 2** deals with the individual functions and processes that are described in ITIL.

Part 1 starts with **Chapter 2**, introducing the Service Lifecycle, in the context of IT service management and IT Governance. It discusses principles of organizational maturity, and the benefits and risks of following a service management framework. This chapter ends with the introduction of the Service Lifecycle.

In **Chapters 3 to 7**, each of the phases in the Service Lifecycle is discussed in detail, in a standardized structure: Service Strategy, Service Design, Service Transition, Service Operation and Continual Service Improvement. These chapters provide a detailed view on the characteristics of the Service Lifecycle, its construct and its elements. The main points of each phase are presented in a consistent way to aid readability and clarity, so that the text is clear and its readability is promoted. Each section follows a consistent structure:
• Introduction
• Basic concepts
• Processes and other activities
• Organization
• Methods, techniques and tools
• Implementation

Part 2 starts with **Chapter 8**, introducing the functions and processes that are referred to in each of the lifecycle phases. This chapter provides general information on principles of processes, teams, roles, functions, positions, tools, and other elements of interest.

Next, the processes and functions are described in detail in **Chapters 9 to 13**. The 27 functions and processes are clustered according to the ITIL core book that contains their detailed description. Each of these processes and functions is described in terms of :
• Introduction
• Activities, methods and techniques
• Interfaces, inputs and outputs
• Metrics and Key Performance Indicators (KPIs)
• Implementation, with Critical Success Factors (CSFs), challenges, risks and traps

The **Appendices** provide useful sources for the reader. A reference list of used sources is provided, as well as the official ITIL Glossary. The book ends with an extensive Index of relevant terms that will support the reader in finding relevant text elements.

1.6 How to use this book

Readers who are primarily interested in the Service Lifecycle can focus on Part 1 of the book, and pick whatever they need on functions and processes from part 2.

Readers who are primarily interested in the functions and processes and are not ready for a lifecycle approach yet, or who prefer a process approach, can read the introductory chapters, and then focus on the functions and processes of their interest.

Readers who want a thorough introduction to ITIL, exploring its scope and main characteristics, can read Part 1 on the Lifecycle, and add as many of the functions and processes from Part 2 as they need or like.

In this way, this new edition of the Foundations book aims to provide support to a variety of approaches to IT Service Management based on ITIL.

PART 1
THE ITIL SERVICE LIFECYCLE

Chapter 2

Introduction to the Service Lifecycle

2.1 Introduction to ITIL

In the 1980s the quality of service provided by both internal and external IT companies to UK government departments was of such a level that the CCTA (Central Computer and Telecommunications Agency, now the Office of Government Commerce, OGC) was instructed by the Government to develop a standard approach for an efficient and effective delivery of IT services. This was to be an approach which was independent of the suppliers (whether internal or external). The result of this instruction was the development and publication of the Information Technology Infrastructure Library™ (ITIL). ITIL is made up of a collection of "best practices" found across the range of IT service providers.

ITIL offers a systematic approach to the delivery of quality of IT services. It gives a detailed description of most of the important processes in an IT organization, and includes checklists for tasks, procedures and responsibilities which can be used as a basis for tailoring to the needs of individual organizations.

At the same time, the broad coverage of ITIL also provides a helpful reference guide for many areas, which can be used to develop new improvement goals for an IT organization, enabling it to grow and mature.

Over the years, ITIL has become much more than a series of useful books about IT service management. The framework for the "best practice" in IT service management is promoted and further developed by advisors, trainers and suppliers of technologies or products. Since the nineties, ITIL represents not only the theoretical framework, but the approach and philosophy shared by the people who work with it in practice.

Being an extended framework of best practices for IT service management itself, the advantages and disadvantages of frameworks in general, described in Section 2.5, are also applicable to ITIL. Of course, ITIL was developed because of the advantages mentioned earlier. Many of the pointers from "best practices" are intended to avoid potential problems, or, should they occur after all, to solve them.

ITIL exams

In 2007 the APM Group launched a new qualification scheme for ITIL, based on ITIL version 3. ITIL version 2 will be maintained for a transition period. **ITIL version 2** has qualifications on three levels:
* **Foundation** Certificate in IT Service Management
* **Practitioner** Certificate in IT Service Management
* **Manager** Certificate in IT Service Management

Until 2000, some 60,000 ITIL certificates had been distributed and by 2006 the number had reached 500,000 certificates.

For **ITIL version 3** a new system of qualifications has been set up. There are four qualification levels:
* **Foundation Level**
* **Intermediate Level (Lifecycle Stream & Capability Stream)**
* **ITIL Expert**
* **ITIL Master**

For more information about the ITIL V3 Qualification Scheme, see http://www.itil-officialsite.com/Qualifications/ITILV3QualificationScheme.asp.

2.2   IT governance

With the growing role of information, information systems and IT service management, the management requirements for IT grew as well. These requirements focus on two aspects: the compliance with internal and external policies, laws and regulations, and the provision of added value to the stakeholders of the organization. IT governance is still a very young discipline, with no more than a few acknowledged standards or frameworks available. In contrast, there are many different definitions of IT governance available. A definition that receives a lot of support is the one by Van Grembergen:

> *IT governance consists of a comprehensive framework of structures, processes and relational mechanisms. Structures involve the existence of responsible functions such as IT executives and accounts, and a diversity of IT Committees. Processes refer to strategic IT decision-making and monitoring. Relational mechanisms include business/IT participation and partnerships, strategic dialogue and shared learning.*

There is a clear distinction between governance and management, suggesting that governance enables the creation of a setting in which others can manage their tasks effectively (Sohal & Fitzpatrick). So IT governance and IT management are two separate entities. IT service management can be considered to be part of the IT management domain, which leaves IT governance in the business or information management domain.

Although many frameworks are characterized as "IT Governance frameworks", such as COBIT and even ITIL, most of them are in fact management frameworks. There is at least one standard for

IT Governance available: the local Australian standard for Corporate governance of information and communication technology (AS8015-2005).

2.3   Organizational maturity

From the moment **Richard Nolan** introduced his "staged model" for the application of IT in organizations in 1973, many people have used stepwise improvement models. These models were quickly recognized as suitable instruments for quality improvement programs, thereby helping organizations to climb up the maturity ladder.

Dozens of variations on the theme can easily be found, ranging from trades such as software development, acquisition, systems engineering, software testing, website development, data warehousing and security engineering, to help desks and knowledge management. Obviously the *kaizen* principle (improvement works best in smaller steps) was one that appealed to many.

After Nolan's staged model in 1973, the most appealing application of this modeling was found when the Software Engineering Institute (SEI) of Carnegie Mellon University, USA, published its Software Capability Maturity Model (SW-CMM). The CMM was copied and applied in most of the cases mentioned above, making CMM something of a standard in maturity modeling. The CMM was later followed by newer editions, including CMMI (CMM Integration).

Later, these models were applied in quality management models, like the European Foundation for Quality Management (EFQM). Apart from the broad quality management models, there are several other industry accepted practices, such as Six Sigma and Total Quality Management (TQM) which are complementary to ITIL.

The available standards, and frameworks of best practice, offer guidance for organizations in achieving "operational excellence" in IT service management. Depending upon their stage of development, organizations tend to require different kinds of guidance.

Maturity model: CMMI

In the IT industry, the process maturity improvement process is best known in the context of the **Capability Maturity Model Integration (CMMI)**. This process improvement method was developed by the Software Engineering Institute (SEI) of Carnegie Mellon University. CMMI provides both a staged and a continuous model. In the continuous representation, improvement is measured using capability levels. Maturity is measured for a particular process across an organization. In the staged representation, improvement is measured using maturity levels, for a set of processes across an organization.

The capability levels in the **CMMI continuous representation** are:
1. **incomplete process** - a process that either is not performed or partially performed
2. **performed process** - satisfies the specific goals of the process area
3. **managed process** - a performed (capability level 1) process that has the basic infrastructure in place to support the process
4. **defined process** - a managed (capability level 2) process that is tailored from the organization's set of standard processes according to the organization's tailoring guidelines, and contributes

work products, measures and other process improvement information to the organizational process assets

5. **quantitatively Managed process** - a defined (capability level 3) process that is controlled using statistical and other quantitative techniques
6. **optimizing process** - a quantitatively managed (capability level 4) process that is improved based on an understanding of the common causes of variation inherent in the process

The **CMMI staged representation** model defines five maturity levels, each a layer in the base for the next phase in the ongoing process improvement, designated by the numbers 1 through 5:

- **initial** - processes are ad hoc and chaotic
- **managed** - the projects of the organization have ensured that processes are planned and executed in accordance with policy
- **defined** - processes are well characterized and understood, and are described in standards, procedures, tools and methods
- **quantitatively managed** - the organization and projects establish quantitative objectives for quality and process performance, and use them as criteria in managing processes
- **optimizing** - focuses on continually improving process performance through incremental and innovative process and technological improvements

Many other maturity models were based on these structures, such as the Gartner Maturity Models. Most of these models are focused at capability maturity. Some others, like KPMG's World Class IT Maturity Model, take a different approach.

Standard: ISO/IEC 20000

Developing and maintaining a quality system which complies with the requirements of the ISO 9000 (ISO-9000:2000) series can be considered a tool for the organization to reach and maintain the system-focused (or "managed" in IT Service CMM) level of maturity. These ISO standards emphasize the definition, description and design of processes. For IT service management organizations, a specific ISO standard was produced: the ISO/IEC 20000 (see Figure 2.1).

Customer maturity

When assessing the maturity of an organization, we cannot restrict ourselves to the service provider. The **level of maturity of the customer** (Figure 2.2) is also important. If there are large differences in maturity between the provider and the customer, then these will have to be considered to prevent a mismatch in the approach, methods and mutual expectations. Specifically, this affects the communication between the customer and the provider.

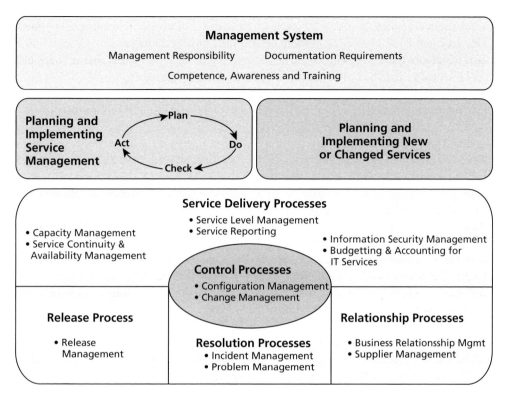

Figure 2.1   Overview of the ISO/IEC 20000 service management system

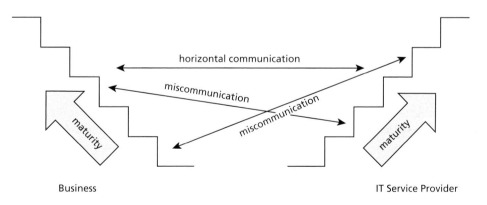

Figure 2.2 Communication and maturity levels: customer and provider

2.4   Benefits and risks of ITSM frameworks

The list below identifies some benefits and possible problems of using IT service management best practices. This list is not intended to be definitive, but is provided here as a basis for considering some of the benefits that can be achieved and some of the mistakes that can be made when using common process-based IT service management frameworks:

Benefits to the customer/user:
- The provision of IT services becomes more customer-focused and agreements about service quality improve the relationship.
- The services are described better, in customer language, and in more appropriate detail.
- Management of service quality, availability, reliability and service costs is improved.
- Communication with the IT organization is improved by agreeing on the points of contact.

Benefits to the IT organization:
- The IT organization develops a clearer structure, becomes more efficient, and is more focused on the corporate objectives.
- The IT organization is more in control of the infrastructure and services it has responsibility for, and changes become easier to manage.
- An effective process structure provides a framework for the effective outsourcing of elements of the IT services.
- Following best practices encourages a cultural change towards providing service, and supports the introduction of quality management systems based on the ISO 9000 series or on ISO/IEC 20000.
- Frameworks can provide coherent frames of reference for internal communication and communication with suppliers, and for the standardization and identification of procedures.

Potential problems/mistakes:
- The introduction can take a long time and require significant effort, and may require a change of culture in the organization; an overambitious introduction can lead to frustration because the objectives are never met.
- If process structures become an objective in themselves, the service quality may be adversely affected; in this scenario, unnecessary or over-engineered procedures are seen as bureaucratic obstacles, which are to be avoided where possible.
- There is no improvement in IT services due a fundamental lack of understanding about what the relevant processes should provide, what the appropriate performance indicators are, and how processes can be controlled.
- Improvement in the provision of services and cost reductions are insufficiently visible, because no baseline data was available for comparison and/or the wrong targets were identified.
- A successful implementation requires the involvement and commitment of personnel at all levels in the organization; leaving the development of the process structures to a specialist department may isolate that department in the organization and it may set a direction that is not accepted by other departments.
- If there is insufficient investment in appropriate training and support tools, justice will not be done to the processes and the service will not be improved; additional resources and personnel may be needed in the short term if the organization is already overloaded by routine IT service management activities which may not be using "best practices".

2.5   Service Lifecycle: concept and overview

The information provision role and system has grown and changed since the launch of ITIL version 2 (in 2000/02). IT supports and is part of an increasing number of goods and services. In the business world, the information provision role has changed as well: IT's role is no longer just supporting, but has become the baseline for the creation of business value.

ITIL version 3 intends to include and provide insight into IT's new role in all its complexity and dynamics. To that end, a new service management approach has been chosen that does not center around processes, but focuses on the Service Lifecycle.

Basic concepts

Before we describe the Service Lifecycle, we need to define some basic concepts.

Good practice

ITIL is presented as a good practice. This is an approach or method that has proven itself in practice. These good practices can be a solid backing for organizations that want to improve their IT services. In such cases, the best thing to do is to select a generic standard or method that is accessible to everyone, ITIL, CobiT, CMMI, PRINCE2® and ISO/IEC 20000, for example. One of the benefits of these freely accessible generic standards is that they can be applied to several real-life environments and situations. There is also ample training available for open standards. This makes it much easier to train staff.

Another source for good practice is proprietary knowledge. A disadvantage of this kind of knowledge is that it may be customized for the context and needs of a specific organization. Therefore, it may be difficult to adopt or replicate and it may not be as effective in use.

Service

A service is about creating value for the customer. ITIL defines a service as follows:

> *A **service** is a means of delivering value to customers by facilitating outcomes the customers want to achieve without the ownership of specific costs or risks.*

Outcomes are possible from the performance of tasks, and they are limited by a number of constraints. Services enhance performance and reduce the pressure of constraints. This increases the chances of the desired outcomes being realized.

Value

Value is the core of the service concept. From the customer's perspective value consists of two core components: utility and warranty. Utility is what the customer receives, and warranty is how it is provided. The concepts utility and warranty are described in the Section "Service Strategy".

Service management

ITIL defines service management as follows:

> *the form of services.*
>
> ***Service management** is a set of specialized organizational capabilities for providing value to customers in*

ITIL discusses some of the fundamental principles of service management that supplement the functions and processes in the ITIL core books. The next principles may help design a service management system:

• **Specialization & coordination** - The goal of service management is to make capabilities and resources available through services that are useful and acceptable to the customer with regard to quality, costs and risks. The service provider takes the weight of responsibility and resource management off the customer's shoulders so that they can focus on the business' core competence. Service management coordinates the business of service management responsibility with regard to certain resources. *Utility* and *warranty* act as a guide.

• **Agency principle** - Service management always involves an agent and a principal that seconds this agent to fulfill activities on their behalf. Agents may be consultants, advisors or service providers. Service agents act as intermediary between service providers and customers in conjunction with users. Usually, these agents are the service provider's staff, but they can also be self-service systems and processes for users. Value for the customer is created through agreements between principals and agents.

• **Encapsulation** - The customer's interest focuses on the value of use; he prefers to be spared from any technical details and structure complexity. The "encapsulation principle" is focused on hiding what the customer does not need and showing what is valuable and useful to the customer. Three principles are closely linked to this:
  – separation of concerns
  – modularity: a clear, modular structure
  – loose coupling: reciprocal independence of resources and users

Systems

ITIL describes the organizational structure concepts which proceed from system theory. The Service Lifecycle in ITIL version 3 is a system; however, a function, a process or an organization is a system as well. The definition of a system:

> *A **system** is a group of, interrelating, or interdependent components that form a unified whole, operating together for a common purpose.*

Feedback and learning are two key aspects in the performance of systems; they turn processes, functions and organizations into dynamic systems. Feedback can lead to learning and growth, not only within a process, but also within an organization in its entirety.

Within a process, for instance, the feedback about the performance of one cycle is, in its turn, input for the next process cycle. Within organizations, there can be feedback between processes, functions and lifecycle phases. Behind this feedback is the common goal: the customer's objectives.

Functions and processes

The distinction between functions and processes is important in ITIL.

What is a function?

> A **function** is a subdivision of an organization that is specialized in fulfilling a specified type of work, and is responsible for specific end results.
> Functions are independent subdivisions with capabilities and resources that are required for their performance and results. They have their own practices and their own knowledge body.

What is a process?

> A **process** is a structured set of activities designed to accomplish a defined objective.
> Processes result in a goal-oriented change, and utilize feedback for self-enhancing and self-corrective actions.

Processes possess the following characteristics:
- They are **measurable** because they are performance-oriented.
- They have **specific results**.
- They provide results to **customers** or stakeholders.
- They **respond to a specific event** - a process is indeed continual and iterative, but is always originating from a certain event.

It can be difficult to determine whether something is a function or a process. According to ITIL, whether it is a function or process depends completely on the organizational design. A good example of a function is a service desk, a good example of a process is change management.
A poor coordination between functions combined with an inward focus leads to the rise of functional silos. This does not benefit the success of the organization as a whole. Processes run through the hierarchical structure of functions; functions often share some processes. This is how processes suppress the rise of functional silos, and help to ensure an improved coordination in between functions.

The Service Lifecycle

ITIL version 3 approaches service management from the lifecycle of a service. The Service Lifecycle is an organization model providing insight into:
- the way service management is structured
- the way the various lifecycle components are linked to each other
- the impact that changes in one component will have on other components and on the entire lifecycle system

So ITIL version 3 focuses on the Service Lifecycle, and the way service management components are linked. The processes are also discussed (both the version 2 processes and some that are new to version 3) in the cycle phases. They describe how things change.

The Service Lifecycle consists of five phases. Each volume of the new ITIL books describes one of these phases:

- **Service Strategy** – the phase of defining the guidelines for creating business value and achieving and maintaining a strategic advantage
- **Service Design** – the phase of designing and developing appropriate IT services, including architecture, processes, policy and documents, in order to meet current and future business requirements
- **Service Transition** – the phase of planning and managing the realization of new and modified services according to customer specifications
- **Service Operation** – the phase of managing and fulfilling all activities required to provide and support services, in order to ensure value for the customer and the service provider
- **Continual Service Improvement** – the phase of continual improvement of the effectiveness and efficiency of IT services against business requirements

Service Strategy is the axis of the Service Lifecycle (Figure 2.3) that "runs" all other phases; it is the phase of policymaking and objectives. The phases Service Design, Service Transition and Service Operation implement this strategy, their continual theme is adjustment and change. The Continual Service Improvement phase stands for learning and improving, and embraces all cycle phases. This phase initiates improvement programs and projects, and prioritizes them based on the strategic objectives of the organization.

Figure 2.3   The Service Lifecycle (Based on OGC ITIL V3 material)

The Service Lifecycle is a combination of many perspectives on the reality of organizations. This offers more flexibility and control.

The dominant pattern in the Service Lifecycle is the succession of Service Strategy to Service Design, to Service Transition and to Service Operation, and then, through Continual Service Improvement, back to Service Strategy, and so on. The cycle encompasses, however, many patterns. Depending on tasks and responsibilities, a manager can choose his own control perspective. If you are responsible for the design, development or improvement of processes, the best perspective to use is a process perspective. If you are responsible for managing SLAs, contracts and services, the Service Lifecycle perspective and its various phases is likely to meet your needs better.

ITIL Library

The IT Infrastructure Library (ITIL) encompasses the following components:
- Core Library - the five Service Lifecycle publications:
  - Service Strategy
  - Service Design
  - Service Transition
  - Service Operation
  - Continual Service Improvement

Each book covers a phase from the Service Lifecycle and encompasses various processes. The processes are always described in detail in the book in which they find their key application.
- Complementary portfolio:
  - introduction guide
  - key element guides
  - qualification aids
  - white papers
  - glossary

Chapter 3
Lifecycle Phase: Service Strategy

3.1 Introduction

In this section, the axis of the lifecycle is introduced. Service Strategy delivers guidance with designing, developing and implementing service management as a strategic resource. The Service Strategy is critical in the context of the processes along the ITIL Service Lifecycle in the Service Design, Service Transition, Service Operation, and Continual Service Improvement (CSI) phases.

The Service Strategy gives a more extensive scope of the ITIL framework. Organizations that are already using ITIL can use this section as a guideline for developing a strategic overview of their ITIL-based capabilities. They can also try to improve the synchronization between IT and business strategies. First consider why something should be done before thinking about how it will be done. The why is more important for the client's business.

This section offers a number of guidelines that will help in setting customer- and market-oriented goals and expectations. A Service Strategy also helps in identifying, selecting and prioritizing opportunities. A clear Service Strategy helps to ensure that an organization is equipped to manage costs and risks within the service portfolios.

The following topics are covered: defining the strategy concept; service assets; service catalogues; implementation of the strategy through the Service Lifecycle; various types of service providers; financial management; service portfolio management; organizational development; and strategic risks.

What is strategy?

Strategy is a term that originated in the military world, where it is primarily defined as the distribution and application of military resources in order to meet the objectives of a plan. In service management the strategy also has to maintain the link between policies and tactics.

The goal of Service Strategy is to identify the competition and to compete with them by distinguishing oneself from the rest and by delivering superior performances. ITIL cites the following building blocks of well-performing service providers:
- **market focus** - know where and how to compete
- **distinctive capabilities** - create distinctive and profitable assets that the business appreciates
- **performance anatomy** - organizational standpoints that are measurable and feasible, such as viewing services as a strategic asset in which constant improvement is necessary

The four Ps of strategy

If a service provider really knows its service objectives and understands the distinguishing factors of its product, then it is ready to begin the Service Lifecycle. The Service Strategy constitutes the axis of the cycle. We can begin with what we call the four Ps (based on Mintzberg, 1994); strategy is perspective, position, plan and pattern:
- **perspective** - have a clear vision and focus
- **position** - take a clearly defined stance
- **plan** - form a precise notion of how the organization should develop itself
- **pattern** - maintain consistency in decisions and actions

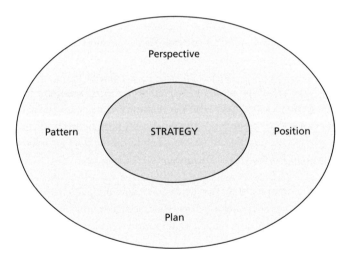

Figure 3.1   The four Ps of strategy, based on Henry Mintzberg

Perspective

Strategy is *perspective* because it provides the vision and focus of an organization. It determines the distinguishing characteristics of the service provider and its interactions with the customer.

> Strategy as **perspective** defines the convictions, values and goals that govern the behavior of the entire organization. A strategic perspective determines the direction through which the service provider can achieve its objectives.

Pose the following questions as a way of testing the perspectives:
* Are they clear and memorable?
* Are they suitable for promoting and conducting activities?
* Do they establish the boundaries within which people are free to experiment?

Position

Strategy is *position* because it provides the decisions that ensure that the services will be offered in a specific market. It is essential that a service provider be conscious of its position in the marketplace.

> *Strategy as **position** defines the distinguishing characteristics of the service provider in the eyes of the customer.*

Several positions are possible:
* positioning based on **variety** - a limited catalogue of services, but with such depth that diverse customers with similar needs can be adequately served
* positioning based on **needs** - a broad catalogue of services that delivers most of the services to a specific type of customer
* positioning based on **access** - ability to deliver services to customers with specific needs, such as location, scale or structures

Pose the following questions to test the organization's position:
* Does the organization help managers test the suitability of a specific procedure?
* Does the organization set clear boundaries within which personnel may or may not operate?
* Is there a degree of freedom for experimenting within these constraints?

Plan

Strategy is a *plan* because it prescribes how an organization handles a development.

> *Strategy as **plan** focuses on the organization's action plan in a competitive market. Service management is a coordinated set of plans through which service providers plan and implement service strategies.*

Pattern

Strategy is a *pattern* because it lays out the activities within the allotted timeframe.

> *Strategy as **pattern** represents an organization's procedures. As a consequence of the perspective, position, and plan of the strategy, characteristic patterns are created that lead to recurring successes.*

Mission and objectives

Specialization and coordination are necessary in the lifecycle approach. Feedback and monitoring during the various processes of the cycle makes this possible.

The dominant pattern in the cycle is the succession of Service Strategy to Service Design, to Service Transition, to Service Operation and back again to Service Strategy via CSI.

Service Strategy assists organizations to think and do business in a strategic manner. The implementation of the strategy takes place through the use of strategic assets.

Finally, a multidisciplinary approach is necessary in order to answer questions such as:
- What kind of services must we offer, and to whom?
- How do we stand out above the competition?
- How can we justify strategic investments?
- How can we actually create value for the customer and our stakeholders?
- How can we efficiently allocate resources in a service portfolio?
- How can we use financial management to ensure insight and control over value creation?

To survive, organizations must understand how they create value for themselves and for the customer. The mission of the Service Strategy phase is to develop the capacity to achieve and maintain a strategic advantage. The associated objectives are:
- defining strategic objectives
- determining the direction for growth opportunities
- setting investment priorities
- defining outcomes, learning about effectiveness
- creating strategic assets
- identifying the competition
- surpassing the competition by delivering distinctive performances
- devising plans that will ensure dominance over the competition now and in the future

The development and application of the Service Strategy requires constant revision, just as in all other components of the cycle. If the strategy is effective, then the efforts that are expended in all of the other phases of the lifecycle will be successful.

3.2   Basic concepts

Utility and warranty
Value is not only discernable in the customer's business outcomes, but is also, to a large extent, dependent on the customer's perception. This refers to the difference between economic value and economic perception. Perception depends on the customer's self-image, the value attributes, and personal experience. It is important to remember that the definition and differentiation of value are mainly in the mind of the customer. Economic value does not have to correspond automatically with the economic perceptions of the customer.

ITIL version 3 uses two important concepts for the value of a service. For customers, the positive effect is the "utility" of a service; the insurance of this positive effect is the "warranty". The **service value** is a combination of utility and warranty, defined by ITIL as:
- **Utility** - *fitness for purpose*. The attributes of the service that have a positive effect on the performance of activities, objects, and tasks with a specific result. Utility stands for the increase of a possible profit.
- **Warranty** - *fitness for use*. Availability and reliability in continuity and security. Warranty stands for the decline in possible losses.

The utility is what the customer receives, and the warranty affirms how it will be delivered. It is advisable to view these two aspects separately in order to arrive at the best possible design and development. See Figure 3.2 for the combined steps towards value creation.

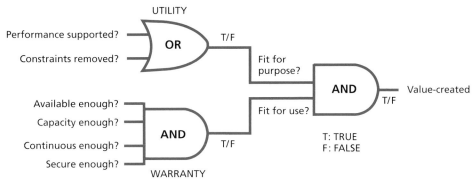

Figure 3.2   Combining utility and warranty for value creation (Source: Service Strategy was produced by OGC)

Communicating utility and warranty

The utility of a service is communicated through the support of certain results or by preventing certain risks and costs. Customers are very eager to outsource the management of assets that remove financial resources in their core assets. They also want to prevent a shortage in capacity.

Customers are unable to use services that are not suitable for use. Warranty guarantees the utility of a service by ensuring that it is available and that it offers sufficient capacity, continuity and security:

- **Availability** - Availability is the most fundamental aspect in the delivery of services to a customer. It offers the customer the assurance that the services are available according to the agreed terms and conditions.
- **Capacity** - Without the effective monitoring of capacity issues, service providers are not in a position to offer the utility of most services.
- **Continuity** - Continuity ensures that the service supports the business even during times of great difficulty or other disasters.
- **Security** - Security assures the customers that they can make use of the service safely and securely.

Value creation is a combination of the effects of utility and warranty. Both are necessary for the creation of value for the customer. See Figure 3.3 for the effect that the combination of utility and warranty has on the customer's assets.

Service structures

The value creation process is complex to such an extent that traditional service models are inadequate. Rather than concentrating on a fixed chronology of activities in a chain, the focus during the Service Strategy phase must be placed on the value creation system itself. Service management stands for patterns of cooperation.

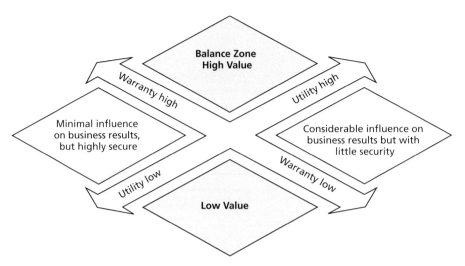

Figure 3.3   Effect of utility and warranty on customer assets

ITIL defines the value network as follows:

> A **value network** is a web of relationships that generates tangible and intangible value through complex and dynamic exchanges through two or more organizations.

The following questions play a role in the construction of a service model:
- Who are the participants in the service?
- What are the patterns in exchanges and transactions?
- What is the impact or what are the products to be delivered from each transaction and each participant?
- What is the best way to generate value?

Service assets

Resources and capabilities
Resources and capabilities are types of assets. Organizations use them to create value in the form of goods and services. Resources comprise the direct input for production. Management, organization, people and knowledge convert resources into value. Capabilities represent the capacity of an organization to coordinate, manage and apply resources in order to produce value.

Resources are often based on experiences; they are knowledge-intensive, based on information, and deeply imbedded in the people, systems, processes and technologies of an organization. It is relatively easy to acquire resources compared to capabilities.

Capabilities develop over the years. The development of distinctive capabilities is stimulated by broadening and deepening of experiences acquired through the number and variety of customer, markets, contracts and services. Experience is gained through problem-solving, handling situations, managing risks and analyzing mistakes. Service providers must develop distinctive capabilities in order to retain customers with services that are difficult to duplicate by the competition. Service providers must also invest substantially in education and training if they are to continue to develop their strategic assets.

Capabilities alone cannot produce value without adequate and appropriate resources. The productive capacity of a service provider depends on the availability of resources. Capabilities are used to develop, implement and coordinate the productive capacity.

Asset types
Together resources and capabilities form the basis for the value of a service (see Figure 3.4).

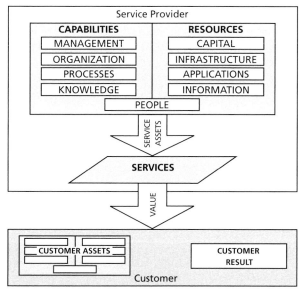

Figure 3.4   Resources and capabilities are the basis for value creation

Below is a list of descriptions of asset types:
- **Management** - Management is a system that includes leadership, administration, policy, performance, regulations and incentives; this layer cultivates, coordinates and oversees other asset types
- **Organization** - Organizational assets are active configurations of people, processes, applications and infrastructures that implement all organizational activities; this layer includes the functional hierarchies, social networks of groups, teams and individuals, and all of the systems that they use for working together towards collective goals.
- **Process** - Process assets consist of algorithms, methods, procedures and routines that drive the implementation and management of activities and interactions.
- **Knowledge** - Knowledge assets are accumulations of realization, experience, information, insight and intellectual property that are associated with specific activities and contexts.
- **People** - People as assets represent the capacity for creativity, analysis, perception, education, assessment, leadership, communication, coordination, empathy and trust.

- **Information** - Information assets are collections, patterns and meaningful abstractions of data that are applied in the context of customers, contracts, services, events, projects and production.
- **Applications** - Application assets are greatly varied in type and include artefacts, automation and tools for supporting the performance of other asset types; applications derive their value from their relationships with other assets.
- **Infrastructure** - Infrastructure assets exist in the form of layers that are defined by their relationships with other assets that they support (people and applications, in particular).
- **Financial capital** - Financial assets are necessary in order to support the ownership or use of all types of assets.

Type of service provider

ITIL distinguishes between the various types of service providers. Although most aspects of service management apply to all types, there are also aspects, such as customers, contracts, competition, markets and incomes, which are different for each type.

ITIL defines the following three archetypes:
type I - internal service provider
type II - Shared Services Unit
type III - external service provider

Type I - Internal service provider

Type I providers are providers who deliver their services within their own business units.

Type I providers (Figure 3.5) are found in organizations where IT, R&D, marketing or manufacturing determine the competitive position of the organization, for which a high degree of control is necessary.

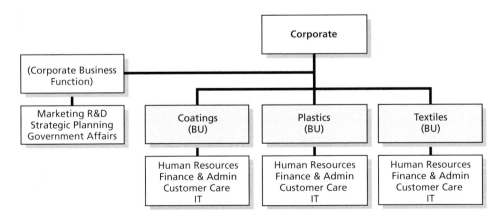

Figure 3.5   Type I providers (Source: Service Strategy was produced by OGC)

Advantages of this type:
- **short lines of communication** - close contact with the customer through which certain costs and risks can be avoided
- **customer-oriented** - specialized in a limited set of business needs, which makes it possible to be very customer-oriented
- **limited decision rights** - decision rights by the manager of the business unit

Disadvantages:
- **limited opportunities for growth** - growth is tied to the growth of the business unit

Competition:
- **open market** - providers outside the business unit

Objective:
- **value contribution** - the attainment of functional excellence and return for the business unit to which they belong

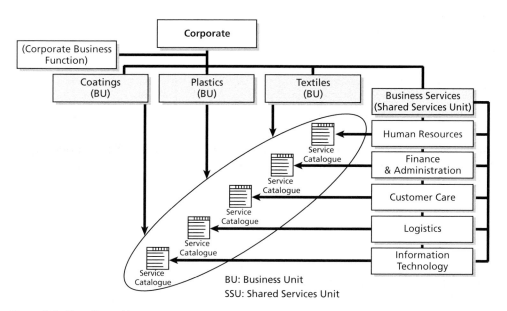

Figure 3.6   Type II provider (Source: Service Strategy was produced by OGC)

Type II - Shared Services Unit (SSU)
Functions such as finance, IT, human resources and logistics are not always at the core of an organization's competitive advantage, and need not be maintained at the corporate level. The services of such shared functions are often consolidated into an autonomous unit called a shared services unit.

Type II providers deliver services to Business Units that operate under the same collective strategy.

The advantages of a Shared Service Unit are (See Figure 3.6):
- **lower prices** - compared with external service providers, through collective benefits, internal agreements and internal bookkeeping
- **broader decision-making authority** - decisions can be made outside the business unit
- **possibility for standardization** - the possibility of the development of a standard, which could be used by various business units
- **competitive position** - possibility of challenging the competition

Disadvantages:
- **replaceable** - customers can compare the provider with external service providers

Objective:
- keep up with the industry's best practice, cultivate the market, formulate business strategies, strive for operational effectiveness and develop distinctive capabilities

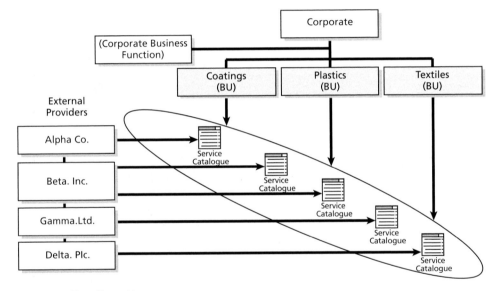

Figure 3.7   Type III provider (Source: Service Strategy was produced by OGC)

Type III - External service provider

> ***Type III providers*** *deliver services to customers in competing business environments that need flexible structures.*

Customers come from various places. Competing customers have access to the same assets with the Type III service provider (see Figure 3.7).

Advantages of this type:
- **more flexibility** - more freedom to exploit more opportunities
- **competitive prices** - more opportunities to vary prices
- **minimizing of system risks** - spreading risks over a larger network

Disadvantages:
- greater risks for the customers
- extra costs

Objective:
- to offer customers flexibility and external knowledge, experience, scale, scope, capabilities and resources

Customers consider the following issues when choosing or changing a certain type of service provider (see Figure 3.8):
- Transaction costs:
  - the total costs of a service provider
  - should we keep the activities in-house (aggregation)?
  - should we outsource (disaggregation)?
- strategic factors
- core competencies
- risk management capabilities

From/To	Type I	Type II	Type III
Type I	Functional reorganization	Disaggregation	Outsourcing
Type II	Aggregation	Corporate reorganization	Outsourcing
Type III	Insourcing	Insourcing	Value net reconfiguration

Figure 3.8   Customer's choice of type of service provider (Source: Service Strategy was produced by OGC)

3.3   Processes and other activities

Activities
The following sections deal with the four most important activities of the Service Strategy process as defined by ITIL (see Figure 3.9):
1. defining the market
   a. understanding the customer
   b. understanding the opportunities
   c. classifying and visualizing the services

2. the development of the offer
3. the development of strategic assets
4. preparation for implementation

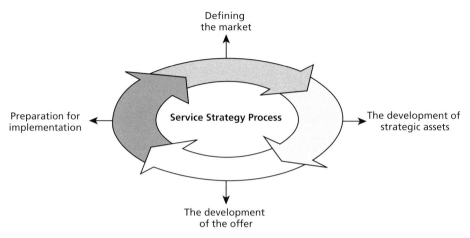

Figure 3.9   The activities of the Service Strategy process

Defining the market

In the context of service management, organizations are interested in strategy from two different but connected perspectives. There are strategies for services and there are services for strategies. From the one perspective, strategies are developed for the services that will be offered. From the other perspective, service management is set forth as a competency for a specific business strategy.

Understanding the customer

For service management professionals it is essential to know the performance of the customer's assets. Without an insight into these assets there is no basis on which to determine the value of a service.

Understanding the opportunities

Customers' unsupported objectives can present an opportunity in which services can be developed that could be offered as a solution to the customer's problem.

In a changing business there are new opportunities. The CMS (Configuration Management System) can make the mapping of customer results into services and service assets a viable option.

Having an insight into the customer's business and being familiar with their objectives are essential factors in the development of a strong business relationship with the customer. Business Relation Managers (BRM) are responsible for this. They are closely involved with the customer and manage the opportunities through the use of a Customer Portfolio. BRMs work closely with Product Managers who are responsible for the development and management of services through the lifecycle. Product Managers focus on the products and maintain contact with the business via a service portfolio.

Classifying and visualizing services

Services vary primarily in how and in what context they create value. Service archetypes serve as the business models for services. They define how service providers behave on behalf of their customers. Customer assets are the context in which value is created because they are the link with the business outcomes that the customer wants.

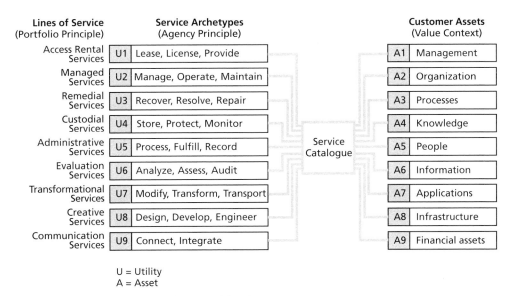

Figure 3.10   Service provider business model and customer assets (Source: Service Strategy was produced by OGC)

Depending on a variety of factors, the customer owns various kinds of assets. A combination of a service archetype and a customer asset (see Ux-Ay in Figure 3.10, and Figure 3.11) represents an item in the service catalogue. Various services can be associated with the same archetype.

The same archetype can be used to service a variety of customer assets under a utility-based Service Strategy. This is a variation of needs-based and access-based positioning. The strategy of the service provider determines the contents of the service catalogue.

Service Strategy results in a specific collection of patterns (intended strategy) or a collection of patterns can make a specific Service Strategy attractive (emergent strategy). This visual method is useful in the communication and coordination between the functions and processes of service management. The right synchronization between the value-creating context (customer assets) and the value-creating concepts (service archetype) helps prevent inadequacies in performance.

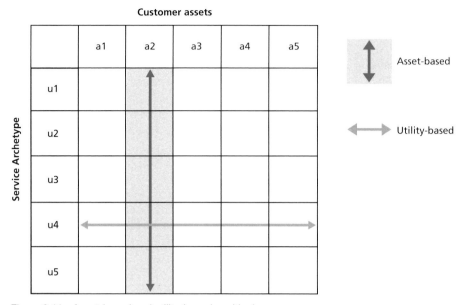

Figure 3.11   Asset-based and utility-based positioning (Source: Service Strategy was produced by OGC)

Developing the offer

The consumers' market
The opportunity for supporting business outcomes with services defines the market. Every market represents a series of opportunities for service providers to serve a customer with one or more services.

Results-oriented definition of services
A results-oriented definition of services ensures that managers view all aspects of service management from the customer's perspective. Services are a way of providing value to customers by facilitating customers' results without having to incur costs and take risks themselves. Well formulated service definitions lead to effective and efficient service management processes.

To ensure that your service definitions are sound, pose the following questions:
• What kind of services do we deliver? (service type)
• Who are our customers? (service type)
• What kinds of results do we support? (utility)
• How do the results create value for the customers of our customers? (utility)
• What constraints do our customers encounter? (utility)

It is impossible to produce value without a complete definition of value.

Service portfolio, pipeline, and catalogue
The service portfolio represents the agreements and investments that the service provider makes with all customers and markets: contractual obligations, service development, Continual Service Improvement (CSI) and third line services (visible or invisible to customers).

The service portfolio also represents all of the resources that are active in the various phases of the Service Lifecycle. An important governance aspect of service portfolio Management (SPM) is that every phase needs resources in order to conclude projects, initiatives and contracts. See the Section on "Processes and activities" for a brief explanation of SPM, or Chapter 9 for a detailed description of SPM and SPM methods.

Summary:

> *The **service portfolio** represents the opportunities and readiness of a service provider to serve the customers and the market. The service portfolio can be divided into three subsets of services:*
> *- the service catalogue*
> *- the service pipeline*
> *- retired services*

The following sections explain the individual components of the service portfolio.

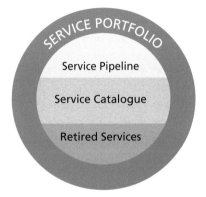

Figure 3.12   The service portfolio

The service catalogue is the expression of the operational capacity of the provider within the context of a customer or market outlet.

The **service catalogue** has two aspects: the business service catalogue and the technical service catalogue (see Chapter 9 for more details). The business service catalogue portion is defined as the mapping of critical business processes to the underlying IT services, and keeping the details of the relationships between those components, supporting the customer view of the service catalogue. The technical service catalogue is the aspect of the service portfolio that is not visible to the customer, containing details on the technical composition of services, supporting the service provider's view of the service catalogue.

The service catalogue consists of services that are active in the Service Operation phase and those approved to be offered. The service catalogue divides services into components. It communicates the policy, guidelines and accountability, and includes prices, service level agreements, and conditions for delivery.

The service catalogue describes the part of the portfolio in which costs are recovered or profits are earned. The service catalogue also serves as the visualization tool for SPM decisions. The issue of services and the capacity to perform them satisfactorily is also raised in the catalogue. Customer assets and business outcomes trigger questions about the expectations of utility and warranty. If there are items in the catalogue pertaining to whether these expectations can be met, it will result in a service contract or agreement. Catalogue items are clustered in Lines of Service (LOS) based on commonly recurring patterns of business activities (see Figure 3.13).

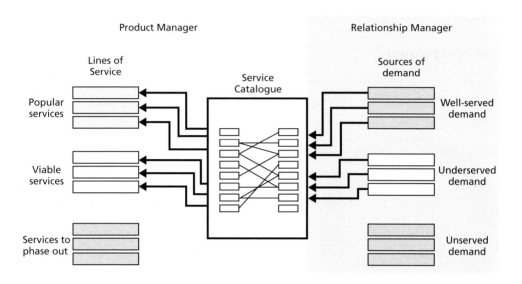

Figure 3.13   Service catalogue, product managers, lines of service, and demand management (Source: Service Strategy was produced by OGC)

The approval of the Service Transition is necessary in adding or deleting services from the catalogue for the following reasons:
• If an item is to be added to the catalogue, it must be available if a customer requests it. Due diligence is necessary for ascertaining the comprehensiveness of and support for a proposed service.
• Items in the service catalogue are mainly in the Service Operation phase, with the related contractual obligations to the customer. An evaluation of all changes to the catalogue will be performed to ascertain that all of the necessary obligations have been satisfied.
• The addition of items to the catalogue requires that capabilities and resources be available in order to satisfy a customer's specific request.

The service catalogue is an essential strategy tool because it can be viewed as the virtual projection of the actual and available capabilities of the service provider. Many customers are only interested in what the provider can attest to at this particular moment.

The **service pipeline** consists of services that are still in development for a specific market or customer. These services are to be applied to the operational phase via Service Transition after the finishing of a design-, development-, and test phase. The pipeline represents the growth and strategic anticipation for the future. It says something about the general health of a provider and indicates how new concepts and improvement ideas are nourished through Service Strategy, Service Design, and CSI. Good financial management is necessary in order to finance the pipeline.

Some services in the catalogue are **retired services**, meaning that they have been phased out or withdrawn. The out-phasing of services is a component of Service Transition and occurs in order to guarantee that all agreements with customers will be kept and that the phased out service assets no longer have any contractual obligations.

Developing strategic assets

Service providers must regard service management as a strategic asset. Service management begins with the capabilities that coordinate and manage resources in order to support a catalogue of services. Capabilities and resources strengthen each other and are modified until the goal of attaining a higher service level is achieved.

Service management as a closed-loop control system

Service management is the capability of an organization to deliver services to customers. Services can improve the performance of customer assets. Improvements in Service Design, Service Transition, and Service Operation enhance the customer performance potential and reduce the risks for the customer.

Services stem from service assets. Service potential is converted into performance potential of customer assets. Enhancing the performance potential often stimulates the request for additional demand for service in terms of scale or scope. This request translates into more use of the service assets and justifies the retention of maintenance activities and upgrades. From this perspective, service management is a closed-loop control system with the following functions:
• developing and maintaining service assets
• understanding the performance potential of customer assets
• mapping of service assets to customer assets through services
• designing, developing and adapting services

Service management as a strategic asset

For service management to be developed as a strategic asset, the value network, within which the service provider operates, must first be identified. This network could exist within only one organization, as is often the case for Type I and Type II providers. More often the value network extends outside the organization's boundaries and includes external customers, providers, and partners.

Strategic assets are dynamic in nature and are expected to continue to perform under changing business conditions and organizational objectives. That makes it necessary for strategic assets to have an instructional capacity. Service management must keep an eye on the interaction between customer assets and service assets (see Figure 3.14).

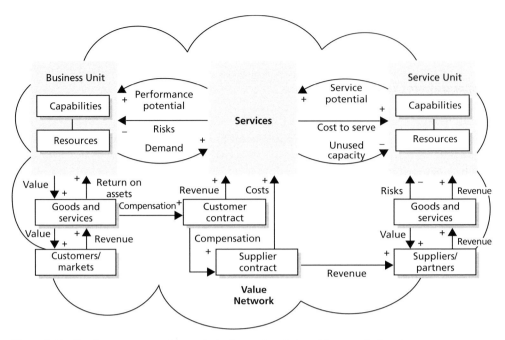

Figure 3.14   Service management as a strategic asset and closed-loop control system (Source: Service Strategy was produced by OGC)

Increasing the service potential

The service assets of a service provider represent the service potential that is available to customers. One of the core objectives of service management is the improvement of the service potential of the capabilities and resources.

> Example: training of personnel increases the service potential as a result of the capability improvement that takes place. This capability improvement is demonstrated in the following aspects:
> • The personnel have more knowledge for monitoring and analyzing the lifecycle.
> • Resources are improved because personnel are added to the core competencies, and the availability hours of the helpdesk are extended.

Increasing the performance potential

The services of a service provider represent the potential for improving the performance of customer assets. Visualize and define the performance potential of services so that all decisions are focused on the creation of value for the customer.

ITIL poses a number of core questions:
• What is our market?
• What does the market want?
• Do we have something unique to offer to the market?
• Do we have the right portfolio for a specific market?
• Do we have the right catalogue for a specific customer?

- Is every service designed so that it leads to the desired result?
- Is the implementation of every service such that it leads to the desired result?
- Do we have the right models and structures to be a service provider?

Preparation for implementation

Strategic audit
Before formulating a Service Strategy the provider must first look at his distinguishing capabilities:
- Which of our services are the most distinctive?
- Which of our services are the most lucrative?
- Which of our customers and stakeholders are the most satisfied?
- Which of our activities are the most effective?

In this way the strong and weak points can be examined, the Critical Success Factors (CSF) determined, and the risks and opportunities delineated.

Setting goals
Clear objectives ensure consistent decision-making. In order to determine its goals and objectives, an organization must know what the customer wants to achieve. ITIL defines three different types of information that determine the objectives of a service:
- **Tasks** - What is the task of the service that is to be provided?
- **Results** - What kind of results does the customer hope to achieve?
- **Constraints** - What are the limiting factors for the customer in achieving these results?

A clear look at what the customer deems valuable is essential. Look at the service from the outside. Begin with the common business objectives because they lead to a better understanding of the service utility and the service warranty. Customers do not buy services; they buy the satisfaction of a specific need.

Defining the Critical Success Factors (CSFs)
For every market there are critical success factors that determine the success or failure of a Service Strategy. These factors are influenced by customer needs, business trends, competition, regulations, providers, standards, best practices and technologies. ITIL contends that critical success factors, also known as Strategic Industry Factors (SIF), share the following general characteristics:
- They are defined in terms of capabilities and resources
- They seem to be the key to success for market leaders
- They are defined at the market level
- They are the basis for competition among rivals
- They are dynamic
- They usually require considerable investment and development time
- Their value is calculated through a combination with other factors

Critical success factors change or are influenced by one or more of the following factors:
- customers
- competition

- suppliers
- regulators

In every market service providers need a series of core assets in order to support the customer's portfolio with a service portfolio (see Figure 3.15).

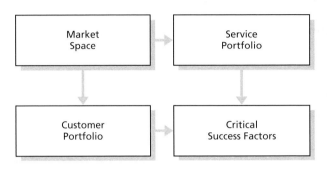

Figure 3.15   Critical success factors in a market (Source: Service Strategy was produced by OGC)

Critical success factors are decisive for success in a market. They are also useful for evaluating the strategic position of a service provider. This means that the critical success factors must be even further defined in specific value propositions to the customer.

Example: to be competitive in a market, it can be necessary to have a high availability; a "fail-safe operation" of the IT infrastructure is essential; and an adequate capacity is needed to guarantee continuity.

In many markets cost effectiveness is a customary Critical Success Factor, while in other markets the specialized domain knowledge or reliability of the infrastructure is much more important.

ITIL advises that a strategic analysis be performed for every market, major customer and service portfolio in order to determine the current strategic positions and the desired strategic positions for success.

Investigation of business potential
Service providers can be active in more than one market. A component of strategic planning is the analysis of the presence in various markets: an analysis of strong and weak points, opportunities and risks in every market. Service providers also analyze the possible expansion of the potential market.

Providers determine which customer needs can be effectively and efficiently satisfied by their services, while at the same time deciding which markets will be served and which will be ignored.

First, identify the:
- markets that can best be served with existing assets
- markets that must be avoided with the existing assets

Next determine for the selected markets:
- what is the service offering (service portfolio)
- which customers (Customer Portfolio)
- Critical success factors
- Underserved market spaces
- service models and service assets
- Service Pipeline and service catalogue

Synchronizing with the customer's needs
It is essential to understand the relationship between the customer and market. Customers can cover one or more markets. Markets can include one or more customer.
- The market of type I providers is internal to the organizational unit of which it is a part.
- The market of type II providers is internal to the enterprise, but is distributed through the business units.
- The market of type III providers is divided over more than one enterprise.

Expansion and growth
When service strategies happen to be linked with a market, it is easier to make decisions about portfolios, designs, production and long-term improvement. The growth and expansion of a business is less risky when it is based on core capabilities and proven performance. Successful strategies for expansion are often based on the effective use of service assets and customer portfolios.

Growth in a specific market is made possible through:
- extensions of existing contracts
- increasing requests
- expansion with complementary services

Processes
ITIL version 3 distinguishes three processes at the strategic level:
- Financial management
- Demand management
- Service portfolio management

These processes will be described briefly here; detailed information on them can be found in Chapter 9 of this book.

Financial management

Financial management is an integral component of service management. It anticipates the essential management information that is required for the guarantee of efficient and cost-effective service delivery. Efficient financial management positions the organization to responsibly account for all expenditures and to apply it directly to services.

How can we use financial management to ensure insights into the value creation process? Service valuation ensures that the business understands precisely what is being delivered through IT. Utility and warranty must be translated into a monetary figure in order to calculate the value. ITIL defines two essential value concepts for service valuation: the **provisioning value** (the production costs) and the **service value potential** (the value-adding component).

One objective of financial management is to ensure that the right financing is obtained for the delivery and purchase of services. A plan provides the financial translation and qualification of the anticipated demand for IT services.

ITIL divides planning into three primary areas, each of which represents the financial results that are necessary for continued transparency and service valuation:
operating & capital planning, demand planning, and regulatory & environmental. A careful plan leads to confidence that the financial data and models will provide accurate information on the development of demand and the supply of services.

Investment analysis

The objective of the investment analysis (Service Investment) is to derive a value-indication of a specific service from the attained value and incurred costs of the total lifecycle.

Accounting

Financial management builds a bridge between collective financial systems and service management. The results from a service oriented bookkeeping function is that far more details and understanding are obtained in regard to the delivery and consumption of services and the production of data that are directly relevant to the planning process.

Variable Cost Dynamics (VCD)

Variable Cost Dynamics (VCD) focuses on analyzing and understanding the many variables that influence service costs. The VCD analysis can be used as an analysis of the anticipated impact of events such as acquisitions, disinvestments and changes to the service portfolio or service alternative.

Fundamental decisions for financial management

Some of the concepts in financial management have a significant impact on the development of service strategies. ITIL explains a number of these concepts so that every organization can decide which options are best suited to their own service strategies:
• Cost recovery, value center, or accounting center?
• Chargeback: to charge or not to charge.
• Financial management implementation checklist.

For detailed information on financial management, see Chapter 9. One of the greatest challenges in the search for financing for ITIL projects is the identification of a specific business objective that is dependent on service management. For a description of the techniques of return on investment (ROI), post ROI, and business case, see the section on "Methods, techniques and tools" later in this chapter.

Demand Management (DM)

Demand management is an essential aspect of service management in which the offer is harmonized with the demand. The goal of demand management is to predict as accurately as possible the purchase of products, and if possible, to regulate it. Poorly managed demand is a risk for service providers because excess capacity can result in costs that will not be compensated in value. Insufficient capacity, on the other hand, influences the quality of the delivered services and limits the growth of the service. Service Level Agreements (SLAs), demand forecasting, planning and close coordination with the customer can minimize the uncertainty regarding demand, but cannot eliminate it completely.

Service management has an additional problem of synchronous production and consumption. Service Operation is not possible without the existence of the demand for the product to be consumed.

Demand management based on activities

Business processes are the primary source of the demand for services. Patterns of Business Activity (PBA) influence the demand pattern. It is crucial to study the customer's business in order to identify, analyze and record these patterns, which can serve as a solid foundation on which to create a capacity management strategy.

Service packages

Core services deliver the basic results to the customer. They represent the value that the customer wants and for which they are willing to pay. Core services serve as the basis for the value proposition for the customer. Support services make that value proposition possible (enabling service or "basic factors") or improve it (enhancing services or "excitement factors"). The bundling of core services and support services is an essential aspect of a marketing strategy. Service providers must conduct a thorough analysis of the principal conditions in their business environment, the needs of the customer segment or the customer types that they serve, and the alternatives that are available to these customers. These decisions are strategic because they comprise the long-term vision that will enable the continued creation of value for customers in the form of business methods, norms and standards, technologies and regulations in a changing industry. The bundling of support services with core services influences the service-production and provides a challenge for the design-, transition-, and CSI phases.

Service packages come with one or more Service Level Packages (SLP). Each SLP covers a definitive level of utility and warranty from the perspective of the customers' results, assets and the Patterns of Business Activity (PBA). Every SLP is able to provide for one or more demand pattern.

See Chapter 9 for more detailed information on demand management.

Service Portfolio Management (SPM)

SPM is a method to manage all service management investments. The objective of SPM is to achieve maximum value creation while at the same time managing the risks and costs.

SPM begins with the documentation of the standardized services of the organization, and in particular, the service catalogue. To be financially feasible, the portfolio must include the right mix of services in the pipeline and a catalogue.

Business value of SPM

The value of a service portfolio strategy is the capacity to anticipate changes while maintaining the strategy and planning.

SPM is a dynamic and ongoing process and comprises the following work methods:
- **Define** - Inventory the services and business cases, and validate the portfolio data; the cyclical nature of the SPM process means that this phase not only inventories the services, but also continually revalidates the data.
- **Analyze** - Maximize the value of the portfolio; synchronize, and set priorities, and balance from request to offer; in this phase, the strategic objectives take shape.
- **Approve** - Completion of the proposed portfolio, authorization of services and resources; decisions for the future.
- **Charter** - Communication of decisions, allocation of resources, and charter services.

See Chapter 9 for an extended description of the service portfolio management process.

3.4   Organization

IT organizations are complex systems within a greater complex system of the business, customers and industry. The transaction costs principle is a simple but powerful way for organizations to explain that the organization's right to exist is easier to justify if the organization is in a position to manage its transaction costs. An adequate amount of resources, a well-considered strategy, and distinctiveness combine to position the organization to deliver superior services in a competitive market while justifying the acquisition of additional resources. See Figure 3.16 for an illustration of this cycle.

The development of an organization

There is not just one way for a company to organize itself. External factors have a significant impact on an organization's Service Strategy. A Service Strategy is the implicit blueprint of the design, the size and the scope of an organization.

Organizations characterize themselves by the dominant management style in which the style corresponds with what the organization needs at a specific moment in time.

ITIL describes five recognizable phases in organizational development along the spectrum of centralization and decentralization. It is essential to know the situation in which the organization finds itself and the range of opportunities.

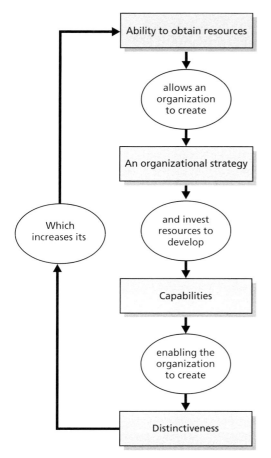

Figure 3.16   Organizational value creation cycle (Source: Service Strategy was produced by OGC)

Phase 1: Network

In phase 1, an organization focuses on fast, informal and *ad hoc* provision of services. The organization is technologically oriented and is uncomfortable with formal structures. For organizations in stage 1 innovation and entrepreneurship are important organizational values.

When the demand for service increases, this model is no longer effective. A network structure is a cluster for the coordination of activities through the making of agreements rather than through formal hierarchies or authority. Staff work closely together in order to complement their capabilities.

Advantages of a network structure:
- avoid high bureaucratic costs associated with complex organizations
- a flat organization in which fewer managers are necessary
- flexibility allows for quick modifications or changes to the structure

Disadvantages of a network structure:
- managers must oversee the integration of activities
- significant coordination problems
- opportunities for outsourcing functional activities

Advice: a change in leadership style is necessary to grow beyond these challenges.

Phase 2: Directive

The phase 1 crisis can be resolved with a strong management team. They assume the responsibility for leading the strategy and for guiding managers to embrace their functional responsibilities. Phase 2 focuses on the establishment of hierarchical structures (line management) that differentiate functional activities. Communication is more formal and various basic processes are used.

The turning point arises if an autonomous crisis emerges because centralization hinders decision-making, and there is no longer the freedom for experimentation or innovation.

Advice: to grow beyond this challenge, more delegation is necessary

Phase 3: Delegation

In phase 3, efforts are made to enhance technical efficiency and provide space for innovation in order to reduce costs and improve services. A decentralized organizational structure is adopted in which the responsibility shifts from functional ownership (line management) to process ownership.

A drawback of Phase 3 is that the objectives of functional ownership and process ownership do not coincide. Functional owners have the feeling that they are losing control. For this reason, the process is usually abandoned.

Advice: improve the coordination within the organization by initiating formal systems and programs

Phase 4: Coordination

In phase 4 the focus is directed towards the use of formal systems as a means of achieving better coordination. Centralization of technical functions and decentralization of service management processes emerge, with the goal of improving response time to market demands.

Advice: if everything is in order internally, the next order of business is to improve cooperation with the customer

Phase 5: Collaboration

During Phase 5, the focus is on the improvement of cooperation with the business. A commonly used structure is the matrix structure with the flow of functional responsibilities (line management) on the vertical line, and the flow of product- or customer-related responsibilities on the horizontal line. An organization with a matrix structure takes on all of the functions that it needs.

Advantages of a matrix structure:
- minimizes and overcomes functional barriers
- increases speed of response to changing product- or customer needs
- opens up communication among the functional specialists
- creates opportunities for team members of diverse functions to learn from each other
- uses the skills of specialist staff who can move from product to product and from customer to customer

Disadvantages of a matrix structure:
- lack of a monitoring structure that the staff can use to build a stable pattern of expectations
- conflicting roles can demoralize staff
- possible conflict situation between functions and product- or customer teams

From work group to department

If a work group grows to the size of a department, then the groups can be divided according to attributes. See Table 3.1 for an overview of the basic organizational structures.

Basic structure	Description	Strategic considerations
Function	Organizing by function is the best way of specializing. Pooling of resources and minimizing duplication.	• Specialization • Development of standards • Small-scale
Product	Organizing by product is preferred by organizations that are focused on new and diverse products. This organization is found primarily in processing industries.	• Focus on product • Strong product knowledge
Market or customer	Organizing by market or customer offers differentiation in the form of increased knowledge and response to the wishes of the customer.	• Service is unique for each segment • Customer service • Powerful consumer • Quick service
Geography	Organizing by geography is preferred when providing services in close proximity. Minimizes travel and distribution costs while benefiting from knowledge of local area.	• On-site services • Close to customers for delivery and support • Organization is viewed as a local enterprise
Process	Organizing by process is preferred in executing processes from start to finish.	• Need to shorten process cycle time • Process excellence

Table 3.1   Basic organizational structures

Organization design

The key to organizational design is strategy. The strategy determines the focus and leads the criteria for every step in the design process. The first order of business is to determine the departmental structure for designing the core processes (Figure 3.17).

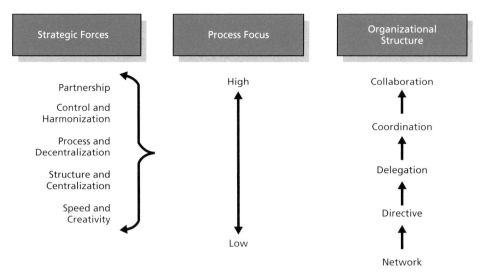

Figure 3.17   Matching strategic strengths with organizational development (Source: Service Strategy was produced by OGC)

Organizational culture

The culture of an organization is a set of collective values and norms that determine the course of both internal and external interactions. A collective culture contributes to the effectiveness of the organization. There are two types of values:

- **end values** - the desired results in terms of quality, excellence, reliability, innovation, and profitability
- **instrumental values** - the desired behavior in terms of standards, respect for tradition and authority, careful and conservative treatment and moderation

You can analyze the culture of a service management organization as follows:

- determine the end values and the instrumental values
- determine whether the objectives, norms and regulations carry over the values of the organizational culture to the personnel
- assess whether new staff is immediately accepted into the organizational culture

Sourcing strategy

The goal of the Service Strategy is to improve the core competencies. Sometimes it is more efficient to outsource certain services. We call this the SoC principle (separation of concerns, SoC): that which results from the search for competitive differentiation through the redistribution of resources and capabilities.

A risk in outsourcing of services is outsourcing them to a competitor:

- **Substitution** - The vendor can replace the sourcing organization.
- **Disruption** - The vendor can damage your reputation.
- **Distinctiveness** - You can develop a dependence on another organization.

Outsourcing structures

The dynamic of the outsourcing of services requires that organizations formally determine the provisions of an outsourcing strategy. This also includes the structure and role of the relevant party, and the impact of outsourcing on decision-making. The following generic forms of outsourcing can be delineated:

- **internal outsourcing**:
  - Type 1 internal - provision and delivery of services by internal staff; this offers the most control, but is limited in scale
  - Type 2 shared services - working with internal BUs; offers lower costs than Type 1 and more standardization, but is still limited in scale
- **traditional outsourcing**:
  - complete outsourcing of a service - a single contract with one service provider; better in terms of scaling opportunities, but limited in best-in-class capabilities
- **multi-vendor outsourcing**:
  - *prime* - a single contract with one service provider who works with multiple providers; improved capabilities and risks, but increased complexity
  - *consortium* - a selection of multiple service providers; the advantage is best-in-class with more oversight; the disadvantage is the risk of the necessity of working with the competition
  - *selective outsourcing* - a pool of service providers selected and managed through the service receiver; this is the most difficult structure to manage
  - *co-sourcing* - a variation of selective outsourcing in which the service receiver combines a structure of internal or shared services with external providers; in this case, the service receiver is the service integrator

In outsourcing services a balance must be found between acceptable risks and control.

Outsourcing with multiple providers

It appears that outsourcing with multiple providers is a good method because the organization can maintain strong relationships with each provider while the risks are spread out and costs are contained. The challenge is the governance and management of these relationships.

Checklist for the selection of providers:

- **demonstrated competencies** - staff, use of technology, innovation, experience, and certification, where applicable
- **track record** - quality, financial value, dedication
- **relationship dynamics** - do the vision and strategy fit with those of the organization?
- **quality of solutions** - have the services been delivered as requested?
- **overall capabilities** - financial stability, resources, management systems, scope and range of services

Service Provider Interfaces (SPI)

Various guidelines and reference points are necessary to support the development of business relationships. Service provider interfaces offer these reference points.

During contract discussions the responsibilities and service levels should be negotiated:
- identification of integration points of various management processes
- identification of specific roles and responsibilities
- identification of management information that is relevant to the customer

Process owners possess SPIs and define and maintain them. SPI definitions consist of:
- technological prerequisites (e.g. management tool standards or prescribed protocols)
- data requirements (e.g. specific events or records), formats (data layout), interfaces (e.g. APIs, firewall ports), and protocols (e.g. SNMP, XML)
- non-negotiable requirements
- required roles/responsibilities
- response times and escalation paths

Sourcing governance
Governance is the framework of decision rights that encourage the desired behavior in outsourcing. The difference between governance and management is that management has to do with decision-making and the implementation of processes; governance has to do with making the right decisions.

Governance is often forgotten and is therefore the weakest link in the service sourcing strategy. With a few simple interventions, the first inroad towards governance can be made:
- **establish a governance body** - decisions can be made on the right level
- **differentiate between governance domains** - with distinctions according to important domains, such as service delivery, communication, and contract management
- **establish a fixed decision rights matrix** - RACI- or RASIC-matrices are the most common forms for decision rights matrices

ISO/IEC 20000 is the first formal international standard specifically designed for IT service management. It provides a foundation for the management structure between internal- and external providers, therefore minimizing the risks with service sourcing. It is especially useful in multisource environments.

Critical success factors
The factors of an outsourcing strategy often depend on:
- desired results
- optimum model for delivering services
- best location from which to deliver services

Recommended approach of the strategy:
- analyze the internal service management competencies of the organization
- compare these findings with the industry benchmarks
- examine the organization's ability to deliver strategic value

To measure the effect of sourcing, the organization must conduct a zero-measure of its performance metrics before commencing implementation. This can be established with two types of metrics:

- **business metrics** - financial savings, service level improvements, business process efficiency
- **customer metrics** - availability and consistency of services, more supply, service quality

Roles and responsibilities

A key role in the implementation of a sourcing strategy lies with the Chief Sourcing Officer, who reports to the CIO and manages the implementation of sourcing. Other important roles may include:

- **Director of service management** - The director supervises the provider on behalf of the business.
- **Contract manager** - The contract manager manages the service contract from the perspective of the service provider.
- **Product manager** - The product manager manages the services in the service provider's organization.
- **Process owner** - The process owner manages the process models that have been developed on behalf of the users
- **Business representatives** - They represent the customers' interests and manage the sourcing relationship from that perspective.

3.5   Methods, techniques and tools

Services are socio-technical systems with service assets as the operational elements. The interactions between two sub-systems in the form of dependencies (passive) and influences (active) are critical for the performance of service management as value-creating systems.

The effectiveness of the Service Strategy depends on a well-managed relationship between the social and technical sub-systems. It is essential to identify and manage these dependencies and influences. Reviews of Service Design, Service Transition, Service Operation, and CSI must include an analysis of possible dysfunction or lack of synchronicity between the two sub-systems. The interest of a balanced approach is apparent from the following observations:

- Improvements in the design and the realization of activities, tasks and interfaces can compensate for inadequacies in human resources.
- Investing in knowledge, skills, behavior and experience can compensate for poorly designed systems.
- Automation of routine activities can reduce unwanted discrepancies and relieve work pressure through a simple technical adjustment.

The design of socio-technical systems is an important consideration in service management. It is important to know that services are much more than a series of activities that produce a certain value. They are systems with complex interactions between different production factors and service assets.

Service automation

Automation can have a significant impact on the performance of service assets such as management, organization, people, processes, knowledge and information.

Service management can benefit from automation in the following areas: design and modeling, service catalogues, identifying and analyzing patterns, classification, investigation and optimization.

To prepare for automation, ITIL recommends the following steps:
• Simplify the service processes before automating, but be careful not to lose any essential information.
• Clarify the flow of activities, allocation of tasks, need for information and interactions.
• In self-service situations, minimize the area in which users come into contact with the underlying systems and processes.
• Do not rush the implementation of automation when it involves tasks and interactions that are not simple and routine.

Service analysis and instrumentation
Service analysis is the placing of information in a context of patterns. Through an understanding of patterns of information we can answer the following questions:
• How does this incident influence the service?
• How does this incident impact the business?
• How should we respond?

In this case, the Data-Information-Knowledge-Wisdom (DIKW) sequence can be used. This series describes the added value that can be given to the data by viewing them in this context.

Instrumentation describes the technologies and techniques that are used to evaluate the behavior of infrastructure elements. Instrumentation can aggregate a very large amount of basic data, but more context is needed to determine the actual relevance of the data and to input that into the information. In order to input data into the information, it is necessary to understand the relationships between the data and to see them in the appropriate context. This can be filled in on the basis of four questions: who, what, when and where. This is comparable to the series event-, fault-, and performance management.

Service interfaces

Characteristics of good service interfaces
The design of service interfaces is crucial for service management. The service interfaces meet the basic requirements of warranty, such as:
• The interfaces must be easy to find, and simple to use.
• The interfaces must be available and in a form that ensures opportunities for choice and flexibility for users.
• The interfaces must have sufficient capacity so that there is no waiting period if a large number of users try to make use of the interface simultaneously.
• The interfaces must accommodate users with varying skills, competencies, backgrounds and handicaps.

Combinations of service and technology

Advances in communication technology influence the interaction between service providers and their customers.

There are five ways in which technology contributes to communication with the customer:
1. **communication without technology** - such as with consulting services
2. **communication assisted by technology** - only the service provider has access to the technology; for example, an airport representative who uses a terminal to check in customers
3. **communication facilitated by technology** - both the customer and the provider have access to the same technology
4. **communication accomplished through technology** - service provider and customer are not in close proximity; for example, a customer who receives information via a service desk
5. **communication generated by technology** - the customer sees the service provider only in the form of technology, via a self-service interface; appropriate for routine activities, such as automated teller machines (ATMs)

Self-service channels

Automation is of added value to capacity. The capacity of channels for self-service has a low marginal cost, is infinitely scalable, does not get tired, offers unlimited consistent performances, and is available 24/7 for a relatively low cost.

Tools for the Service Strategy

Simulation

System dynamics is a methodology for understanding and managing the complex problems of IT organizations. It offers a way to get a handle on and to model feedback processes, supplies and flows, delays and other complex problems. It is a tool for evaluating the consequences of new policies and new structures before they are put into practice. System dynamics can provide insights into the following situations:
- **Capability trap** - In order to pressure the staff to work harder, the organization unconsciously sets the stage in which an increasingly higher level of tension is needed to arrive at the same level of performance.
- **Tool trap** - Although tools are often very useful, they also require the development of knowledge and experience; organizations overlook the impact of the increased short-term work pressure through training and learning and practical activities, and end up running additional unintended risks.
- **Fire-fighter trap** - When an organization rewards managers for putting out fires quickly, the performance can suffer over the long-term; in this case it might be better not to reward extinguishing fires.

Analytical modeling

There is a lot of depth and diversity in analytical modeling. The Service Strategy as well as other functions and processes in the Service Lifecycle can benefit from the knowledge that comes from analytical modeling for improving performance in light of technical, financial and time constraints. Six Sigma, PMBOK® and PRINCE2® offer well tested methods based on analytical models. They must be evaluated and adopted within the context of the Service Strategy and service management.

Return on investment
One of the greatest challenges in seeking financing for ITIL projects is identifying a specific business objective, which is dependent on service management. To that end, this section will cover the following three techniques:
- **business case** - a way of identifying business objectives that are dependent on service management
- **pre-program ROI** - techniques for quantitatively analyzing investments in service management
- **post-program ROI** - techniques for retroactively analyzing investments in service management

Business case
A way to justify investments in service management initiatives is to make a business case.

> A **business case** is a decision-making-, support-, and planning instrument that plans for the likely consequences of a business action.

The consequences can be qualitative as well as quantitative. A financial analysis is often central to a good business case. The business impact has to be directly linked to the business objectives. A business objective is the reason for considering a service management initiative. A strategic objective in the area of increasing productivity, for example, can be the introduction of competitive products. While a business case usually rests on a cost analysis, there are many other matters that are also important for a service management initiative.

Pre-program ROI
Capital budgeting is the investment of financing now in order to yield increasing cash inflows or decreasing cash outflows in the future. Capital budgeting decisions fall into two categories:
- **screening decisions (NPV)** - because you have to spend money to make money, the time value of money (discounted cash flow) plays a role; capital budgeting decisions can be based on analyses of the cash flows
- **preference decisions (IRR)** - decisions can also be based on preferential approaches

In this chapter, a distinction is made between two approaches: the Net Present Value (NPV) and the Internal Rate of Return (IRR). NPV is based on the comparison between cash inflows and cash outflows, where the difference, the "net present value", determines whether or not the investment is valuable. With IRR the yields over the entire lifecycle of a service are compared with the cash inflow (rate of return). Both approaches must decide if a proposed service management initiative will outlive a previously determined financial barrier (e.g. minimum return).

For service management programs, the NPV offers the following advantages over the IRR method:
- In general, NPV is easier to use.
- IRR accepts that the rate of return is, in fact, the rate of return of the program. This is a dubious assumption for environments with minimal experience with service management programs.

When NPV and IRR are not in agreement about the attractiveness of a project, then NPV is the best choice. NPV will make the more realistic assumption for the rate of return.

Post-program ROI

If a service management initiative is launched without prior ROI analysis, it is wise to do the analysis retroactively. The calculation of a service management ROI is illustrated in the basic model in Figure 3.18.

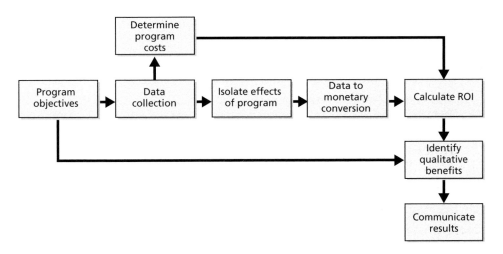

Figure 3.18   Post-program ROI approach (Source: Service Strategy was produced by OGC)

The Post-Program ROI approach comprises the following steps:
- **Program objectives** - Objectives must be clear because they convey the depth and scope of the ROI-analysis.
- **Data collection** - Examples include the metrics for the service quality, the transaction costs, customer satisfaction surveys, etc.
- **Isolation of the program's effects** - Various techniques are available to ensure that the program is effective; for example, the future analysis, which denotes what would have occurred if the program had not been started.
- **Monetary conversion of data** - In order to calculate the ROI, the data must be depicted as monetary values, so that the values can be compared with the costs.
- **Determining the program costs** - All of the related costs of the ITIL program are calculated (including, for example, planning, design, and implementation costs, technology costs, and training costs).
- **Calculate the ROI** - See the NPV - and IRR techniques in the previous sections.
- **Identify the qualitative benefits** - Qualitative benefits begin with how they are defined in the business case; the qualitative benefits are checked for a second time during the CSI phase.

Service delivery models and analysis

Organizations that analyze the existing methods for the delivery of services can make use of various models for the analysis:

- **Managed services** - The most traditional variant in which the business unit that needs the service handles the financing itself. This is the most expensive variant because the costs of the service are completely covered by the business unit.
- **Shared services** - Delivery of multiple services to one or more business unit through the collective use of infrastructures and resources. Cost savings through increased use of existing resources.
- **Utility-based services** - Maximizes the combination of delivered services over the same infrastructure so that even more services can be provided using the same resources. This is possible by providing services based on utility, depending on how much, how often and when the customer needs them. This model is the most cost-effective and the most refined because it requires a knowledge and capability level that most organizations do not have. These cost savings are possible through a deeper understanding of the architecture of the technology and the customers' needs, whereby a combination of services and architecture is achieved that makes maximum use of existing resources.
- **On-shore, off-shore, or near-shore?** - Determine what mix of on-shore, near-shore and off-shore services are right for a specific organization at a specific time. If an organization is not aware of its most important service cost components and the dynamic of variable costs, then it will be difficult to make a logical and fact-based decision about outsourcing. The cost analysis of service delivery (service provisioning cost analysis) is the statistical estimation of the various forms of delivery and the determination of the most beneficial model.
- **Service provisioning cost analysis** - Statistically ranks the various forms of provisioning (and often providers) to determine the most beneficial model.

3.6   Implementation

From Strategy to Tactics and Production

Implementation based on the lifecycle

Strategic positions are converted into plans with objectives and ultimate goals, based on the lifecycle. Plans are a means for reaching these positions. Plans ensure that each phase in the Service Lifecycle have the capabilities and resources that are needed for achieving the strategic positions. The lifecycle provides the clarity and context for the development of the necessary capabilities and resources.

Plans translate the intentions of the strategy into actions, through Service Design, Service Transition, Service Operation, and CSI. The Service Strategy provides every phase of the lifecycle with input. CSI ensures that there is feedback by which the implementation of the strategy can be monitored during the entire lifecycle. (See Figure 3.19.)

The Service Strategy defines the portfolio of services that are offered and the customers that are supported for a specific market.

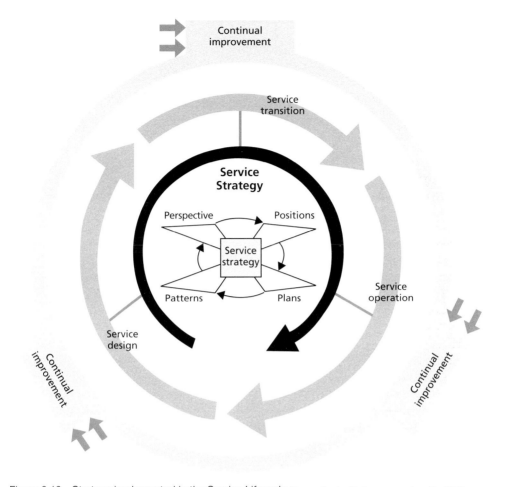

Figure 3.19   Strategy implemented in the Service Lifecycle (Source: Service Strategy was produced by OGC)

Customers and service providers must both face the strategic risks that arise out of uncertainties. It is essential that risks be translated into opportunities and challenges, depending on the harmonization of service management capabilities with the existing needs of the customer. The Service Strategy needs CSI in order to guide the lifecycle elements to be certain that they have not missed any opportunities or challenges.

Patterns that emerge in implementing the Service Lifecycle ultimately lead to the assumption of new strategies. This bottom-up development of the Service Strategy, along with the traditional top-down approach, comprises a closed planning and management system for service strategies. This feedback- and learning process is an essential success factor for service management to make the necessary changes and innovations. (See Figure 3.20.)

Strategy and design
Service strategies arrive at implementation through the delivery and support of the Contract Portfolio in a specific market area. Contracts specify the terms and conditions under which value is provided to the customer through delivered services. Because every service is linked to one or

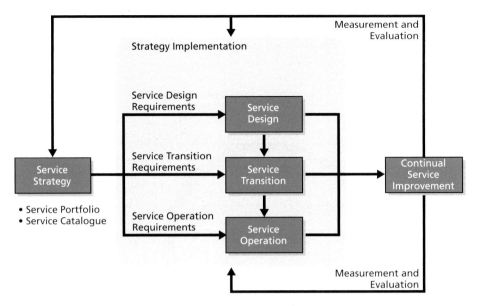

Figure 3.20   Closed-loop planning and monitoring system for strategy (Source: Service Strategy was produced by OGC)

more market area, the design of the service is related to the categories of customer assets and to the service models. They comprise the high-level input for the Service Design phase.

Service models
Factors from the utility and warranty that the customer wants influence the structure and dynamic of the models.

> **Service models** describe how service assets interact with customer assets and create value for a given portfolio of contracts.

The structure and dynamic have consequences for the Service Operation phase which are evaluated during the Service Transition phase.

Service models are developed by the market. (Figure 3.21)

Outcome-oriented design
The attributes of a service constitute the characteristics that provide the service with form and function from the customer's perspective. It is a design challenge to determine which attributes must be adopted. Look at the business outcomes, for example, on the basis of the Kano model. A model developed by Noriaki Kano can be used to help understand customer preferences. The Kano Model considers attributes of an IT service grouped into areas such as Basic Factors, Excitement Factors, Performance Factors, etc.

Design focused on constraints
The development of a list of constraints and the visualization of the interaction requires a team of specialists from business and technology. They can observe and record the interaction among

customers, providers, partners and advisors. All five phases of the Service Lifecycle provide input for those constraints. The method is a means for the Service Strategy to communicate the challenges and opportunities to the Service Design phase.

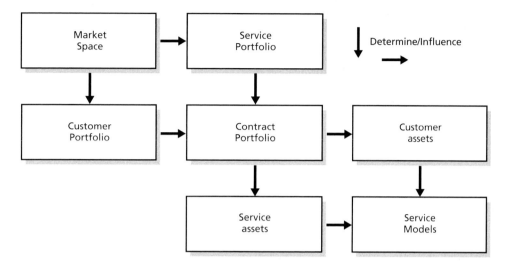

Figure 3.21   Service models are developed by the market (Source: Service Strategy was produced by OGC)

Strategy and transition

Service Strategy is dependent on the dynamic capabilities of service providers who make possible an effective response to the challenges and opportunities of customers and markets. Strategic plans always cost money. There are always costs and risks involved with decisions, such as introducing a new service, entering new market areas and serving new customers.

Service Transition represents one of the most important components of service management, with processes such as change management, configuration management and service deployment. The ability to carry out quick changes in service portfolios and contracts is a critical success factor in certain markets and strategies. Therefore the Service Transition is an important element in service management.

Strategy and operation

The ultimate achievement of strategies occurs in the operations phase. Therefore in developing strategies, it must always be kept in mind as to what is operationally feasible. Operations, on the other hand, must understand what kind of outcomes are needed in order to attain a particular strategy and must provide for adequate support.

Deployment patterns

Arrange service assets in patterns that are most effective in delivering value to the customer in every segment of the service catalogue. Deployment patterns in the Service Operation phase define the operational strategies for customers.

Hosting the contract portfolio
The need to provide service contracts influences the deployment patterns. Service contracts comprise the context in which the service portfolio provides services that are of value to the customer. Every contract represents the agreements that have been made with a customer regarding the utility and warranty of the services.

Hosting decisions require close coordination between Service Strategy and Service Operation. The strategy for a market influences the content of the customer portfolio and the service portfolio. Specific perspectives, positions, plans and patterns (the 4 Ps) determine the service offer, the associated contractual agreements and conditions, and the customers to whom they will be provided. The combination of service portfolios and the customer portfolio generates the contract portfolio.

Strategy and CSI

Quality perspective
Experience shows that SLA-metrics are necessary, but that they are not sufficient for measuring the quality of services that are provided to the customer. The quality of services, such as that experienced by customers, is based on the utility and warranty that are provided. Service quality depends on the positive impact of the service (utility) and the certainty of that impact (warranty).

The many definitions of quality can be summarized in four broad perspectives:
• level of excellence
• price-quality relationship
• conformity to specifications
• meeting or exceeding expectations

The most dominant perspective influences the assessment and management of services, especially in the context of service level management.

One of the most important decisions is the definition of the significance of service quality. Quality itself is a basis for strategies in a market. Therefore the definition of quality influences strategic decisions and objectives. It affects the design and the implementation of a service. It also influences the internal performance measures, policy and incentives that managers employ.

Warranty factors
There are differences and similarities in the methods of production of goods and services; how the value they create is transferred to the customer; how it is verified and how this certainty is established. Some factors are visible and measurable (tangible factors), while others are much more difficult to pin down (intangible factors).

Reliability
• **Applications and infrastructure** - In order to fulfill the warranty aspect of value to the customer, services must be reliable. This is essential input of the Service Strategy for Service Design and Service Operation. The provision of services with a high level of reliability can be

the basis for strategic positioning. The reliability of a service depends on the reliability of the underlying service assets and their configuration. The reliability of an asset again depends on a variety of factors such as the quality of the design, development, installation, etc.

• **People and processes** - Reliability in terms of availability serves as an important factor for all service assets and infrastructures, as well as for people and processes. If support staff are not available, the service can ultimately fail as a result. The availability of all components, therefore, must also be managed. It is difficult to define the reliability and availability of people and processes. A factor, such as Mean Time Between Failures (MTBF), is much more difficult to calculate than hardware or network components. MTBF records the reliability of a service asset: the higher the MTBS, the higher the reliability.

Maintainability

Services must be quickly restored when they are unavailable to users. The Mean Time to Restore Service (MTRS) is the average recovery time within which a function (service, system or component) is operational again after a breakdown. The MTRS depends on several different factors, such as configuration of service assets, MTRS of individual components, the competence of support personnel, available resources, policy plans, procedures and redundancy.

Analyses of how the MTRS responds to each factor are useful for improving the performance and the design of services.

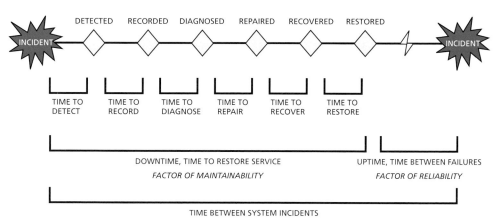

Figure 3.22   Improvement opportunities within the incident lifecycle

The MTRS can be reduced by reducing each of the components in the extended incident lifecycle (see Figure 3.22). More details on how this works can be found in Chapter 10, availability management.

Redundancy

Redundancy is a way of increasing reliability and sustainability of systems. ITIL defines four redundancy types that can be used individually or in combination: Active and passive redundancy (for essential services), and diverse and homogeneous redundancy (for similar and specific service assets). This can be supported by various infrastructural methods that increase the accessibility of services. More details can be found in Chapter 10.

Interactions between availability factors
The various factors that contribute to highly available services have a mutual effect on each other and can be managed together (See Figure 3.23).

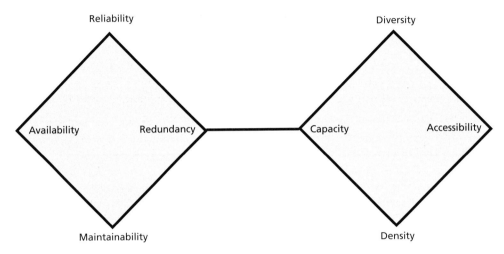

Figure 3.23   Interaction between factors that influence the availability of services (Source: Service Strategy was produced by OGC)

Benefits, bottlenecks and risks

Complexity
IT organizations are complex systems. This explains why some service organizations are not inclined to change. Organizations are not always in a position to anticipate the long-term consequences of decisions and actions. This often results in their aversion to policy changes. Without continual learning processes, today's decisions often end up as tomorrow's problems.

A natural reaction is to divide services into processes that are managed by groups with specialized knowledge, experience and resources. This is fine as long as the mutual connection is not lost. Service management processes are a means, not an end.

Coordination and control
The people who make the decisions often have limited time, attention and capacity. Therefore they delegate the roles and responsibilities to teams and individuals who are specialized in specific systems, processes, performances and results.

Service management is an interconnected set of specialized competencies that are defined around processes and lifecycle phases. An increase in the level of specialization leads to a requisite increase in coordination. Improved coordination is possible through the cooperation and monitoring between teams and individuals.

Problems with cooperation call for a way of connecting those groups with varying and possibly conflicting interests and objectives. This also applies to the cooperation between the service provider and the client.

Possible solutions:
- Make agreements in which everyone benefits.
- Maintain the shared views and agreed goals of service management; these are defined in service strategies, objectives, policy, rewards and incentives.
- Use collective processes that integrate groups and functions, shared applications that integrate the processes and shared infrastructures that integrate the applications.

Control perspectives are based on the objectives of one or more service management process or lifecycle phase. They help managers to focus on what is important and relevant to the processes that they control, and guarantee that high quality information is available to ensure effectiveness and efficiency.

Preserving Value

Deviations in performance
Mature customers are not only interested in the utility and warranty that they receive for the price they pay. They want to know the Total Cost of Utilization (TCU). The TCU concept is based on the principle of transaction costs. Customers see not only the costs of the actual consumption, but are also aware of all of the other related costs that are incurred indirectly during the process.

The creation of value for customers is a clearly visible objective for providers. The creation of value for their stakeholders is also of great importance. With Type I providers these two objectives are closely connected. With type III providers they can easily diverge or even conflict.

The exclusion of hidden costs is a challenge, a Critical Success Factor, and a risk.

Operational effectiveness and efficiency
Services must have a beneficial use from the perspective of both the customer and the service provider. This collective interest is essential to the economic feasibility of the services. Both the provider and the customer must, therefore, derive an economic value from the service.

Value is intangible and thus difficult to predict. Therefore efficiency must be created on the basis of a desired result. Effectiveness is the quality of being in a position to create a specific desired effect. In the context of service, the two effects are utility and warranty.

The increase of the efficiency of a process can result in the availability of extra capacity for other demands from the market, whereby the additional demand can be served with the same resources. Improvements in Service Design and Service Operation can drive this type of profit in efficiency. Thus, there is feedback and interaction between efficiency and desired effectiveness.

Increasing efficiency can lead to increasing effectiveness, which then can again lead to an increase in efficiency until a certain optimization limit has been reached.

Reducing hidden costs

One category of hidden costs includes transaction costs. These comprise, for example, resources that the provider supplies for determining the needs of the customer, the preferences of users, quality criteria and prices.

Standardization, shared services and reuse, coupled with segmentation and differentiated service levels can help recoup some of the transaction costs.

Confirmation of hidden benefits

Services offer an attractive alternative to the acquisition of assets. They offer the customer the utility of an asset while they can outsource the Maintenance and Repair Operations (MRO). MRO services belong to a separate category of services.

Standardization of service management processes for a specific industry leads to a higher level of efficiency and flexibility from consolidation, disaggregation, and flexible configuration of business processes, infrastructure components and human resources.

Effective use of intangible assets

Intangible assets are non-physical claims for future benefits generated through innovation, unique systems, processes, designs and competencies. The combination with tangible and financial assets ensures the creation of an economic value for the owner. Tangible assets include rival assets (or scarce assets): physical assets, human resources and financial assets. The specific use of this type of asset ensures that they cannot be used elsewhere. For example: people who assist the customer, equipment space, invested financial capital. Intangible assets, on the other hand, are not contentious because they are put in place simultaneously for different demands. The use of intangible assets, such as Web-based technologies and software-based automation of processes, can increase the scalability of service systems. Effective use of knowledge-intensive systems and processes is, in this respect, possible against virtual low costs.

From a service management perspective, the structure of service models, designs, and infrastructure can be analyzed in order to determine the ratio of intangible elements to tangible elements. Wherever possible, tangible elements should be replaced by intangibles so that the Service Design becomes scalable.

Measuring effectiveness

Measurements focus the organization on its strategic goals, follow the progression and provide the organization with feedback. Most IT organizations are good at monitoring data, but often they are not very good at providing insights into the effectiveness of the services that they offer. The "what" and the "where" can usually be answered accurately, while the "how" and the "why" are seen to be less important. It is crucial to perform the right analyses and to modify them as the strategy changes. In this case, organizations can apply the previously mentioned DIKW (Data-Information-Knowledge-Wisdom) knowledge management method.

Risks

The implementation of strategy leads to changes in the service portfolio. This then leads to the management of related risks. Decisions regarding risks must be balanced so that the potential benefits provide more value to the organization than the costs of addressing the risks. For example: innovation can be risky, but it can also result in greater benefits in the improvement of services.

For analysis purposes it can be useful to visualize the positive risk types that are related to opportunities, investments, and innovations in contrast to the negative risks such as failing to exploit opportunities, not succeeding in investing appropriately and ignoring innovation opportunities.

Definition of risk
ITIL defines risk as follows:

> **Risk** *is an uncertain outcome, or in other words, a positive opportunity or a negative threat.*

The task of risk management is to ensure that the organization makes use, in a cost-effective manner, of a risk framework that consists of a set of well-defined steps. (See Figure 3.24.)

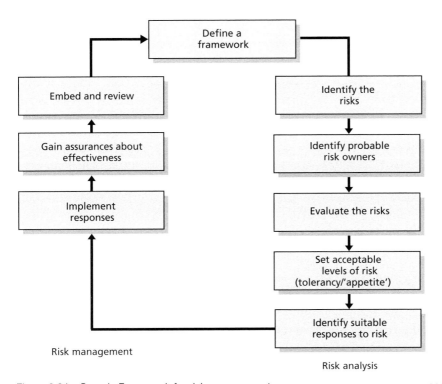

Figure 3.24   Generic Framework for risk management (Source: Service Strategy was produced by OGC)

The goal is to support better decision-making through the use of a good understanding of the risks and their probable impact. There are two phases: risk analysis and risk management:

- **Risk analysis** - Risk analysis is involved with the gathering of information regarding the exposure to risks so that the organization makes the right decisions and oversees the risks in the appropriate the manner.

• **Risk management** - Risk management ensures that there are processes in place that are focused on monitoring risks, that reliable and current information about risks is available, that the right control balance for proceeding with the risks is applied, and that the decision-making is supported by a framework of risk analysis and evaluation.

Transfer of risks

Risk management plays a crucial role in service management (Figure 3.25). Services reduce the risk to the client's business, but they also bring risks to the service providers. Clients compensate service providers for these risks in a variety of ways: first and foremost by paying for the services (not possible with Type I).

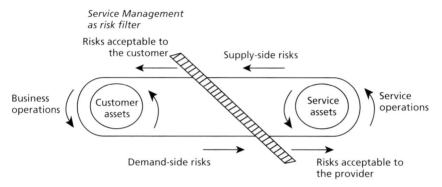

Figure 3.25   Risk management plays an important role in service management (Source: Service Strategy was produced by OGC)

Service providers must ensure that sufficient compensation occurs but at the same time, they must remain reasonable. Costs are facts, but prices are a matter of policy. That means that certain investments, for example, can yield a profit over the course of time. In addition, with new services and customers, the risks can pay for themselves in the form of new customers (scale) or demand for other services (scope).

Supplements or changes to the client's portfolio must be preceded by an evaluation of the risks that the service provider is willing to assume on behalf of the client.

Risk analysis and risk management must be applied to the Service Pipeline and service catalogue in order to identify, curb and mitigate the risks within the lifecycle phases.

Risks for service providers

Risks for service providers arise when uncertainty from the customer's business is combined with uncertainties in their operations, and have an adverse effect across the lifecycle. It is useful to communicate risks in financial terms, which can be used as indicators instead of measures.

ITIL recognizes the following types of risks:
• **Contract risks** (a contract includes formally legal binding agreements between business and service providers) - Risks that the service provider will make it impossible to satisfy

the contractual agreements are strategic risks, because they not only threaten the current production, but they also damage the trust for future interactions. The impact of contract risks and the underlying dangers and weaknesses may not be limited to just one specific function of the process. The customer makes no distinction between the source of risks. Coordination throughout the entire lifecycle is necessary in order to manage risks effectively.

- **Design risks** - Customers expect services to have a specific impact on the performance of their assets, which is a utility from their perspective. There is always a risk that the services will achieve undesired results. This is a performance risk. A poor performance is usually the result of a bad design.
- **Operational risks** - Every organization deals with operational risks. Viewed from a service management perspective, there are two types to distinguish: risks for the business units and risks for the service units.
- **Market risks** - Effective service management helps reduce the competitive risks by increasing the scale and scope of the demand for a service catalogue. Another approach is to modify the contents of the service catalogue so that customers can find the depth and breadth that they are looking for. Market risks can be reduced through:
  - *Differentiation* - From the customer's perspective, assets that are scarce and complementary are interesting. Service providers can thus concentrate on providing the important assets that have not been provided by others. Un-served and underserved markets offer attractive opportunities.
  - *Consolidation* - Consolidation of the demand reduces the financial risks for service providers as well as the operational risks for the customer.

Chapter 4
Lifecycle Phase: Service Design

4.1 Introduction

Objective

Service Design follows the Service Strategy in the Service Lifecycle, and deals with the design and development of services and their related processes. It refers not only to completely new services, but also to modified service delivery.

According to ITIL, the most important objective of Service Design is:

> *The design of new or modified services for introduction into a production environment.*

The objectives of Service Design include, but are not limited to:
* to contribute to the business objectives
* where possible, to contribute to saving time and money
* to minimize or prevent risks
* to contribute to satisfying the current and future market needs
* to assess and improve the effectiveness and efficiency of IT services
* to support the development of policies and standards regarding IT services
* to contribute to the quality of IT services

In order to ensure that the services that are developed meet the customer's expectations, the following actions must be undertaken:
* The new service must be added right from the concept phase of the service portfolio and it must be kept up-to-date throughout the process.
* The Service Level Requirements (SLR) must be clear before the service is delivered.
* Based on the SLRs, the capacity management team can model these requirements within the existing infrastructure.
* If it appears that a new infrastructure is needed or more support is desired, then financial management must be involved.

- Before the implementation phase begins, a Business Impact Analysis (BIA) and a risk assessment must be performed. This will provide valuable information for IT Service Continuity Management (ITSCM), availability management and capacity management.
- The service desk must be brought up to speed regarding the new service delivery before the new services are delivered.
- Service Transition can make a plan for the implementation of the service.
- Supplier management must be involved if there are purchases to be made.

To satisfy the changing needs and demands of the business, the design of effective and efficient IT services is a process of balancing among functionality, available resources (human, technical, and financial) and available time. This is a continual process in all phases of the lifecycle of IT services.

The Service Design phase in the lifecycle begins with the demand for new or modified requirements from the customer. Ultimately at the end of the design process, a service solution must be designed that satisfies the requirements before including the service in the transition process. Good preparation and an effective and efficient infusion of personnel, processes, products (services, technology and tools) and partners - ITIL's four Ps - is a must if the design plans and projects are to succeed.

Considering the mutual dependence of departments, IT services cannot be designed, transitioned or implemented in isolation. And everyone in the organization must be informed of the underlying components and mutual relationships of IT service delivery (and the related involved departments). This process requires a holistic approach, clear communication and the requirement that everyone can have access to the correct, most recent and unambiguous IT plans, and be provided with the appropriate information.

Design aspects
In order for the organization to strive to attain the highest possible quality with a continual "improvement focus", a structured and results-oriented approach is necessary in each of the five separate aspects of design. Results-oriented in this case means aiming "to satisfy the wishes of the customers/users." These five aspects are as follows:
1. service solution (including functional requirements, resources and capacities)
2. service portfolio (support systems and tools)
3. architecture (technological and management)
4. processes
5. measurement systems and metrics

The design of service solutions
A structured design approach is necessary in order to produce a new service against agreed costs, functionality, quality and within the agreed time scale. The process must be iterative and incremental in order to satisfy the customers' changing wishes and requirements. The following matters should be taken into consideration:
- analysis of agreed business requirements
- revision of existing IT services and infrastructures and development of alternative services
- design of the services on the basis of new requirements

- the contents of the Service Acceptance Criteria (SAC) must be included in the initial design
- evaluation of costs of alternatives
- agreed expenditures and costs
- evaluation and confirmation of benefits for the business
- decide on the desired solutions, results and objectives (SLR)
- monitor the services in light of the overall strategies
- ensure that corporate and IT governance and security controls are satisfied
- ensure that the service functions effectively and satisfies the requirements
- support agreements are necessary to deliver the service
- assemble the Service Design Package (SDP); this includes all aspects of the service and the requirements for all successive stages in the lifecycle

The design of the service portfolio

The service portfolio is the most critical management system for supporting all of the processes. It describes the service delivery in terms of value for the customer and must include all of the service information and its status. The portfolio illustrates the status of a service, whether in development, operational or retired. The following is an overview of the service portfolio, highlighting the various phases. It is important to note that the customer has an insight only into the service catalogue, see Figure 4.1. The other sections of the portfolio are not available to the customer.

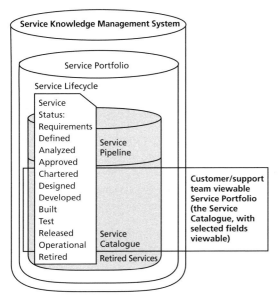

Figure 4.1   Content of the Service Portfolio (Source: Service Design was produced by OGC)

Although the service portfolio is designed during the Service Design phase (see the service catalogue management process), the portfolio is managed by the Service Strategy. Further information on the portfolio can be found in the chapter on Service Strategy.

The design of the architecture

The architecture design activities include preparing the blueprints for the development and deployment of an IT infrastructure, the applications and data (according to the needs of the business). It should be noted that during this design aspect, the provision of quality, high value services is possible only by the personnel, the processes and the partners that are involved in this production aspect. ITIL describes this architecture design as follows:

> **Architecture design** is the development and maintenance of IT policy, strategies, architectures, designs, documents, plans and processes for deployment, implementation and improvement of appropriate IT services and solutions throughout the organization.

The design of an architecture is not simple and varying - sometimes conflicting - needs must be taken into account. In any case, it must be ensured that:
- it satisfies the needs of the business, its products and services
- a proper balance is found among innovation, risks and costs
- it conforms to relevant frameworks, strategies, policies, etc.
- there is coordination among the designers, planners, strategists, etc.

Every enterprise is a complex system of functions, processes, structures and information sources. The architecture of the enterprise must offer insights into how these matters connect with each other in order to achieve the enterprise objectives. The enterprise architecture is, in its own right, equally large and complex.

There are various frameworks for the development of enterprise architectures. The enterprise architecture must include the following elements:
- **service architecture** - translates the applications, infrastructure, organization and support activities into services to the business
- **application architecture** - ensures the development of blueprints for the development of individual applications
- **information architecture** - describes how the information sources are managed and distributed
- **IT infrastructure architecture** - describes the structure, function and geographic distribution of hardware and software
- **environment architecture** - describes all of the aspects, types and levels of the environment controls

In addition to a technical component (applications, system software, information and data, infrastructure and environment systems), a management architecture must also be developed. In this regard, there are five elements that must be taken into consideration, namely: the sector (needs, requirements), personnel, processes, tools and technology (IT products that are used in providing the services). It is important that the technology is not the primary focus, but rather the wishes and requirements of the customer.

The design of processes

Working with defined processes is the basis of ITIL. By defining what the activities are and what the input and output are, it is possible to work more efficiently and effectively, and especially in a more customer-oriented way. By assessing these processes, the organization can enhance its efficiency and effectiveness even further. The next step is to establish norms and standards. In this way the organization can link the quality requirements with the output. This approach corresponds with Deming's *Plan-Do-Check-Act* Management Cycle.

Every process must have a process owner who is responsible for the process and for its improvement. Service Design offers the process owner support in the design process by standardizing terms and templates and ensuring that processes are consistent and are integrated.

ITIL describes a process as follows:

> A **process** is a structured set of activities designed to achieve a specific goal. A process makes defined outputs out of one or more inputs. A process includes all roles, responsibilities; resources and management controls that are needed to deliver reliable output and can possibly define policy, standards, guidelines, activities, procedures and work instructions, if necessary.

A process consists of the implementation of activities and the monitoring of that implementation. Process control is defined further as:

> **Process control** consists of the planning and regulation of a process, with the purpose of executing that process in an efficient, effective and consistent manner.

The design of measurement systems and metrics

In order to lead and manage the development process effectively, regular assessments must be performed. The selected assessment system must be synchronized with the capacity and maturity of the processes that are assessed. Care should be taken as it will affect the behaviour of delivering the service. Immature processes are not capable of supporting refined assessments. There are four elements that can be investigated, namely **progress**, **fulfillment**, **effectiveness** and **efficiency** of the process. As the processes develop over time, the units of measure also must develop. Therefore, the emphasis in mature processes is more on the assessment of efficiency and effectiveness. Additional information can be found in the chapter on Continual Service Improvement.

Value of Service Design

Good Service Design offers the following benefits:
- lower Total Cost of Ownership (TCO)
- improved quality of service delivery
- improved consistency of the service
- simpler implementation of new or modified services
- improved synchronization of services with the needs of the business
- improved effectiveness of performances
- improved IT administration
- more effective service management and IT processes
- more simplified decision-making

Design constraints and opportunities

Although designers are free to design services, it must be understood that they are dependent on internal resources (including available financial resources) and external circumstances (e.g. the impact of ISO, SOX and COBIT). In addition, the design process offers opportunities to enhance the effectiveness and efficiency of IT facilities through the use of a Service Oriented Architecture (SOA) approach, considering the resulting decrease in time for delivering service solutions to the business.

It is important that the services are kept up-to-date in the service catalogue (part of the service portfolio and the configuration management system, or CMS). In general, this will position the organization to link IT facilities with the objectives (business service management). This will allow them to predict the impact of technology on the business and vice versa.

Business Service Management (BSM) enables the organization to:
• synchronize IT facilities with the business objectives
• set the priorities of IT activities on the basis of their impact on the business
• increase productivity and profitability
• support "corporate governance"
• enhance competitive advantages
• increase the quality of service delivery and customer satisfaction

4.2   Basic concepts

Service Design models

Which model should be used for the development of IT services largely depends on the model that is chosen for the delivery of IT services. Before a new design model is adopted, an overview of the available IT capacities and equipment should be made. This overview should focus on the following elements:
• business drivers and demands
• the scope and capability of the current service provider
• the requirements and goals of the new service
• the scope and capability of current external service providers
• the maturity of the organizations and their processes
• the culture of the organizations
• IT infrastructure, applications, data, services and other components
• the level of corporate and IT governance
• available budget and resources
• staff levels and available skills

Insights into the above issues will help determine what the opportunities for the organization are and whether they are in a position to take the next step of providing new or changed services. The manner in which the next step is taken should be based on the business drivers and on the capabilities of the IT organization (and its partners).

Delivery options for IT services

The gap (between the current and the desired situation) does not necessarily have to be bridged by the organization itself. There are various strategies that can be considered for outsourcing some or all of the services, each with advantages and disadvantages. The most common of these are summarized in Table 4.1.

Delivery strategy	Characteristics	Advantages	Disadvantages
in-sourcing	Internal capacities are used for the design, development, maintenance, execution, and/or offer of support for the service.	- direct control - freedom of choice - familiarity with internal processes	- cost and time for delivering services - dependence on internal resources and competencies
outsourcing	Engaging an external organization for the design, development, maintenance, execution, and/or offering of support of the service.	- focus on core competencies - reducing long-term costs	- less direct control - unfamiliarity with the skills of the supplier
co-sourcing	A combination of in- and outsourcing in which various outsourcing organizations work co-operatively throughout the lifecycle.	- time to deliver services - better control	- complexity of projects - intellectual property and copyright protection
multi-sourcing	Multiple organizations make formal agreements with the focus on strategic partnerships (creating new market opportunities).	- expanded market opportunities - competitive response opportunities	- complexity of projects - 'culture clash'
business process outsourcing (BPO)	An external organization takes over a business process, or part of one, at a cheaper location, eg a call center.	- one-counter functionality - access to specialized skills	- loss of knowledge - loss of relationship with the business
application service provision	Computer-based services are offered to the customer over a network.	- access to complex and expensive solutions - support and upgrades included	- access only to facilities, not knowledge - 'culture clash'
knowledge process outsourcing (KPO)	This goes one step further than BPO, and rather than offering knowledge of a (part of a) process, knowledge of an entire work area is offered.	- knowledge and expertise - cost savings	- loss of internal knowledge - loss of relationship with the business

Table 4.1   IT services delivery strategies

The choice of one of the above delivery strategies depends on the specific situation in which the organization finds itself. Various issues play a role in the decision. The organization's available internal capacities and needs and the personnel (culture) have a significant impact on the delivery strategy. Whichever strategy is chosen, it is always essential to assess and review the performances in order to remain ultimately able to satisfy the changing demands of the market.

Design- and development options for IT services

In order to make the appropriate decision regarding the design and delivery of IT services, it is crucial to understand the current lifecycle stages, methods and approaches for service development. Insights into the following aspects of lifecycle approaches for service development are essential:
- the structure (milestones)
- activities (work flows, tasks)
- primary models associated with the chosen method giving various perspectives (process-, data-, event- and users' perspectives)

Rapid Application Development

It is necessary to understand the differences between object-oriented and structured system development and the basic principles of Rapid Application Development (RAD) in order to recognize how the choice of a software solution changes the structure of the lifecycle approach.

Traditional development approaches are based on the principle that the requirements of the customer/client can be determined at the beginning of the lifecycle and that the development costs can be kept under control by managing the changes. RAD-approaches begin with the notion that change is inevitable and that discouraging change simply indicates passivity in regard to the market. The RAD-approach is an incremental and iterative development approach.

The incremental approach implies that a service is designed bit by bit. Parts are developed separately and are delivered piecemeal. Each piece is supported by one of the business functions and together they support the whole. The big advantage in this approach is its shorter delivery time. The development of each part, however, requires that all phases of the lifecycle are continued.

The iterative approach implies that the lifecycle is repeated many times through the design. Prototypes of the entire process are used in order to understand the customer-specific requirements better, after which the design is adapted to it.

A combination of the two approaches is possible. An organization can begin by specifying the requirements for the entire service, followed by an incremental design and the development of the application.

RAD-approaches, such as the Unified Process and the Dynamic Systems Development Method (DSDM), are a response to the customer's demand to keep costs low during the development project. Thus DSDM involves the user in the development process of developing a software system that satisfies the expectations (demands) that can be adjusted, for on-time delivery within the allotted budget.

RAD-approaches not only provide a substantial savings in time, they also reduce development and implementation risks. Although they might be more difficult to manage than conventional approaches and involve more requirements regarding the skills and experience of the personnel, they make a positive contribution to the implementation and overall acceptance in the organization. They also support developers to anticipate changing organization demands more quickly, so that they can modify the design. Contrary to traditional approaches, the RAD-teams are smaller and are made up of generalists. In addition, it is easier to insert critical decisions during the process.

Commercial of the shelf solutions

Many organizations choose standard software solutions to satisfy needs and demands. A framework is needed for the selection, modification and implementation of packages of this kind, and it is especially important to know at the outset what requirements are set at management and operational levels. It is equally important in regard to purchasing, to have an understanding of the advantages and disadvantages of such packages.

Besides defining the functional requirements, it is also crucial to determine the requirements in regard to the product, the supplier and the integration of the service package.

4.3   Processes and other activities

Processes

In this section is a description of Service Design processes and activities that are responsible for the delivery of important information for the design of a new or changed service solution. A results-oriented, structured approach, together with consideration of the five aforementioned design aspects, guarantees service delivery of the highest quality and consistency in the organization as a whole. A more extensive description of the processes can be found in Chapter 10 of this book.

All of the design activities in this phase of the lifecycle stem from the needs and demands of the customer and are a reflection of the strategy, planning and policy produced by the Service Strategy. Each phase of the lifecycle is input for the following phase of the lifecycle. Service Strategy provides important input into the Service Design, which in turn provides input for the Transition phase. Therefore it is, in fact, the backbone of the Service Lifecycle.

In order to develop effective and efficient services that satisfy the customers' needs, it is essential that the output from the other areas and processes be included in the Service Design process. The seven tightly connected processes in the Service Design phase are:
• service catalogue management
• service level management
• capacity management
• availability management
• IT service continuity management
• information security management
• supplier management

Service Catalogue Management (SCM)

Service catalogue management is an important component of the service portfolio. The two comprise the backbone of the Service Lifecycle by providing information to every other phase. Although the overall portfolio is produced as a component of the Service Strategy, it needs the cooperation of all of the successive phases. At the moment that a service is ready for use, the Service Design produces the specifications that can be included in the service portfolio. The ultimate goal of service catalogue Management is the development and maintenance of a service catalogue that includes accurate details of all services, whether operational, in development or retired, and the business processes they support. It comprises, thus, the portion of the portfolio that is visible to the customer.

Service Level Management (SLM)

Service level management represents the IT service provider to the customer, and the customer internally to the IT service provider. The goal of this process is to take responsibility for ensuring that the levels of IT service delivery are achieved, both for existing services and future services in accordance with the agreed targets. SLM includes the planning, coordinating, providing, agreeing, monitoring and reporting of service level agreements (SLAs), including the revision of attained service delivery, to ensure that the quality satisfies, and where possible, exceeds, the agreed requirements. An SLA is a written established agreement between a service provider and a customer that records the goals and responsibilities of both parties. This process supports the service catalogue Management by providing information and trends regarding customer satisfaction.

Capacity management

Capacity management is the central point for all designs regarding IT performance and capacity issues. The goal of capacity management is to ensure that the capacity corresponds to both the existing and future needs of the customer (recorded in a capacity plan). The engine behind the process of capacity management is the requirements that the customer poses and that are recorded in the SLA.

Synchronization between capacity management and the service portfolio and SLM within the lifecycle of Service Design is essential. Thus capacity management provides information on existing and future resources through which the organization can decide which components will be renewed and when and how that will be done. For its part, capacity management must also have a view regarding the plans of the organization as outlined in the IT Service Strategy.

Availability management

The availability and reliability of IT services have a direct influence on customer satisfaction and the reputation of the service provider. Availability management is, therefore, essential and must be involved at an early stage in the lifecycle, just as is the case with capacity management. Availability management includes the entire process of designing, implementing, assessing, managing and improving IT services and the components included therein. The goal of this process is to ensure that the availability level of both new and modified services corresponds with the levels as agreed with the customer. In order to achieve that, availability management can implement both proactive and reactive activities that include monitoring and reporting of the availability metrics, and must maintain the availability management information system, which includes all of the necessary information, and this forms the basis of the availability plan.

IT Service Continuity Management (ITSCM)

IT service continuity management plays a valuable role in the support of the process of business continuity planning. This process can be applied by organizations as a means of focusing attention on continuity and recovery requirements, and to justify the decision to implement a business continuity plan. The ultimate goal of ITSCM is to support business continuity by ensuring that the required IT facilities can be restored within the agreed time. The process focuses on occurrences that can be considered as disasters (calamities). The focus in the first instance is solely on IT-related matters that support the business processes. Less significant catastrophes will be handled through the incident management process.

Information security management

Information security management ensures that the information security policy satisfies the organization's overall security policy and the requirements originating from corporate governance.

Security is not really a step in the lifecycle. Information security is a continual process and is an integral component of all of the services. This process supports the consciousness of the entire organization in regard to service delivery. Information security management must understand the entire playing field of IT and business security so that it is in a position to manage existing and future security aspects of the business. The Information security management system (ISMS) serves as the basis for a cost-effective development of an information security program that supports the business objectives.

Supplier management

The process of supplier management draws attention to all of the suppliers and contracts in order to support the delivery of services to the customer. The goal is to guarantee a constant level of quality for the right price. All activities in this process stem from the suppliers strategy and the policy originating with the Service Strategy. In order to achieve consistency and effectiveness during the implementation of the policy, a suppliers and contracts database must be established which includes suppliers and contracts as well as the execution of the supported services. All of this should be done with an eye towards valuable, high-quality IT service delivery. The supplier management process must be "in sync" with the demands of the organization as well as the requirements of information security management and ITSCM.

Activities

In addition to the seven processes mentioned earlier, three activities can be differentiated in the Service Design process. They are:
• development of requirements
• data- and information management
• application management

Development of requirements

Type of requirements
ITIL assumes that the analysis of the existing and required business processes results in functional requirements that fall under IT services (consisting of applications, data, infrastructure, environment and skills).

There are three types of requirements for each system, namely:
- **Functional requirements** - These describe matters for which a service could be done and that can be expressed as a task or function of which a component must be carried out. Various models can be considered for specifying the functional requirements, such as:
  - system context diagram
  - use case model
- **Management- and operational requirements** - These define the non-functional requirements of the IT service. The requirements serve as a basis for the first systems, the estimation of costs and support for the viability of the proposed service. Requirements from the management and execution can relate to a large number of quality aspects:
  - manageability
  - efficiency
  - availability and reliability
  - capacity and performance
  - security
  - installation
  - continuity
  - controllability
  - maintainability
  - operability
  - measurability and reportability
- **Usability requirements** - Ensure that the services satisfy the expectations of the users in terms of ease of use and user friendliness. In order to achieve this, the following must be done:
  - develop performance standards for evaluations
  - define test scenarios

Just as with management- and operational requirements, usability requirements can be adopted to test applications for compliance with the usability requirements.

Requirement investigation
There are various investigation techniques for arriving at clearer requirements. Considering that customers are often unsure about the requirements, the support of a developer is sometimes necessary. This person must be aware of the fact that people may see him/her as "someone from the IT department", which dictates the requirements. A certain amount of care is therefore called for. Possible investigation methods are:
- interviews
- workshops
- observation
- protocol analysis
- shadowing

- scenario analysis
- prototyping

Problems in the development of requirements

There are various problems that can occur in developing requirements:
- lack of relevance to the objectives of the service
- lack of clarity or ambiguity in the wording
- duplication between requirements
- conflicts between requirements
- uncertainty on the part of users
- inconsistent levels of detail

In order to face these and other problems, it is important to appoint participants. Three groups need to be involved in the establishment of requirements:
- the customer
- the users' community
- the service development team

Documenting requirements

The requirements document is the core of the process. This document contains every individual requirement in a standard template. The requirements that eventually come from the users must also be included. Every requirement must be SMART (Specific, Measureable, Achievable/ Appropriate, Realistic/Relevant and Timely/Time-bound) formulated. In addition, they should be checked to make sure they are clear, unambiguous and reasonable, synchronized with the customer's objectives, and not in conflict with any of the other requirements.

The result can then be recorded in the requirements catalogue. This should be a component of the requirements portfolio in the overall service portfolio. The users' requirements should be included here and labeled with an identification number, the source, the owner, the priority (e.g. according to the MoSCoW-approach: must have, should have, could have, won't have), description, involved business process, and so on.

The requirements analysis is an iterative process. In other words, the requirements change during the course of the development process of the service. It is therefore also important that the users be involved throughout the entire process.

Data- and information management

Data is one of the most critical matters that must be kept under control in order to develop, deliver and support effective IT services. Factors for successful data management include:
- the users have access to the information that they need for their work
- information is shared in the organization
- the quality of the information is maintained at an acceptable level
- legal aspects in the areas of privacy, security and confidentiality are taken into account

If data assets are not effectively managed, there is a risk that people will collect information and data that are not necessary; emphasis will be placed on outdated information; a lot of information is no longer accessible; and information is made accessible to those who are not authorized to have it.

Scope
There are four management areas in the field of data and information management:

- **Management of data sources** - The sources should be clear and responsibilities must be entrusted to the right person. This process is also known as data administration. This activity includes the following responsibilities:
  - define the need for information
  - a data inventory and an enterprise data model must be developed
  - identify shortages and ambiguities
  - maintain a catalogue
  - assess the costs and the rewards of the organization data
- **Management of data- and information technology** - This area relates to the management of IT and includes matters such as the design of databases and database management. This is covered in the chapter on Service Operation.
- **Management of information processes** - The data lifecycle (process of creating, collecting, accessing, modifying, storing, deleting and archiving of data) must be controlled. This often occurs in conjunction with the application management process.
- **Management of data standards and policy** - The organization must formulate standards and policy for data management as a component of the IT strategy.

Data management and the Service Lifecycle
In order to understand the use of data in business processes, it is recommended that a lifecycle approach be followed that looks into subjects such as:

- What data do we have at this time and how are they classified?
- What data should be collected through the business processes?
- How will the data be stored and maintained?
- How are the data accessed and by whom?
- How are the data disposed of and by whom?
- How is the data quality protected?
- How can the data be made more accessible and available?

Data has an important connotation; not only for organizations for which the provision of data is a core business; consider, for example, a press bureau such as Reuters. Data is increasingly viewed as a common property with a value that can be placed in financial terms. Various opportunities for this exist:

- **Valuing data by its availability** - This approach looks at which business processes would not be possible if a certain portion of the data were not available, and what this would cost the organization.
- **Valuing lost data** - This approach examines the cost of having to replace data if it were lost or destroyed.
- **Valuing data by considering the data lifecycle** - This approach focuses on issues such as how data is created; how it is made available; and how it is archived; the lifecycle differs (and thus,

so do the costs) depending on the demand, or if these steps can be performed by an internal or external party.

Classifying data
Data can be classified on three levels:
- **Operational data** - This data is necessary for the continued functioning of the organization and is the least specific.
- **Tactical data** - This is data that is needed for line- or higher management; among other things, this refers to quarterly data, distilled from management information systems.
- **Strategic data** - Refers to the long-term trends compared with external (market) information.

Data owner
Responsibilities of the data owner include:
- determining who can create, revise, read and delete data
- consent given regarding the way in which data are stored for modification
- approves level of security
- agreeing business description and a purpose

Data integrity
In defining IT services, it is important that management and operational data requirements be considered. Specifically in the following areas:
- restoration of lost data
- controlled access to data
- implementation of policy on archiving of data
- periodic monitoring of data integrity

Application management
An application is defined by ITIL as:

> An **application** is a software program(s) with specific functions that offer direct support to the execution of business processes and/or procedures.

Applications, along with data and infrastructure, comprise the technical component of IT services. It is crucial that the applications that are provided correspond with the requirements of the customer. Organizations often expend a great deal of time on the functional requirements of the new service, while too little time is spent on the design of the management- and operational (non-functional) requirements of the service. That means that when the service is performed, it completely caters to the functional requirements, but not to the expectations of the business and the customer in the area of quality and performance.

Two alternative approaches are necessary to implement application management, namely:
- **Service Development Lifecycle** - (SDLC) is a systematic problem-solving approach for supporting the development of an IT service. This consists of the following steps:
  - feasibility study
  - analysis
  - design

- testing
- implementation
- evaluation
- maintenance
- **Application maintenance** - The other approach looks globally at all of the services in order to ensure a continuing process of managing and maintaining the applications. All applications are described consistently in the application portfolio, which is synchronized with the customers' requirements.

Application frameworks

The application framework includes all management- and operational aspects and provides solutions for all of the management- and operational requirements for an application.

Architecture-related activities must be planned and managed separately from the individual system-based software projects. Application designers must concentrate on one application, while application framework developers focus on more than one application and on the opportunities.

A method which is often employed is to distinguish between different types of applications. For example, not every application can be used on a Microsoft Windows platform, coupled with a UNIX server in which HTML, Java-applets and JavaBeans must be used. The different application types can be viewed as an application family. Every application in the same family is based on the same application framework.

In this concept the first step of the application design phase is the identification of the right framework. As the application framework matures, various decisions can be made. If it is not mature then the right strategy is to collect and analyze the requirements that do not fit with the existing framework. Based on the application requirements, new requirements can be defined for the application framework, after which the framework can be modified so that it satisfies all of the requirements.

CASE tools

An aspect of overall alignment is the need to align applications with their underlying support structures. Development environments traditionally have their own Computer Assisted/Aided Software Engineering tools (CASE) that, for example, offer the means to specify requirements, draw design diagrams or generate applications. They are also a location for storage and for managing the elements that are created.

Application development

After the design phase, the application must be further developed. Both the application and the environment must be prepared for the launch. The application development phase includes the following issues:
- consistent coding conventions
- independent structural guidelines for applications
- business-ready testing

- management checklist for the building phase
- organization of the team roles for the structure

Important outputs of application development include:
- scripts for starting and stopping an application
- scripts for monitoring both hardware- and software configurations
- specifications of the unit of measure that can be obtained from the application
- SLA-objectives and requirements
- operational requirements and documentation
- support requirements

4.4   Organization

Roles and responsibilities

Well performing organizations can quickly and accurately make the right decisions and execute them successfully. In order to achieve this, it is crucial that the roles and responsibilities are clearly defined. This is also an essential issue in the Service Design process. One of the possible models that can be helpful in this regard is the RACI model. RACI is an acronym for the four most important roles:
- **Responsible** - the person who is responsible for completing the task
- **Accountable** - just one person who is accountable for each task
- **Consulted** - people who give advice
- **Informed** - people who must be kept in the loop regarding the progress of the project

In establishing a RACI system, the following steps are necessary:
- identify activities and processes
- identify and define functional roles
- conduct meetings and delegate the RACI-codes
- identify gaps and potential overlaps
- distribute the chart and build in feedback
- ensure that the allocations are followed

Skills

Despite the fact that every position brings with it specific skills and competencies (see "Roles" below), the responsible person must:
- be aware of the business priorities and objectives
- be aware of the role that IT plays
- possess customer service skills
- be aware of what IT can provide to the customer
- have the competencies and knowledge that are needed in order to perform the function well
- have ability to use, understand and interpret the best practice policies and procedures to ensure adherence

Roles

In this section is a description of the roles and responsibilities of the most important positions in the Service Design process. Depending on the size of organizations these roles can be combined. The most important roles are:

- **The process owner** is responsible for ensuring that the process is implemented as agreed and that the established objectives will therefore be achieved. Tasks are:
  - documenting and recording the process
  - defining the KPIs and if necessary revising them
  - improving the effectiveness and efficiency of the process
  - providing input to the Service Improvement Plan
  - reviewing the process, the roles and responsibilities
- **The service design manager** is responsible for the overall coordination and inputting of the service designs. Tasks include:
  - ensure that the Service Strategy corresponds with the design process and that the designs satisfy the established requirements
  - design the functional aspects of the services
  - produce and maintain the design documentation
  - assess the effectiveness and efficiency of the design process
- **The service catalogue manager** is responsible for the production and maintenance of the service catalogue. In addition, the service catalogue manager must:
  - ensure that the services are recorded in the service catalogue
  - ensure that the information that has been included is up-to-date and is consistent with the information in the service portfolio
  - ensure that the catalogue is secure and that there are backups
- **The service level manager** has as their most important responsibilities to:
  - have an insight into the changing demands of the customer and the market
  - ensure that the customers' existing and future requirements have been identified
  - negotiate and make agreements on the delivery of services
  - assist in the production and maintenance of an accurate services portfolio
  - ensure that the objectives that have been ratified in underlying contracts are synchronized with the SLA
- **The availability manager** is responsible for:
  - ensuring that the existing services are available as agreed
  - assisting in investigating and diagnosing all incidents and problems
  - contributing to the design of the IT infrastructure
  - proactively improving the availability of services
- **The security manager** has as their most important tasks to:
  - design and maintain the information security policy
  - communicate with the involved parties on matters pertaining to the security policy
  - assist in the business impact analysis
  - perform risk analyses and risk management together with availability management and ITSCM

In addition, there are still the following responsible positions to recognize in this process:

- IT planner
- IT designer/architect

- service continuity manager
- capacity manager
- supplier manager

4.5   Methods, techniques and tools

Technological considerations

It is extremely important that someone ensures that the tools to be used support the processes and not the other way around. There are various tools and techniques that can be used for supporting the service and component designs. They not only make the hardware and software designs possible, but also enable the development of environment designs, process designs and data designs. The great variety of tools and techniques offer the following benefits:

- attainment of speed in the design process
- adherence to standards
- the development of prototypes and models
- take into account diverse scenarios (what if…?)

The design process can be simplified by making use of tools that give a graphic image of the service and its components; from the business processes to the service and the SLA, through the infrastructure, environment, data and applications, processes, OLAs (operational level agreements), teams, contracts and suppliers. If the tool also contains financial information and is coupled with a "metrics tree", the service can be guarded and managed through all of the phases in its lifecycle.

These tools not only facilitate the design process, they also support all of the phases in the Service Lifecycle, including:

- management of all levels of the Service Lifecycle
- all aspects of the service and the performances
- management of costs
- management of the service portfolio and catalogue
- a Configuration Management System (CMS) and a Service Knowledge Management System (SKMS)

The following generic activities must be performed:

- ensure that there is a generic lifecycle for IT assets
- formalize relationships between different types of IT assets
- define the roles and responsibilities
- ensure that a study is performed in order to understand the TCO of an IT service

Even more can be added for application assets:

- define an acquisition strategy for IT assets and analyze how this can be synchronized with both the IT- and the business strategy
- document the role that the application plays in the provision of IT services
- determine standards for the use of various approaches to the design of applications

For data/information assets still more can be added:
- ensure that data designs are made in the light of:
  - the importance of standardization
  - the need for qualitatively valuable data
  - the value of data to the organization

For IT infrastructure assets more can be added:
- establish standards for the acquisition and management of IT- and environmental infrastructure (electricity, space, middleware, database systems etc.)
- determine activities for the optimum use of the IT infrastructure assets
- specify the need for tools and describe how they would be used

For skills assets more can be added:
- formalize how competencies could be considered as assets in the organization
- ensure that the competencies are documented

In order to establish interfaces and dependencies the following can be added:
- formalize the interfaces that the acquisition and management of IT assets have with functions and processes outside the IT sphere
- formalize quality control in the acquisition and management of IT assets

Service management tools

Tools help ensure that Service Design processes can function effectively. They enhance efficiency and provide valuable management information on the identification of possible weak points. The long-term benefit is that the use of tools serves to reduce costs and increase productivity, in the interest of improving the quality of IT service delivery. In addition, the use of tools makes possible the centralization of essential processes, as well as the automation and integration of "core" service management processes.

Considerations in the evaluation of service management tools include:
- data structure, data handling and integration
- conformity with international standards
- flexibility in implementation, use, and sharing of data
- support in the monitoring of service levels

The tool serves to support the process rather than the other way around. If possible, it is recommended that a completely integrated tool be acquired, that supports the many service management processes. If this is not possible, then interfaces among the various tools should be taken into consideration. During the selection process it is advisable to employ a Statement of Requirements (SoR). The requirements should be considered using the MoSCoW analysis:
- **M** - must have this
- **S** - should have this
- **C** - could have this
- **W** - won't have this now, but would like in the future

The tool must be flexible so that it can support individual access rights. It is necessary to determine who has access to the data and with what objective. In addition, it must be decided as to which platform the tool can work on. During the first consideration it is wise to look into the credit worthiness of the supplier and find out if they offer support (training) for a few months or years. In this process it is important to realize that a solution almost never satisfies 100% of the requirements. The 80/20 rule is perhaps more realistic in this framework. In other words, the tool is likely to satisfy closer to 80% of the established requirements.

4.6   Implementation

Implementation considerations

In this section the implementation considerations for Service Design are addressed. In addition, the interfaces of Service Design with the other phases of the Service Lifecycle will be discussed.

Business impact analysis

The Business Impact Analysis (BIA) is a valuable source of information for establishing the customer's needs, and the impact and the risk of a service. The BIA is an essential element in the business continuity process and dictates the strategy to be followed for risk reduction and recovery after a catastrophe. The BIA consists of two parts: on the one hand is the investigation of the impact of the loss of a business process or function; on the other hand is the stopping of the effect of that loss.

The BIA must be conducted in order to support the definition of the business continuity strategy, and makes it possible to better understand the function and the importance of the service. In this way the organization can determine, among other things:
• what the critical services are
• what an acceptable time is for the service to be unavailable
• what an acceptable level of unavailability of the service is
• what the costs of the loss of the service are
• what are the critical business & service periods

Implementation of Service Design

The process, policy and architecture for the design of IT services, as described in this book, must be documented and used in order to design and implement appropriate IT services. In principle, it is recommended that all of the processes be implemented at the same time since all of the processes are related to each other and often are also dependent on each other. What is ultimately needed is an integrated set of processes that IT services can manage and oversee throughout the entire lifecycle. Since organizations can rarely implement everything at once, the process for which there is the greatest need should be the first to be done, realizing that all processes are interlinked. In addition, this also depends on the maturity of the organization's IT service management. The implementation priorities must correspond with the objectives of the Service Improvement Program (SIP). If, for example, availability of IT services is an important point, then the organization must focus on those processes that will improve availability; in this case, incident management, problem management, change management and availability management. Various other processes, such as capacity management, security management and continuity management also influence availability, as illustrated by the intertwining of the ITIL processes.

It is important that a structured project management method be used during the implementation phase. The CSI model is a good example of such a method. The success of the Service Design and the success of the improvement of the Service Design processes must be assessed. The results must then be analyzed and reported. If it does not satisfy the requirements, then an adjustment is probably needed. During the entire process assessments must be made. One of the possible methods is the Balanced Scorecard, which was developed by Robert Kaplan and David Norton as a method for measuring business activities in terms of its strategy and vision, and with which a good image of the organization's performance can be sketched.

Prerequisites
There are various prerequisites for new or revised processes. They are often requirements of other processes. For example, before Service Level Management (SLM) can design the Service Level Agreement (SLA) a business service catalogue and a technical service catalogue are necessary. Problem management depends on a mature incident management process. These things are much bigger than just ITSM: availability and capacity management need information of the business plan. There are more of these examples which need to be considered first before high process maturity can be achieved.

Critical success factors and KPIs
It is recommended that every IT service provider focuses on a number of critical success factors and KPIs. They should be determined at the beginning of the Continual Service Improvement Program.

KPIs for Service Design are:
• percentage of specifications of the requirements of Service Design produced on time
• percentage of specifications of the requirements of Service Design produced within budget
• percentage of Service Design packs produced on time
• accuracy of Service Design
• accuracy of the SLAs, OLAs and contracts

Challenges
Examples of challenges that are faced during implementation include:
• the need for synchronization of existing architecture, strategy and policy
• the use of various technologies and applications
• unclear or changing customer requirements
• lack of awareness and knowledge of service delivery
• resistance to working systematically
• inefficient use of resources

In order to overcome the challenges, consideration may be given to the following matters:
• insights into the customer's requirements and priorities
• adequate communication with involved parties, but equally, be a "listening ear"

- involve as many people as possible in the design process
- ensure the involvement of management and personnel

Risks

There are several risks during the Service Design phase, including:
- if the level of maturity in one of the processes is low, it is impossible to reach a high level of maturity in other processes
- business requirements are not clear for the IT personnel
- too little time is allotted for Service Design
- synchronization among infrastructure, customer and partners is not good, which means the requirements cannot be satisfied
- the Service Design phase is not clear or on the whole is not available

Interfaces with other phases in the lifecycle

All activities in the Service Design phase originate from the customer's needs and requirements, and are then also a reflection of the strategy, plans and policy produced by the first phase of the lifecycle: the Services Strategy.

The Service Design phase in the lifecycle begins with the new or changed requirements of the customer. Ultimately, by the end of the design process, a service solution must be designed which satisfies those requirements before they begin the transition process together with the service package. In the transition phase, the service will be evaluated, structured, tested and deployment will take place after which the implementation will be transferred to Service Operation.

Figure 4.2 makes clear that the output from every phase is input for the next phase in the lifecycle. Thus Service Strategy provides important input to Service Design, which in turn, provides input to the transition phase.

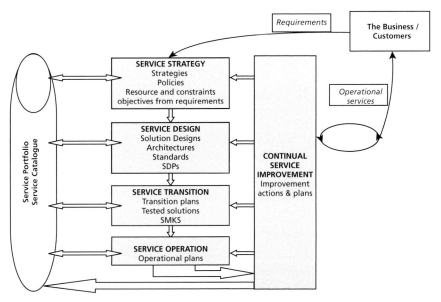

Figure 4.2   The most important relationships, inputs and outputs of Service Design (Based on OGC ITIL V3 material)

The service portfolio provides information to every process in every phase of the lifecycle. In this respect it is in fact the backbone of the Service Lifecycle. The service portfolio must be a component of the service knowledge management system and be included as a document in the configuration management system. This will be described in greater detail in the following Section, "Service Transition".

Chapter 5

Lifecycle Phase: Service Transition

5.1 Introduction

This chapter explains how the specifications from Service Design can be effectively converted to a new or changed service.

Objectives

The **goals** of Service Transition include:
- supporting the change process of the business (client)
- reducing variations in the performance and known errors of the new/changed service
- ensuring the service meets the requirements of the service specifications

The **objectives** of Service Transition include:
- the necessary means to realize, plan and manage the new service
- ensuring the minimum impact for the services which are already in production
- improving customer satisfaction and stimulate the proper use of the service and mutual technology

Scope

ITIL defines the **scope** of Service Transition as follows:

> **Service Transition** *includes the management and coordination of the processes, systems and functions required for the packaging, building, testing and deployment of a release into production, and establish the service specified in the customer and stakeholder requirements.*

A Service Transition generally comprises the following steps:
- planning and preparation
- building and testing
- any pilots
- planning and preparation of the deployment
- deployment and transition
- review and closing of Service Transition

Although change management, service asset and configuration management and knowledge management support all phases of the Service Lifecycle, the ITIL Service Transition book covers these. Release and deployment management, service validation and testing, and evaluation are included in the scope of Service Transition.

Value for the business
An effective Service Transition ensures that the new or changed services are better aligned with the customer's business operation. Specifically:
• the capacity of the business to react quickly and adequately to changes in the market
• changes in the business as a result of takeovers, contracting, etc. are well managed
• more successful changes and releases for the business
• better compliance of business and governing rules
• less deviation between planned budgets and the actual costs
• better insight into the possible risks during and after the input of a service
• higher productivity of customer staff

Optimization
A Service Transition is effective and efficient if the transition delivers what the business requested within the limitations in terms of money and other necessary means. Additionally, it is important

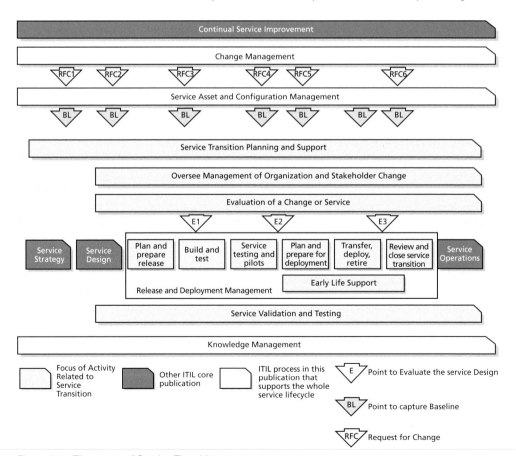

Figure 5.1   The scope of Service Transition (Based on OGC ITIL V3 material)

that the phase and release plans are coordinated with the business, the service management and the IT strategy.

That is why it matters the extent to which the results of the transition correspond with the specifications of the Service Design: what are the differences between the actual values and those from the specifications? These can influence aspects such as time, money, quality and risks.

5.2   Basic concepts

The following policies are important for an effective Service Transition and apply to every organization. The approach must still be adjusted to the conditions which differ from organization to organization:

- **Define and implement guidelines and procedures for Service Transition** - Define and document policies for Service Transition. The management team must approve the policies. The management team must pass the policies on to the organization, service providers and partners.
- **Always implement all changes through Service Transition** - All changes in the service portfolio or service catalogue undergo the change management process and the Service Transition phase.
- **Utilize frameworks and standards** - Base Service Transition on generally accepted frameworks, processes and systems. This promotes cooperation between the parties involved in the Service Transition and ensures that they "speak the same language".
- **Re-use of existing processes and systems** - Service Transition processes must be aligned with the processes and systems that the organization already applies. This promotes efficiency and effectiveness. If new processes are developed, re-use is an important design criterion.
- **Align service transition plans with the needs of the business** - Align transition plans, and new or changed services to the requirements and needs of the customer organization.
- **Create relations with stakeholders and maintain these** - During Service Transition, build up a relationship with customer (representatives), users and suppliers, to map their expectations of the new or changed service.
- **Set up effective "controls"** - Set up suitable control mechanisms for the entire lifecycle to guarantee a smooth transition of service changes and releases.
- **Deliver systems for knowledge transfer and decision support** - Service Transition develops systems and processes for knowledge transfer as necessary for an effective delivery of the service, and in order to make decision-making possible.
- **Plan releases and deployment packages** - Release packages must be clear, traceable, clearly planned, designed, built, tested, delivered, distributed and deployed for everyone involved.
- **Anticipate and manage changes in direction** - Ensure that the staff is trained in order to see when "direction adjustments" are necessary during the transition.
- **Manage resources proactively** - Deliver (and manage) shared and specialist resources for the different Service Transition activities in order to avoid delays.
- **Ensure the involvement in an early stage in the Service Lifecycle** - Consult stakeholders at an early stage, so that new or changed services are actually delivering what has been agreed.
- **Assure the quality of a new or changed service** - Verify and validate that the proposed changes can deliver the required service requirements.
- **Proactively improve the quality during a Service Transition** - Proactively plan and improve the quality of a new or changed service.

5.3   Processes and other activities

This section explains the processes and activities of a Service Transition:
- transition planning and support
- change management
- service asset and configuration management
- release and deployment management
- service validation and testing
- evaluation
- service knowledge management

Some of these processes and activities occur in more than one phase of the Service Lifecycle, but are stated in this section as they are central during the Service Transition.

Extensive information about each of these processes can be found in Chapter 11 of this book. The following sections only cover a short summary of the processes.

Transition planning and support

Transition planning and support ensures the planning and coordination of resources in order to realize the specification of the Service Design. Additionally, the process ensures the identification, management and minimization of risks which can interrupt the service during the transition phase.

The scope of transition planning consists of:
- design specifications and requirements of the production department in the transition planning process
- management of:
  - planning
  - support activities
  - transition progress
  - changes
  - issues
  - risks
  - deviations
  - processes
  - supported systems and tools
- monitoring the Service Transition performance
- communication with the client, users and stakeholders

The planning and support activities are:
1. set up transition strategy
2. prepare Service Transition
3. planning and coordination of Service Transition
4. support

Change management

The objective of the change management process is to ensure that changes are deployed in a controlled way, evaluated, prioritized, planned, tested, implemented and documented. There can be different reasons for a change such as: cost reduction, service improvement, failure of the service provision or a changed environment.

> A **change** is the addition, modification or removal of authorized, planned or supported service or service component and its associated documentation.

In the change management process it is important to ensure that:
- standardized methods and procedures are used
- all changes are kept in the CMDB
- consideration is given to the risks for the business

Universally the change management activities are comprised of:
- change planning and management
- release planning
- communication
- change authorization
- set up recovery plan
- reporting
- impact assessment
- continual improvement

The specific activities for the management of individual changes are comprised of:
1. create and record the Request for Change (RFC)
2. review the RFC
3. assess and evaluate change
4. authorize change
5. plan updates
6. coordinate change implementation
7. review and close change

Service Asset and Configuration Management (SACM)

SACM manages the service assets in order to support the other service management processes.

The objective is: the definition of service and infrastructure components and the maintenance of accurate configuration records. For this it is important that:
- the integrity of the service assets and configuration items (CIs) is protected
- all assets and CIs are categorized in configuration management
- the business and service management processes are effectively supported

SACM may cover non-IT assets and CIs of work products which support the development of services. The scope of the process also includes assets and CIs of other suppliers ("shared assets") in as far as these are important for the service.

The SACM activities are:
- management and planning
- configuration identification
- configuration management (control)
- status accounting and reporting
- verification and audits

Release and deployment management

Release and deployment management is aimed at the building, testing and deploying of the services specified in the Service Design, and ensuring that the client utilizes the service effectively.

The objective of release and deployment management is to ensure that:
- there are release and deployment plans
- release packages (composition) are successfully deployed
- the IT organization transfers knowledge to the clients
- there is minimal disturbance to the services

The process activities of release and deployment management are mainly comprised of:
1. planning
2. preparation of building, testing and deployment
3. building and testing
4. service tests and pilots
5. planning and preparation for deployment
6. transfer, deployment or retirement
7. verify deployment
8. Early Life Support (ELS)
9. review and close

Service validation and testing

Service tests deliver an important contribution to the quality of IT service provision. Tests ensure that the new or changed services are "fit for purpose" and "fit for use".

The goal of service validation and testing is to deliver a service which is of added value to the client's business. When not properly tested, additional incidents, problems and costs occur.

The objectives of service validation and testing are to ensure that:
- the release fulfils the expectation of the client
- the services are "fit for purpose" and "fit for use"
- the specifications (requirements) of the client and other stakeholders are defined

Service validation and testing are applied during the entire Service Lifecycle and are intended to test the quality of the service (parts). Testing directly supports the release and deployment process. The output from testing is used by the evaluation process.

The test process activities are not conducted in a fixed order and can be implemented in parallel. In any case they include:
• validation and test management
• planning and design test
• verification of test plan and design
• preparing the test environment
• testing
• evaluation of exit criteria and reports
• cleaning up and closure

There are many different test techniques and approaches, including: document review, simulation, scenario and laboratory tests, and role plays. The best choice depends on the type of service, the risk profile, the test goal and the test level.

Evaluation

Evaluation is a generic process that is intended to verify whether the performance of "something" is acceptable; for example, whether it has the right price/quality ratio, whether it is continued, whether it is in use, whether it is paid for, and so on.

In the context of Service Transition, the objective of evaluation is the definition of the performance of a service change. Evaluation delivers important input for Continual Service Improvement (CSI) and future improvement of service development and change management.

The evaluation process is comprised from the following activities:
• planning the evaluation
• evaluation of the predicted performance
• evaluation of the actual performance
• risk management

Knowledge management

The goal of knowledge management is the improvement of the quality of decision-making by ensuring that reliable and secure information is available during the Service Lifecycle. See also the DIKW model in Chapter 11.

The objectives of knowledge management include:
• enabling the service provider to improve the efficiency and quality of the services
• ensuring that the service provider's staff have access to adequate information

Knowledge management is used in the entire lifecycle, but is particularly relevant during the Service Transition: A successful transition depends to a large degree on the information available and knowledge of users, service desk, support and service provider.

Effective sharing of knowledge requires the development and maintenance of a service knowledge management system (SKMS). This system should be available to all information stakeholders and suit all information requirements.

Knowledge management is comprised of the following activities, methods and techniques:
- knowledge management strategy
- knowledge transfer
- data and information management
- the use of the SKMS

Other activities

Communication is central during every Service Transition: the greater the change, the greater the need for communication of the reasons for the change, the possible advantages, the plans for implementation and the effects.

Other operational activities of Service Transition such as the management of organizational changes and the management of stakeholders are explained in the Section "Organization".

5.4   Organization

On the whole, the activities of a process are not carried out by a single department. The different activities, for example of SACM, are carried out by departments such as service operation, application management, network management and system management. Therefore, the process activities are related to the different IT departments and their respective staff. Roles and responsibilities are also defined.

Generic roles

Process owner - The process owner ensures that all process activities are carried out and:
- is responsible for the process strategy, and assists in the design
- provides process documentation, guidelines and procedures and their application
- ensures there are adequate resources

Service owner - The service owner holds the responsibility, toward the client, for the initiation, transition and maintenance of a service and:
- is the contact person and ensures that the service meets the requirements
- identifies improvement points and provides data and reports for service monitoring
- is accountable for the delivery of the service to IT Management

Organizational context

The interfaces of other departments and third parties in Service Transition must be clearly defined and known. Programs, projects, Service Design and service provider all contribute towards the Service Transition.

Service Transition is actively managed by a **service transition manager**. The Service Transition manager is responsible for the daily management and control of the Service Transition teams and their activities. An example of a Service Transition organization is presented in Figure 5.2.

Service Transition roles and responsibilities

This section describes a number of roles and responsibilities within Service Transition, although some roles also fall within other lifecycle phases. Depending on the size of the organization and the scope of the service which is changed, some of these roles can be carried out by one person.

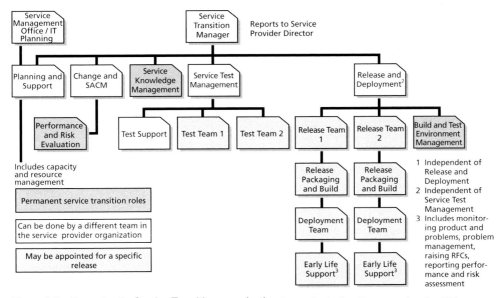

Figure 5.2   Example of a Service Transition organization (Source: Service Transition was produced by OGC)

The responsibilities of the **service asset manager** include:
- formulating process objectives and implementing the policy, the process standards, plans and procedures
- indicating the scope and function of the process, which items must be managed and the information that must be established
- taking care of communication about the process and making it known
- taking care of resources and training
- setting up the identification and the naming conventions of assets
- taking care of the evaluation of the use of tooling
- setting up interfaces with other processes
- planning the completion of the asset database
- making reports
- assisting with audits and taking care of corrective actions

The responsibilities of the **configuration manager** include:
- formulating process objectives and implementing the policy, the process standards, plans and procedures
- evaluating the existing configuration management systems and implementing the new systems
- indicating the scope and function of the process, which items must be managed and the information that must be established
- taking care of communication about the process and making it known
- taking care of resources and training
- setting up the identification and the naming conventions of CIs
- taking care of the evaluation of the use of tooling
- setting up interfaces with other processes
- evaluating existing CMS systems and implementation of new systems

- planning the filling in of CMS in the CMDBs
- making reports
- assisting with audits and taking corrective actions

The **change manager** has responsibilities (some of which can be delegated) including:
- receiving, logging and prioritizing (in collaboration with the initiator) RFCs, rejecting RFS based on the criteria
- preparing and chairing CAB and ECAB meetings
- deciding who attends which meeting, who receives RFCs, what must be changed there
- publishing Changes Schedules (SCs)
- maintaining change logs
- closing RFCs
- reviewing implemented changes
- making reports

The **Change Advisory Board (CAB)** is an advisory consultation body. The specific roles and responsibilities of the CAB will be explained in Section 11.2.

The responsibilities of the **release packaging and build manager** include:
- final release configuration
- building the final release and testing it (prior to independent testing)
- reporting known faults and workarounds
- input to the final implementation sign-off

The **deployment manager** is responsible for the following including:
- the final service implementation
- coordination of all release documentation, release notes and communication
- planning of the deployment, in combination with change management, knowledge management and SACM
- providing guidance during the release process
- giving feedback concerning the effectiveness of a release
- recording metrics for deployment to ensure within agreed SLAs

ITIL recognizes the following roles in the Service Transition phase of the Service Lifecycle, but this falls outside the scope of this book and the ITIL Foundations exams:
- configuration analyst
- configuration manager
- CMS manager
- configuration management team
- change authority
- risk-evaluation manager
- service knowledge manager
- test support
- Early Life Support (ELS)
- building and test environment management

Organizational change management

Significant change of a service also means a change of the organization. This can vary from "the transfer of a staff member to another department" to large changes such as "the manner of working in the organization". For example: a mail order company no longer sells its products by a printed catalogue but via a website.

The following aspects are important in organizational change management:
- **The emotional change cycle** - One of the biggest causes of failure of changes is not sufficiently considering the way in which the changes affect people. Therefore consider the emotional phases that people can experience before accepting changes. The emotional phases are: shock, avoidance, external blame, self blame and acceptance.
- **The role of Service Transition in organizational changes** - The management of change is the responsibility of the managers and heads of department involved in this specific change. However, the Service Transition manager or process owner is an important party in the change, and therefore Service Transition plays an important role in organizational changes. Service Transition must:
  - show awareness of the different cultures at organizational and individual levels
  - include active participation in the changing of people's attitudes (who are active within the lifecycle)
  - support individuals in such a way that the implementation of changes is consistently executed
  - evaluate whether the IT organization is sufficiently capable
  - guarantee that the change is accepted by the majority in their daily work method
  - take care to ensure that knowledge transfer, training, team building, process improvement and evaluation of staff are sufficiently competent
- **Planning and implementation of organizational changes** - In the planning and design of changes there is often insufficient consideration for the organizational side and the people. The focus lies on the technical aspect of the change. That is why it is important that the project plans also state the organizational changes caused by the change.
- **Products** - Service Strategy and Service Design result in several work products which support the management of organizational changes during the Service Transition, for example:
  - stakeholder analysis
  - organizational and competency assessments
  - service management process models
  - guidelines for processes and procedures
  - communication plan
  - RACI matrix (Responsible, Accountable, Consulted, Informed)
- **Evaluation of readiness for organizational change** - It is good practice to make a checklist to assess if the organization fulfills the requirements for transition in terms of roles and skills.
- **Monitoring of progress** - Research and surveys must be carried out on a regular basis at different levels in the organization concerning the effectiveness and the success of a Service Transition program. Use the result of the research to define how much progress is achieved with the transition. It will also indicate to staff that they are being heard and that their input is important in the transition.

- **Manage organizational changes in sourcing** - Sourcing IT services is one of the most serious organizational changes. There are many consequences for the personnel which must be considered and carefully prepared, such as:
  - the shock for staff
  - changes in the way in which the business and the service provider do business with each other
  - change of location with all the associated risks
- **Methods and techniques for organizational changes** - Numerous methods, techniques and best practices exist for management of changes, such as J.P. Kotter's "Changes in eight steps" and Rosabeth Moss Kanter's theory about the reasons why people resist change. It is important to make the best possible use of these.

Stakeholder management

Stakeholder management is a Crucial Success Factor in Service Transition. This is why a strategy should be developed in the Service Design phase. Explain:
- who the stakeholders are
- what their interest are
- what their influence is
- how they are included in the project or program
- what information is shared with them

A stakeholder map is a useful tool to map the different interest of the stakeholders. (See Figure 5.3.)

Stakeholders	Strategic direction	Financial	Operational changes	Interface with customers	Public safety	Competitive position
Business partner	●	●		●		●
Project teams			●			
Customers		●		●	●	
Press and media						●
Trade unions			●			
Staff	●		●			
Regulatory bodies		●			●	

Figure 5.3   Example stakeholder matrix (Source: Service Transition was produced by OGC)

Further a **stakeholder analysis** assists in finding out what the requirements and interests of the stakeholders are, and what their final influence and power will be during the transition.

Finally, the turnover of stakeholders during the Service Lifecycle must also be considered.

5.5   Methods, technology and tools

Technology plays an important part in the support of Service Transition. It can be divided into two types:

- **IT service management systems**:
    - enterprise frameworks which offer integration capabilities to integrate and link in the CMDB or other tools
    - system, network and application management tools
    - service dashboards and reporting tools
- **Specific ITSM technology and tools**:
    - service knowledge management systems
    - collaboration tools, content management systems and workflow tools
    - tools for data mining, data extraction and data transformation
    - tools for measuring and reporting
    - test (management) tools
    - publication tools
    - release and deployment technology

In addition specialized tools are available for change management, configuration management and release management, such as:

- configuration management
- tools for version control
- document management systems
- design tools
- distribution and installation tools
- construction and deployment tools

A more elaborate description of the various tools for Service Transition and the underlying processes is beyond the scope of this book.

5.6   Implementation

The implementation of Service Transition in a "greenfield" situation (from zero) is only feasible when establishing a new service provider. Most service providers focus on the improvement of the Service Transition (processes). For the improvement of Service Transition (processes) the following five aspects are also important:

1. **Justification** - The benefits of effective Service Transition are not always immediately visible to the client. Gathering evidence of the damage caused by an ineffective transition phase can justify the establishment or improvement of Service Transition. Take into consideration aspects such as: the costs of failed changes or errors in services in the production environment which could have been avoided if a good test process had been used.

2. **Design** - Factors to take into account when designing Service Transition are:
   - standards and guidelines to which the design must adhere
   - relationships with other supporting services (HRM, telecommunications, facilities management), project and program management, clients, end users and other stakeholders
   - budget and means
3. **Introduction** - Experience has taught us that it is unwise to apply the improved or newly implemented (and therefore unproven) Service Transition to current projects. In all likelihood the advantages do not outweigh the disadvantages resulting from the disruption of the project.
4. **Cultural aspects** - Even formalizing existing procedures will lead to cultural changes in an organization. Take this into consideration and do not only think of those staff that are directly involved in the Service Transition, but consider all stakeholders.
5. **Risks and advantages** - Do not make any decisions about the introduction or improvement of Service Transition without an insight into the risks and advantages to expect.

Relationships with other lifecycle phases

Even though this book presents Service Transition as a more or less delimited lifecycle phase, this does not mean that it can be viewed on its own. Without the input from Service Design and the output to Service Operation, Service Transition has no purpose.

There is also the input and output of knowledge and experience from and to Service Transition. This flow of knowledge and experience works both ways:

- **Against the flow** - For instance Service Operation shares practical experiences with Service Transition as to how similar services behave in the production environment. Experiences from Service Transition supply input for the assessment of the designs from Service Design.
- **With the flow** - Service Design supplies Service Transition with the knowledge needed to implement a change (for instance the different designs), and Service Transition supplies production experiences (for instance from testing) which could prove to be important for the daily management of the service.

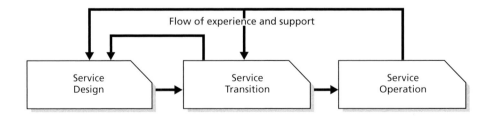

Figure 5.4   Flow of knowledge and experience from and to other lifecycle phases (Source: Service Transition was produced by OGC)

Challenges and critical success factors

For a successful Service Transition, several challenges need to be conquered, such as:

- taking into account all stakeholders (and their different perspectives) and maintaining relationships which could be important within Service Transition
- the lack of harmonization and integration of processes and disciplines which influence Service Transition
- finding the balance between a stable operation environment and being able to respond to changing business requirements in a flexible manner
- finding the balance between pragmatism and bureaucracy
- creating an environment in which standardization and knowledge sharing is stimulated
- creating a culture in which one is responsive to cooperation and cultural changes
- ensuring that the quality of services corresponds to the quality of the business
- finding the balance between "taking risks" and "avoiding risks"; this balance must correspond to that of the business
- the integration with other lifecycle phases, processes and disciplines
- a clear definition of the roles and responsibilities
- having the correct tools for managing the IT infrastructure
- developing good quality systems, tools, processes, procedures for Service Transition

Risks

Potential risks of Service Transition are:

- de-motivation of staff as a result of changed responsibilities and roles
- unforeseen expenses
- resistance to change
- lack of knowledge sharing
- poor integration between processes
- lack of maturity and integration of systems and tools

Finally, there can be circumstances in which Service Transition can have additional risk, for instance as a result of a lack of money or resources, or political problems.

Chapter 6
Lifecycle Phase: Service Operation

6.1 Introduction

Well designed and implemented processes are of little value when the day-to-day fulfilment of these processes is not well organized. Nor are service improvements possible when the day-to-day performance measuring and data gathering activities are not fulfilled systematically during the Service Operation.

Objectives

The goals of Service Operation are to coordinate and fulfill activities and processes required to provide and manage services for business users and customers with a specified agreed level. Service Operation is also responsible for management of the technology required to provide and support the services.

Scope

Service Operation is about fulfilling all activities required to provide and support services. These include:
* the services
* the service management processes
* the technology
* the people

Optimizing the Service Operation performance

Service Operation can be improved in two ways:
* Long-term incremental improvement - This is based on the review of the performances and output of all Service Operation processes, functions and outputs over time; examples include putting new tools into use or changes in the design process.
* Short-term ongoing improvement of existing situations within the Service Operation processes, functions and technology - These are small changes that are implemented to change the fundamental significance of a process or technology; examples are tuning, training or staff transfer.

6.2   Basic concepts

Service Operation is responsible for the fulfillment of processes that optimize the service costs and quality in the service management lifecycle. As part of the organization, Service Operation must help ensure that the customer (business) achieves its goals. Additionally, it is responsible for the effective functioning of components supporting the service.

Functions, groups, teams, departments and divisions
The Service Operation book refers, with various terms, to the way people are organized to fulfill processes or activities:
* **function** - a logical concept that refers to the people and automated actions that execute a defined process, an activity or a combination of processes and activities
* **group** - a number of people who are similar to each other in some way; in this book, group refers to people fulfilling similar activities
* **team** - a more formal type of group of people working together to achieve a common goal, for example, project teams or application development teams; this does not necessarily have to take place in the same organizational structure
* **department** - a formal organizational structure that performs a specific series of defined activities
* **division** - refers to a number of departments that are clustered, often based on geographic location or product line
* **role** - refers to a series of connected behaviors or actions that are performed in a specific context by an individual, team or group. A chief system manager can, for example, perform the role of problem manager, and a technical management department can perform the role of technical observation point

Achieving balance in Service Operation

Procedures and activities take place in a continually changing environment. This can give rise to a conflict between maintaining the current situation and reacting to changes in the business and technical environment. Consequently, one of the key roles of Service Operation is handling this conflict. It must try to achieve a balance between conflicting priorities.

The internal IT view versus the external business view

The view that IT is part of IT services (the external business view) is the opposite of the idea that IT is a series of technological components (the internal IT view). This causes the key conflict in all phases of the IT service management lifecycle.

The external IT view is about the way users and customers experience services. The internal IT view is about how the IT organization manages IT components and systems to provide services.

Both views are necessary to provide services. The organization that is exclusively focused on business requirements without thinking about how they will provide services will eventually only make promises they are unable to live up to. An organization that is exclusively focused on internal systems without thinking about which services they will support, will eventually support expensive services that are of little use. It is a matter of achieving a balance between these two extremes. (See Figure 6.1.)

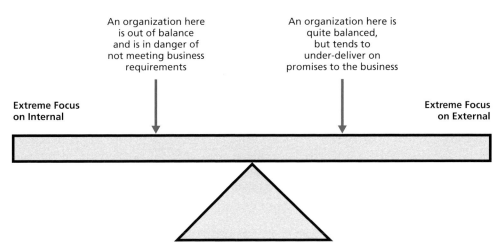

Figure 6.1   Achieving a balance between external and internal focus (Source: Service Operation was produced by OGC)

Stability versus responsiveness

On the one hand, Service Operation must ensure that the IT infrastructure is stable and available. At the same time, Service Operation must recognize that business and IT requirements change.

Some changes take place gradually and can be planned. They do not jeopardize stability. The platform functionality, performance and architecture will change over a number of years.

However, other changes can happen very quickly, sometimes under extreme pressure. For example, a business department wins a contract that suddenly requires additional IT services and more capacity.

To achieve an IT organization in which stability and response are in balance:
- Invest in adaptable technologies and processes, for example, virtual server and application technology.
- Build a strong service level management process that is active from the Service Design phase to the Continual Service Improvement phase of the IT service management Lifecycle.
- Encourage integration between service level management and the other Service Design processes, so that business requirements match the operational IT activities and components of the IT infrastructure.
- Initiate changes in the IT service management lifecycle as soon as possible; they can be taken into account in the functional and management requirements.
- Involve IT as soon as possible in the change process in case of business changes; this helps ensure scalability, consistency and IT services that include the business changes.
- Have the Service Operation teams provide input for the design and the refining of architecture and IT services.
- Implement and use service level management to prevent that business and IT managers and staff negotiate agreements informally.

Service quality versus service costs

Service Operation must provide IT services to customers and the users continually, and to the agreed level. At the same time, they have to keep the costs and use of resources at an optimal level. Many organizations are strongly pressured to enhance the service quality, while they have to reduce costs.

Achieving an optimal balance between costs and quality is a key task of service management. Many organizations leave this to the Service Operations team, who lack the authority, but the Service Strategy and Service Design phase are more appropriate for this. Service level requirements and a clear understanding of the goals and dangers of service business can help ensure that the service is provided with the right costs.

Reactive versus proactive

A reactive organization does nothing until an external stimulus forces it to act. For instance, it only develops a new application when a new business requirement demands. A proactive organization always looks for new opportunities to improve the current situation. Usually, proactive behavior is viewed positively, because it enables the organization to keep a competitive advantage in a changing environment. An over-proactive attitude can be very costly, and can create distracted staff. For an optimal result, reactive and proactive behavior must be well-balanced.

Providing a service

All Service Operation staff members must be aware that they are providing a service to the business. Do not only train staff to provide and support IT services, but also teach them the attitude with which they should provide these services.

Involving operational staff in design, transition and CSI

It is very important that the Service Operation staff are involved in Service Design, Service Transition and Continual Service Improvement, and, if necessary, in Service Strategy.

One way to achieve a balance in Service Operation is an effective set of Service Design processes. This will provide IT operations management with:
- a clear definition of IT service goals and performance criteria
- a link between IT service specifications and the IT infrastructure performance
- a definition of the operational performance requirements
- service and technology planning
- the ability to model the impact of changes in technology and business requirements
- an appropriate cost model to review the return on investment (ROI), and cost reduction strategies

Operational health

An organization can determine its operational health by isolating some "vital characteristics" of devices or services that are essential to the execution of a critical business function. Consider, for example, the bandwidth usage on a network segment, or the memory usage on an important server. If the value of these characteristics lies within the normal system range, the system is sound, and will not require any additional attention.

From time to time though, it is necessary to check the systems thoroughly for problems that do not directly affect the vital characteristics. The operational soundness also depends on the ability to prevent incidents and problems. Invest in a reliable and well-maintainable infrastructure for this. Create a solid availability design and practice proactive problem management.

Finally, the operational health depends on the ability to identify and effectively locate defects once they have occurred, so that they have little impact on the service. This also requires effective incident and problem management processes.

Communication

IT teams and departments, as well as users, internal customer and Service Operation teams, have to communicate effectively with each other. Good communication can prevent problems. Any communication must have a certain goal or result. Every team and every department must have a clear communications policy.

Service Operation has various types of communication:
- routine operational communication
- communication between shifts
- performance reports
- communication during projects
- communication in case of changes
- communication in case of exceptions
- communication in case of emergencies
- training on new or adjusted processes and service designs
- communication of Service Strategy and Service Design with Service Operation teams

Documentation

IT operation management and all technical and application management teams and departments are involved in recording and maintaining the following documents:
- process manuals for all the processes they are involved with
- technical procedure manuals
- planning documents such as capacity and availability plans
- service portfolio
- work instructions for the service management tools, in order to comply with the reporting requirements

6.3 Processes and other activities

This section devotes its attention to the following processes, activities and functions:
- event management
- incident management
- problem management
- request fulfilment
- access management
- monitoring and control (activity)
- IT operations (function)

Additionally, there are other processes that will be executed or supported during Service Operation, but are driven by other phases of the service management lifecycle:
• change management
• capacity management
• availability management
• financial management
• knowledge management
• IT Service Continuity Management (ITSCM)
• service reporting and measurement

Event management

An event is an occurrence that affects the IT infrastructure management or the provision of an IT service. For the most part, events are notifications created by an IT service, configuration item or monitoring tool. For an effective Service Operation, the organization must know its infrastructure status, and be able to trace deviations of the regular or expected performance. Good monitoring and control systems provide information for this.

Event management surveys all events that occur in the IT infrastructure in order to monitor the regular performance, and which can be automated to trace and escalate unforeseen circumstances.

Event management can be applied to any aspect of service management that must be managed and can be automated.

The most important activities of the event management process are:
• event occurs
• event notification
• event detection
• event filtering
• the event significance (event classification)
• event correlation
• trigger
• response selection
• action assessment
• close event

There is no standard record for event management; metrics should be set accordingly.

Incident management

The incident management process focuses on restoring failure of service as quickly as possible for customers, so that it has a minimal impact on the business. Incidents can be failures, questions or queries.

Incident management includes any event that interrupts or can interrupt a service; so they also include events reported by customers, either by the service desk or through various tools.

The incident management process consists of the following steps:
- identifying
- recording/logging
- categorizing
- prioritizing
- initial diagnosing
- escalating
- investigating and diagnosing
- resolving and restoring
- closing

Request fulfilment

Request fulfilment is the process of handling service requests, where a separate process is utilized that initiates the need for a request.

The goals of the request fulfilment process are:
- offering users a channel where they can request and receive standard services (changes); there must be an agreed approval and qualification process for this
- providing information to customers about the availability of services and the procedure to obtain them
- providing the standard services components (such as licenses and software media)
- assisting with general information, complaints or remarks

Request fulfilment consists of the following activities, methods and techniques:
- menu selection
- financial approval
- other approval
- fulfilment
- closure

Problem management

Problem management is responsible for analyzing and resolving the causes of incidents. In addition, it develops proactive activities to prevent current and future incidents, using a so-called "known error sub process" that enables a quicker diagnosis when new incidents happen.

Problem management includes all activities that are needed for a diagnosis of the underlying cause of incidents, and to determine a resolution for those problems. It must also ensure that the resolution is implemented through the appropriate control procedures (i.e. with change management and release management).

Problem management consists of two important processes:
- reactive problem management
- proactive problem management

Reactive problem management consists of:
- detection
- logging
- categorizing
- prioritizing
- investigating and diagnosing
- determining workarounds
- identifying a known error
- finding a resolution
- closing
- reviewing major problems
- mistakes in development environment

Access management

Access management is the process of allowing authorized users access to use a service, while access of unauthorized users is limited. In some organizations this is also known as rights or identity management.

Access management helps ensure that this access is always available at agreed times. This is provided by availability management.

A service request through the help desk can initiate access management.

Access management consists of:
- requesting access
- verification
- assigning rights
- monitoring of the identity status
- logging and tracking access
- removing or restricting rights

Monitoring and control

Service monitoring and control is based on a continual cycle of monitoring, reporting and undertaking action. This cycle is crucial to providing, supporting and improving services.

Monitoring and control cycle

The best-known model for describing control is the **monitor control loop**. Although a simple model, it has many complex applications in IT service management.

There are two types of monitoring and control cycles:
- open loop systems
- closed loop systems

There are two monitoring levels:
- internal monitoring and control
- external monitoring and control

In practice, many organizations have combinations of internal and external monitoring, but in many cases they are not linked.

There are various types of monitoring tools; the situation determines which **type of monitoring** is adopted.

IT operations

IT Operations activities refer to the day-to-day operational activities that are needed to manage the IT infrastructure.

Console management/operations bridge

The operations bridge is a central coordination point that controls various events and routine operational activities; it detects incidents and reports the performance status of technological components.

An operations bridge gathers all the crucial observation points in the IT infrastructure, so that they can be monitored and controlled from a central location with minimum effort.

The operations bridge combines many activities such as console management, event handling, first-line network management, job scheduling and support after regular office hours. In some organizations, the service desk is part of the operations bridge.

Job scheduling

IT Operations perform the standard routines, queries or reports that technical management and application management teams have transferred as part of the service or as part of routine day-to-day maintenance tasks.

Backup and restore

Backup and restore is essentially a component of well planned continuity. Service Design must help to ensure that there are good backup strategies for each service. Service Transition must help to ensure that they are tested correctly. The only point of taking backups is to ensure that information can be restored.

Other operational activities

The remainder of this section focuses on a number of operational activities which ensure that the technology matches the service and process goals. Sometimes these activities are described as processes, but they actually concern a series of specialized technical activities that help to ensure that the technology needed for providing support to the services works effectively and efficiently.

Mainframe management

Mainframes form the central part of many services, and their performance forms a baseline for service performance and user and customer expectations.

The way in which mainframe management teams are organized varies substantially. In some organizations a specialized team fulfills all aspects of mainframe management. In other organizations this is done by several teams or departments.

Server management and support

Most organizations use servers to offer flexible and accessible services for hosting applications or databases, fulfilling client/server services, storage, print and file management.

The server team or department must fulfil the following procedures and activities:
* supporting the operating system
* license management for all configuration items
* third-line support
* procurement advice
* system security
* definition and management of virtual servers
* capacity and performance

Network management

Since most IT services are dependent on connectivity, network management is crucial to service provision. Service Operation staff access important service components, via network management.

Network management is responsible for all Local Area Networks (LANs), Metropolitan Area Networks (MANs) and Wide Area Networks (WANs) within an organization.

Storage and archiving

Many services require that data must be stored for a specific time. Often, such data must be made available as an offline archive when it is no longer required on a daily basis. This is not only for compliance with external regulations and legislation, but also because data may be invaluable internally to an organization for a variety of other reasons.

Storage and archiving does not only demand infrastructure component management, but also policy that prescribes where data must be stored, for how long, in which form, and who can access the data.

Database administration

Database administration must work closely together with key application management teams or departments. In some organizations the functions can be combined or can be brought under one management structure.

Database administration must ensure optimal database performance, security and functionality. Database administrators have, among others, the following responsibilities:
* designing and maintaining database standards and policies
* database design, creation and testing

Directory services management

A directory service is a specialized software application that manages information about the available resources on a network, and to which users it is accessible. It is the basis for providing access to those resources, and for detecting and preventing unauthorized access.

Directory services look at every resource as an object of the directory server, and name them. Every name will be linked to a resource network address, so that users do not have to remember confusing and complex addresses.

Desktop support

Many users have access to IT services through a desktop or laptop. Desktop support is responsible for all desktop and laptop hardware, software and peripheral equipment in an organization. Specific responsibilities include:
- **desktop policy and procedures** - for example, license policy, personal use of laptops and desktops, etc.
- **desktop maintenance** - such as release implementation, upgrades, patches and hot fixes
- **support of connectivity problems** (together with network management) - for home-workers and field staff

Middleware management

Middleware connects software components, or integrates them with distributed or unlike applications and systems. Middleware enables effective data transfer between applications. For this reason middleware is important for services that depend on multiple applications or data resources. This is especially relevant in the context of service orientated software/architecture (SOA).

Internet/web management

Many organizations use the internet for their business operations, and are therefore heavily dependent upon the availability and performance of their websites. In such cases, a separate internet/web support team is required. This team has, among others, the following tasks:
- designing internet and web services architecture
- the specification of standards for the development and management of web based applications, content, websites and web pages; this is usually addressed during Service Design
- maintaining all web development and management applications
- supporting interfaces with back-end and legacy systems
- monitoring and managing web based performance, such as user experience simulation, benchmarking and virtualization

Facility and data center management

Facility management refers to management of the physical environment of IT operations, usually located in data centers or computer rooms. This is an extensive and complex subject. Service Operation only provides an overview of the most important roles and activities, and emphasizes the role of facility management in data center management.

Data center strategies

Managing a data center is much more than hosting an open room where technical groups install and manage equipment for which they use their own approach and procedures. It requires a series of processes and procedures; it involves all IT groups in every phase of the IT service management lifecycle. Data center activities are determined by strategic and design decisions about management and control, and are fulfilled by operators.

Information security management and Service Operation

Service Design discusses information security management as process. Information security management is responsible for setting policy, standards and procedures that ensure protection of organization assets, data, information and IT services. Service Operation teams play a role in fulfilling these policy regulations, standards and procedures, and work closely together with the teams or departments that are responsible for information security management. The role of a service operation team consists of:

- **Policing and reporting** - Operational staff check system journals, logs, event/monitoring alerts, hacker detections and actual or potential security breach reports; to do this, they work closely with information security management; this is how a "check and balance system" comes into existence, which ensures effective detection and control of security issues.
- **Technical assistance** - Sometimes IT security staff need support for their security incident research, for report creation or for gathering forensic evidence that will be used for disciplinary actions or criminal prosecution.
- **Operational security management** - For operational reasons technical staff need access to important technical areas (root system passwords, physical entry into data centers or communication rooms, etc.); it is crucial that all these activities are checked and recorded so that security events can be detected and prevented.
- **Screening and vetting** - To ensure that every member of the Service Operation staff will meet the security requirements of the organization, each member's background is checked; the background of service providers and third parties may also need to be security cleared.
- **Training and awareness** - Service Operation staff must be trained regularly in the security policy and the procedures of an organization; this cultivates awareness; this training must include details on disciplinary actions.

Operational activity improvement

Service Operation staff must be looking continually for process improvement opportunities in order to achieve a higher service quality or a more efficient service provision. This can be done with the following activities:

- automating manual tasks
- reviewing makeshift activities or activities
- operational audits
- utilizing incident and problem management
- communicating
- education and training

6.4 Organization

Functions
A function is a logical concept that refers to the people and automated measures that execute a defined process, an activity or a combination of processes and activities.

Figure 6.2 shows the service operation functions needed to manage a stable operational IT environment.

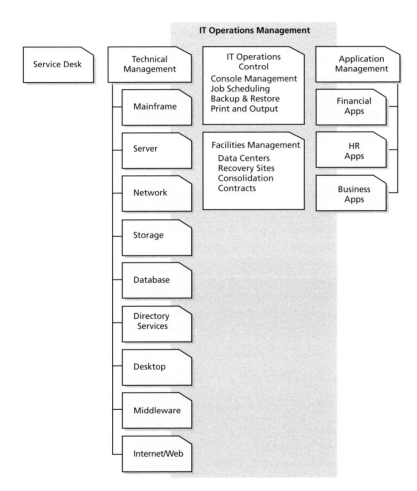

Figure 6.2   Service operation functions (Source: Service Operation was produced by OGC)

Functions and activities
Due to the technical character and special nature of certain functions, teams, groups and departments are often named after the activities that they undertake. Thus network management

is often fulfilled by a network management department. However, this is not an absolute rule. There are a few options available when assigning activities to a team or department:
- an activity can be performed by several teams or departments
- a department can perform several activities
- an activity can be performed by groups

Service desk

A service desk is a **functional unit** with a number of staff members who deal with a variety of service events. Requests may come in through phone calls, the internet or as automatically reported infrastructure events.

The service desk is a very important part of the organization's IT department. It should be the prime contact point for IT users, and it processes all incidents and service requests. Often the staff use software tools to record and manage events.

Justification and the role of a service desk

Many organizations consider a service desk as the best resource for first-line support of IT problems. A service desk provides the following advantages:
- improved customer service, improved customer perception of the service and increased customer satisfaction
- increased accessibility due to a single point of contact, communication and information
- customer and user requests are resolved better and faster
- improved cooperation and communication
- an improved focus on service and a proactive service approach
- reduced negative business impact
- improved infrastructure management and control
- improved use of resources for IT support, and increased business staff productivity
- more meaningful management information for decision support
- it is a good entry position for IT staff

Service desk objectives

The principal goal of the service desk is to restore the "normal service" for users as soon as possible. This could entail resolving a technical error, fulfilling a service request or answering a question.

Organizational structure of a service desk

There are all sorts of ways to structure a service desk. The solution will vary for each organization. The most important options are:
- local service desk
- centralized service desk
- virtual service desk
- follow the sun - "24/7" service
- specialized service desk groups

A local service desk example

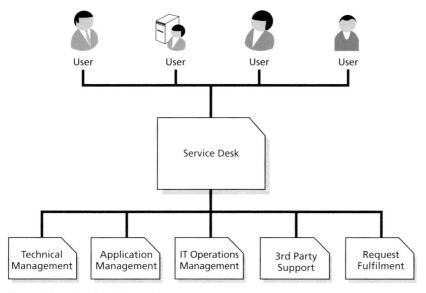

Figure 6.3   A local service desk (Source: Service Operation was produced by OGC)

A virtual service desk example

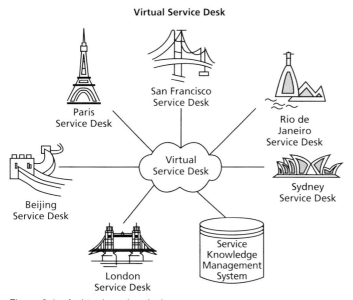

Figure 6.4   A virtual service desk (Source: Service Operation was produced by OGC)

Service desk staff

It is important to ensure the availability of the correct **number of staff members**, so that the service desk can meet the business demands at any time. The number of calls can fluctuate significantly each day and from hour to hour. When scheduling, a successful organization takes both the peak hours and the slow times into account.

The necessary levels and skills required for service desk staff are also important. The agreed solution times should be balanced against the complexity of the supported systems and "what the business is willing to pay" to determine the required **skill level**. Most of the time, the optimal and most cost-effective approach is first-line support through the service desk, which records the calls and transfers escalations quickly to the second-line and third-line support groups who have more expertise. However, this basic starting point can be improved over time by providing first-line staff with an effective knowledge-base, diagnostics scripts and integrated tools as well as ongoing training and awareness, so that first-line resolution rates can be increased.

Metrics for the service desk

Define realistic **metrics** to review the service desk performance at regular points in time. This way, the maturity, efficiency, effectiveness and opportunities can be assessed, and the service desk activities improved. Do ensure that the service desk performance metrics are realistic and carefully selected.

In addition to the "hard" measurements of the service desk performance, it is also important to conduct "soft" measurements in the form of customer and user satisfaction surveys. Do customers and users think that their calls are answered correctly, was the service desk agent friendly and professional? This type of measurement can best be answered by the user.

Service desk outsourcing

The decision to outsource is a strategic topic for senior managers, and will be discussed in detail in the domains of Service Strategy and Service Design.

Technical management

Technical management refers to the **groups, departments or teams** who offer technical expertise and general management of the IT infrastructure.

The role of technical management

Technical management has a dual role:
- It is the custodian of technical knowledge and expertise in relation to managing the IT infrastructure. In this role, technical management helps ensure that the knowledge required for designing, testing, managing and improving IT services is established, developed and refined.
- It takes care of the actual resources that are needed to support the IT service management lifecycle. In this role, technical management helps ensure that the resources are trained and implemented effectively, so that it can design, build, transfer, process and improve the required technology that is needed to provide and support IT services.

By fulfilling these two roles, technical management helps ensure that the organization is able to access the correct type and level of human resources to manage the technology, and consequently, meet the business goals.

Technical management also drives IT operations while managing the technology operations and providing guidance to IT operations.

Objectives of technical management

Technical management assists in the planning, implementation and maintenance of a stable technical infrastructure to support the organization's business processes. This is done by:

- well-designed and cost-effective technical topology
- using the appropriate technical skills to maintain the technical infrastructure in a optimal condition
- using technical skills effectively, to diagnose and resolve technical failures quickly

General technical management activities

Technical management is involved in several general activities, such as:

- starting training programs
- designing and carrying out training for users, the service desk and other groups
- researching and developing resolutions that may help to expand the service portfolio, or may be used to simplify or automate IT operations
- releases that are often implemented with the assistance of technical management staff

The technical management organization

Generally speaking, technical management is not provided by one department or group. One or more technical support teams are needed to provide technical management and support for the IT infrastructure.

IT operations management consists of a number of technological areas. Each area requires a specific set of skills to manage and operate it. Some skills are related to each other, and can be performed by generalists, while others apply specifically to a component, system or platform.

Technical design and technical maintenance and support

Technical management consists of specialized technical architects, designers, maintenance specialists and support staff.

Metrics for technical management

Specific metrics for technical management depend largely on which technology is being managed. Some general metrics include:

- measuring the agreed output
- process values
- technological performance
- Mean Time Between Failures (MTBF) of specific equipment
- maintenance activity measurement
- training and skill development

Technical management documentation

Among others, technical management documentation consists of:

- technical documentation (manuals, management and administration manuals, user manuals for CIs)
- maintenance schedules
- an inventory of skills

IT operations management

IT operations management is the **function** that is responsible for performing the day-to-day operational activities. They ensure that the agreed level of IT service is provided to the business.

IT operations management plays a dual role:

- It is responsible for implementation of activities and performance standards that have been defined during Service Design and have been tested during Service Transition. In this sense, the role of IT operations focuses on maintaining the status quo, whereby stability of the IT infrastructure and consistency of IT services are the most important tasks of IT operations.
- Simultaneously, IT operations is part of the process that adds value to the business and supports the value network (see *Service Strategy*). IT operations must be capable of continual adaptation to business requirements and demands.

IT operations management objectives

Objectives of IT operations management are:

- maintaining the existing situation to achieve stability in the processes and activities of the organization
- continual research and improvement to achieve better service at lower costs while maintaining stability
- rapid application of operational skills to analyze operational failures and to resolve them

IT operations management organization

IT operations management is seen as a separate function, but in many cases technical and application management workers contribute to this function.
The assignment of activities depends on the maturity of the organization.

IT operations management metrics

IT operations management measures both the effective implementation of defined activities and procedures, as well as execution of process activities. Examples include:

- successful completion of planned tasks
- the number of exceptions to planned activities and tasks
- process metrics
- metrics of maintenance activities
- metrics related to facility management

IT operations management documentation

IT operations management generates and uses a number of documents, including:

- **Standard Operating Procedures (SOP)** - A series of documents providing detailed instructions and activity schedules for each IT operations management team, department or group.

- **Operations logs** - Each activity that is performed as part of IT operations must be registered for a variety of reasons, in order to:
  - confirm successful completion of specific tasks or activities
  - confirm that an IT service was provided as agreed
  - provide a basis for problem management to research the underlying cause of incidents
  - provide a basis for reports about performance of IT operations teams and departments
- **Shift schedules and reports** - Documents that display the exact activities that must be performed during a shift; there is also a list showing all dependencies and the sequence of activities; there may be more than one operational schedule because each team may be provided with a version for its own systems.

Application management

Application management is responsible for the management of applications during their lifecycle. The application management **function** is executed by a department, group or team that is involved with management and support of operational applications. Application management also plays an important role in designing, testing and improving applications that are part of IT services.

Application management role

Application management is for applications what technical management is for IT infrastructure. It plays a role in all applications, whether they are purchased or have been internally developed. One of the most important decisions to which they contribute is whether to purchase an application or to develop it internally (discussed in detail in Service Design). When this decision has been made, application management plays a dual role:

- it is the custodian of technical knowledge and expertise for the management of applications
- it provides actual resources for the support of the IT service management lifecycle

Two other roles filled by application management:

- it provides advice to IT operations about the best way to carry out the ongoing operational management of applications
- it integrates the Application Management Lifecycle with the IT service management lifecycle

Application management objectives

The objectives of application management are to support the business processes of the organization by determining functional and management requirements for applications. Another objective is to assist in design and implementation of the applications and to support and improve them.

Application management principles

One of the most important decisions in application management is whether to **develop or purchase** an application which supports the requested functionality. The Chief Technical Officer (CTO), or steering group, makes the ultimate decision, but in doing so, both depend on a number of information sources. If the decision maker wants to have the application developed, they will also have to decide whether to have it developed by staff or to outsource the development. This is further discussed in detail in Service Design.

Application management lifecycle

The lifecycle that is followed to develop and manage the application goes by many names, such as the Software Lifecycle (SLC) and the Software Development Lifecycle (SDLC). These are mostly used by application development teams and their project managers to define their involvement in designing, developing, testing, implementing and supporting applications. Examples of this approach include Structured Systems Analysis and Design Methodology (SSADM) and Dynamic Systems Development Method (DSDM).

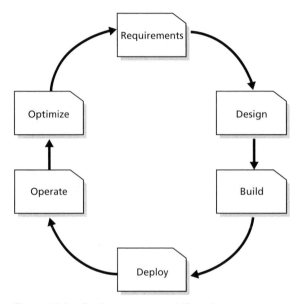

Figure 6.5 Application management lifecycle (Source: Service Operation was produced by OGC)

Application development and operations are part of the same lifecycle and must be involved through all Service Lifecycle phases, although the degree of involvement depends on the lifecycle phase.

Relation between application management lifecycle and service management lifecycle

The application management lifecycle is not an alternative for the service management lifecycle. Applications are part of services and must be managed as such. Nevertheless, applications are a unique mix of technology and functionality and this requires a special focus during each phase of the service management lifecycle.

Each phase of the application management lifecycle has its own specific objectives, activities, deliverables and dedicated teams. Each phase also has a clear responsibility to ensure that its output corresponds with the specific objectives of the service management lifecycle.

The phases of applications management within Service Operation are: requirements
- design
- build
- deploy
- operate
- optimize

During the first phase, the **requirements** for a new application are collected, based on the business needs of the organization. There are six requirement types for an application, whether it is developed in-house, outsourced or purchased:
- **functional requirements** - what is necessary to support a certain business function?
- **management requirements** - concentrate on the need for responsive, available and secure service, and involve things like deployment, system management, and security
- **usability requirements** - what are the needs of the user, and how can they be satisfied?
- **architecture requirements** - especially if it requires a change in the existing architecture standards
- **interface requirements** - where dependencies occur between existing applications or tools and the new application
- **service level requirements** - specify how the service is to be delivered, what the quality of the output has to be and other qualitative aspects that are measured by the user or client

The **design phase** will translate the requirements into specifications. Design of the application and the environment or the operational model in which the application is run will also take place during the Design Phase. Architectural considerations for design and operation are the most important aspect of this phase, because they can impact the structure and content of both the application and the operational model.

The **build phase** gets the application and the operational model ready for deployment. Application components are coded and purchased, integrated and tested. Testing is not a separate phase in the lifecycle although it is a separate activity. Testing forms an integral part of the development and roll-out phase, as validation of the activity and output of those phases.

The **deployment phase** deploys the operational model and the application. The existing IT environment absorbs the operational model and the application is installed on top of the operational model. This involves the processes of release and deployment management that are described under Service Transition.

During the **operate phase** the service organization uses the application as part of providing services requested by the business. The performance of the application in relation to the total service is measured continually in relation to the service levels and the most important business drivers.

The **optimize phase** reviews and analyzes the results of the service level performance metrics. Possible improvements are discussed and the necessary developments are initiated. The two main strategies involve maintaining and iteratively improving service levels at lower costs. This can lead to a change in the lifecycle of an application or to its retirement. Good communication with users is important during this phase.

Generic application management activities

Although most application management teams and departments are dedicated to specific applications, they share a number of activities. These include:

* identifying the knowledge needed to manage and operate applications in the Service Operation phase
* initiating training programs to develop and refine skills in the appropriate application management resources and to maintain training reports for these resources
* defining standards for designing new architectures and determining application architectures during Service Strategy processes
* testing, designing and executing the functionality, performance and controllability of IT services
* defining event management standards
* defining, managing and maintaining attributes and relations of application CIs in the configuration management system

Application management organization

Although application management departments, groups and teams all perform similar functions, each application has its own set of management and operational requirements. Differences may include:

* the purpose of the application
* the functionality of the application
* the platform on which the application is run
* the type or the brand of technology that is used

Application management teams and departments are mostly organized on the basis of the categories of the applications that they support. Examples of typical application management organization include:

* financial applications
* HR applications
* manufacturing support
* sales support
* call center and marketing applications
* business specific applications
* IT applications
* web portals

Traditionally, application development and management teams/departments have operated as autonomous units. Each team manages its own environment in its own way and they all have a separate interface to the business. Recent attention for object-oriented and *Service Oriented Architectures* and the growing pressure from business that demands a faster response and improved cooperation has brought these two worlds closer together. This requires a higher involvement of Service Operational personnel in the Service Design phase.

Application management roles and responsibilities
Application management has two roles:
- **the application manager** - supervises and has overall responsibility for management and the decisions that are made
- **the application analyst/architect** - is responsible for requirements that meet the application specifications

Application management metrics
The application management metrics mainly depend on the way in which the applications are managed, but general metrics include:
- measuring agreed-upon outputs
- process metrics
- performance of the application
- measuring maintenance activities
- application management teams cooperate closely with application development teams and the correct metrics must be used to measure this
- training and skill development

Service Operation roles and responsibilities
The key to effective ITSM is ensuring that there is clear accountability and roles defined to carry out the practice of Service Operation.

Service desk roles
The following roles are needed for the service desk:
- service desk manager
  - manages service desk activities
  - acts as escalation point for supervisors
  - takes on wider customer service role
  - reports to senior managers about any issue that could significantly impact the business
  - attends Change Advisory Board meetings
  - overall responsibility for processing incidents and service requests
- service desk supervisor
  - ensures that staffing and skill levels are maintained
  - is responsible for production of management reports
  - acts as escalation point for difficult calls
- service desk analysts
  - deliver first line support by accepting calls and processing the resulting incidents or service requests, using incident and request fulfilment processes
- super users
  - business users who act as liaison points between business and IT

Technical management roles
The following roles are needed for the technical management areas:
- technical managers/team leaders
  - responsible for leadership, control and decision-making

- technical analysts/architects
  - defining and maintaining knowledge on how systems are related and ensuring that dependencies are understood
- technical operators
  - performing day-to-day operational tasks

IT Operation management roles

The following roles are needed for IT Operations management:
- IT operations manager
- shift leader
- IT operations analysts
- IT operators

Application management roles

Application management requires Application Managers and Team Leaders. They have overall responsibility for leadership, control and decision making for the applications team or department.

Application Analysts and Architects are responsible for matching business requirements to technical specifications.

Event management roles

It is unusual to appoint an 'event manager' but it is important that event management procedures are coordinated. The service desk is not typically involved in event management, but if events have been identified as incidents, the service desk will escalate them to the appropriate service operation teams.

Technical and application management play an important role in event management. For example, the teams will perform event management for the systems under their control.

Incident management roles

The **incident manager** is responsible for:
- driving the effectiveness and efficiency of the incident management process
- producing management information
- managing the work of incident support staff (first tier and second tier)
- monitoring the effectiveness of incident management and making recommendations for improvement
- managing major incidents
- developing and maintaining incident management systems and processes
- effectively managing incidents using first, second, and third tier support

Request fulfilment roles

Initial service request handling is done by the service desk and incident management staff. Actual fulfilment will be undertaken by the appropriate service operation team(s) or departments and/or external suppliers.

Problem management roles

One person (or, in larger organizations, a team) should be responsible for problem management. The **problem manager** is responsible for coordinating all problem management activities and is specifically responsible for:

- liaison with all problem resolution groups to accomplish quick solutions to problems within SLA targets
- ownership and protection of the Known Error Database
- formal closure of all problem records
- liaison with vendors and other parties to ensure compliance with contractual obligations
- managing, executing, documenting and planning all (follow-up) activities that relate to major problem reviews

Access management roles

Since access management is the execution of security and availability management, these two areas will be responsible for defining the appropriate roles. Although usually no access manager is appointed by an organization, it is important there should be one process for managing privileges and access. This process and the related policy are usually defined and maintained by information security management and executed by various service operation functions, such as the service desk, technical management and application management.

Service Operation organization structures

There are several ways to organize Service Operation functions, and each organization will come to its own decisions based on its size, geography, culture and business environment.

Organization by technical specialization

This organization type creates departments according to the technology, the skills and activities necessary to manage that technology. IT operations follows the structure of the technical management and application management departments. As a consequence IT operations is geared to the operational agendas of the technical management and application management departments, and all groups have to be defined during the Service Design phase.

Organization by activity

This type of organization structure focuses on the fact that similar activities are performed on all technologies within an organization. This means that people who perform similar activities, regardless of the technology, are grouped together, although teams may occur within each department that is involved with a specific technology, application, etc.

Organizing to manage processes

It is not a good idea to structure the entire organization according to processes. Processes are used to eliminate the "silo effect" of departments, not to create silos.

In process-based organizations, people are organized in groups or departments that perform or manage a specific process. However, this type of organization structure should only be used if IT operations management is responsible for more than IT operations. In some organizations IT operations is also responsible for defining SLAs and negotiating UCs.

Process-based departments are only effective if they are capable of coordinating process execution throughout the entire organization. This means that process-based departments can only be considered if IT operations management can play the role of process owner for specific processes.

Organizing IT operation by geography

IT operations can be physically spread out, and in some cases each location must be organized according to its own context. This structure is usually used in the following circumstances, when:

- data centers are geographically distributed
- different regions or countries possess different technologies or offer a different range of services
- there are different business models or organizational structures in the different regions; in other words, the business is decentralized according to geography and the each business unit is fairly autonomous
- legislation differs between country or region
- different standards apply, per country or region
- there are cultural or language differences between the personnel who are managing IT

Hybrid organization structures

It is unlikely that IT operations management will be structured using only one type of organizational structure. Most organizations use a technical specialization combined with some extra activity or process-based departments:

- **Combined functions** - The IT operations, technical management and application management departments are included in one structure; this sometimes occurs when all groups are co-located in one data center; in these situations, the data center manager assumes responsibility for technical, application and IT production management.
- **Combined technical and application management structure** - Some businesses organize their technical management and application management functions according to systems; this means that every department contains application specialists and IT infrastructure technical specialists who manage services based on a series of systems.

6.5 Methods, techniques and tools

The most important requirements for Service Operation are:

- an integrated IT service management technology (or toolset)
- self-help (e.g. FAQ's on a web interface)
- workflow or process management engine
- an integrated CMS
- discovery/deployment/licensing technology
- remote control
- diagnostic utilities
- reporting capabilities
- dashboards
- integration with business service management

6.6   Implementation

General implementation guidelines for Service Operation:

Managing change in Service Operation

Service Operation staff must implement changes without negative impact on the stability of offered IT services.

Change triggers

There are many things that can trigger change in the Service Operation environment, including:

- new or to be upgraded hardware or software
- legislation
- obsolete components
- business imperatives
- process enhancements
- changes in management or personnel
- change in service levels
- new services

Change assessment

Involve Service Operation as early as possible in assessment of all changes. This way, operational issues will be handled properly.

Assessing and managing risk in Service Operation

In a number of cases, it is necessary that risk evaluation is conducted swiftly, in order to take appropriate action. This is especially necessary for potential changes or known errors, but also in case of failures, projects, environmental risks, vendors, security risks and new clients that need support.

Operational staff in Service Design and Transition

Service Operation staff should be particularly involved in the early stages of Service Design and Transition. This will ensure that the new services will actually work in practice and that they can be supported by Service Operation staff.

Planning and implementation of service management technologies

There are several factors that organizations must plan before and during deployment of ITSM support tools, such as:

- licenses
- deployment
- capacity checks
- timing of technology deployment
- the type of introduction - the choice of a big-bang introduction or a phased approach

Next, we will discuss some challenges that Service Operation must overcome.

Lack of engagement with development and project staff

Historically, there is a separation between Service Operation staff and staff involved in the development of new applications or in the execution of projects that deliver new functionality in an operational environment.

This image is damaging because contemplating Service Operation issues is best done at the beginning of new developments or projects, when there is still time to include these factors in the planning stages.

Service Design and Service Transition describe the steps necessary to include IT production issues in new developments and projects right from the start.

Justifying funding

Often is it difficult to justify expenditure for Service Operation because funds spent are often considered to be "infrastructure" costs.

In reality, many investments in IT service management, especially for Service Operation, can save money and show a positive ROI as well as improving service quality.

Challenges for Service Operation managers

Managers in Service Operation can be faced with the following challenges:
- Service Design has the tendency to focus on one service while Service Operation aims at delivering and supporting all services.
- Service Design will often be conducted in projects while Service Operation focuses on continual management processes and activities that recur.
- The two phases of the lifecycle possess different metrics that encourage Service Design to conclude the project on time, as specified and within the arranged budget. However, it is hard to predict how the service will look, and what will be the costs after roll-out and some initial time in service. If the service does not work as expected, IT operations management will be responsible.
- Ineffective Service Transition may hamper the transition from design to production.

Another series of challenges involves metrics. Each alternative structure will introduce a different combination of items that can be easy or difficult to measure.

A third set of challenges concerns the use of virtual teams. Traditional, hierarchical management structures are unable to handle the complexity and diversity of most organizations. Knowledge management and mapping authority structures becomes increasingly important as organizations expand and diversify. Service Strategy will expand on this further.

One of the most important challenges facing Service Operation managers is the balance between the many internal and external relationships. There is an increasing use of networks, partnerships and shared services models. A Service Operation manager must invest in relation management knowledge and skills in order to handle the complexity of these challenges.

Critical success factors

Management support

Support from higher and middle management is necessary for all IT service management activities and processes, especially in Service Operation. It is crucial for obtaining sufficient financing and resources. Senior management must also offer visible support during the launch of new Service Operation initiatives.

Middle management must also provide the necessary support and actions.

Business support

It is also important that Service Operation is supported by the business units. This works better if the Service Operation staff involve the business in all their activities, and are open about successes and failures.

Regular communication with the business is crucial to building a good relationship and to ensuring support; Service Operation will be better placed to understand the aspirations and concerns of the business. Additionally, the business can provide feedback on the efforts of Service Operation to satisfy the business needs.

Hiring and retaining staff

The correct number of staff with the correct skills is critical for successful Service Operation. Consider the following challenges:

- Projects for new services often clearly specify what the new skills must be, but may underestimate how many staff are needed and how skills can be retained.
- There may be a lack of staff with solid knowledge of service management; having good technicians is important, but there must also be a certain number of people who have knowledge of both technological and service problems.
- Because staff with both technological and service knowledge are fairly rare, they are often specially trained; it is important to retain them by offering a clear career path and solid compensation.
- Staff are often assigned new tasks too quickly, while they are still extremely busy with their current workloads. Successful service management projects may require a short term investment in temporary workers.

Service management training

Good training and awareness can provide great advantages. In addition to increasing expertise, they can generate enthusiasm in people. Service Operation staff must be aware of the consequences of their actions for the organization. A "service management culture" must be created. Service management will only be successful if the people are focused on overall service management objectives.

Appropriate tools

Many service management processes and activities cannot be effectively executed without proper support tools. Senior management must ensure that financing for such tools is included in annual budgets, and must support acquisition, implementation and maintenance.

Test validity

The quality of IT services provided by Service Operation depends on the quality of systems and components that are delivered in the operational environment.

The quality level will improve considerably if solid and complete testing of new components and releases is performed in a timely manner. Also, the documentation should be independently tested for completeness and quality.

Measuring and reporting

Clear agreements are necessary regarding the way in which things are measured and reported; all staff will have clear targets to aim for, and IT and business managers will be able to evaluate quickly and simply whether progress is being made and which areas deserve extra attention.

Risks

Consider the following risks:

- **Service loss** - The greatest risk run by Service Operation is the loss of essential IT services with adverse impact on staff, customers and finances. In extreme cases, loss may occur to life and health, when IT services are used for essential health and security purposes.
- **Risks to successful Service Operation**:
  - insufficient financing and resources
  - loss of momentum
  - loss of important staff
  - resistance to change
  - lack of management support
  - if the design fails the requirements, successful implementation will never deliver the required results; this will require new design
  - in some organizations, service management is viewed with suspicion by both IT and the business; the advantages of service management must be clear for all stakeholders; this problem can be solved by clear service level management and careful communication during Service Design

Chapter 7

Lifecycle Phase: Continual Service Improvement

7.1 Introduction

IT must continually align and re-align IT services to the changing business needs by identifying and implementing improvements to IT services that support the business. ITIL version 3 places this within the lifecycle phase of **Continual Service Improvement**.

In English there is a difference between *continual* and *continuous*:
- *continuous* means that the organization is involved in an activity without interruption; the efforts are constantly at the same level; for example, *continuous operation*
- *continual* means a succession of closely placed activities; in this way a sequence of improvement efforts is created: *continual improvement*

An IT service is created by a number of activities. The quality of these activities and the process which links these activities determine the quality of the eventual service. CSI focuses on the activities and processes to improve the quality of services. To this end, it uses the *Plan-Do-Check-Act* Cycle of Deming (PDCA). This cycle prescribes a consolidation phase for each improvement, to engrain the new procedures in the organization. This implies a repeating pattern of improvement efforts with varying levels of intensity, instead of a single continuing improvement effort which is always on the same level. This is the reason why, in ITIL version 3, the "C" of CSI stands for continual and not continuous.

Measuring and analyzing is crucial to CSI; by measuring it is possible to identify which services are profitable and which services can do better. The **CSI improvement process** has a seven step plan. Creating a **Service Improvement Plan** (SIP) is an SLM activity within the CSI scope. The Section "Processes and other activities" pursues this matter in more depth. Next we will describe the roles which execute the core activities, followed by the methods, techniques and technology which assist them. The interfaces between service level management and CSI are dealt with in the last section on interfaces with the other phases and IT service management processes from the ITIL lifecycle. First of all, we will consider the justification of CSI and a number of basic concepts.

Goal and objectives

The **goal** of CSI is for continual improvement of the effectiveness and efficiency of IT services, allowing them to meet the business requirements better. This entails both achieving and surpassing the objectives (**effectiveness**), and obtaining these objectives at the lowest cost possible (**efficiency**). To increase the effectiveness you can, for instance, reduce the number of errors in a process. To make a process more efficient you can eliminate unnecessary activities or automate manual operations.

By measuring and analyzing the process results in all Service Lifecycle phases you can determine which results are structurally worse than others. These offer the highest improvement probability.

CSI mainly measures and monitors the following matters:
- **Process compliance** - Does the organization follow the new or modified service management processes and does it use the new tools?
- **Quality** - Do the various process activities meet their goals?
- **Performance** - How efficient is the process? What are the elapsed times?
- **Business value of a process** - Does the process make a difference? Is it effective? How does the client rate the process?

The main **objectives** of CSI are:
- to measure and analyze **service level achievements** by comparing them to the requirements in the Service Level Agreement (SLA)
- to recommend improvements in all phases of the lifecycle
- to introduce activities which will increase the quality, efficiency, effectiveness and customer satisfaction of the services and the IT service management processes
- to operate more cost effective IT services without sacrificing customer satisfaction
- to use suitable quality management methods for improvement activities

Scope

The scope of CSI contains three important areas:
- general quality of the IT management
- continual tuning of the IT services to the current and future needs of the business
- continual tuning of the IT service portfolio
- the maturity of the IT processes which make the services possible

7.2   Basic concepts

CSI and Organizational Change

In order to make continual improvement a permanent part of the organizational culture, a change in mentality is often needed. This is one of the most difficult aspects of CSI and, in reality, a lot of CSI programs fail because they do not (or cannot) achieve this cultural change. John P. Kotter, *Professor of Leadership* at the Harvard Business School, examined over a hundred companies and discovered eight crucial steps needed to successfully change an organization:
- **create a sense of urgency** - for instance, answer the question "what if we do nothing?"

- **form a leading coalition** - a single pioneer cannot change an entire organization; a small key team is needed with the necessary authority and resources; this team can be expanded as the support grows
- **create a vision** - a good vision formulates the goal and the purpose of CSI, provides direction, motivates, coordinates and formulates goals for the senior management; make these goals SMART: *Specific, Measurable, Achievable/Appropriate, Realistic/Relevant* and *Timely/Time-bound*; without a vision, a CSI program will soon become a repository of projects which do not have obvious benefits for the organization; tailor the vision to the client's requirements
- **communicate the vision** - each stakeholder must know what the vision is, what is its use for them, and why CSI is needed; to achieve this, put together a communication plan, and demonstrate by example
- **empower others to act on the vision** - remove obstacles, give direction by setting clear goals and supply people with the proper resources such as tools and training; create security and self confidence; only then will they be able to take responsibility for their part in CSI
- **plan for and create quick wins** - evaluate per service or process what can be improved rapidly; plan this, execute it and communicate it in order to increase support
- **consolidate improvements and create more change** - quick wins convince and motivate; medium term successes offer confidence in the organization's own improvement capabilities and foresee a set of standard procedures; but in the long run improvement can only be considered a success if people and processes are continually improving themselves
- **institutionalize the changes**:
  - hire personnel with experience in best practices in the field of IT management
  - from day one hand out work instructions
  - clarify what the procedures are
  - train staff in IT management
  - match the goals and reports to changing demands
  - define clear action points in the minutes
  - integrate new IT solutions and development projects in existing processes

Combined with good project management, these steps will considerably increase the chances of success.

The PDCA Cycle

A "*big bang*" approach does not usually result in a successful improvement program. That is why the American statistician Dr W Edwards Deming developed a step-by-step improvement approach in the 1980s: the ***Plan-Do-Check-Act* Cycle** (**PDCA**):

- **Plan** - what needs to happen, who will do what and how?
- **Do** - execute the planned activities
- **Check** - check whether the activities yield the desired result
- **Act** - adjust the plan in accordance to the checks

Next is a consolidation phase to engrain the changes into the organization. The Cycle is also known as the **Deming Cycle** (Figure 7.1).

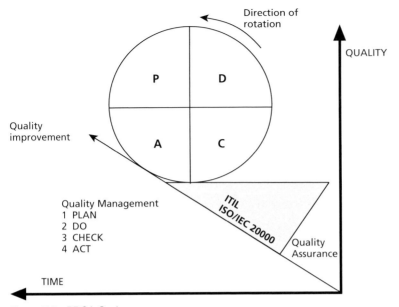

Figure 7.1   PDCA Cycle

CSI uses the PDCA Cycle in two areas:
- implementation of CSI
- continual improvement of services and processes

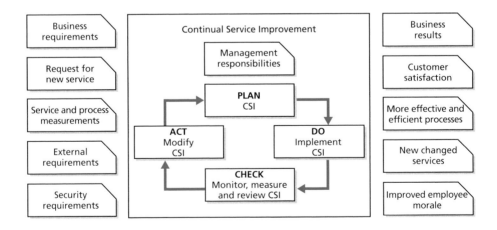

Figure 7.2   P-D-C-A Cycle for the improvement of services, applied to the introduction of CSI (in accordance to ISO/IEC 20000) (Source: Continual Service Improvement was produced by OGC)

First, we discuss the Cycle for the *implementation of CSI* (Figure 7.2):
- **plan CSI**:
    – determine the scope
    – determine the requirements CSI must meet
    – set goals, for instance using gap analysis

      – define action points

      – determine which checks need to be executed during the check phase

      – determine the interfaces between CSI and the rest of the lifecycle

      – determine which process activities need to be introduced

      – set (management) roles and responsibilities

      – find out which tools are needed to support and document processes

      – select the methods and techniques to measure and document the quality and effectiveness of the services and processes

- **implement CSI (*do*):**
  - determine the budget
  - document roles and responsibilities
  - determine the CSI policy, plans and procedures, maintain these, communicate about them and train your staff
  - supply monitoring, analysis and reporting tools
  - integrate CSI with Service Strategy, Service Design, Service Transition and Service Operation
- **monitor, measure and evaluate CSI (*check*):**
  - report on the accomplishments with regard to the plans
  - evaluate the documentation
  - perform process assessments and audits
  - formulate proposals for process improvement
- **adjust CSI (*act*):**
  - introduce the improvements
  - adjust the policy, procedures, roles and responsibilities

During the implementation of CSI all phases play an important part. In the second area where the PDCA Cycle is used - *continual improvement of services and processes* - the focus is mainly on the "check" and "act" phase. There are, however, also activities in the "plan" and "do" phase which are involved:

- plan improvement initiatives:
  - set goals and check methods
  - perform gap analysis
  - determine action points
- implement the improvement initiative:
  - eliminate the discrepancies found
  - provide a smooth execution of the process
- monitor, check and evaluate services and processes:
  - compare the checks after the improvement to those prior to the improvement and to the goals set in the plan phase
  - determine whether the discrepancies found need to be eliminated
  - make recommendations for the improvement such as adjusting the service catalogue and the new SLA checks
- continual improvement of services and processes:
  - introduce the improvements
  - determine which discrepancies need to be addressed, this constitutes the input for the plan phase

Metrics, KPIs and CSFs

An IT service manager needs to know whether their organization as a whole meets its goals and which processes contribute to this. A **metric** measures the results of a process or activity by determining whether a certain variable meets its set target. For instance, a metric measures whether the required number of incidents are resolved within one hour.

Metrics are mainly interpreted on a strategic and tactical level. They must describe all processes within an organization. Three types are needed for CSI:
- **technology metrics** - measure the performance and availability of components and applications
- **process metrics** - measure the performance of service management processes; they stem from **Key Performance Indicators** (**KPIs**), which in turn stem from **Critical Success Factors** (CSFs); also see step four of the CSI improvement process: "process data"; these metrics help to determine the improvement opportunities for each process
- **service metrics** - the results of the end service; these are measured using component metrics

A metric stems from the goal set by an organization. If the business views IT as a *cost center* then it will probably want to decrease the costs. If, however, it sees IT as the enabler of the company, then the goal will probably be to develop flexible services which will decrease the *time-to-market*. The measuring system should not focus solely on only one of the three aspects of money, time and quality, otherwise the remaining two aspects will receive insufficient attention.

For the business mission, **CSFs** are defined: these are elements essential to achieving the mission. The **KPIs** following on from these CSFs determine the quality, performance, value and process compliance. They can either be *qualitative* (such as customer satisfaction), or *quantitative* (such as costs of a printer incident).

At the start of the improvement program two to three KPIs per CSF will already supply a great deal of information which will need to be processed. The KPIs can be extended or adjusted later according to new developments. For instance, if the organization has achieved its goals or when new service management processes are introduced.

Determine if the KPI is suitable by answering these questions:
- Do we achieve our goals if we achieve the KPI?
- Can the KPI be interpreted correctly? Does it help in determining the action needed?
- Who needs the information? When? How often? How fast does the information need to be available?
- Is the KPI stable and accurate or subject to external, uncontrollable influences?
- How easy is it to adjust the KPI to new developments?
- To what extent can the KPI be measured now? Under what circumstances?
- Who collects and analyzes the measurements? Who is responsible for the improvements resulting from this information?

Data, information, knowledge and wisdom (DIKW)

Metrics supply quantitative **data**; for instance, that the service desk registers 12,000 incidents each month. CSI transforms this data into qualitative **information**, a received and understood message which stems from processed and grouped data; such as the fact that 18% of the incidents reported are related to the organization's email facility. By combining information with experience, context, interpretation and reflection it becomes **knowledge**; for example, since we know that the organization is a web store, we can determine the impact of the incidents concerning the email facility.

What it comes down to in CSI is **wisdom**: being able to make the correct assessments and the correct decisions by using the data, information and knowledge in the best possible way. For example, because we know the impact of the email incidents on the client, we can decide to focus on this service because we want to improve our customer service. The CSI improvement process focuses on the acquirement of wisdom (see the Section "Processes and other activities" and step 6 in the CSI improvement process about service reporting).

Governance

Governance drives organizations and controls them. *Corporate governance* provides a good, honest, transparent and responsible management of an organization. *Business governance* results in good company performances. Together they are known as *enterprise governance*.

IT governance is also part of *enterprise governance*. It shapes the processes and structure of an IT organization and ensures that it achieves its goals. Complying with the new rules, such as the American *Sarbanes-Oxley Act* from 2002 (corporate governance), and constantly performing better at a lower cost (business governance) are both part of IT governance.

These two developments are the main motive for CSI: IT service providers must offer their services from a strategic rather than a tactical perspective. IT departments which only focus on technology will soon become less appealing to their business.

An ITSM standard such as ITIL helps to control an organization by forging it into a coherent system of roles, responsibilities, processes, policy and *controls*.

CSI policies and procedures

CSI policies capture agreements about measuring, reporting, service levels, CSFs, KPIs and evaluations. These must be known to the whole organization. Most organizations assess the process results each month. It is wise to evaluate new services more often.

An IT organization should implement the following CSI policies:
- all improvement initiatives must go through the change management process
- all functional groups are responsible for CSI activities
- CSI roles and responsibilities are recorded and announced (see Section "Organization")

7.3   Processes and other activities

To improve the services of the IT organization CSI measures the yield of these services. The main CSI activities are:

- check:
  - check the results of the processes
  - examine customer satisfaction
  - assess process maturity
  - check whether the staff follow the internal guidelines
  - analyze the measurement data and compare these to the goals set in the SLA
- report:
  - propose improvements for all phases in the lifecycle
  - consider the relevance of existing goals
- improve:
  - introduce activities which increase the quality, efficiency, effectiveness and customer satisfaction of the services
  - use appropriate quality management methods for improvement activities

Setting directions

The effect of the improvement is greatly determined by the direction in which the improvement takes place.

> "Would you tell me, please, which way I ought to go from here?"
> "That depends a good deal on where you want to get to," said the Cat.
> "I don't much care where -" said Alice.
> "Then it doesn't matter which way you go," said the Cat.
> "- so long as I get somewhere," Alice added as an explanation.
> "Oh, you're sure to do that," said the Cat, "if you only walk long enough."
>
> Source: Lewis Carroll, Alice's Adventures in Wonderland, 1865

Without a vision about the direction of the improvement, an improvement has only a limited value. Because of this, determine a vision including its goals before you start with an improvement process.

The organization must continually assess its current improvement course (CSI goals) on relevance, completeness and feasibility. The **CSI model** in Figure 7.3 can provide some support.

This continual cycle consists of six phases:
1. **Determine the vision** - IT gets an insight into the goals of its business, and together with the business formulates a vision to tune the IT strategy to the business strategy; together they formulate a mission, goals and objectives.
2. **Record the current situation** - Record the starting point (baseline) of the client, organization, people, process and technology.
3. **Determine measurable targets** - Set priorities together with the client based on the vision: what do we improve first, how extensive must the improvement be and when should it be finished?

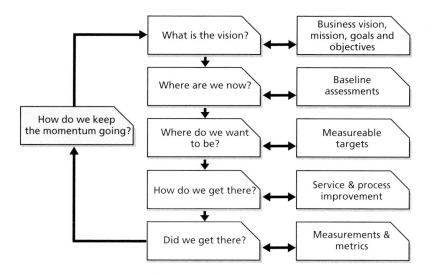

Figure 7.3   CSI model (Source: Continual Service Improvement was produced by OGC)

4. **Plan** - Draw up a detailed service improvement plan (SIP) including actions to achieve the desired situation.
5. **Check** - Measure whether the objectives have been achieved, and check whether the processes are complied with.
6. **Assure** - Engrain the changes in order to maintain them.

Announce this plan to the whole organization in order to create a consciousness, understanding, enthusiasm and support. Create a dialogue with the organization and regularly communicate and report on the actual achievements.

Service measurement
In order to determine the current situation, step two of the CSI model must measure an organization. This means that they must be able to determine the value of their services with regard to the service levels which have been agreed upon. They must also be able to report on this to their client. This requires that the organization knows which components, systems and applications are responsible for which part of the service.

By measuring an organization can also prove when the client itself is responsible for a failure. As a result the client can increase its knowledge level through training.

The section on the CSI improvement process in Chapter 13 goes deeper into the subject of service measurement.

The CSI improvement process
The **CSI improvement process** or 7-step improvement process describes how you should measure and report. The plan phase in CSI yields a **Service Improvement Plan (SIP)**.

If service level management discovers that something can be improved, it will pass this on to CSI. CSI can then formulate activities which will bring about the improvement. For the execution CSI generates a SIP. This turns "improvement" into an IT process with input, activities, output, roles and reporting.

CSI measures and processes these measurements in a continual improvement process. This goes **from measuring to improving in seven steps**:

- what *should* you measure?
- What *can* you measure?
- Gather data (measure).
- Process data.
- Analyze data.
- Present and use the information.
- Implement corrective action.

Chapter 13 contains an elaborate section on the CSI improvement process.

Service reporting

Service reporting is the process which is responsible for the generation and supply of reports about the results achieved and the developments in service levels. An extensive description of the service reporting process can be found in Chapter 13.

7.4 Organization

Process activities are not limited to one part of the organization. Because of this the process manager must map the defined process roles and activities to existing staff. Clear definitions of the responsibility and accountability are required, for instance in a **RACI matrix** (*Responsible, Accountable, Consulted, Informed*).

Roles and responsibilities

CSI comprises permanent production roles such as **service manager**, **service owner**, **process owner** and analysts, and temporary project roles such as project managers and project team members.

Table 7.1 provides an overview of the accompanying key activities and roles. Not all roles are full-time. Make a global division and adjust this later on if needed.

Key activity	Key role
Gather data from the measurement of service results and service management processes and compare these to the starting point (baseline), goals, SLAs and benchmarks; analyze trends	Service manager, service owner, IT process owner
Set targets for efficiency improvement and cost effectiveness throughout the entire Service Lifecycle	Service manager
Set targets for service improvements and use of resources	Service manager, service owner, business process owner

Key activity	Key role
Consider new business and security requirements	Service manager, business process owner
Create a SIP and implement improvements	Service manager, service owner, process owner
Enable personnel to propose improvements	Service manager
Measure, report and communicate about improvement initiatives	Service manager
Revise policy, processes, procedures and plans if needed	Service manager
Ensure that all approved actions are completed and that they achieve the desired result	Service manager, business manager, IT process owner, business process owner

Table 7.1   Key activities and the roles to be divided

Table 7.2 provides an overview of the roles, activities and skills needed for the different steps in the CSI improvement process.

Step	Roles	Activity types	Skills
1. What should you measure?	Decision makers, such as the **service manager, service owner, service level manager, CSI manager, process owner**	• high management level • high variation • action oriented • communicative • focus on future	• management skills • communicate • create and use concepts • handle complex and uncertain situations • education and experience
2. What can you measure?	Internal and external service providers who know the possibilities, such as the **service manager, service owner, process owner** and the **process manager**	• intellectual • investigative • medium to high variation • goal oriented • specialized in business management	• analyze • model • inventive attitude • education • program
3. Gather data (measure)	Personnel who supply services in the *Service Transition* and *Service Operation* life phases, such as the service desk personnel on a daily basis	• standardized • routine (low variation) • automated • clerical level • procedural	• accuracy • precision • applied training • technical experience
4. Process data	See step 3	• specialized • structures • automated • medium variation • procedural	• numerical skills • methodical • accurate • applied training • programming • experience with tools
5. Analyze data	Internal and external service providers who know the possibilities, such as the **service owner, process owner** and the business and IT analysts	See step 2	See step 2

Step	Roles	Activity types	Skills
6. Present and use the information (reporting)	Internal and external service providers who know the possibilities and the main decision makers, such as the **CSI manager, service manager, service owner, service level manager, process owner**	See step 1	See step 1
7. Implement corrective actions	See step 6	See step 2	See step 2

Table 7.2   Roles for the CSI improvement process

For the ITIL Foundations exam, knowledge is required on the roles printed in bold in Table 7.2. We will discuss these further, except for the role of **service level manager**. The Section on "Service Design" describes this role. The Section "Other roles" mentions other roles present in CSI.

Figure 7.4 shows how the various roles can cooperate.

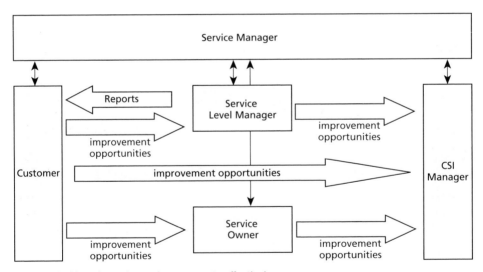

Figure 7.4   How the various roles cooperate effectively

Service manager

The **service manager** manages the development, implementation, evaluation and ongoing management of new and existing products and services. The service manager is responsible for:

• achieving company strategy and goals
• benchmarking
• financial management
• customer management
• vendor management

- full lifecycle management
- inventory management

The service manager must know a great deal about market analysis, be able to anticipate new market needs, formulate complex programs, guide personnel and sell services.

CSI manager

Without a clear and unambiguous responsibility, improvement will not occur. As a result this new role is essential for a successful improvement program. The **CSI manager** is responsible for CSI in the organization. The CSI manager manages the measuring, analysis, investigating and reporting of trends and initiates service improvement activities. In addition, they also makes sure that sufficient CSI supporting resources are available. They are responsible for:
- development of the CSI domain
- awareness and communication of CSI throughout the organization
- allocating CSI roles
- identifying and prioritzing improvement opportunities to senior management together with the service owner
- identifying monitoring requirements together with the service level manager
- ensuring that the proper monitoring tools are installed
- creating SIPs together with the service level manager
- capturing baseline data to measure improvement against it
- defining and reporting upon CSFs, KPIs and activity metrics
- using supporting frameworks and models
- making knowledge management an integral part of the daily routine
- evaluating analyzed data

The CSI manager must be able to lead projects throughout the organization, build good relationships with the business and IT management, have a flair for improvement opportunities throughout the company and be able to counsel staff.

Service owner

It is crucial to appoint one person responsible for each service: this is the **service owner**. They are the central point of contact for a specific service. It does not matter where the underlying technological components, process or functions are located. The main responsibilities are:
- owning and representing the service
- understanding which components make up the service
- measuring the performance and availability
- attending *Change Advisory Board* (CAB) meetings if these changes are relevant to the service they represent
- working with the CSI manager to identify and prioritize improvements
- participating in internal and external service reviews
- maintaining the service entry in the service catalogue
- participating in the negotiation of SLAs and OLAs

Process owner

Having an owner is just as crucial to a process as a service owner is to a service. The **process owner** ensures that the organization follows a process. They must be a senior manager with enough credibility, influence and authority in the organization departments which are part of the process. The process owner performs the essential role of process champion, design lead, advocate, coach and protector. See also the Section on "Service Design".

Other roles

Other roles which are important to CSI:
- **Service knowledge manager** - designs and maintains a knowledge management strategy and implements this
- **Reporting analyst** - evaluates and analyzes data, and identifies trends; often cooperates with SLM roles (see Service Design); must have good communication skills because reporting is an essential element of communication
- **Communication responsibility** - designs a communication strategy for CSI

7.5   Methods, techniques and tools

There are various methods and techniques to check whether planned improvements actually produce measurable improvements. One method or technique is not usually enough: you need to find the best mix for your organization. Check whether the chosen methods and techniques are suitable to measure the results of your processes, document them thoroughly and instruct staff who will be using the method or technique.

Implementation review

To determine whether the improvements produce the desired effects, you have to ask whether the original problem situation has actually improved, and how the organization has planned and implemented the improvement. The following questions help with this:
- Have we correctly assessed the present situation and have we properly formulated the problem?
- Have we taken the correct decisions with respect to our strategy?
- Have we adopted the strategy in the right way?
- Have we formulated the right CSI goals?
- Have the goals been reached?
- Do we now provide better IT services?
- What are the lessons learned and where are we now?

Assessments

An assessment compares the performance of an operational process against a performance standard. This can be an agreement in an SLA, a maturity standard, or a benchmark of companies in the same industry. By conducting assessments, IT organizations show their commitment to improvement in maturity.

Assessments are very well suited to answer the question "where are we now?", and to determine the extent of the gap with "where we want to be". A well-designed maturity assessment framework evaluates the viability of all aspects of the process environment including the people, process and technology as well as factors effecting overall process effectiveness in the business. Keep in mind that the desired performance or maturity level of a process depends on the impact that the process has on the customer's business processes.

First determine the relationship between business processes, IT services, IT systems and components. CSI can separately assess the effectiveness and efficiency results for each component. This helps in identifying areas for improvement.

It is crucial to clearly define what is being assessed. Base this on the goals and the expected future use of assessment and assessment reports. An assessment can take place on three levels:
- **process only** - only assess process attributes based on the general principles and guidelines of the process framework which defines the subject process
- **people, process and technology** - also assess skills, roles and talents of managers and staff who participate in the process; also assess the process-supporting technology
- **full assessment** - also assess the culture of acceptance within the organization, the ability of the organization to articulate a process strategy, the definition of a vision for the process environment as an "end-state", the structure and function of the process organization, and so on

All these factors are compared to the maturity attributes of the selected maturity model.

Assessments are useful in the:
- **planning phase** - as starting point (baseline) for process performance
- **implementation phase (*do*)** - to check that the estimates are correct
- **measurement phase (*check*)** - to complete the balance and to identify further possible improvements

Advantages of assessments:
- they can measure certain parts of a process independently of the rest and determine the impact of that specific component on the rest of the process
- they can be repeated

Disadvantages of assessments:
- they only offer a snapshot in time and do not give insight into the cultural dynamics of an organization
- they can become a goal in themselves instead of a means to an end
- they are labour intensive
- the results are still dependent on subjective assessors and therefore not entirely objective, even if the measurements are

This applies to both internal and external assessments. Table 7.3 gives an overview of the advantages and disadvantages of both forms.

Internal assessment	
Advantages	**Disadvantages**
• no expensive consultants • self assessment sets are available for free • promotes internal co-operation and communication • promotes internal level of knowledge • good starting point for CSI • internal knowledge of existing environment	• less objective • disappointing acceptance of findings • internal politics can get involved • limited knowledge of skills • labour intensive
External assessment	
Advantages	**Disadvantages**
• objectivity • expert ITIL knowledge • wide experience with several IT organizations • analytical skills • credibility • minimal impact on the provision of services	• high costs • risk as to acceptance • limited knowledge of existing environments • insufficient preparation limits effectiveness

Table 7.3　Internal versus external assessment

Benchmarks

A benchmark is a particular type of assessment: organizations compare (parts of) their processes with the performance of the same types of processes that are commonly recognized as "best practice". This can be done in four ways:
- **internal** - against an earlier starting point (baseline)
- **internal** - against another system or department
- **external** - against industry standards
- **external** - directly with similar organizations; this is only useful, however, if there are enough similar organizations in terms of environment, sector and geographical placement

The form you choose depends on the purpose of the benchmark:
- measurements of costs (price) and performance of internal or external service providers
- compare process performance with the existing industry standard
- compare the financial performance of high-level IT costs with industry standard or other organizations
- measure effectiveness in achieving the required customer satisfaction

To determine this you can set up an organizational profile, which consists of four key components:
- **company information profile** - basic information such as scope and type of organization
- **current assets** - hardware such as desktops and servers
- **current best practices** - policy, procedures and tools and the degree to which they are used in the organization
- **complexity** - the number of end users and the quantity and type of technology in your organization

In all cases a benchmark provides the following results:
- represents performance
- shows the gaps
- shows the risk of not closing these gaps

- helps set priorities
- helps in communicating the information well

In this way organizations discover whether their processes are cost effective, whether they meet customer needs and how effective they are in comparison to other organizations. They become aware of the need to improve and the ways they can do so, for example in the areas of economies of scale, efficiency and effectiveness. Management can then act on this. In the ideal case benchmarking forms part of a continual cycle of improvement and is repeated regularly.

Studies into the performance of one's own organization and other departments or organizations takes time. Setting up a benchmark database and visiting other organizations also involves costs.

Benchmarking is done in cooperation with:
- the business
- users or consumers
- internal service providers
- external service providers
- users in "public domain"
- benchmark partners (other organizations who are involved in the comparison)

First look to see if there are any problem areas. Use the steps from the CSI improvement process, supported by (some of) the following techniques:
- informal discussions with the business, staff or suppliers
- focus groups
- market research
- quantitative research
- surveys
- questionnaires
- re-engineering analysis
- process mapping
- quality control variation reports
- financial ratio analysis

Two special forms of benchmarking are:
- **Process maturity comparison** - as opposed to an assessment, this is not a comparison with the maturity model, but the maturity level is compared with that of other organizations; for example, CMMI can be used as a maturity model
- **Total cost of ownership (TCO**™**)** - the sum of all the costs of the design, the introduction, operation and improvement of services (developed by Gartner); it is often used to compare specific services in one organization with those of another organization

Balanced Scorecard (BSC)

Kaplan and Norton developed the **Balanced Scorecard (BSC)** in the 1990s. Define a balanced scorecard for each business unit. Begin carefully: select two to four goals. Then you can extend this as a "waterfall" to the underlying components, such as the service desk. After successful implementation keep measuring regularly.

Gap analysis

This analysis naturally flows on from assessments and benchmarks. Having determined where the organization is now, the gap analysis will determine the size of the gap with where the organization wants to be. In this way light is shed on new opportunities for improvement. The *service gap model* in Figure 7.5 shows possible gaps or discrepancies.

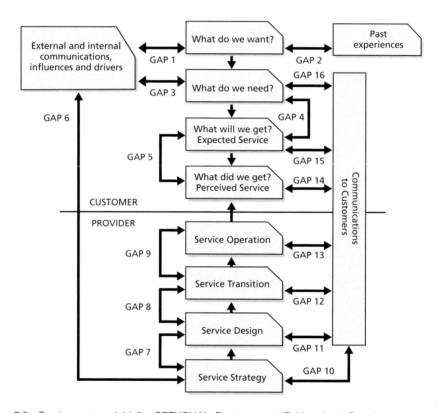

Figure 7.5   Service gap model (after SERVQUAL: Parasuraman, Zeithaml and Berry)

Gap analyses can be the result of a benchmarking on service or process maturity investigations. They can be done on a strategic, tactical or operational level. It gives an overview of the amount of resources and money which an organization has to spend to reach specific goals.

SWOT-analysis

A **SWOT-analysis** looks at the *Strengths, Weaknesses, Opportunities and Threats* of an organization (component) or project. The organization then answers the following questions:

- How can we profit from strong points?
- How can we remove weak points?
- How can we use opportunities optimally?
- How can we manage and eliminate threats?

Set your end goal before you perform a SWOT analysis. Look at which strong points help achieve a goal, which weaknesses prevent you from doing this, what external conditions promote the goal, and what external conditions prevent it.

To arrive at a SWOT of the whole organization, you can first make a SWOT for each organization component or function and then integrate them into a company SWOT. See Table 7.4 for sample aspects of SWOTs.

Possible strenghts	Possible weaknesses
• core competences • financial means • recognized as a market leader • proven management	• no clear strategic direction • outdated facilities • low profits • little insight into performance
Possible opportunities	Possible threats
• creation of new customer groups • application of skills and knowledge for new products	• foreign competition with lower prices • lower market growth • expensive legislation and regulation

Table 7.4   Examples of aspects from SWOT analyses

Rummler-Brache swim-lane diagram

Geary Rummler and Alan Brache introduced the idea of representing the relationships between processes and organizations or departments with "swim lanes" in a Rummler-Brache **swim-lane diagram**. This maps the flow of a process: from the customer through the department to the technology (Figure 7.6). The horizontal rows divide the separate organizations or departments from each other. Activities and decisions are connected through arrows to indicate the flow.

The row in which these components are placed indicates which organizational component is responsible for the activity or decision.
Because this instrument places the whole process within a recognizable structure of organizations, it is very useful as a communication tool with the management.

Tools

CSI needs different types of software to support, test, monitor and report on the ITSM processes. As part of the assessment of "where do we want to be?" the requirements for enhancing tools will be addressed and documented. The need and sophistication of the tools required depend on the business need for IT services and to some extent the size of the organization.

In any case, tools must monitor and analyze the most important components of a service, in a manner that supports the CSI Improvement Process. They can also centralize, automate and integrate the key processes. This then produces new data for trend analysis.

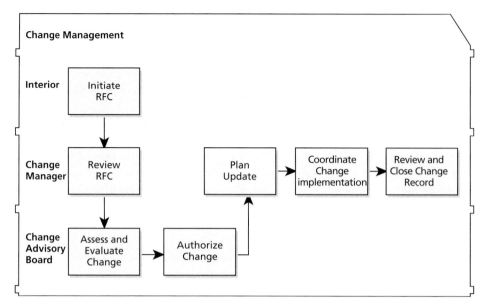

Figure 7.6   Rummler-Brache swim-lane diagram (Source: Continual Service Improvement was produced by OGC)

Tools to be used for CSI are for example:
- **IT service management suites** - tools and suites that are compatible with the ITIL process framework providing significant levels of integration between the processes and their associated record types. This functionality creates a rich source of data and creates many of the inputs for CSI. The Configuration Management System (CMS) is the foundation for the integration of all ITSM tool functionality and is a critical data source for CSI.
- **event management** - events are status messages from, for example, servers and systems; tools for event management assess these status reports for impact and origin, and categorize the reports
- **system and network management** - monitors technology platforms; the tools generate error messages for event management, providing input to performance management
- **automated incident and problem solving** - proactive detection monitors, pre-programmed scripts that automatically repair the technology; they also record information for analysis for possible improvements
- **Knowledge management** - databases with descriptions of earlier incidents and problems, and their proven solutions; also measurement of the use of the database and the effectiveness of the solution
- **service request and fulfillment (service catalogue and workflow)** - helps with defining a service catalogue and automates service requests and their settlement
- **performance management** - collects data about availability, capacity and performance to develop availability and capacity information systems
- **application and service performance monitoring** - monitors the service of the technology from an end user perspective; the tools measure availability, reaction and transaction times and efficiency of the servers

- **statistical analysis tools** - central collection point for raw data from the above tools; the analysis instruments group these data logically, creating models for current services and making predictive models for future services
- **software version control/software configuration management** - creates an overview of all software for the development environment, thus providing the Definitive Media Library (DML)
- **software test management** - supports the test and roll-out activities of release management
- **security management** - protects against intruders and unauthorized use; all hardware and software that is under security management must automatically give a warning as soon as a security incident threatens
- **project and portfolio management** - registers new functionality and the services and systems that they support; the tools help to map the service portfolio and keep it up-to-date; they can also automate organizational aspects such as plans
- **financial management** - monitors the use of resources and services for the invoicing process
- **business intelligence/reporting** - collects data from all the above mentioned tools, with which it generates important information for the business

7.6   Implementation

Before you implement CSI you must make sure that:
- the critical roles of CSI manager, service owner and reporting analyst have been filled
- monitoring and reporting on technology metrics is in place
- internal review meetings are scheduled
- external review meeting scheduled to follow internal review meetings

Communication forms an important part of any service improvement project. A communications plan is required which will need to deal with the responses and feedback from the target audience.

Define a communication plan that always states the messenger, what is the message, target audience, timing and frequency of communication, method of communication and a feedback mechanism.

CSI can be implemented through various approaches:
- **service approach** - with this you define the issues with certain services; you create an action plan with the owner of the service: how are we going to remove the issue?
- **lifecycle approach** - with this you look at the results of the various lifecycle phases and you look for possible improvements
- **functional approach** - if many incidents occur with one specific function in an organization, for example in the server group, you can remove as many problems in this function group as possible with a test project

See also "Basic concepts": Organizational Change and the PDCA Cycle.

Business case

The business case must make it clear whether it is useful to start with CSI. It must indicate what exactly will change in the intended future situation with respect to the starting situation. From a set **baseline** an organization can estimate what the present situation provides and costs, and how much the improvement of the situation will provide and cost. Formulate this in the language that the business understands. In any case answer the following questions:

- **Where are we?** - Determine the present service levels.
- **What do we want?** - Determine the company vision, mission, goals and objectives.
- **What do we need?** - Determine what services are essential for the fulfillment of the mission and set priorities on the basis of this.
- **What can we afford?** - With the help of service level management (SLM) and financial management, set the budget for IT services and see what actions are feasible.
- **What will we get?** - Determine the required results together with the business
- **What did we get?** - Have Service Operation monitor the service levels and report on them.
- **Does it still meet our wants/needs?** - Look at further possible improvements with the business.

Answer these questions by testing. In the Section "Processes and other activities" testing is discussed in detail.

For a business case, it is important to have an overview of the **costs** and benefits of CSI. Extra information about the measurement and estimation of costs and benefits can be found in the Section "Processes and other activities" and in "Methods, techniques and tools".

Costs

When deciding on an improvement initiative, always keep an eye on the costs of development, operations and ongoing maintenance. Examples of this are:

- labor costs
- training costs
- tools to process measurement data
- assessments or benchmark studies
- management time to follow progress
- communication campaigns to create awareness and to change the culture

Benefits

Results of a service improvement plan can be divided into:

- **improvements** - measurable improvements with respect to the starting situation
- **benefits** - profit that is the result of improvements (usually in financial terms)
- **Return on Investment (ROI)** - the difference between the costs and benefits of the improvement
- **Value on Investment (VOI)** - ROI, plus the extra value that cannot be expressed in money or that only becomes clear in the long-term; it is difficult to quantify extra value such as higher customer satisfaction; if there are enough "hard numbers", it still does not add much; a narrative appendix as to this qualitative value is more useful

Define both direct and indirect benefits and consider each group of **stakeholders** for each organizational level. Define the benefits such that they are measurable. Put the business first. Added value for the business can mean:

- shorter time to market
- customer bonding
- lower maintenance costs for the inventory
- larger market share

CSI can provide the following benefits:

- **to the business**:
  - more reliable support for business processes through incident, problem and change management
  - higher productivity through increased quality and availability of IT services
  - the business knows what they can expect of the IT department and what the IT department expects of them
  - procedures to ensure the continuity of IT service are oriented to the needs of the business
  - better management information about business processes and IT services
  - the IT department has more knowledge of the business processes, so that it can respond better to the desires of the business
  - quality projects, releases and changes run according to plan and provide the agreed quality at the agreed costs
  - minimal number of unused opportunities
  - better relationship between the business and IT
  - higher customer satisfaction
- **financial**:
  - efficient IT services
  - cost effective IT infrastructure and services
  - cost reduction, for example though lower costs for the implementation of changes and less excess processes and equipment
  - changes have less (financial) impact on the business
  - services meet the requirements but do not over perform
  - better division of resources, such that expenditures for the continuity of IT services are in proportion with the importance of the business processes that they support
  - cost structure is tuned to business needs
  - minimal costs and risks with checks that legislation is followed
- **innovative**:
  - more proactive development of technology and services through better information on the areas in which changes can lead to profits
  - the IT department reacts better to changes in demands from the business or the market and to new trends
  - a business which trusts their IT service providers dares to "think big"
- **internal benefits for the IT organization**:
  - more competent IT department, less chance of errors
  - integration of people and processes
  - more communication and teamwork (also with the business)
  - more productive and more motivated staff

- defined roles and responsibilities
- more effective processes, better use of resources
- IT repeats and increases profit points through increased process maturity
- better metrics and management reports through structured approach to measurement and knowledge gathering
- better picture of and more trust in present and future IT improvement opportunities
- services and systems achieve feasible goals within a realistic schedule
- better direction of service providers
- better relationship with the business
- cost alignment with business needs

Critical Success Factors (CSFs)

A **Critical Success Factor** (CSF) is a necessary condition for a good result of a service or process. Critical success factors for CSI are:

- appoint a **CSI manager** (see also "Organization")
- adoption of CSI by the whole organization
- constant visible management participation in CSI activities, for example by creating a vision and communicating about it
- clear criteria for the prioritization of improvement projects
- adoption of the service cycle approach
- sufficient funding
- resource allocation - people are dedicated to the improvement effort not just as an add-on to their already long list of tasks to perform
- technology to support improvement activities
- embrace service management processes and do not adapt it to meet personal needs and agendas

Challenges and risks

Introduction of CSI comes with the following challenges and risks:

- lack of management commitment
- poor relationship and communication between IT and the business
- too little knowledge of the IT impact on the business and its important processes
- too little knowledge of the business' priorities
- lack of information, monitoring and measurement
- not using the information from reports
- insufficient resources, budget and time
- immature service management processes
- too little or no knowledge management (see also "Organization")
- trying to change everything at once
- resistance against (cultural) changes
- not enough business or IT objectives, strategies and policy
- poor supplier management
- not testing
- tooling is too complex or insufficient
- difference in used technology

Interfaces

CSI uses a lot of data from the entire lifecycle of a service. The information that results from this, together with the demands of the business, the technical specifications, the opportunities of IT, the budget, trends and legislation, gives insight into the opportunities for the improvement of an organization.

Service Level Management (SLM)

Service level management is the most important process for CSI: it discusses with the business what the IT organization needs to measure and what the results should be. That is why this section begins with information on what SLM and CSI have in common. For more information about the service level management process see the Section about "Service Design".

After each phase of the lifecycle, test whether the improvement initiative has met its goals. This can be done using the **Post Implementation Review (PIR)** from the change management process.

Because steps 1 and 2 of the CSI improvement process lie primarily with SLM and CSI, an overview of the common ground between CSI and the other ITIL processes and the different Service Lifecycle phases is given starting from step 3 only. Service Operation also provides information about what *can* be measured before step 2.

In the light of CSI, the objective of SLM is to maintain and improve the quality of IT services. SLM does this by making a constant cycle of agreements, monitoring and reporting about IT service levels.

In the CSI improvement process, SLM plays a role with:
• What you should measure:
  – consult with the business as to what it would like
• What you can measure:
  – see what has already been measured
  – determine what can and should be measured (SLA, OLAs and Underpinning Contracts)
• Data gathering (measurement):
  – determine what happens with the data: who receives them, what analyses are needed?
• Data processing:
  – evaluate the processed data from the business perspective
  – consider how often the data must be processed and how often they must be reported on
• Data analysis:
  – compare the Service Level achievements (performance, results) with the SLAs
  – identify and record trends to expose possible patterns
  – determine the need for SIPs
  – the need to adjust existing OLAs or Underpinning Contracts (UCs)
• Presenting the information:
  – reporting to and communicating with the business
  – organizing internal and external service evaluations
  – helping to prioritize activities

- Implementing corrective actions:
  - together with problem and availability management, set up an SIP and ensure that the organization carries out this plan

In this way SLM determines what the organization measures and monitors together with the business, it reports on the performance and signals new business demands. Using this information CSI identifies and prioritizes improvement opportunities. This is the most important input for the SIP (Figure 7.7).

It is recommended that an annual budget is set for SIPs. SLM and CSI can then take quick action, which leads to a proactive attitude.

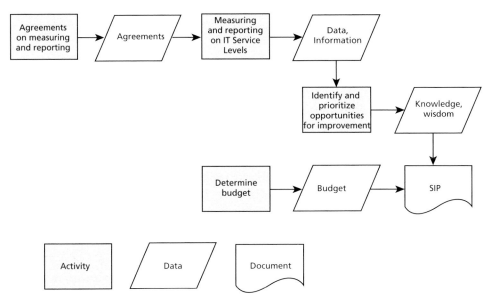

Figure 7.7   SLM and SIP

If an organization outsources its Service Delivery processes, it must also negotiate regarding CSI and include this in the SLA. Otherwise the acting party will no longer be motivated to deliver more than is agreed upon in the contract.

Monitor and gather data (measurement, step 3)
In the Service Lifecycle, *Service Strategy* monitors the effect of strategies, standards, policy and design decisions.

Service Design monitors and collects information related to the design and modification of services and service management processes. This phase also tests whether the CSFs and KPIs agreed upon with the business are measurable and effective. They also determine what should be measured and set schedules and milestones for this.

Service Transition monitors and measures data about the actual usage of services and service management processes. It develops the monitoring procedures and sets measurement criteria for after implementation.

Service Operation measures the performance of the services and components in the production environment. Once again this forms input for the CSI improvement process: what can be measured and what do these data say?

Apart from SLM, availability management also plays an important role in step 3. This process:
- creates metrics in consultation with the business to measure availability
- determines which tools are needed to make these measurements
- monitors and measures the performance of the infrastructure and frees up enough resources for this
- provides data to CSI
- updates availability plans

Capacity management also undertakes these actions; it does this in order to measure whether the IT organization can provide the requested services. This can be done from three perspectives:
- **business capacity management** - answers the question "what do we need?" and "how to we measure that?" together with the business
- **service capacity management** - answers the question "what do we need?" from the service perspective and provides information about this to CSI
- **component capacity management** - looks at the components a service is comprised of and what needs to be measured to monitor this in its entirety

Incident management defines monitoring requirements to track events and incidents, preferably automated, before they cause problems. It also monitors the reaction, repair, and resolution time and the number of escalations. For example, the service desk monitors the number of reports, the average response time and the percentage of callers who hang up prematurely.

Security management monitors and measures the security and records security incidents and problems.

And, finally, financial management monitors and measures the costs and keeps an eye on the budget. It also contributes to the reports as to the costs and ROI of improvement initiatives.

Process data (step 4)

Service Operation processes the data in logical groups. Within these groups availability management and capacity management process the data at the component level regarding availability and capacity. They work together with SLM to give these data an "end-to-end" perspective and use the agreed upon reporting form to do this.

Incident management and service desk check and process data about incidents and service requests, and the KPIs related to this. Security management checks and processes data about security incidents and reports on them.

Analyze data (step 5)

Service Strategy analyzes trends, looks at whether the strategies, policy and standards introduced achieve their goal, and whether there are opportunities for improvement. *Service Design* analyzes the results of design and project activities, and researches trends and opportunities for improvement. It also looks at whether the CSFs and KPIs set in step 2 are still adequate. *Service Operation* also analyzes results, trends and opportunities for improvement.

The most important Service Operation process for CSI is problem management. This process finds the underlying causes of problems, and these form important opportunities for improvement.

Availability management analyzes performance and trends about components and service data. It compares data with earlier months, quarters and years. It also looks at whether the correct information is being measured and whether SIPs are needed. It uses the following techniques:

- **Component Failure Impact Analysis (CFIA)** - an availability matrix updates which components are strategically important for each service and what role they play (Figure 7.8); a well-arranged configuration management database (CMDB) is required for this; identifies single points of failure
- **Fault Tree Analysis (FTA)** - determines the chain of events that can lead to the failure of an IT service (Figure 7.9)
- **Service Failure Analysis (SFA)** - looks at what a failure means for the business (impact) and what the business expects and aims at end-to-end availability improvement; on the basis of this, CSI can determine and prioritize possible improvements
- **Technical Observation Post (TOP)** - a meeting of IT personnel with different specializations to discuss one aspect of availability
- **Expanded Incident Lifecycle** - calculates the mean time to restore a service (MTRS); see also the Section on "maintainability" under Service Strategy

Capacity management analyzes when which customer uses what services, how they use them and how this influences the performance of one or more systems or components. This again provides improvement opportunities to CSI.

Configuration Item:	Service A	Service B
PC #1	B	B
PC #2		B
Cable #1	B	B
Cable #2		B
Outlet #1	X	X
Outlet #2		X
Ethernet segment	X	X
Router	X	X
Wan Link	X	X
Router	X	X
Segment	X	X
NIC	A	A
Server	B	B
System software	B	B
Application	B	B
Database	X	X

X = Fault means service is unavailable
A = Failsafe configuration
B = Failsafe, with changeover time
" " = No impact

Figure 7.8   CFIA matrix

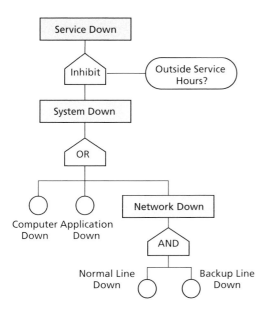

Figure 7.9   Fault Tree Analysis

Whereas problem management is oriented toward resolving problems that have already occurred in the past, capacity management tries to prevent problems proactively, by making extra storage capacity ready on time, for example. Often this is done by reproducing the situation in a model, and then asking a number of "what if" questions.

Incident management and the service desk can compare the collected data with earlier results and the agreed service levels. They can also propose SIPs or corrective actions.

Security management uses all the other processes to find the origin of security incidents and problems. It looks for trends and possible improvements in the area of monitoring and looks at whether security strategies produce the intended results.

Every improvement initiative must consult IT Service Continuity Management (ITSCM) to make sure that the IT services are not put at risk. **Risk management** plays a central role in this. It analyzes what effects an improvement can have, while in turn CSI analyzes the results of risk management activities, to discover opportunities for improvement. See also Service Design regarding risk management.

Present and use (step 6)

Service Strategy presents results, trends and recommendations for the improvement of adopted strategies, policy and standards. *Service Design* does this for design improvements and project activities and *Service Transition* and *Service Operation* for service and service management processes.

Availability management, capacity management, incident management, service desk, problem management, and security management help with creating reports and prioritizing corrective actions.

Knowledge management is very important in presenting and using the information for CSI. This is the only way CSI can get a good overview of the knowledge of the organization and the opportunities for improvement. It is also important in order to ensure continual improvement and that all the knowledge and experience gathered is shared and stored. For more information about knowledge management see also the Section about "Service Transition".

Implement corrective actions (step 7)
Availability management, capacity management, incident management, service desk, problem management and security management perform incremental or corrective actions where approval from the business is not required.

Capacity management can also proceed by introducing **demand management** measures to influence the behavior of the end user:
• calculation of costs
• making policy for the proper use of the services
• communicating expectations
• education about proper use
• negotiating maintenance times
• setting use restrictions, such as limiting the amount of storage space

As with all other changes in the lifecycle, CSI changes must go through the change, release, and deployment process. CSI must therefore submit a Request for Change (RFC) with change management and conduct a PIR after implementation. Also consider the updating of the CMDB by means of configuration management. After this, IT Service Continuity Management (ITSCM) must keep the continuity plan up-to-date.

Finally
The introduction of CSI is not simple. It requires conscious striving toward continual improvement as part of the culture and behavior of the organization, and a proactive attitude. In a world where the technology changes very quickly, such a proactive attitude is a big challenge; after all we are constantly controlled by the changes. In a situation of increasing outsourcing and professional development of IT service management, service quality is progressively becoming a distinguishing factor. To get "in control" and to achieve the desired quality it is preferable to work proactively. CSI is essential to this.

As with many other domains, a step-by-step approach is needed for this. Do not begin with a big-bang approach with all the processes at once, but first determine the biggest problem areas (for example with SWOT) and choose a well-considered approach for the improvements. Recognizing the critical success factors is very important here.

PART 2
FUNCTIONS AND PROCESSES

Chapter 8
Introduction to Functions and Processes

8.1 Introduction

Processes are *internal* affairs for the IT service provider. An organization that is still trying to gain control of its processes therefore has an **internal focus**. Organizations that focus on gaining control of their systems in order to provide services are still internally focused. The organization is not ready for an **external focus** until it controls its services and is able to vary them on request. This external focus is required to evolve into that desirable customer-focused organization.

Because organizations can be in different stages of maturity, IT managers require a broad orientation in their discipline. Most organizations are now working on the introduction of a process-focused or customer-focused approach, or still have to start working on this. Process control is therefore a vital step on the road towards a **mature customer-focused organization**.

ITIL has made an important contribution to the organization of that process-focused operating method in the past decade. The development started in North-western Europe and has made some progress on most other continents in the last few years also. On a global scale, however, a minimal number of organizations have actually started with this approach - and an even smaller number have made serious progress at this point. The organization change projects that were thought to be necessary to convert to a process-focused organization were not all successful.

These findings lead us to conclude that the majority of organizations in the world require access to good information and best practices concerning the **business processes of IT organizations**. Fortunately, that information is abundant. The ITIL version 2 books provide comprehensive documentation on the most important processes, while ITIL version 3 adds even more information.

The **process model** is at least as important as the processes because processes must be deployed in the right relationships to achieve the desired effect of a process-focused approach. There are many different process models available. The experiences gained with these processes and process models in recent years have been documented comprehensively in books, magazines and white papers, and have been presented at countless conventions.

8.2   Management of processes

Every organization aims to realize its vision, mission, strategy, objectives and policies, which means that appropriate activities have to be undertaken.

For example, a restaurant will have to purchase fresh ingredients, the chefs will have to work together to provide consistent results, and there should be no major differences in style among the waiting staff. A restaurant will only be awarded a three-star rating when it manages to provide the same high quality over an extended period of time. This is not always the case: there will be changes among the waiting staff, a successful approach may not last, and chefs often leave to open their own restaurants. Providing consistently high quality means that the component activities have to be coordinated: the better and more efficiently the kitchen operates, the higher the quality of service that can be provided to the guests.

In the example of the restaurant, appropriate activities include buying vegetables, bookkeeping, ordering publicity material, receiving guests, cleaning tables, peeling potatoes and making coffee. With just such an unstructured list, something will be left out and staff will easily become confused. It is therefore a better idea to structure the activities. Preferably these will be structured in such a way as to allow us to see how each group of activities contributes to the objectives of the business, and how they are related to other activities.

Such groups of activities are known as **processes**. If the process structure of an organization is clearly described, it will show:
• what has to be done
• what the expected inputs and results are
• how we measure whether the processes deliver the expected results
• how the results of one process affect those of another process

Processes can be defined in many ways. Depending upon the objectives of the creator, more or less emphasis will be on specific aspects. For example, a highly detailed process description will allow for a high level of control. Superficial process definitions will illustrate that the creator does not care much about the way in which the steps are executed.
Once the processes are defined, the roles, responsibilities and people can be assigned to specific aspects, bringing the process to the level of a *procedure*.

Processes

When arranging activities into processes, we do not use the existing allocation of tasks, nor the existing departmental divisions. This is a conscious choice. By opting for a process structure, it often becomes evident that certain activities in the organization are uncoordinated, duplicated, neglected or unnecessary.

> A **process** is a structured set of activities designed to accomplish a defined objective.

Instead, we look at the **objective** of the process and the **relationships** with other processes. A process is a series of activities carried out to convert input into an output, and ultimately into an outcome. The **input** is concerned with the resources being used in the process. The (reported) **output** describes the immediate results of the process, while the **outcome** indicates the long-term results of the process (in terms of meaningful effect). Through **control** activities, we can associate the input and output of each of the processes with **policies and standards** to provide information about the results to be obtained by the process. Control regulates the input and the **throughput** in case the throughput or output parameters are not compliant with these standards and policies. This produces chains of processes that show the input that goes into the organization and what the result is, and it also monitors points in the chains in order to check the quality of the products and services provided by the organization.

The standards for the output of each process have to be defined, in such a way that the complete chain of processes in the process model meets the corporate objective. If the output of a process meets the defined requirements, then the process is **effective** in transforming its input into its output. To be really effective, the outcome should be taken into consideration rather than merely focusing on the output. If the activities in the process are also carried out with the minimum required effort and cost, then the process is **efficient**. It is the task of process management to use **planning and control** to ensure that processes are executed in an effective and efficient way.

We can study each process separately to optimize its quality. The **process owner** is responsible for the process results. The **process manager** is responsible for the realization and structure of the process, and reports to the process owner.

The logical combination of activities results in clear transfer points where the quality of processes can be monitored. In the restaurant example, we can separate responsibility for purchasing and cooking, so that the chefs do not have to purchase anything and can concentrate on their core activities.

The management of the organization can provide control on the basis of the process quality of the process as demonstrated by data from the results of each process. In most cases, the relevant **performance indicators** and standards will already be agreed upon. In this case the process manager can do the day-to-day control of the process. The process owner will assess the results based on a **report** of performance indicators and checks whether the results meet the agreed standard. Without clear indicators, it would be difficult for a process owner to determine whether the process is under control, and if planned improvements are being implemented.

Processes are often described using **procedures** and **work instructions**.

> *A **procedure** is a specified way to carry out an activity or a process.*
> *A procedure describes the "how", and can also describe "who" carries the activities out. A procedure may include stages from different processes. A procedure can vary depending on the organization.*
>
> *A set of **work instructions** defines how one or more activities in a procedure should be carried out in detail, using technology or other resources.*

A process is defined as a logically related series of activities executed to meet the goals of a defined objective. Processes are composed of two kinds of activities: the activities to realize the goal (operational activities concerned with the throughput), and the activities to manage these (control activities). The control activities make sure the operational activities (the workflow) are performed in time, in the right order, etc. (For example, in the processing of changes it is always ensured that a test is performed *before* a release is taken into production and not *afterwards*.)

Processes and departments

Most businesses are hierarchically organized. There are departments that are responsible for the activities of a group of employees. There are various ways of structuring departments, such as by customer, product, region or discipline. IT services generally depend on several departments, customers or disciplines. For example, if there is an IT service to provide users with access to an accounting program on a central computer, this will involve several disciplines. The computer center has to make the program and database accessible, the data and telecommunications department has to make the computer center accessible, and the PC support team has to provide users with an interface to access the application.

Processes that span several departments (teams) can monitor the quality of a service by monitoring particular aspects of quality, such as availability, capacity, cost and stability. A service organization will try to match these quality aspects with the customer's demands. The structure of such processes can ensure that good information is available about the provision of services, so that the planning and control of services can be improved.

Figure 8.1 shows a basic example of the combinations of activities in a process (indicated by the dashed lines).

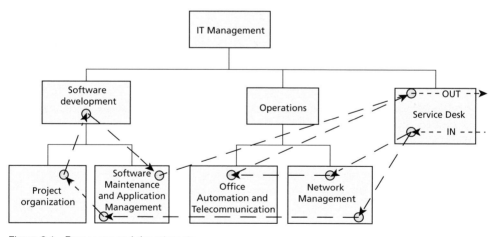

Figure 8.1   Processes and departments

IT service management and processes

IT service management has been known as the process and service-focused approach of what was initially known as Information Technology management. The shift of management from infrastructure to processes has paved the way for the term IT service management as a process and customer-focused discipline. Processes should always have a defined objective. The objective of IT service management processes is to contribute to the quality of the IT services. Quality management and process control are part of the organization and its policies.

By using a process approach, best practices for IT service management describe how services can be delivered, using the most effective and efficient series of activities. The Service Lifecycle in ITIL V3 is based on these process descriptions. The structure and allocation of tasks and responsibilities between functions and departments depends on the type of organization, and these structures vary widely among IT departments, and they often change. The description of the process structure however, provides a common point of reference that changes less rapidly. This can help to maintain the quality of IT services during and after reorganizations, and also among service providers and partners as they change. This makes service providers far less sensitive to organizational change, and much more flexible: providers can continually adapt their organization to changing conditions, leaving the core of their processes in place. In this way the shop can stay open during reconstruction work. However, reality may pose some practical problems, making this more difficult in practice than it seems in theory.

Applying the best process definitions of the industry allows IT service providers to concentrate on their business. As with other fields of industry, the processes in the IT industry are similar for all organizations of the same nature. Many of the process descriptions documented in ITIL have been recognized as the best that the industry could hope to adopt.

8.3 Teams, roles and positions in ITSM

Organizations divide the various tasks for carrying out processes or activities in many different ways. Tasks can be covered by organizational bodies, such as groups, teams, departments or divisions. These organizational bodies are then managed in **hierarchical organizations** by a line manager, who has a certain "span of control" and who manages one or more of these bodies. **Flat organizations** have relatively few layers in this hierarchy. Organizations can also divide the tasks more in the spirit of equality, such as, for example, **network organizations**, in which the cooperation between the various bodies is paramount.

Besides hierarchical organizations, which manage through "the line", there are also **project organizations**, which manage primarily by using temporary forms of project cooperation, while **process organizations** are managed primarily by means of an agreed work method. Obviously, these types of management can be combined in innumerable ways. As a result of this, we are seeing a great number of unique organizational configurations in the field.

Organizations can distinguish themselves from other organizations, particularly in respect to the type of organization they operate. An organization that is directed toward hierarchy will have a staff primarily of senior line management. A process-oriented organization will have staff that are responsible for processes. Depending on the degree to which management is based on processes, the line or projects, the staff will consist of a mix of the relevant responsible managers.

When setting up an organization, positions and roles are also used, in addition to the various groups (teams, departments, divisions). **Roles** are sets of responsibilities, activities and authorities granted to a person or team. One person or team may have multiple roles; for example, the roles of Configuration Manager and Change Manager may be carried out by a single person. **Positions** (functions) are traditionally recognized as tasks and responsibilities that are assigned to a specific person. A person in a particular position has a clearly defined package of tasks and responsibilities which may include various roles. Positions can also be more broadly defined as a logical concept that refers to the people and automated measures that carry out a clearly defined process, an activity or a combination of processes or activities.

8.4   Tools used in ITSM

In the performance of tasks in IT service management, innumerable automated support aids can be used: these are referred to as tools. With the help of these tools, management tasks can be automated; for example, monitoring tasks or software distribution tasks. Other tools support the performance of the activities themselves; for example, service desk tools or service management tools. The latter category, in fact, supports the management of several processes and are therefore often referred to as workflow tools - although they may not have actual workflow engines.

The fact that the IT field is fundamentally focused on automated facilities (for information processing) has led to a virtual deluge of tools appearing on the market, which have greatly increased the performance capacity of IT organizations.

8.5   Communication in IT service organizations

People, process, partners and technology provide the main "machinery" of any organization, but they only work well if the machine is oiled: **communication** is an essential element in any organization. If the people do not know about the processes or use the wrong instructions or tools, the output may not be as anticipated.

People are core assets of the organization. This is not only due to the fact that they need to be in place to perform certain activities or to take decisions, but also because people have the good habit of communicating. When an organization applies highly detailed instructions for all its activities, it will end up in a bureaucracy. On the other hand, an organization without any rules will most likely end up in chaos. Whichever balance an organization is trying to find here, it will always benefit enormously from communication between the people in the organization. A regular and formal meeting culture will support this, but organizations should not underestimate the important role of informal communication: many projects have been saved by means of a simple chat in the tea room, or in the car park.

Formal structures on communication include:
* **reporting** - internal and external reporting, aimed at management or customers, project progress reports, alerts
* **meetings** - formal project meetings, regular meetings with specific targets
* **online facilities** - email systems, chat-rooms, pagers, groupware, document sharing systems, messenger facilities, teleconferencing and virtual meeting facilities
* **notice boards** - near the coffee maker, water cooler, at the entrance of the building, in the company restaurant

IT teams and departments, as well as users, internal customers and service production teams, must communicate with each other. The **stakeholders** for communication can thus be found among all managers and employees who are involved in service management, in all the layers of the organization, and with all customers, users and service providers. Good communication can prevent problems. All communication must have a particular goal or result. Every team, process and every department must have a clear **communications policy**.

IT service management includes several types of communication, such as:
- routine operational communication
- communication between teams
- performance reports
- communication during projects
- communication when there are changes
- communication in case of exceptions
- communication in case of emergencies
- training for new or adapted processes and service designs
- communication with service production teams regarding service strategies and design

8.6   Culture

Organizations that want to change, for example to improve the quality of their services, will eventually be confronted with the current organizational culture and will have to deal with any changes to this culture as a consequence of the overall change. The organizational culture, or corporate culture, refers to the way in which people deal with each other in the organization; the way in which decisions are made and implemented; and the attitude of employees to their work, customers, service providers, superiors and colleagues.

Culture, which depends on the standards and values of the people in the organization, cannot be controlled, but it can be influenced. Influencing the culture of an organization requires leadership in the form of a clear and consistent policy, as well as a supportive personnel policy.

The corporate culture can have a major influence on the provision of IT services. Businesses value innovation in different ways. In a stable organization, where the culture places little value on innovation, it will be difficult to adjust its IT services in line with changes in the organization of the customer. If the IT department is unstable, then a culture which values change can pose a serious threat to the quality of its services. In that case, a "free for all" culture can develop where many uncontrolled changes lead to a large number of faults.

8.7   Processes, projects, programs and portfolios

Activities can be managed from a process perspective, from an organizational hierarchy (line) perspective, from a project perspective, or from any combination of these three. Organizations that tend to apply just one of these management systems often miss the benefits of the others. The practical choice often depends upon history, culture, available skills and competences, and personal preferences. The optimum choice may be entirely different, but the requirements for applying this optimum may be hard to realize and vary in time.

There are no "hard and fast laws" for the way an organization should combine processes, projects and programs. However, it is generally accepted that there are some consequences attached to modern practices in IT service organizations, since the most widely accepted approach to service management is based on process management. This means that whenever the organization works with projects or programs, it should have established how these approaches work together.

The practical relationship between projects and processes is determined by the relative position of both in terms of "leading principles for the management of the organization": if projects are considered more important than processes, then decisions on projects will overrule decisions on processes; as a consequence, the organization will not be able to implement a stable set of processes. If it is the other way around, with projects only able to run within the constraints of agreed processes, then project management will be a discipline that will have to adapt to new boundaries and definitions (e.g. since projects always change something from A to B, they will most likely fall under the regime of Change, Release and Deployment Management).

The most suitable solution is dependent upon the understanding of the role of IT service management in the organization. To be able to find a solution for this management challenge, it is recommended that a common understanding of processes, projects, programs, and even portfolio's is created. The following definitions may be used:
- **Process** - A process is a structured set of activities designed to accomplish a defined objective.
- **Project** - A project is a temporary organization, with people and other assets required to achieve an objective.
- **Program** - A program consists of a number of projects and activities that are planned and managed together to achieve an overall set of related objectives.
- **Portfolio** - A portfolio is a set of projects and/or programs, which are not necessarily related, brought together for the sake of control, coordination and optimization of the portfolio in its totality. NB: In ITIL, a service portfolio is the complete set of services that are managed by a service provider.

Since the project/program/portfolio grouping is a hierarchical set of essential project resources, the issue can be downscaled to that of a relationship between a project and a process.

The most elementary difference between a process and a project is the one-off character of a project, versus the continuous character of the process. If a project has achieved its objectives, it means the end of the project. Processes can be run many times, both in parallel and in sequence. The nature of a process is aimed at its repeatable character: processes are defined only in case of a repeatable string of activities that are important enough to be standardized and optimized.

Projects are aimed at changing a situation A into a situation B. This can involve a simple string of activities, but it can also be a very complex series of activities. Other elements of importance for projects include money, time, quality, organization and information. Project structures are normally used only if at least one of these elements is of considerable value.

Actually, projects are just ways of organizing a specific change in a situation. In that respect they have a resemblance with processes. It is often a matter of focus: processes focus at the specific sequence of activities, the decisions taken at certain milestone stages, and the quality of the activities involved. Processes are continuously instantiated and repeated, and use the same approach each time. Projects focus more at the time and money constraints, in terms of resources spent on the change and the projects end, and projects vary much more than processes.

A very practical way of combining the benefits of both management systems might be as follows:

• Processes set the scene for how specific series of activities are performed.
• Projects can be used to transform situation A into situation B, and always refer to a change.
• If the resources (time, money, or other) involved in a specific process require the level of attention that is normally applied in a project, then (part of) the process activities can be performed as a project, but always under the control of the process: if changes are performed, using project management techniques, the agreed change management policies still apply.

This would allow organizations to maintain a continuous customer focus and apply a process approach to optimize this customer focus, and at the same time benefit from the high level of resource control that can be achieved when using project management techniques.

8.8 Functions and processes in the lifecycle phases

For the sake of readability and uniformity, the following structure for the descriptions was used as much as possible:

1. **introduction** - describes the purpose and aims of the process or function, its scope, value to the business, principles, guidelines, starting points and basic concepts
2. **activities, methods and techniques** - explains the process or function in greater detail based on the workflow of activities (if possible); also describes commonly used methods and techniques
3. **interfaces** - describes how the process or function is triggered, its inputs and outputs, and its links to other functions and processes
4. **metrics** - describes the process metrics, in particular the Key Performance Indicators (KPIs)
5. **implementation** - describes the Critical Success Factors (CSFs), challenges, risks and traps that may apply for the introduction of a process or function

Chapter 9
Functions and Processes in Service Strategy

9.1 Financial Management

Introduction

Financial management is an integrated component of service management. It provides vital information that management need to ensure efficient and cost-effective service delivery. Efficient financial management enables the organization to provide a full justification of expenditures and allocate them directly to services.

IT organizations are increasingly aware of the fact that they are essentially equivalent to market-oriented organizations. Like the latter, IT organizations must understand and control the factors that influence demand. An IT organization also tries to reduce costs whilst improving its offering.

If implemented correctly, financial management generates meaningful and critical data on performance. It is also able to answer important organization issues, such as:
- Does our differentiation strategy result in higher profits and revenue, reduced costs or increased coverage?
- Which services cost most and why?
- Where are our greatest inefficiencies?

Financial management ensures that the costs of IT services are clear (e.g. via the service catalogue) and that the business understands them. The benefits are:
- improved decision-making
- speed of change
- service portfolio management
- financial compliance and control
- operational control
- value capture and creation

Service valuation

How can we achieve insight into the value creation process with the aid of financial management? Service valuation quantifies, in financial terms, the funding sought by the business and IT for service delivered, based on the agreed value of those services.

The main part of **service valuation** is to determine the value of services at a level the business considers realistic. This allows the provider to gain insight into which customer interests are served. An additional goal is improved management of demand and consumption behavior.

Translate utility and warranty to a monetary figure to calculate the value. ITIL defines two vital value concepts for service valuation:
- **Provisioning value** - The actual underlying costs to IT related to provisioning a service including all fulfillment elements, both tangible and intangible. These are costs like:
  - hardware and software license costs
  - annual maintenance costs for hardware and software
  - personnel that work to support or maintain a service
  - paid facilities
  - taxes, capital or interest charges
  - compliance costs
- **Service value potential** - The value-adding component based on the customer's perception of value from the service or expected marginal utility and warranty from using the service, in comparison with what is possible using the customers' own assets. Look at the service's individual value components to determine the true value of the service. Determine the eventual value of the service by adding these components and comparing them against the costs (provisioning value). Figure 9.1 shows the related concepts of value in greater detail. Consider the section on "Service Design" in Chapter 4 for details about the identification of service value potential.

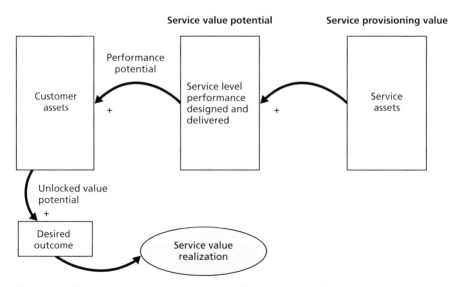

Figure 9.1   Customer assets constitute the basis for value definition (Source: Service Strategy was produced by OGC)

Demand modeling

In adequate management of service demand results in costs and risks. Demand modeling uses service-oriented financial information with factors of demand and supply in order to model anticipated usage by the business, and provisioning requirements of IT.

Service portfolio management

Financial management provides vital input for service portfolio management. By applying cost structures to services, companies can compare their service costs with those of other providers.

Service provisioning optimization

Financial management provides vital input for optimizing the service delivery (*Service Provisioning optimization*, SPO). SPO investigates the financial inputs and constraints of service components or delivery models to determine if alternatives should be explored relating to how a service can be provisioned differently to make it more competitive in terms of cost or quality. It is this financial analysis of service components, constraints and value that is at the heart of financial management's interaction with service provisioning optimization.

Planning confidence

One objective of financial management is to ensure proper funding for delivery and consumption of services. Planning provides financial translation and qualification of expected future demand to IT services.

Planning can be split up into three primary areas. Each area represents financial results that are necessary to ensure continued visibility and service valuation:
- **operating & capital planning** (general and fixed asset ledgers) - translation of IT expenditures to collective financial systems as part of the collective planning cycle
- **demand planning** - need for and use of IT services as described earlier
- **regulatory and environmental planning** (compliance) - is controlled from the business

Careful planning results in confidence that the financial data and models provide accurate information on the development of service demand and offer.

Service investment analysis

Financial management provides the shared analytical models and knowledge to assess the expected value and/or return of a given initiative, solution, program or project in a standardized manner.

The objective of service investment analysis is to derive a value indication for the total lifecycle of a service based on (a) the value received and (b) costs incurred during the lifecycle of the service.

Accounting

Financial management plays a transitional role between corporate financial systems and service management. The results of a service-orientated accounting function is that far greater detail and understanding is achieved regarding service provisions and consumption, and the generation of data that feeds directly into the planning process.

Related functions and accounting properties are:
- **service recording** - assignment of a cost entry to the appropriate service
- **cost types** - high-level expenses categories such as hardware, software, labour, administration; once the basis for cost administration (e.g. per department, service or customer) is established, cost types are determined for cost entry; the number of cost types can vary depending on the organization's size; cost types must have a clear and recognisable description, so that costs can be easily allocated; the cost types can then be split up into *cost items*; settlement for each cost item may be established at a later stage
- **cost classification** - to ensure good cost control, it is important to gain insight into the types of costs that occur costs can be split up according to various aspects:
  - *Capital/operational costs*:
    - Capital costs have to do with the purchase of assets that generally last several years. The expenditure is written down over several years. Only the write-down amount is counted as costs.
    - Operational costs are costs that occur regularly and are not offset by tangible production assets (e.g. a maintenance contract for hardware, license costs, insurance premiums).
  - *Direct/indirect costs* - What costs contribute directly to a product or service and what costs do not:
    - Direct costs are costs that can be identified specifically and exclusively for an IT service. For instance activities and materials that are associated directly and exclusively with a specific service (e.g. a broadband connection).
    - Indirect costs cannot be identified directly for an IT service (e.g. facilities, supporting services and administrative costs).
  - *Fixed/variable costs* - Costs that vary or not with the production level:
    - Fixed costs are costs that do not vary due to production changes, such as investments in hardware, software and buildings. Generally the monthly or annual write-downs and interest are entered as costs instead of the acquisition costs. Fixed costs are ongoing, even if the service is reduced or terminated.
    - Variable costs are costs that do vary due to production changes, such as hiring external staff.
  - *Cost units* - The identified unit of consumption that is accounted for a particular service or service asset.

Variable Cost Dynamics (VCD)

Variable Cost Dynamics (VCD) focuses on analyzing and understanding the multitude of variables that impact service cost, how sensitive those elements are to variability, and the related incremental value changes that results. Among other benefits, VCD analysis can be used to identify a marginal change is unit cost resulting from adding or subtracting one or more incremental units of a service. This is helpful when applied toward the analysis of expected impacts from events such as acquisitions, divestitures, changes to the service portfolio or service provisioning alternatives etc.

Examples of variable service cost components are:
- number and type of users
- number of software licenses
- cost/operating footprint of data center

- delivery mechanisms
- number and type of resources
- cost of adding one more storage device
- costs of adding one more end user license

Activities, methods and techniques

Service valuation
During service valuation activities, the following decisions are made:
- **Direct costs versus indirect costs** - Can costs be attributed directly to a specific service or are they shared by several services (indirect costs)? Once the depth and breadth of the cost components are appropriately identified, rules or policy to guide how costs are to be spread among multiple services may be required.
- **Labour costs** - Develop a system to calculate the labor costs for a certain service.
- **Variable costs** - Include expenditures that are not fixed, but which vary depending on things such as the number of users or the number of running instances. To predict variable costs, you can use:
  - *Tiers* - identifying price breaks where plateaus occur within a provider so that customers are encouraged to obtain scale efficiencies familiar to the provider
  - *Maximum costs* - prescribing the cost of service based on the maximum level of variability
  - *Average costs* - this involves setting the cost of the service based on historical averaging of the variability.
- **Translation of cost account data to service value** - This is only possible once costs are attributed to service rather than, or in addition to, traditional cost accounts.

After having established the fixed and variable costs for each service, you need to think about the variable cost drivers and variation level of a service.

Funding model alternatives
This section summarises several traditional models to fund IT services:
- **rolling plan funding** - a constant funding cycle; suitable for a Service Lifecycle for which a funding obligation is incurred at the start of a cycle and continues until changes occur or the lifecycle ends
- **trigger based plans** - critical triggers activate a planning for a specific event; the change management process, for instance, could act as a trigger for the planning process for all approved changes that have financial consequences
- **zero based funding** - funding only the actual costs to deliver an IT service

Business Impact Analysis (BIA)
A BIA seeks to identify an organizations most critical business services through an analysis of outage severity translated into a financial value, coupled with operational risk.

This information can help shape and improve operational performance. By enabling better decision making regarding prioritization of incident handling, problem management focus, change and release management operations, project priority and so on. It is a beneficial tool for identifying the costs of service failure and the relative worth of a service.

The cost of service outage is a financial value placed on a specific service and is meant to reflect the value of lost productivity and revenue over a specific period of time.

Key decisions for financial management

Some concepts in financial management have a big impact on the development of service strategies. ITIL highlights a number of these, allowing each organization to determine which the best alternatives are for its Service Strategy:

- **Cost recovery, value center, or accounting center?** - The IT financial cycle starts with funding applied to resources that create output. That output is identified as value by the customer, and this in turn induces the funding cycle to begin again. IT is typically referred to as a cost center, with funding based only on replenishing actual costs expended to deliver service.
- **Chargeback: to charge or not to charge?** - A chargeback model for IT can provide accountability and transparency. Charging costs increases the customer organization's awareness of the costs incurred to provide it with information. There are several chargeback models:
  - *notional charging* - an accounting method that provides insight into the costs that would be charged for a specific settlement method
  - *tiered subscription* - involves varying levels of warranty and/or utility offered for a service or service bundle, all of which have been priced, with the most appropriate chargeback models applied
  - *metered usage* - settling costs on the basis of carefully established consumption units; applies exclusively for organizations that have made serious progress in introducing financial management
  - *direct plus* - a more simplistic model where costs that can be attributed directly to a service are charged accordingly with some percentage of indirect costs shared amongst it
  - *fixed or user cost* - the simplest chargeback model in which the costs are divided on the basis of an agreed denominator, such as the number of users; this model contributes little to affecting customer behavior
- **Financial management implementation checklist** - A number of example implementation steps for phased implementation could include: plan, analyze, design, implement and measure.

9.2 Service Portfolio Management (SPM)

Introduction

A service portfolio describes the services of a provider in terms of business value. It articulates business needs and the service provider's response to those needs. Business values correspond to marketing terms; they assure that the competitiveness of the service provider is measurable with regard to the competitors.

With SPM, managers are better able to assess the quality requirements and accompanying costs. They can look for cost cutting action points, while at the same time maintaining the service quality.

> *Service Portfolio Management (SPM)* is a dynamic method for governing investments in service management across the enterprise and managing them for value.

The **goals** of service portfolio management are to realize and create maximum value, while at the same time keeping a lid on risks and costs.

SPM starts with documenting the standardized services of the organization and then those of the service catalogue. In order to be financially feasible, the portfolio must be a good mix of a service catalogue and services in pipeline.

The product manager plays an important role in the service portfolio management. He or she is responsible for managing services as a product during the entire lifecycle. Product managers coordinate and focus the organization and own the service catalogue. They work closely together with the Business Relationship Managers (BRM), who coordinate and focus on the client portfolio. In essence, SPM is a Governance method.

Value for the business

The service portfolio functions as basis of the decision-making framework. It helps answer the following strategic questions:
- Why should a customer buy these services?
- Why should a customer buy these services *from us?*
- What are the pricing and charge back models?
- What are our strengths and weaknesses, our priorities and our risks?
- How should our resources and capabilities be allocated?

Activities, methods and techniques

SPM is a dynamic and continuous process that entails the following work methods (see also Figure 9.2):
- **Defining** - Making an inventory of services, business cases and validating the portfolio data; start with collecting information on all *existing and proposed* services in order to determine the costs of the existing portfolio; the cyclic nature of the SPM process signifies that this phase does

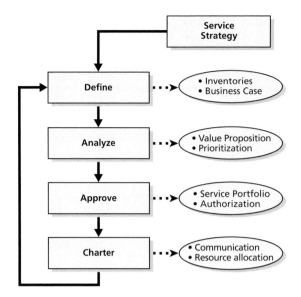

Figure 9.2   Service Portfolio Process (Source: Service Strategy was produced by OGC)

not only make the inventory of the services, but also validates the data over and over again; each service in the portfolio should have a business case.
- **Analyzing** - Maximizing the portfolio value, tuning, prioritizing and balancing supply and demand; in this phase, the strategic goals are given a concrete form.
  Start with a series of top/down questions such as:
  – What are the long-term goals of the service organization?
  – Which services are required to realize these goals?
  – Which capabilities and resources are necessary to achieve those services? In other words, what are the four Ps?
  – how will we get there?
The answers to these questions form the basis of the analysis, but also determine the desired result of SPM. Service investments must be subdivided into three strategic categories:
  – **Run the Business (RTB)** - RTB investments concentrate on maintaining the service operations
  – **Grow the Business (GTB)** - GTB investments are intended to expand the scope of services
  – **Transform the Business (TTB)** - TTB investments are moves into new market spaces
- **Approving** - Finishing the proposed portfolio, authorizing services and resources and making decisions for the future; there are six different outcomes: retain, replace, rationalize, refactor, renew and retire.
- **Charter** - Communicating decisions, allocating resources and chartering services; start with a list of decisions and action items; communicate about this clearly and unequivocally with the organization; these decisions must be in tune with the budget decisions and financial plans; the expected value of each service must have been incorporated into the financial forecasts and

resource planning; new services are promoted to Service Design existing services are refreshed in the service catalogue. Retired services begin their sunset to Service Transition.

With an efficient portfolio having optimal ROI and risk levels, an organization creates maximum value while using limited resources and capabilities.

9.3   Demand Management

Introduction

Challenges in managing service demand

Demand Management (DM) is a vital aspect of service management. It aligns supply with demand and aims to predict demand as closely as possible and, if possible, even regulate it. Badly managed demand represents a risk for service providers. Too much capacity, for instance, results in costs that do not yield value. Inadequate capacity, however, affects the service quality and limits service growth. Service Level Agreements (SLAs), demand prognosis, planning and strict coordination with the customer can reduce demand-related uncertainty, but they cannot eliminate it altogether.

Service management must deal with the additional problem of *synchronous production and consumption*. Service Operation is impossible without the existence of a demand that consumes the output. It is a pull-system, in which consumption cycles stimulate the production cycles (see Figure 9.3).

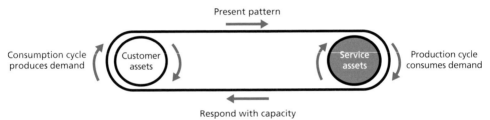

Figure 9.3   Close relationships between demand and capacity (Source: Service Strategy was produced by OGC)

Unlike goods, services cannot be manufactured in advance and stocked in a finished goods inventory in anticipation of demand. The productive capacity of resources available to a service is adjusted according to demand forecasts and patterns.

Activity-based demand management

Business processes are the primary source of demand for services. Patterns of Business Activity (PBAs) influence demand patterns as seen by the service providers (see Figure 9.4).

It is extremely important to study the customer's business to identify, analyze and codify such patterns to provide sufficient basis for capacity management.

Activities, methods and techniques

Core services and supporting services

Core services deliver the basic outcomes desired by the customer. They represent the value that customers want and for which they are willing to pay. Core services anchor the value-proposition for the customer and provide a basis for their continued utilization and satisfaction. Supporting services either enable or enhance the value proposition. Enabling services are basic factors and enhancing services are excitement factors.

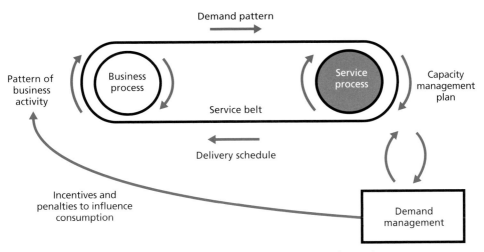

Figure 9.4   Business operations have an impact on demand patterns for services (Source: Service Strategy was produced by OGC)

Developing a differentiated offering

The packing of core and supporting services is an essential aspect of market strategy. Service providers should thoroughly analyze the prevailing conditions in their business environment, the needs of the customer segments or types they serve, and the alternatives that are available to those customers. The decisions are strategic because they hold a long-term view for maintaining value for customers even as industry practices, norms, technologies and regulations change. Bundling of supporting services with core services has implications for the design and operation of services. Decisions have to made whether to standardize on the core or the supporting services.

Service providers must focus on the effective delivery of value through core services, whilst at the same time keeping an eye on the supporting services. Research has shown that customers are often dissatisfied with supporting services. Some supporting services, such as the service desk or technical support, are generally bundled but can also be offered separately. This is an important consideration in the strategic planning and review of the plans. These strategic decisions can have a major impact on the service provider's success at the portfolio level. They are important primarily to service providers who supply multiple organizations or business units (BUs) while at the same time being forced to reduce costs in order to preserve the competitiveness of their portfolio.

Services packages

ITIL defines a service packages as follows:

*A **service package** is a detailed description of an IT service that is available to be delivered to customers. A service package includes a Service Level Package (SLP) and one or more core services and supporting services.*

The definition of a Service Level Package (SLP) is:

> A **Service Level Package (SLP)** is a defined level of utility and warranty for a particular Service Package. Each SLP is designed to meet the needs of a particular Pattern of Business Activity.

SLPs are associated with a set of service levels, a pricing policy, and a **Core Service Package (CSP)**. ITIL defines a Core Service Package as follows:

> A **Core Service Package (CSP)** is a detailed description of a core service that may be shared by two or more Service Level Packages.

A Line of Service (LOS) is being defined as:

> A **Line of Service (LOS)** is a core service or supporting service that has multiple Service Level Packages. A Line of Service is managed by a Product Manager and each Service Level Package is designed to support a particular market segment.

Combinations of CSPs and SLPs are used to serve customer segments with differentiated values. CSP and SLP are loosely bundled to enable local optimization and maintain the service catalogue's efficiency as a whole (Figure 9.5).

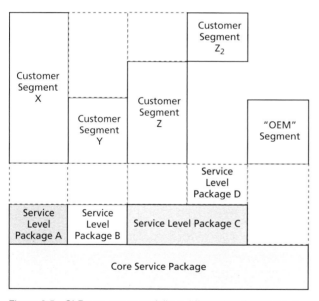

Figure 9.5   SLPs are a way to deliver differentiated services (Source: Service Strategy was produced by OGC)

The advantage of CSPs is that they provide for strict control of core services used by all BUs. It controls complexity and assures the business outcome. Every BU can develop SLPs on the basis of applications and processes that serve their own market spaces.

Chapter 10
Functions and Processes in Service Design

10.1 Service Catalogue Management

Introduction

The **purpose** of Service Catalogue Management (SCM) is to provide a single source of consistent information on all of the agreed services, and ensure that it is widely available to those who are approved to access it.

The **goal** of service catalogue management is the development and upkeep of a service catalogue that contains all accurate details, the status, possible interactions and mutual dependencies of all current services and those being prepared to run operationally.

Value for the business

The service catalogue is the central resource of information on the IT services delivered by the service provider organization. This ensures that all areas of the business can view an accurate, consistent picture of the IT services, their details and their status. It contains a customer facing view of the IT services in use, how they are intended to be used, the business processes they enable, and the level of quality of service the customer can expect for each service.

Basic concepts

Over the years, the IT infrastructures of organizations grow at a rapid pace and there may not be a clear picture of the services offered by the organizations and whom they are offered to. To get a clearer picture, a service portfolio is developed (with a service catalogue as part of it), and maintained. The development of the service portfolio is a component of the Service Strategy phase. The Portfolio needs subsequent support from the other phases in the lifecycle.

It is important to make a clear distinction between the portfolio and the catalogue:
- **Service portfolio** - The portfolio contains information about each service and its status. As a result, the Portfolio describes the entire process, starting with the client requirements for the development, building and execution of the service. The service portfolio represents all active and inactive services in the various phases of the lifecycle.

- **Service catalogue** - The catalogue is a subset of the service portfolio and consists only of active and approved services (at retail level) in Service Operation. The catalogue divides services into components. It contains policies, guidelines and responsibilities, as well as prices, service level arrangements and delivery conditions. The client gets to review the largest part of the service catalogue.

Many organizations integrate and maintain the portfolio and catalogue as a part of their Configuration Management System (CMS). By defining every service, a Configuration Item (CI) must be defined and, when possible, incorporated into a hierarchy, the organization can relate the incidents and requests for change to the services in question. It is for this reason that changes in both portfolio and catalogue must be part of the change management process.

The service catalogue can also be used for a Business Impact Analysis (BIA) as part of IT Service Continuity Management (ITSCM), or as a starting point for the re-distribution of the workload as part of the capacity management. These benefits justify the investment (in time and money) involved in preparing a Catalogue and making it worthwhile.

The service catalogue has two aspects:
- **The business service catalogue** contains details of the services that are being supplied to the customer together with the relationships to the business units and the business processes that rely on the IT services. This is the customer view of the service catalogue. The business service catalogue facilitates the development of proactive and preemptive SLM processes, allowing it to develop more into the field of Business Service Management (BSM).
- **The technical service catalogue** contains details of the IT services supplied to the customer, together with relationships to the supporting and shared services, components and CIs. This is the part that is not visible to the client. The technical service catalogue explains which technical aspects (and departments) are necessary to render the service.

A combination of both catalogues provides a quick overview on the impact of incidents and changes on the business. For this reason, many mature organizations combine both aspects in a service catalogue, as part of a service portfolio.

Activities, methods and techniques
The service catalogue is the only resource which contains constant information about all services of the service provider. The catalogue should be accessible to every authorized person. Activities in this process include:
- agreeing and documenting a service definition with all relevant parties
- interfacing with service portfolio management to agree the contents of the service portfolio and service catalogue
- producing and maintaining an accurate service catalogue and its contents in conjunction with the service portfolio
- interfacing with the business and IT service continuity management on the dependencies of business units and their business processes with the supporting IT services, contained within the business service catalogue
- interfacing with support teams, service providers and configuration management on interfaces and dependencies between IT services and the supporting services, components and CIs contained within the technical service catalogue

- interfacing with business relationship management and service level management to ensure that the information is aligned to the business and business process

Interfaces
Inputs are:
- business information from the organization's business and IT strategy, plans and financial plans etc.
- business impact analysis
- service portfolio
- CMS
- Feedback from other processes

Outputs are:
- documentation and agreement of a "definition of the service"
- updates to the service portfolio
- updated to the service catalogue

Metrics
KPIs are:
- the number of services recorded and maintained within the service catalogue as a percentage of those being delivered and transitioned in the live environment
- the number of differences discovered between the information from the service catalogue and reality
- percentage increase in the completeness of the business service catalogue, compared with the operational services
- percentage increase in the completeness of the technical service catalogue, compared with the IT components in support of the services
- access of the service desk to information in support of the services, expressed by the percentage of incidents without the appropriate service-related information

Implementation
The most important challenge in the service catalogue management process is maintaining an accurate service catalogue (containing both the Business and the Technical aspect) as part of the service portfolio. In order to achieve this, spreadsheets or databases must be developed before integrating the service catalogue or service portfolio into the Configuration Management System (CMS) and Service Knowledge Management System (SKMS). In addition, it is important that all parties involved recognize that both catalogues are essential sources of information which must be used and maintained by everyone in the IT organization.

Critical success factors are:
- accurate service catalogue
- business users' awareness of the services being provided
- IT staff awareness of the technology supporting the services

Risks include:
- inaccurate information in the catalogue and it not being under change management control
- poor acceptance of the service catalogue and its use in the operational processes
- inaccuracy of the information supplied by the business, IT and service portfolio
- tools and resources needed to keep the information up-to-date
- poor access to accurate change management information and processes
- circumvention of the use of the service portfolio and service catalogue
- information too detailed to maintain accurately or at too high level to be of any value

10.2 Service Level Management

Introduction
The **goal** of the Service Level Management (SLM) process is to ensure that an agreed level of IT service is provided for all current IT services, and that future services are delivered to agreed achievable targets.

The **objectives** are:
- defining, documenting, agreeing, monitoring, measuring, reporting and executing a review of the service level
- delivering and improving the relation and communication with the business and the clients
- ensuring that specific and measurable targets are being developed
- monitoring and improving customer satisfaction with the quality of service being delivered
- ensuring that the IT and the customers have a clear and unambiguous expectation of the level of service to be delivered
- ensuring that proactive measures to improve levels of service delivered are implemented wherever it is cost-justifiable to do so

Scope
SLM represents the IT service provider client the business, and the business to the IT service provider. There is regular bi-directional contact, whereby both the present service and the future service are discussed. SLM has to manage the expectations of both parties (both internal and external). In addition, SLM assures the quality of service delivered meets the expectations.

The SLM process should include the following items:
- development of business relationships
- development and management of Operational Level Agreements (OLAs)
- reviewing underpinning supplier contracts
- proactive prevention of service failures, reduction of service risks and improvement in service quality
- reporting and managing all services and review of SLA breaches and weaknesses

Value for the business
SLM provides a consistent interface to the business for all service related issues. It provides the business with the agreed service targets and the required management information to ensure that those targets have been met. Where targets are breached, SLM should provide feedback on the cause of the breach and details of the actions being taken to prevent the breach recurring.

The service level management process entails planning, coordinating, drafting, agreeing, monitoring and reporting on Service Level Agreements (SLAs), and the ongoing review of service achievements to ensure that the required and cost-justifiable service quality is maintained and gradually improved. The SLA is a written agreement between a Service Provider and its customers defining service targets and responsibilities of both parties.

On the other hand, an OLA is an agreement between an IT service provider and another part of the same organization that assists with the provision of services.

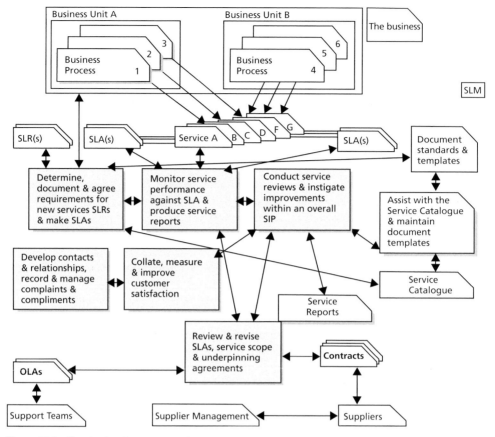

Figure 10.1   Service level management process (Source: Service Design was produced by OGC)

Activities, methods and techniques

The activities of service level management (Figure 10.1) are:

- **Design of SLA Frameworks** - SLM has to design the most appropriate SLA structure, so that all services and all customers are covered in a manner best suited to organizational needs. There are a number of options including the following:
  - **service-based SLAs** - an SLA covers one service for all customers of that service; an SLA can be established for e-mail services or for supplying certain telephone facilities, for example. This framework can cause difficulties if the specific requirements of one customer vary for the same service.
  - **customer-based SLAs** - an agreement with a customer containing all services they use; the customer often prefers this SLA because all of their requirements are captured in one single document
  - **multi-level SLAs** - a combination having for example the following structure:
    - corporate level, covering all generic SLM matters
    - customer level, covering all SLM issues which are relevant to a specific group of customers or business units
    - service level, covering all subjects that are relevant to a specific service relating to a specific customer

The multi-level SLA keeps the SLAs to a manageable size and reduces the need for frequent updates.

- **Determining, documenting and agreeing on the requirements for new services and production of Service Level Requirements (SLRs)** - Once the service catalogue is produced and the SLA structure determined, the first SLR needs to be drafted; at this stage, both customer and the other departments should be involved, in order to prevent the situation where the customer is faced with a "fait accompli" at a later stage and in order to find out how realistic the arrangements are.

- **Monitoring the performance with regard to the SLA and reporting the outcome** - Everything that is incorporated into the SLA must be measurable; otherwise disputes may arise, which may eventually result in confidence loss of faith; for example, the service provider can measure incident response time; report regularly regarding the results and use these reports for discussion with the customer; it is also recommended that all complaints and compliments are recorded and then discussed these with the relevant parties.

- **Improving customer satisfaction** - Besides the "hard" monitoring listed, customer satisfaction with the service provision should be taken into account; this can be done by using questionnaires, for example.

- **Review and revise underpinning agreements** - The IT service provider is dependent to some extent on their own internal technical services (or external partners and suppliers); in order to meet the SLA targets, the underpinning agreements with internal departments (OLAs) must support the SLA as must the contracts with external parties; the agreements must at all times be up-to-date and incorporated into the change management and configuration management processes.

- **Produce service reports** - Communication is a core activity in service management and requires adequate reporting. Reporting mechanisms should be specified and agreed, and reports should be delivered at regular intervals. Service reports are input to service review meetings. The reports should contain accurate information from all areas and processes that is integrated into a comprehensive report on service performance, measured against agreed business targets.

- **Reviewing and improving services** - Consult regularly with the customer to evaluate the services and identify possible improvements in the service provision; focus on those improvement items that yield the greatest benefit to the business; report regularly on the progress of the improvements and incorporate them in the Service Improvement Plan (SIP).

- **Review and revise SLAs** - All agreements should be subject to change and configuration management and reviewed periodically, to make sure that changes to the service infrastructure haven't invalidated the agreements.

- **Developing contacts and relations** - SLM has to instill confidence in the business; by using the service catalogue, SLM can start working proactively; the catalogue supplies information with which the relation between services and the business units and the business processes which are dependent on these services, can be better understood; in order to do this thoroughly, SLM can carry out the following activities among others:
  - consulting and informing stakeholders, customers and managers
  - maintaining accurate information in the service portfolio and service catalogue
  - adopting a flexible and responsive attitude towards customer needs
  - developing a full understanding of the business and customer
  - undertake customer satisfaction surveys

With regard to *information management*:
- supplies crucial information to SLM regarding operational services, goals set and "infractions"
- supports SLM service catalogue management by means of the service catalogue
- supplies information and trends to SLM concerning customer satisfaction

Interfaces

Inputs are:
- business information arising from the organization's business strategy, plans and financial plans
- business requirements
- service portfolio and service catalogue
- change information
- Configuration Management System (CMS)

Outputs are:
- service reports
- Service Improvement Plan (SIP)
- Service Quality Plan (SQP)
- standard document templates
- SLA, SLR and OLAs
- Service review meeting minutes

Metrics

KPIs include:
- percentage reduction in SLA targets missed
- percentage increase in customer satisfaction
- percentage reduction in SLA breaches

Implementation

Possible **triggers** for SLM activity are:
- changes in service portfolio
- new or modified agreements
- changes in strategy or policy
- compliments and complaints
- service review meetings and actions

10.3 Capacity Management

Introduction

The **goal** of capacity management is to ensure that cost-justifiable IT capacity in all areas of IT always exists and is matched to the current and future agreed needs of the business in timely manner.

Capacity management is supported initially in Service Strategy where the decisions and analysis of business requirements and customer outcomes influence the development of Patterns of Business Activity (PBA), Lines of Service (LOS) and Service Level Packages (SLPs). This provides the predictive and ongoing capacity indicators needs to align capacity to demand.

The **objectives** of capacity management are:
- creating and maintaining an up-to-date capacity plan that reflects the current and future needs of the customer
- internal and external consulting on services in terms of capacity and performance
- ensuring that the services provided comply with the defined objectives by managing both the performance and the capacity of services
- contributing to diagnosis of performance and capacity-related incidents and problems
- investigating the impact of all changes to the capacity plan
- taking proactive measures to improve performance

Scope

The capacity management process should be the focal point for all IT performance and capacity issues. Network and server support or operation management may take on the majority of day-to-day operational duties, but will provide performance information to the capacity management process. In addition, capacity management also considers space planning and environmental systems capacity. It may also have a task in certain human resource aspects but only where a lack of human resources could result in a breach of OLA or SLA. However, Human Resource Management (HRM) is the main responsibility of line management though the staffing of a service desk could use identical capacity management techniques.

The drivers behind this process are the customer requirements as laid down in the SLA. Because capacity management understands the total IT and customer environment, it is able to comply with current *and* future capacity and performance requirements in a cost-effective manner. Managing large IT infrastructures is a difficult and demanding task, in particular if the IT capacity and required financial investments are growing. Planning is vital to realize economies of scale, for instance, when buying components.

Capacity management should have input to the service portfolio and procurement process to ensure that the best deals with IT service providers are negotiated. Capacity management provides the necessary information on current and planned resource utilization of individual components to enable organizations to decide with confidence:
- which components to upgrade
- when to upgrade
- how much the upgrade will cost

Capacity management has a close two-way relationship with Service Strategy since the latter is based on the organization plans, which in turn are derived from the strategy. In other words, it must understand the short, medium and long-term plans of the organization in order to function properly.

Other processes are less effective as well if they do not receive input from capacity management. For example what is the effect of a change (change management) on the available capacity or are the agreed service level requirements of a new service achievable (SLM). Thorough capacity management is able to predict events (and their impact) before they occur.

Value for the business

Capacity management is responsible for planning and scheduling IT resources to provide a consistent service level that matches the current and future requirements of the customer. Capacity management delivers a capacity plan in consultation with the customer. The plan specifies the IT and financial resources that are necessary to support the business, including a cost justification of expenditure.

The capacity management process involves balancing cost against resources needed and balancing supply against demand.

Capacity management processes and planning must be involved in every phase of the Service Lifecycle, from strategy and design through Transition and Operation to Continual Service Improvement.

Activities, methods and techniques

The capacity management process (Figure 10.2) consists of:
- **reactive activities**, such as:
  - monitoring
  - measuring
- **proactive activities**, such as:
  - predicting future requirements
  - producing trends

The more proactive the capacity management process, the lesser the need for reactive activities.

Capacity management is an extremely technical, complex and demanding process that comprises three sub-processes (Figure 10.2):
- **Business Capacity Management (BCM)** - Translates the customer's requirements to specifications for the service and IT infrastructure; it focuses on current and future requirements; involve business capacity management in:
  - **support** - when establishing Service Level Requirements (SLRs), capacity management must support SLM in understanding the requirements defined by the customer for capacity and performance
  - **designing and changing service configurations** - capacity management must be involved in the development of new and modified services and make recommendations for purchasing hardware and software if performance and capacity factors have an impact

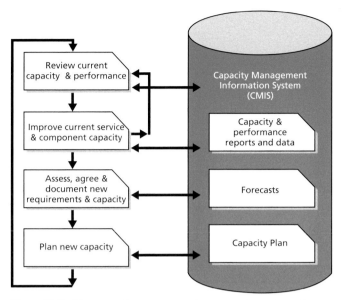

Figure 10.2   The capacity management process (Source: Service Design was produced by OGC)

- **verifying the SLA** - capacity management advises SLM on achievable targets that can be measured
- **approving the SLA** - providing support to SLM if new negotiations are necessary by mapping possible solutions and related costs
- **controlling and implementing** - all changes to service and resource capacity must follow all IT processes such as change, release, configuration and project management to ensure that the right degree of control and coordination is in place on all changes and that any new or changed components are recorded and tracked through their lifecycle
- **Service capacity management** - The main purpose of this sub-process is to identify and understand the IT services (including the resources, working patterns, peaks and troughs etc.) and to ensure that the services meet their SLA targets; service capacity management monitors services, measures their performance, records the data, analyzes the data, and reports on this information; this sub-process focuses on managing, controlling and predicting the performance and capacity of (existing) operational IT services.
- **Component Capacity Management (CCM)** - This sub-process focuses primarily on managing, controlling and predicting the performance, use and capacity of individual IT components, such as processors, network and bandwidth; the emphasis is on IT infrastructure that supports the services; this is primarily an activity executed in the Service Operation phase (see also Chapter 12).

Supporting activities of capacity management

Some activities must be executed repeatedly (proactively or reactively) (Figure 10.3). They provide basic information and triggers for other activities and processes in capacity management. These activities include:

- tuning and optimization
- utilization monitoring
- response time monitoring

- analysis
- implementation
- exploitation of new technology
- designing resilience

Capacity management also includes:
- threshold management and control
- demand management
- predicting "the behavior" of IT services by using modeling methods such as:
  - baseline model
  - trend analysis
  - analytical model
  - simulation model
- application sizing, estimating the requirements for resources to support proposed changes

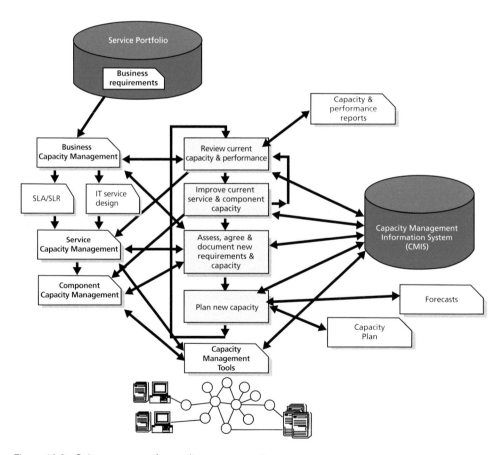

Figure 10.3   Sub-processes of capacity management (Source: Service Design was produced by OGC)

Information management and the capacity management information system

The aim of the Capacity Management Information System (CMIS) is to provide relevant information on the capacity and performance of services and infrastructure in order to support the capacity management process. This information system is one of the most important elements in the capacity management process. All of the capacity management sub-processes analyze the information stored. For instance, it contains business information on the current and future needs of the customer. It also contains data on services, such as response times, information on component usage (e.g. server traffic), and financial data (such as the costs involved in updates).

Interfaces

Capacity management activities can be **triggered** by, among other things, disruptions in services, capacity and performance warnings, new and changed services, changes to business and IT plans and strategies and the review and revision of SLAs, OLAs, contracts or any other agreement.

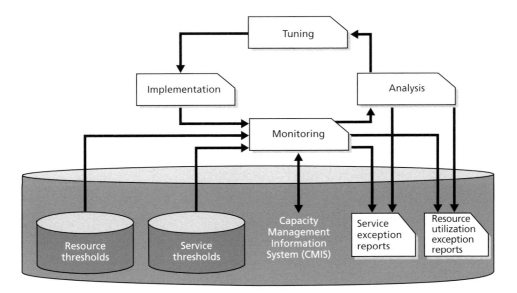

Figure 10.4   Iterative activities in capacity management (Source: Service Design was produced by OGC)

Input

- business information from the organizations business strategy, plans and financial plans, and information on their current and future requirements
- service and IT information from IT strategy and plans
- component performance and capacity information
- service performance issues from incident and problem management
- financial information
- change and performance information
- CMIS
- Workload information from Operations team

Output
- Capacity Management Information System (CMIS)
- Capacity plan with information on current usage of services and components as well as plans to meet the growth in services and new services
- service performance information and reports
- workload analysis and reports
- forecasts and predictive reports
- thresholds, alerts and events

Metrics
To evaluate efficiency and effectiveness activities should include:
- percentage accuracy of forecasts of business trends
- production of workload forecasts on time
- increased ability to monitor performance and throughput of services and components
- timely justification and implementation of new technology
- reduction in use of old technology
- reduction in Incidents and Problems related to inadequate capacity

Implementation
One of the main **challenges** is to convince the customer to supply more strategic information. This enables the service provider to ensure effective business continuity management. This can be particularly important when services are provided via outsourcing. Another challenge is to integrate the component capacity management (CCM) information so that it can be analyzed in a consistent manner. As a result, capacity management is able to supply detailed information on component usage.

Critical success factors include:
- accuracy of business predictions
- knowledge of current and future technologies
- ability to demonstrate cost effectiveness
- ability to plan and implement the appropriate IT capacity to meet business needs

The **risks** include:
- lack of commitment from the business
- lack of accurate information on the strategy and organization plans
- the creation of bureaucratic or manually intensive processes

10.4 Availability Management

Introduction
The **goal** of availability management is to ensure that the level of service availability delivered in all services is matched to or exceeds the current and future agreed needs of the business, in a cost effective manner.

Its **objectives** are:
• creating and maintaining an up-to-date availability plan that reflects the current and future needs of the customer
• advising on availability-related issues
• guiding the customer and IT service provider
• ensuring that availability results meet or exceed the defined requirements
• providing assistance in diagnosis and resolution of availability-related incidents and problems
• assessing the impact of changes have on the availability plan and the performance and capacity of the services and resources
• taking proactive measures to improve availability

Scope
Availability management includes designing, implementing, measuring, managing and improving IT services and the components availability. It must understand the service and component availability requirements from the business perspective in terms of the:
• current business processes (their operation and requirements)
• future business plans and requirements
• service targets and the current Service Operation and delivery
• IT infrastructure, data, applications and the environment (including performance)
• business impacts and priorities n relation to the services and their usage

By understanding these issues, availability management is able to ensure that all services and components are designed and delivered in order to meet their targets in terms of agreed business need. Availability management should be applied to all operational services, new, modified and supporting services. It covers all service aspects that have an impact on availability, such as training, competencies, procedures and tools.

Value for the business
The availability and reliability of IT services has a direct impact on customer satisfaction and company reputation. As such, availability management is vital. It should therefore be included (just like capacity management) in all stages of the Service Lifecycle.

Activities, methods and techniques
The main activities of availability management are (Figure 10.5):
• determining the availability requirements of the business
• determining the Vital Business Functions (VBFs)
• determining the impact of failing components
• defining the targets for availability, reliability and maintainability of the IT components
• monitoring and analyzing IT components

- establishing measures and reporting of availability, reliability, and maintainability that reflect the business user and IT support organization perspectives
- investigating the underlying reasons for unacceptable availability
- creating and maintaining an availability plan

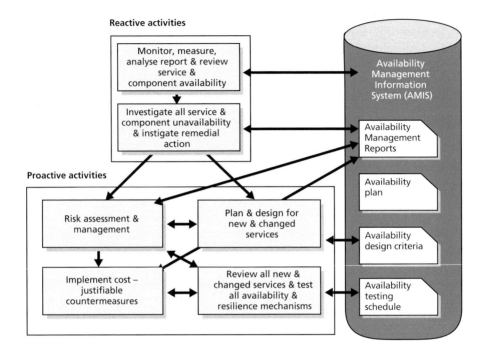

Figure 10.5   The availability management process (Source: Service Design was produced by OGC)

Availability management monitors, measures, analyzes and reports on the following aspects:
- **availability** - the service, component or CIs ability to perform its agreed function when required
- **reliability** - the length of time a service, component or CI can perform its agreed function without interruption
- **maintainability** - how quickly and effectively a service, component or CI can be restored to normal working after a failure
- **serviceability** - the ability of an external IT service provider to meet the terms of their contract

Measuring is extremely important. It can be done from three perspectives:
- **business perspective** - looks at IT availability in terms of its contribution to or impact on the Vital Business Functions that drive the business operation
- **user perspective** - views the availability of IT services as a combination of three factors: frequency, duration and scope of impact (how many users or organization parts are affected), and also response times

- **the IT service provider's perspective** - considers IT service and component availability in regard to availability, reliability and maintainability

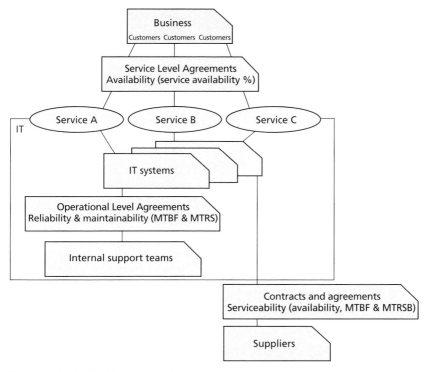

Figure 10.6   Availability terms and measurements (Source: Service Design was produced by OGC)

Availability management must ensure that all services meet their agreed targets. New or changed services must be designed in such a way that they will meet their agreed targets. To achieve this, availability management can perform reactive and proactive activities:

- **reactive activities** - are executed in the operational phase of the lifecycle:
  - monitoring, measuring, analyzing and reporting the availability of services and components
  - unavailability analysis
  - the expanded incident lifecycle
  - Service Failure Analysis (SFA)
- **proactive activities** - must be executed in the design phase of the lifecycle:
  - identifying Vital Business Functions
  - designing for availability
  - Component Failure Impact Analysis (CFIA)
  - Single Point of Failure (SPOF) analysis
  - Fault Tree Analysis (FTA)
  - modeling
  - risk analysis and management
  - availability testing schedule

    – planned and preventive maintenance
    – production of the Projected Service Availability (PSA) document
    – continual review and improvement

Leading principles

Effective availability management consists of both reactive and proactive activities. Do not lose sight of the following things:

- The availability of services is one of the most important aspects to satisfy customers.
- In the event of failures, an effective response can still result in high customer satisfaction.
- Improving availability is possibly only by understanding how the services support the customer's operations.
- Availability can only be managed as well as the weakest link in the chain.
- It is not just a reactive process, but also - and particularly - proactive.
- It is wiser and more cost-effective to build in the right availability level from the start, i.e. in the design of new services.

Starting points for availability management

Figure 10.7 illustrates a number of starting points for availability management. The unavailability of services can be reduced by aiming to reduce each of the phases distinguished in the extended incident lifecycle.

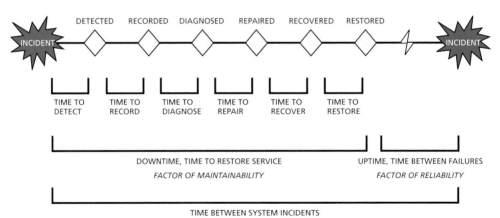

Figure 10.7   The extended incident lifecycle (Note: combination of figures from Service Strategy and Continual Service Improvement)

Services must be restored quickly when they are unavailable to users. The **Mean Time to Restore Service (MTRS)** is the time within which a function (service, system or component) is restored to operational use after a failure. The MTRS depends on a number of factors, such as:

- configuration of service assets
- MTRS of individual components
- competencies of support personnel
- available resources
- policy plans

- procedures
- redundancy

Analysis of the MTRS in relation to each factor is useful to improve the performance and design of services.

The MTRS can be reduced through management for each of its composite components (Figure 10.7). Reducing the duration of the following factors limits the unavailability time of a service:
- **incident detection** - the time between occurrence of an incident and its being detected
- **incident diagnosis** - the time at which diagnosis to determine the underlying cause has been completed
- **incident repair** - the time at which the failure has been repaired/fixed
- **incident recovery** - the time at which component recovery has been completed
- **incident restoration** - the time at which normal business service is resumed

Other metrics for measuring availability include:
- **Mean Time Between Failures (MTBF)** - The average time that a CI or service can perform its agreed function without interruption.
- **Mean Time Between Service Incidents (MTBSI)** - The mean time from when a system or service fails, until it next fails.
- **Mean Time To Repair (MTTR)** - The average time taken to repair a CI or service after a failure. MTTR is measured from when the CI or service fails until it is repaired. MTTR does not include the time required to recover or restore.

Redundancy
Redundancy is a way of increasing reliability and sustainability of systems. ITIL defines the following redundancy types:
- **Active redundancy** - This type is used to support essential services that absolutely cannot be interrupted. The productive capacity of redundancy assets is always available. With active redundancy all redundant units are operating simultaneously. For example mirrored disks in a server computer.
- **Passive redundancy** - The use of redundant assets that are left inoperative until the event of a failure (reactive). For example stand-by servers or clustered systems.

ITIL also uses the following differentiation to explain redundancy types:
- **Diverse redundancy (heterogeneous redundancy)** - Redundancy through various types of service assets that share the same capabilities (spreading the risk). This type is used when the cause of the failure is difficult to predict. For example, use of different storage media, programming languages, or development teams.
- **Homogeneous redundancy** - Refers to using extra capacity of the same type of service assets. With this type there is a high certainty about the causes of failure. For example use of two identical processors.

The active and passive redundancy types can be used individually or in combination with the homogeneous and heterogeneous types. For example: redundancy that is both active and homogeneous has a low tolerance of failure and a high certainty about the causes of failure.

The following approaches improve the accessibility of services:
- **various channels** - the demand is led through various types of access channel; this means it is resistant to the failure of a single channel (active diverse redundancy)
- **closed network** - multiple access gates increase the network's capacity (homogeneous redundancy)
- **loose link** - interfaces are based on public infrastructure, open source technologies and omnipresent access options, such as mobile phones and browsers; it offers users access to the service via multiple channels and in multiple sites; security developments are making this method increasingly accessible

Information management and the availability management information system

Availability management must maintain an information system. The Availability Management Information System (AMIS) contains all of the measures and information required to complete the availability management process. It also provides the business with the right information on the level of the service to be delivered in terms of components and supporting services.

The information system constitutes the basis for the availability plan. The availability plan is not the same as an availability management implementation plan, while it can initially be developed jointly with the implementation plan. Availability management changes all the time, which is why the availability plan must contain the following elements:
- current levels of availability compared against the agreed levels (from the customer's perspective)
- actions taken to resolve shortcomings in availability
- details of changed availability requirements for existing and future services
- a forward looking schedule for Service Failure Analysis (SFA) assignments
- regular review of the SFA assignments
- benefits and opportunities of planned upgrades

The plan should complement the capacity plan and the financial plan and cover a period of two years. The first six months should be covered in more detail. The plan should be updated with minor revisions every quarter, and major revisions occurring every six months.

Interfaces

Activities in the field of availability management are **triggered** by, among other things:
- new or changing customer needs
- new objectives in agreements e.g. SLAs, OLAs or contracts
- service failures
- availability events and alerts

Relationships with other functions and processes are:
- Availability management supports **incident and problem management** to resolve availability incidents and problems.
- Availability management provides **capacity management** with resilience and spare capacity.
- Availability management provides **IT Service Continuity Management (ITSCM)** with assessment on the impact and risks for the business and of restore mechanisms.

- Availability management assists **SLM** in determining the availability objectives and studies, and makes improvement proposals in the event of service and component failures.

The **input** of availability management is:
- business information, such as organization strategies, (financial) plans and information on the current and future requirements of IT services
- risk analyses, business impact analyses and studies of Vital Business Functions
- service information from the service portfolio and service catalogue and from the SLM process
- change calendars and release schedules from change management and release management
- service targets
- unavailability and failure information

The **output** of availability management is:
- the Availability Management Information System (AMIS)
- the availability plan
- availability and recovery design criteria
- reports on the availability, reliability and maintainability of services
- updated risk register
- monitoring, management and reporting
- availability management test schedule
- planned and preventive maintenance schedule
- Projected Service Outage (PSO)

Metrics

Organizations can use various **KPIs** to measure the effectiveness and efficiency of availability management, such as:
- percentage reduction in the unavailability of services and components
- percentage increase in the of reliability of services and components
- percentage improvement in overall end-to-end availability of service
- percentage reduction of the cost of unavailability
- percentage increase in customer satisfaction

Implementation

Availability management has the following **challenges**:
- meeting the expectations of customers, the business and the management
- integrating all availability information into an availability management information system
- convincing the business and management of the need to invest in proactive availability measures

Critical success factors for availability management are:
- managing the availability and reliability of IT services
- availability of IT infrastructure (as agreed in the SLAs) provided at optimal costs
- satisfying business needs for access to IT services

Risks for availability management are:
- lack of commitment from the business to the availability management process
- lack of adequate information on plans and strategies for the future
- lack of resources and funds
- increasing labor-intensive reporting

10.5 IT Service Continuity Management

Introduction

The **goal** of IT Service Continuity Management (ITSCM) is to support the overall business continuity process by ensuring that the required IT technical and service facilities (including computer systems, networks, applications, data repositories, telecommunications, environment, technical support and service desk etc.) can be resumed within required and agreed business timescales.

Objectives include:

- maintaining a set of continuity plans and recovery plans
- performing regular Business Impact Analysis (BIA)
- conducting regular risk estimates and management exercises
- provide advice and guidance to all other areas of the business and IT on all continuity and recovery-related issues
- ensuring that the appropriate continuity and recovery mechanisms are put in place to meet or exceed the agreed business continuity targets
- assessing the impact of all changes on the continuity and recovery plans
- implementing proactive measures to improve the availability of services (where cost-justifiable to do so)
- negotiating agreements with IT service providers in relation to the required recovery capability to support continuity plans

Scope

ITSCM focuses on those events that the business considers a disaster. The incident management process handles less significant events. ITSCM primarily considers the IT assets and configurations that support the business processes. If it is necessary to move to an alternative work environment as a result of a disaster, the process also covers office spaces, personnel accommodation and telephone facilities, for example.

ITSCM does not usually directly cover longer-term risks such as those from changes in business direction. While these can have a huge impact, there is generally enough time to identify them and take action. Minor technical problems, such as non critical disk failures, are not covered by this process - they are handled by incident management. ITSCM does cover:

- agreements on ITSCM's scope
- a business impact analysis to quantify the impact of disasters
- Risk Analysis (RA) - risk identification and risk assessment to identify potential threats to continuity and the likelihood of the threats becoming reality
- creating an overall ITSCM strategy that must be integrated into the business continuity management strategy
- creating continuity plans
- testing the plans
- ongoing operation and maintenance of the plans

Value for the business

ITSCM has a valuable role in supporting the business continuity planning process. Organizations often use it to create awareness of continuity and recovery requirements and justify their decision to implement the process of business continuity planning (including plans).

Activities, methods and techniques

ITSCM is a cyclic process. It keeps the developed service continuity plans and recovery plans in line with the business continuity plans as these are updated.

The process consists of four phases (Figure 10.8):
1. **Initiation** - This phase covers the entire organization and includes the following activities:
   - defining the policy
   - specifying terms of reference and scope
   - allocating resources (people, resources and funds)
   - defining the project organization and control structure
   - agree project and quality plans
2. **Requirements and strategy** - Determining the business requirements for ITSCM is vital when investigating how well an organization can survive a disaster. This phase includes *requirements* and *strategy*. The *requirements* involve undertaking a business impact analysis and risk analysis:
   Requirement 1: Business Impact Analysis
   - *(BIA)* - Its purpose it to quantify the impact caused by the loss of services. If the impact can be determined in detail, it is called "hard impact" - e.g. financial losses. "Soft impact" is less easily determined. It represents, for instance, the impact on public relations, morale and health. The BIA identifies the most important services for the organization and as such provides important input for the strategy. Among other things, the analysis identifies:
     * the type of damage or loss (e.g. income, reputation)
     * how the damage could escalate
     * the required competencies, facilities and services to continue important processes
     * the timeframe within which partial (the most vital processes) and full recovery must occur
     * determination of recovery periods for every individual service
   Generally speaking, more preventive measures need to be taken with regards to those processes and services with earlier and higher impacts. Greater emphasis should be placed on continuity and recovery measures for those where the impact is lower and takes longer to develop.
   - *Requirement 2: Risk estimate* - There are various risk analysis and management methods. Risk analysis is an assessment of risks that may give rise to service disruption or security violation. Risk management identifies the response and cost-justifiable counter-measures that can be taken. A standard method like Management of Risk (M_o_R) can be used to investigate and manage the risks. This method consists of:
     * M_o_R principles
     * M_o_R approach (organization approach)
     * M_o_R processes (identification, assessment, planning, implementation)
     * M_o_R embedding and review
     * communication (up-to-date and adequate information provision)

- *Strategy 1: Risk response measures* - Measures to reduce risks must be implemented in combination with availability management since failure reduction has an impact on service availability. Measures may include: *fault tolerant systems*, good IT security controls, and *off site storage.*
- *Strategy 2: ITSCM recovery options* - The continuity strategy is a balance between the cost of risk reduction measures and recovery options to support the recovery of critical business processes within agreed timescales. A number of recovery options are possible:
  - Manual workarounds: temporary manual solution for a limited period of time
  - Reciprocal arrangements: support agreements between parties with similar infrastructures (not used often these days)
  - Gradual recovery *(or cold standby)*: method that makes basic facilities such as accommodation and computer space available at limited costs within several days
  - Intermediate recovery *(warm standby)*: recovery within two to three days, generally based on a prepared facility that is often shared with several other parties
  - Fast recovery *(hot standby)*: recovery within 24 hours that focuses on the main services, involving e.g. shadow sites that can be operational very quickly and with very low data loss
  - Immediate recovery (also *hot standby*): option for the immediate recovery of mainly business-critical services with the aid of *mirroring* techniques, *dual sites*, and other redundancy solutions; no data loss involved

3. **Implementation** - The ITSCM plans can be created once the strategy is approved. You should remember, however, that the organization structure (leadership and decision-making processes) changes in the event of a disaster recovery process. Set this up around a senior manager generally in charge, with a coordinator below them and the recovery teams below that. Test the plans in full, e.g. using the following test types:
   - walkthrough tests
   - full tests
   - partial test (e.g. a single service or server)
   - scenario test (testing for specific responses/scenarios)

4. **Ongoing operation** - This phase includes:
   - education, awareness and training of personnel
   - review
   - testing
   - change management (ensures that all changes have been assessed for their potential impact)
   - ultimate test (invocation)

Information management

Record all of the information that is required to maintain the ITSCM plans. Align the plan with the BCM (Business Continuity Management) information. At the very least, it should contain information about:

- the most recent version of the BCM strategy and business impact analysis
- risks within a risk register including, risk assessment and possible responses to these
- executed and planned tests
- details of the ITSCM and related plans
- existing recovery facilities, suppliers, partners and agreements
- details on backup and restore processes

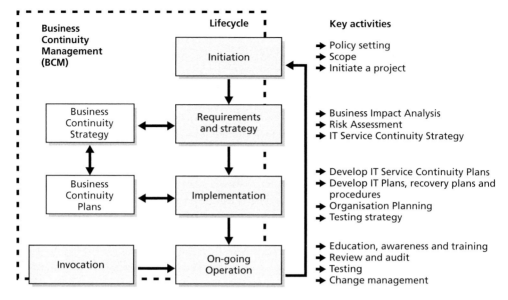

Figure 10.8   The lifecycle of IT Service Continuity Management (ITSCM) (Source: Service Design was produced by OGC)

Interfaces

ITSCM can be **triggered** by various events:

• new or changed business needs
• new or changed targets in the agreements e.g. SLAs, OLAs or contracts
• occurrence of a major incident that requires assessment for potential invocation of ITSCM or BCM plans
• periodical activities, such as business impact analysis or risk analysis

It has **interfaces** with, for example:

• **Incident and problem management** - Incidents and problems can easily evolve into major incidents and disasters.
• **Availability management** - Undertaking risk analysis and implementing risk response should be closely coordinated with the availability management process.
• **Service level management** - Recovery requirements are agreed and documented in SLAs.

ITSCM's **input** includes:

• business information (organization strategy, plans)
• IT information
• financial information
• BCM strategy and plans
• change information (from change management)
• CMS
• testing schedules

ITSCM **outputs** include:
* revised ITSCM policy and strategy
* business impact analysis exercises and reports
* risk analysis and management reviews and reports
* continuity plans
* test scenarios
* test reports and reviews

Metrics
ITSCM's success can be measured by the following **KPIs**:
* the outcome of regular audits of the ITSCM plans
* the extent to which service recovery targets are agreed and documented in the SLA
* the test results of the ITSCM plans
* the regular review of the ITSCM plans

Implementation
The following **challenges** apply for ITSCM:
* providing continuity plans when there is no BCM process
* if there is a BCM process, the challenge is to integrate the ITSCM plan with it and keep it that way

The **success** of ITSCM is influenced strongly by the question whether:
* services can be delivered and restored in accordance with the customer's objectives
* the entire organization is aware of the BCM and ITSCM plans

Its **risks** include:
* lack of commitment from the business and management
* lack of resources and budget
* excessive focus on technology and not on services and the customers' needs
* risk investigation and management are executed in isolation, not in collaboration with availability management and security management

10.6 Information Security Management

Introduction

The **goal** of information security management is to align IT and business security and ensure that information security is managed effectively in all services and service management activities.

Its **objectives** are:
- information is available and usable when required (availability)
- information is available exclusively to authorized persons (confidentiality)
- the information is complete, accurate and protected against unauthorized changes (integrity)
- transactions and information exchange between companies and partners can be trusted (authenticity and non-repudiation)

Scope

Information security management needs to understand the total IT and business security environment. This means, among other things:
- the current and future business security policy and plans
- security requirements
- legal requirements
- obligations and responsibilities
- business and IT risks (and their management)

This enables information security management to manage the current and future security aspects of the business cost effectively. The process should include the following elements:
- production, maintenance, distribution and enforcement of an information security policy
- understanding agreed current and future security requirements of the business
- implementing (and documenting) controls that support the information security policy and manage risks
- managing IT service providers and contracts concerning access to the system and services
- management of security breaches and incidents
- proactive improvement of the security control systems

Value for the business

Information security management ensures that the information security policy complies with the overall business security policy of the organization and the requirements of corporate governance. It raises internal awareness of the need for security within all services and assets. Executive management is responsible for organizations information and is tasked with responding to issues that affect its protection. Boards of directors are expected to make information security an integral part of corporate governance. All IT service provider organizations must therefore ensure that they have a comprehensive information security management policy in place to monitor and enforce the policies.

Basic concepts

The information security management process and framework include:
- information security policy
- Information Security Management System (ISMS)

- comprehensive security strategy (related to the business objectives and strategy)
- effective security organizational structure
- set of security controls to support the policy
- risk management
- monitoring processes
- communication strategy
- training and awareness strategy

Activities, methods and techniques

Information security management system

The Information Security Management System (ISMS) provides the basis for cost-effective development of an information security program that supports the business objectives. Use the four Ps of Personnel, Processes, Products (including technology) and Partners (including service providers) to ensure high levels of security are in place.

ISO 27001 is the formal standard against which organizations may seek certification of their ISMS. Figure 10.9 is based on various recommendations, including ISO 27001, and provides insight into the five elements and their objectives.

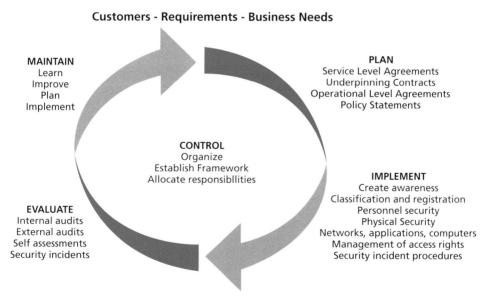

Customers - Requirements - Business Needs

MAINTAIN
Learn
Improve
Plan
Implement

PLAN
Service Level Agreements
Underpinning Contracts
Operational Level Agreements
Policy Statements

CONTROL
Organize
Establish Framework
Allocate responsibllities

IMPLEMENT
Create awareness
Classification and registration
Personnel security
Physical Security
Networks, applications, computers
Management of access rights
Security incident procedures

EVALUATE
Internal audits
External audits
Self assessments
Security incidents

Figure 10.9   Framework for managing IT security (Source: Service Design was produced by OGC)

Security governance

IT security governance can have six outcomes:
- strategic alignment:
  - security requirements should be driven by enterprise requirements
  - security solutions must fit enterprise processes

- value delivery:
  - standard set of security practices
  - properly prioritized and distributed effort to areas with the greatest impact and business benefit
- risk management:
  - risk profiles
  - awareness of risk management priorities
- performance management:
  - defined, agreed and meaningful metrics
  - measurement process that will help that identify shortcomings
- resource management:
  - knowledge is recorded and available
  - security processes are documented
- business process assurance

The information security manager must understand that security is not merely a step in the lifecycle and that it cannot be solved by technology alone. Information security must be an integral part of all services (and systems) and is an ongoing process that needs to be continually managed. Figure 10.10 describes controls that can be used in the process.

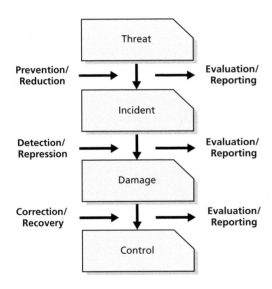

Figure 10.10   Security controls for threats and incidents (Source: Service Design was produced by OGC)

The figure shows that a risk may result in a **threat** that in turn causes an **incident**, the consequence of which is damage. Measures of varying nature can be taken between these phases:
- **preventive measures** - prevent effects (e.g. access management)
- **reductive measures** - limit effects (e.g. backup and testing)
- **detective measures** - detect effects (e.g. monitoring)

- **repressive measures** - suppress effects (e.g. blocking)
- **corrective measures** - repair effects (e.g. rollback)

Information management

All of the information required by information security management should be stored in an information security management system. This system includes all security controls, risks, failures, processes and reports necessary to support and maintain the information security policy and the information security management system. The information must cover all IT services and be integrated with other IT management systems, particularly the service portfolio and the CMS.

Interfaces

Security management can be **triggered** by:
- new or changed company policy
- new or changed business security policy
- new or changed corporate risk management processes
- changed or new business requirements or needs in the agreements - SLAs, OLAs or contracts

Security management has **interfaces** with, among other things:
- **Incident and problem management** - Information security management provides support in the decision-making process relating to and the correction of security incidents and problems.
- **ITSCM** - Information security management has a relationship in reviewing the impact and risks for the company, as well as the provision of recovery mechanisms. ISO 27001 requires a functioning ITSCM plan.
- **SLM** - This provides support for the establishment of security requirements and responsibilities and their inclusion in the SLR and SLA.
- **Change management** - Information security management supports change management in determining the possible impact of changes on security.

Input for the information security management process is:
- business information (strategy, plans)
- corporate governance and business security policies and guidelines
- IT information
- service information from the SLM process
- risk analysis processes and reports
- details of security events and breaches
- change information from the change management process
- CMS
- details of partner and service provider access

Output of the information security management process is:
- overall information security management policy
- ISMS
- revised security risk assessment processes and reports

- security controls, audits and reports
- security test schedules

Metrics

KPIs include:
- percentage decrease in security breaches
- percentage decrease in the impact of security breaches and incidents
- increasing awareness of security procedures in the organization

Implementation

The main **challenge** in this process is to ensure adequate support of the company, business security and senior management. If this is missing, it is impossible to establish an effective security process. If there is senior IT management support but no business support, IT security controls and risk assessment will be severely limited in what they can achieve.

If there is a business security policy established then a challenge becomes one of integration and alignment. Strict change management and configuration management are required to maintain such integration.

The **success** of information security management is influenced strongly by:
- business protected against *security violations*
- determination of a clear policy integrated with the business needs
- security procedures that are justified and supported by the senior management
- effective marketing and education in security requirements
- an improvement mechanism

Risks in information security management include:
- increased danger of information system abuse in terms of privacy and ethics
- danger of hackers
- lack of commitment from the company, senior management, lack of adequate information
- excessive focus on technical aspects and no focus on service and the customer's needs

Too often research into and management of risks is undertaking in isolation instead of in conjunction with availability management and ITSCM.

10.7 Supplier Management

Introduction
The **goal** of the supplier management process is to manage suppliers and the services they supply, to provide seamless quality of IT service to the business, ensuring value for money.

Objectives are:
- obtain value for money from suppliers and contracts
- ensure that underpinning contracts and agreements with suppliers are aligned to business needs
- manage relationships with suppliers and their performance
- negotiate and agree contracts with suppliers
- maintain a supplier policy and a supporting supplier and contract database (SCD)

Scope
The supplier management process includes the management of all suppliers and contracts needed to support the provision of IT services to the business. The greater the contribution of a supplier, the more effort the service provider must put in managing the (relationship with the) supplier, and the more they should be involved with the development and implementation of the strategy. The smaller the supplier's value contribution, the more likely it is that the relationship will be managed mainly at an operational level. The process should include the following aspects:
- implementation and enforcement of the supplier policy
- maintenance of a supplier and contract database (SCD)
- categorizing of suppliers and contracts and risk assessment
- evaluation of contracts and suppliers
- developing, negotiating and agreement of contracts
- revising, renewing and terminating contracts

Value for the business
One of the most important goals of supplier management is to get value for money from supplier and contracts and to ensure that all targets in underpinning contracts and agreements are aligned to business needs and agreed targets within the SLAs. This ensures the delivery of end-to-end seamless, quality IT services that are aligned to the business expectation. The supplier management process should align with all corporate requirements and the requirements of all other IT and service management processes particularly information security management and ITSCM.

Basic concepts
All activities in this process should be driven by a supplier strategy and the policy from Service Strategy. Create a **Supplier and Contract Database (SCD)** to achieve consistency and effectiveness in implementing policy. Ideally, this database would be an integrated element of CMS or SKMS. The database should contain all details regarding suppliers and contracts, together with details about the type of service or product, and any information and relationship to other configuration items.

The data stored here will provide important information for activities and procedures such as:
* categorizing of suppliers
* maintenance of supplier and contract database
* evaluation and set-up of new suppliers and contracts
* establishing new suppliers
* supplier and contract management and performance
* renewed and terminated contracts

Activities, methods and techniques

For external suppliers, it is recommended to draw up a formal contract with clearly defined, agreed upon and documented responsibilities and goals. Manage this contract during its entire lifecycle (Figure 10.11).

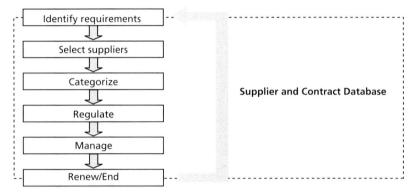

Figure 10.11   Contract lifecycle

These phases are:
* **identify** business need and preparation of business case
  - produce a Statement of Requirement (SOR) and/or a Invitation to Tender (ITT).
  - ensure conformity to strategy and policy.
  - prepare initial business case.
* **evaluate and procure new contracts and suppliers**
  - identify method of purchase or procurement
  - establish evaluation criteria
  - select
  - negotiate
  - agree and award contract
  - establish new suppliers and contracts
  - set up supplier service and contract within SCD
  - transition of service
  - establish contacts and relationships
* **categorize suppliers and contracts**
  - assessment or reassessment of supplier and contract
  - ensure changes progressed through service transition
  - categorization of supplier

- update SCD
- maintain SCD
- **manage the supplier and contract performance**
  - management and control of the operation and delivery of service
  - monitor and report
  - review and improve
  - management of supplier and relationship
  - review at least annually service scope against business need, targets and agreements
  - plan for possible closure
- **end of term**
  - review
  - renegotiate and renew or terminate

Interfaces
The supplier management process can be **triggered** by:
- new or changed corporate governance guidelines
- new or changes business and IT strategies
- new or changed business requirements or changed services

Inputs to supplier management are:
- business information (strategy, plans)
- supplier and contract strategies
- business plan details
- supplier strategies
- supplier contracts
- performance information

Outputs from supplier management are:
- Supplier and Contract Database
- information about performance
- supplier improvement plans (Supplier Service Improvement Plans, SIPs)
- research reports

Relations to other processes are:
- **SLM** - assisting in determining goals, requirements and responsibilities
- **information security management** - manage suppliers and their access to services
- **Service portfolio management** - ensure that the service portfolio accurately depicts all supporting systems and details

Metrics
The performance of supplier management can be measured according to:
- the increase in the number of suppliers that meet contract agreements
- the increase in the number of contract targets aligned with the SLA and SLR

All of the information required by supplier management should be stored in the Supplier and Contract Database. This should also contain information about suppliers and contracts and the execution of supporting services. Also include the latter in the service portfolio.

Implementation

Supplier management has the following **challenges**:
• constantly changing business and IT needs
• existing imperfect contracts
• insufficient experience in the organization
• tied to long-term contracts

In order to meet these challenges, attention might be paid to the following elements:
• clearly written, well-defined service management processes on both sides
• mutually advantageous relations
• clear roles
• good communication

The **success** of supplier management will be determined in part by:
• protection against poor supplier performance
• services (and goals) adjusted to the requirements of the business
• clarity on suppliers and contracts

Supplier management has the following **risks**:
• lack of commitment from the business and senior management
• lack of information on future business goals and policy
• lack of resources or budget
• impossible contract agreements to be met

Chapter 11

Functions and Processes in Service Transition

11.1 Transition Planning and Support

Introduction
The **goals** for transition planning and support include:
- planning and coordinating resources in order to ensure that the specifications of the Service Design are realized
- starting with the transition phase, identify, manage and limit risks that could interrupt the service

The **objectives** for transition planning and support include:
- plan and coordinate people and means within the frameworks
- make sure that everyone applies the same frameworks and standards
- report service issues
- provide clear and extensive plans
- support transition teams and others involved
- controlled planning of changes
- report issues, risks and other deviations

Scope
The following activities are included in the scope of transition planning:
- include design specifications and product requirements in the transition plans
- manage:
  - plans
  - supporting activities
  - transition progress
  - changes
  - issues
  - risks
  - deviations
  - processes
  - supporting systems and tools

- monitor Service Transition achievements
- communicate with clients, users and stakeholders

Value for the business
An integrated approach to planning improves the alignment of transition plans with the customer, service provider, business and change project plans.

Basic concepts
The **Service Design Package** (**SDP**) contains the following information required by the service transition team:
- applicable service packages (e.g. core service package, service level package)
- service specifications
- service models
- architectural design required to deliver the new of changed service including constraints
- definition and design of each release package
- detailed design of how the components will be assembled and integrated into a release package
- release and deployment plans
- service acceptance criteria

In the **release guidelines and policy**, the following subjects are addressed:
- naming conventions, distinguishing release types, such as: **major release**, **minor release** and **emergency release**
- roles and responsibilities; many people from different organizations can be involved with a release; it is useful to set up a responsibility matrix for this purpose
- release frequency, the expected frequency of each type of release
- approach for accepting and grouping changes in to a release
- how the configuration baseline for the release is captured and verified against the actual release contents e.g. hardware, software, documentation and knowledge
- entry and exit criteria and authority for acceptance of the release into each Service Transition stage and into the controlled test, training, disaster recovery and production environments
- the criteria authorization for leaving *Early Life Support* (ELS) and handover to service operations

Activities, methods and techniques
The activities for planning and support consist of:
1. set up transition strategy
2. prepare Service Transition
3. plan and coordinate Service Transition
4. support

1. Set up transition strategy
The transition strategy defines the overall approach to organizing Service Transition and allocating resources. Aspects that may be addressed in the transition strategy are:
- purpose, goals and objectives
- context and scope

- applicable standards, agreements, legal, regulatory and contractual agreements
- organizations and stakeholders involved in the Service Transition
- framework for Service Transition
- criteria for success and failure
- people; roles and responsibilities
- approach including transition model, plans for managing changes, assets, configurations and knowledge; transition estimation; preparation; evaluation; error handling; KPIs
- the products (deliverables) that are the result of the transition activities such as transition plans, schedule of milestones, financial requirements

The SDP defines the various phases of the Service Transition. These may consist of: acquiring and testing components, testing service release, Service Operation ready test, rollout, ELS, review and close service transition.

2. Prepare Service Transition

Preparatory activities consist of:
- review and acceptance of inputs from other Service Lifecycle phases review and check the input deliverables e.g. SDP, Service Acceptance Crtiteria (SAC) and evaluation report
- identifying, raising and scheduling RFCs
- checking the configuration baselines are recorded in configuration management before the start of service transition
- checking transition readiness

3. Plan and coordinate Service Transition

A **service transition plan** describes the tasks and activities required to release and deploy a release into the test environments and into production including
- work environment and infrastructure
- schedule of milestones
- activities and tasks to be performed
- staffing, resource requirements, budgets and timescales at each stage
- lead times and contingency

Good **integrated planning** and management are essential to deploy a release across distributed environments and locations into production successfully An **integrated set of transition plans** should be maintained that are linked to lower level plans such as release, build and test plans.

It is *best practice* to manage several releases in a **program**, with each significant deployment run as a **project**.

Implement **quality reviews** for all Service Transition, release and deployment plans. Questions that might be asked are:
- Are the service transition plans and release plans up-to-date, authorized and are the release dates known?
- Were any risks related to impact on costs, organization and technology taken into account?
- Are new configuration items (CIs) compatible with each other and with configuration items in the target environment?

- Are the people who need to work with it sufficiently trained?
- Have potential changes in the business environment been taken into account?

4. Transition process support

Service Transition advises and **supports** all stakeholders. The planning and support team will provide insight for the stakeholders regarding Service Transition processes and supporting systems and tools. In addition, the team will perform **management/administration** of changes, work orders, issues, risks, communication and deployment. The team will also update stakeholders regarding planning and process.

Finally, Service Transition activities are **monitored**: the implementation of activities is compared with the way they were intended (as formulated in the transition plan and model).

Interfaces

The **trigger** for service transition is an approved (authorized) RFC. **Inputs** for Transition planning include:
- authorized RFCs
- SDP
- definition of the release package and design specifications
- SAC

Outputs for transition planning include:
- transition strategy
- integral collection of Service Transition plans

Metrics

The most important **KPIs** for transition planning and support are:
- the number of implemented releases that met the customers agreed requirements
- decrease in the number of deviations with respect to intended scope, quality, costs and resources
- increased customer and user satisfaction regarding plans and communication
- decrease in the number of issues, risks and delays as a result of improved planning

11.2 Change Management

Introduction

Changes have a proactive or reactive **reason**. Examples of a proactive reason are cost reduction or service improvement. Examples of reactive changes are solving service disruptions or adapting the service to a changing environment.

Changes must be **controlled** adequately, so that:
- exposure to risks is minimized
- the severity of the impact and service interruption is minimized
- the change is implemented successfully on first attempt

The **goals** of change management are:
- respond to the customer's changing business
- responding to Requests for Change (RFCs) from the business and IT

The **objective** of the change management process is ensuring that changes are recorded, assessed, authorized, prioritized, planned, tested, implemented and documented and reviewed in a controlled manner.

The change management process must:
- use standardized methods and procedures
- record all changes in the CMDB
- take account of risks for the business

Scope

The ITIL definition of a change is:

> A **change** is the addition, modification or removal of authorized, planned or supported service or service component and its associated documentation.

The scope of service management covers changes to baselined service assets and CIs across the whole Service Lifecycle. The Section "Service asset and configuration management" later in this chapter discusses these issues in greater detail.

Every organization must itself define which changes its change management process does and does not cover. For instance, changing a defective hard drive of a pc may not be part of the change management process.

Figure 11.1 shows the scope of the change management process as well as the interfaces of the process with the business at the strategic, tactical and operational levels.

Value for the business

Service and infrastructure changes can have a negative impact on the business through service disruption and delay in identifying business requirements, but change management enables the service providers to add value to the business.

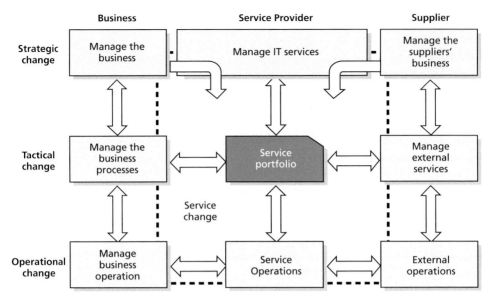

Figure 11.1   Scope of change management (Source: Service Transition was produced by OGC)

For example:
- changes relating to financial regulations, such as SOX, or other rules of good governance
- timely implementation of changes so that the business' deadlines are achieved
- reducing the number of failed changes, thereby reducing the number of service interruptions
- prioritizing changes and responding adequately to change requests from the customer
- reducing the mean time to restore services (MTRS)

Thanks to the increased dependency on IT services, and because the underlying information technology has become so complex, significant efficiency benefits can be realized by means of well structured and planned changes and releases. Some indicators of inadequate change management are:
- unauthorized changes
- unplanned downtime
- implemented changes with little success
- high number of "emergency changes"
- delayed project implementations

Policies
Policies for supporting change management are:
- creating a zero tolerance culture in relation to unauthorized changes
- aligning the change management process with other change processes in the organization
- effective prioritization, e.g. innovative versus preventive versus detective versus corrective changes
- establishing accountability and responsibilities for changes through the lifecycle
- establishing a single focal point for changes

- ensuring integration with other service management processes
- setting up "change windows", performance and risk assessments, performance measures

Design and planning

The change management process is planned in combination with release and configuration management. This makes it possible to assess the impact of changes on services and releases.

The requirement and design for the change management processes include:
- requirements relating to relevant laws and regulations
- an approach to eliminate unauthorized changes
- identification and classification
- organization, roles, responsibilities
- stakeholders
- grouping and relating changes
- procedures
- interfaces with other service management processes

Basic concepts

A **Request for Change (RFC)** is a formal request to change one or more CIs.

A **standard change** is a change of a service or infrastructure component that change management must register, but is of low risk and is pre-authorized. These are routine changes, such as PC upgrades.

An **emergency change** is intended to repair a failure (ASAP) in an IT service that has a large negative impact on the business. If this requires permission from the CAB, but the full CAB cannot be convened, it is necessary to identify a smaller group to make emergency decisions: the **Emergency CAB (ECAB)**.

An emergency change, too, must be tested and documented to the greatest possible extent.

The **Change Advisory Board (CAB)** is a consultation body that meets at fixed intervals to assess changes and help change management prioritize the changes. It may include representatives from all key stakeholders and departments, including:
- customers
- end users
- application developers
- system administrators
- experts
- service desk representatives
- production
- service provider representatives

The CAB must have a number of standard agenda items, including:
- unauthorized changes
- authorized changes not handled by the CAB

- RFCs that must be reviewed by the CAB members
- ongoing or closed changes
- assessment of implemented changes

No change should be approved without having an answer to the following question: "what will we do if the change is unsuccessful?" You must always ensure that a **fallback situation (remediation planning)** is available.

Activities, methods and techniques

Overall the change management activities include:
- change planning and control
- change and Release scheduling
- communications
- change decision making and authorization
- ensuring there are remediation plans
- measurement and control
- management reporting
- understanding impact
- continual improvement

The specific activities to manage individual changes are discussed in subsequent sections (see Figure 11.2):
1. create and record RFC
2. review the RFC and change proposal
3. assess and evaluate the change
4. authorize the change
5. plan updates
6. coordinate change implementation
7. review and close change

This section outlines the aspects followed within a "normal" change. The general principles set out apply to all changes and the "normal" change procedure is modified accordingly to deal with standard and emergency changes for example.

1. Create and record

The change is raised by a request from the initiator - the individual or organizational group that requires the change. For example, this may be a business unit that requires additional facilities, or problem management staff instigating an error resolution from many other sources.

All RFCs are registered and it must be possible to identify them via a unique identification number.

The scope and impact of the eventual change determine how much information is required for the change.

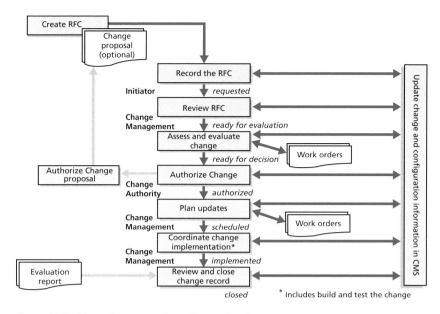

Figure 11.2   Example process flow of a regular change (Source: Service Transition was produced by OGC)

2. Review the RFC

After registration, the stakeholders verify whether the RFC is: totally impractical, repeats of earlier RFCs, accepted, rejected or still under consideration, incomplete submissions e.g. inadequate description, without necessary budgetary approval. Such requests are rejected and returned to the initiator with details of the reason for the rejection. The initiator should have a right of appeal against rejection.

3. Assess and evaluate changes

This step starts with **categorizing** the change. The issue of risk must be considered prior to the authorization of any change. The **likelihood** that the risk will occur and its possible **impact** determine the **risk category** of the change. In practice, a risk categorization matrix is generally used for this purpose (Figure 11.3).

After the change has been categorized, it is **evaluated**. Based on the impact, risk assessment, potential benefits and costs of the change, the **change authority** (e.g. the change manager and/or CAB) determine whether the change is supported or not

The following questions must be answered for all changes. Without this information, the impact assessment cannot be completed, and the balance of risk and benefit to the live service will not be understood. The **seven Rs of change management** represent a good starting point for impact analysis:
1. Who raised the change? (**R**aised)
2. What is the reason for the change? (**R**eason)
3. What is the return required from the change? (**R**eturn)
4. What are the change's risks? (**R**isk)
5. What resources does it require? (**R**esources)

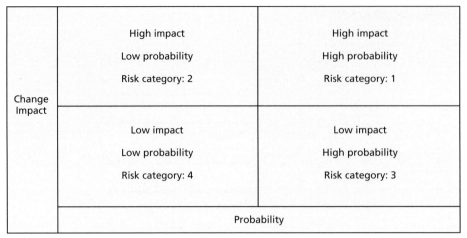

Figure 11.3   Example of a risk categorization matrix (Based on OGC ITIL V3 material)

6. Who are responsible for build, testing and implementation? (**R**esponsible)
7. Which relationships exist between this and other changes? (**R**elationship)

Determine the change's **priority** to establish the order in which the changes put forward must be considered. Priority is derived from the agreed impact and urgency. **Impact** is based on the beneficial change to the business that will result or on the degree of damage and cost to the business if it fails. **Urgency** indicates how long implementation can be delayed.

Examples of priority codes are:
• **low priority** - a change is desirable but can wait until a suitable opportunity occurs
• **medium priority** - no huge urgency or high impact, but the change must not be delayed until a later time; the Change Advisory Board gives this change average priority when allocating resources
• **high priority** - this change represents a serious failure for a number of users or an annoying failure for a large group of users, or it is related to other urgent issues; the Change Advisory Board gives this change top priority in its next meeting
• **immediate priority** - causing significant loss of revenue or the ability to deliver important public services; immediate action is required

Change planning and scheduling
Change management schedules the changes on the change calendar: the **Schedule of Change** (SC). The SC contains the details for all approved changes and their planning e.g. implementation dates.

Changes can be bundled into a release. In consultation with the relevant IT departments, the CAB may set up fixed times to implement changes - moments where services will be hindered as little as possible by changes. A recovery plan must be prepared in case a change implementation is unsuccessful.

4. Authorize the change

Formal authorization from a change authority is required for every change. This may be a role, person or group of people. The level at which approval is required depends on the change type. An example is shown in Figure 11.4.

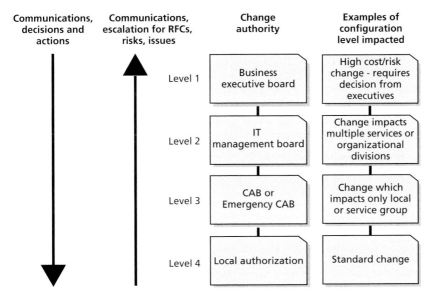

Figure 11.4 Example of an Authorization model (Source: Service Transition was produced by OGC)

5. Coordinate change implementation

Authorized RFCs should be passed on to the relevant technical groups for building of the changes. Building and creating a release are issues discussed in the Section on "Release and deployment management".

You should **test** the changes, the remediation and the implementation method for the changes thoroughly. Section "Service validation and testing" discusses testing in detail.

6. Review and close change record

Implemented changes - perhaps with the exception of standard changes - are evaluated after some time. The CAB then determines whether further follow-up is required. The CAB pays attention to the following matters:
- Did the change realize its intended purpose?
- Are all the stakeholders satisfied with the outcome?
- Did any side-effects occur?
- Were the estimated costs and effort exceeded?

If the change is successful, it can be closed. The outcome should be included in the **Post Implementation Review (PIR)**: the change evaluation. If the change is unsuccessful, change management or the CAB decides what should be done. A new or modified RFC may result.

Interfaces

Examples of change types that **trigger** the change management process:
* strategic changes
* changes to one or more services
* operational changes
* changes for continual improvement (See also CSI in Chapter 13)

The **input** of change management includes:
* policies and strategies for change and release
* RFCs
* Change proposal
* Plans - change, transition, release and deployment test, evaluation, remediation
* Schedule of Change and Projected Service Outages (PSOs)
* assets and CIs
* test results, test report and evaluation report

The **output** of change management includes:
* rejected and approved RFCs
* new or changed services, CIs, assets
* adjusted PSO
* updated Schedule of Change
* change decisions, actions, documents, records and reports

Change management has **interfaces** with the change processes of the business, and with program and project management, and with sourcing and partnering. Interfaces with other service management processes:
* **asset and configuration management** - the information from the configuration management system (CMS) helps to determine the impact of the proposed changes and track the workflow of the changes; it also shows which related CIs (those not included in the RFC) are impacted by the change; Figure 11.5 shows how change and configuration management collaborate
* **problem management** - problem management is one of the parties that most frequently submits RFCs and makes an important contribution to CAB discussions
* **IT service continuity management** - this process has many procedures and plans that are updated by the change management process
* **information security management** - all changes relating to security issues are handled via the change management process
* **capacity and demand management** - badly managed demand results in a great many risks; capacity management plays an important part in the assessment of changes

Metrics

KPIs for the change management process include:
* the number of implemented changes that comply with the customer specifications
* the benefits of the change compared to the costs
* the reduction of the number of service interruptions
* the reduction of the number of unauthorized changes
* the reduction of the number of backouts

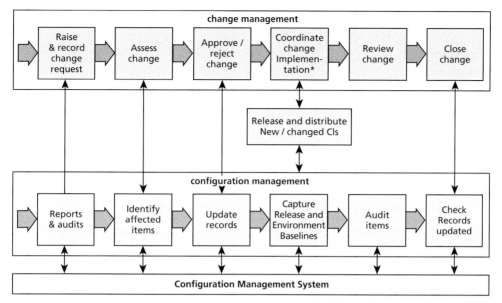

*Includes build and test where applicable

Figure 11.5   The workflow of change and configuration management (Source: Service Transition was produced by OGC)

- change success rate after evaluation compared to the number of approved RFCs
- the reduction of the number of unplanned changes

Examples of metrics for the change management process:
- **Output metrics**, such as:
  - number of disruptions, incidents and problems resulting from changes
  - number of inaccurate change specifications
  - number of incomplete impact analyses
  - service/application repair work resulting from inaccurate change specifications
- **Workload metrics**, such as:
  - frequency of changes
  - number of changes
- **Process metrics**, such as:
  - people's satisfaction with speed, clarity and ease of use
  - number and rate of changes that follow formal change management procedures
  - ratio of planned versus unplanned RFCs
  - ratio of accepted versus rejected RFCs
  - staff utilization
  - costs versus budget

11.3 Service Asset and Configuration Management

Introduction

The **purpose** of Service Asset and Configuration Management (SACM) is to provide a logical model of the IT infrastructure. In this model the IT services are related to the different IT components needed to supply these services.

The **objective** is: to define service and infrastructure components and maintain accurate configuration records. In this context it is important that:
- the integrity of the service assets and Configuration Items (CIs) are protected
- all assets and CIs are located in configuration management system
- the operational and service management processes are supported effectively

Scope

All assets that are used during the Service Lifecycle fall within the scope of asset management. The process offers a complete overview of all assets, and shows who is responsible for the control and maintenance of these assets.

Configuration management ensures that all components (CIs) that form part of the service or product are identified, **baselined** (the configuration) and maintained. It ensures that releases into controlled environments and operational use are on the basis of formal approvals. The process also provides a logical model of all services, assets, the physical infrastructure and the mutual relations.

SACM also relates to non-IT assets and CIs, such as work products used to develop the services and configurations items required to support the service that are not formally classified as assets. The scope of the process also includes assets and CIs of other suppliers ("shared assets"), to the extent that they are relevant to the service.

Value for the business

SACM increases the visibility and performance of the service, release or environment. Among other things this results in:
- better forecasting and planning of changes
- changes and releases to be assessed, planned and successfully delivered
- incidents and problems to be resolved within the service level targets
- better adherence to standards, legal and regulatory obligations (less non-conformances)
- ability to identify the costs for a service

Policies

The first step is to develop and maintain the SACM policies that set the objectives, scope and principles and critical success factors for what is to be achieved by the process. There are significant costs and resource implications to implementing SACM and therefore strategic decisions need to be made about the priorities to be addressed. Many IT service providers focus initially on the basic IT assets (hardware and software) and services that are business critical or covered by legal and regulatory compliance e.g. SOX, software licensing.

Starting points

The policies describe the starting points for the development and control of assets and CIs, for instance:

- the costs of SACM are proportionate to the potential risks to the service if SACM were not implemented
- the need to provide specifications for "corporate governance"
- the need to guarantee the agreements in the SLA and other contracts
- the specifications for available, reliable and cost-effective services
- the specifications for performance criteria
- the transition from reactive maintenance to proactive control
- the requirement to maintain adequate asset and configuration information for stakeholders

Basic concepts

By maintaining relations between CIs a **logical model** of the services, assets and infrastructure (Figure 11.6) is created. This enables other processes to access valuable information:

- impact analysis for proposed changes
- investigations into the cause of incidents and problems
- the planning and design of changes, software upgrades and technological refresh
- the planning of release and deployment packages
- optimization of the use of assets and costs

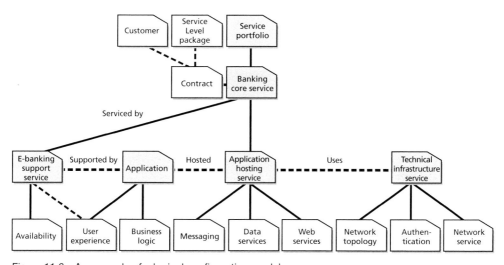

Figure 11.6   An example of a logical configuration model (Source: Service Transition was produced by OGC)

ITIL defines a **configuration item** as follows:

> *A **configuration item** is an asset, service component or other item that is (or will be) under the control of configuration management.*

There are many types of CIs, such as:
- service lifecycle CIS - CIs for the support of the Service Lifecycle activities, such as the business case and release and change plans
- service CIs, such as service capability assets, service resource assets, service model, service package, release package, service acceptance criteria
- organizational CIs, such as the documentation relating to the strategy of the organization
- internal CIs, for instance those associated with individual projects
- external CIs, such as specifications of external customer requirements and agreements
- interface CIs that are required to deliver the end to end service across a Service Provider Interface (SPI)

In order to manage large and complex IT services and infrastructures SACM needs to use a supporting system: a **Configuration Management System (CMS)**.

A CMS generally consists of four layers:
- a **presentation layer** with different "views" for the different target groups
- a **knowledge processing layer** for, for instance, producing reports and queries
- an **information integration layer** that collates and structures the data
- a **data layer** with the data and information from different sources such as configuration management databases (**CMDB**s), discovery and inventory tools, project information, etc.

Figure 11.7 shows an example of a CMS.

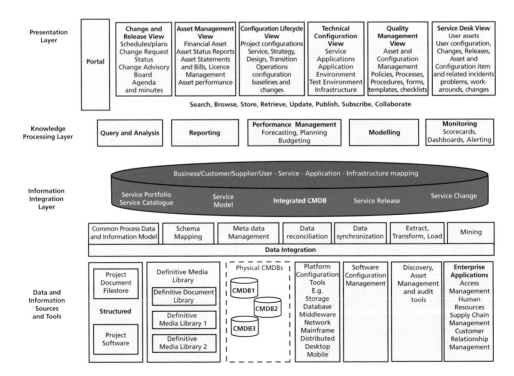

Figure 11.7　Example of a CMS (Source: Service Transition was produced by OGC)

At data level it may be that the CMS gets its data from different CMDBs that, together, form a **federated CMDB**. In practice, it frequently happens that some elements of a service are outsourced, whereas others are performed in-house. For instance, the network is outsourced to service provider A and the server management to service provider B, whereas the application management is performed in-house. In this case the CMS will need data from three different CMDBs that are controlled (and owned) by three different parties.

Where possible, use automated tools (such as discovery, inventory and audit tools) to populate and maintain the CMDB. This minimizes the opportunity for error and saves costs.
ITIL defines various **libraries**:
- A **secure library** is a collection of software, electronic or document CIs of a known type and status.
- A **secure store** is a secure location where IT assets are stored.
- The **Definitive Media Library (DML)** is a secure store where the definitive, authorized (approved) versions of all media CIs are stored and protected.
- **Definitive spares** are an area set aside for secure storage of definitive hardware spares.

It must be possible for all libraries of physical and electronic media to be uniquely identifiable and to be documented in the CMS.

A **configuration baseline** is a configuration of a service, product or infrastructure that has been formally reviewed and agreed on that thereafter serves as the basis for further activities, and that can be changed only through formal change procedures. Among other uses a baseline is used:
- to mark a milestone in the development of a service (e.g. Service Design baseline)
- to build a service component from a defined set of inputs
- to change or rebuild a specific version at a later stage
- to assemble all relevant components in readiness for a change or release
- as a fall-back in the case of problems with new configurations (after changes)

Baseline configurations are included in the CMS.

A **snapshot** (moment in time) is the most recent status of a CI or environment (for instance as it was inventoried by a discovery tool). A snapshot is stored in the CMS and is kept as a read-only historical record (i.e. it cannot be changed). A snapshot:
- is convenient for problem management to analyze what the situation was at the time incidents occurred
- facilitates system restore to support security scanning software

Activities, methods and techniques
The basic SACM process activities consist of:
1. management and planning
2. configuration identification
3. configuration control
4. status accounting and reporting
5. verification and audit

1. Management and planning

The management team and configuration management decide what level of configuration management is needed and how this level will be achieved. This is documented in a **configuration management plan**. Contents of a configuration management plan include:

- context and objective
- scope
- requirements
- applicable policies and standards
- organization for configuration management including roles and responsibilities
- SACM systems and tools
- selection and application of processes and procedures to implement SACM activities including configuration identification, version management, build management, etc.
- reference implementation plan
- relationship management and interface controls e.g. with financial asset management, with projects, with development and customers, etc.
- relationship management and control of service providers and sub-contractors

2. Configuration identification

Configuration identification focuses on determining and maintaining the naming and version numbering of assets and CIs, the mutual relations and the relevant attributes. The most important activities of configuration identification are:

- defining and documenting criteria for the selection of CIs and the components within them
- selecting the CIs on the basis of the defined criteria
- giving all CIs unique numbers for identification purposes
- specifying the attributes of each CI
- indicating when each CI will be placed under configuration management
- identifying the "owner" of each CI

Create a **configuration structure** for each IT service. This structure shows the relations and hierarchy between CIs for a certain service. The configuration structure has a top-down approach. The highest level is the service in question. The lowest CI level is determined by:

- the available information
- the necessary level of control
- the necessary resources required to maintain that CI level

It is only useful to include a certain CI if it supports the other service management processes.

Document **naming conventions** and apply them in the identification of CIs, documents and changes, but also, for instance, in basic configurations, releases and compilations.

Each CI must be uniquely identifiable by means of a version number, as there may be several versions of the same CI; for example different versions of software. When planning naming conventions allow for future growth. The names must also be short but meaningful, and correspond with the existing conventions as much as possible.

Provide all physical CIs, such as hardware, with **labels**, so that they are easy to identify. The labels must be easy to read and accessible, so that a user can pass the information on the label on to the service desk. Labels with a barcode are very efficient for physical audits of the CIs. During such audits it is checked whether the CIs in the organization correspond with those within the CMS.

With the aid of **attributes** information is stored that is relevant for the CI in question. When structuring the CMDB the following attributes, among others, can be used:
• CI number/label or barcode number - unique identifier
• CI type
• name/description
• version
• location
• supply date
• licence details e.g. expiry date
• owner
• status
• supplier/source
• related documents
• related software
• historical data e.g. audit trail
• relationship type
• applicable SLA
• purchase date
• acceptance date
• current status
• planned status
• purchase value
• residual value after depreciation
• comments

The characteristics of a CI are often recorded in **configuration documentation**. Table 11.1 is a RACI table (*Responsible, Accountable, Consulted, Informed*) that shows different documentation types of service CIs and indicates who takes responsibility for the documents in the different phases of the Service Lifecycle.

Relationships describe how CIs work together to provide a service. The CMDB maintains these relations to demonstrate the interdependencies between CIs, for instance:
• a CI **is part of** another CI - a software module is part of an application (parent-child relation)
• a CI **is connected to** - a PC that is connected to the LAN
• a CI **uses** another CI - a business service uses a server
• a CI **is installed on** another CI - MS Word is installed on a PC

Relationships are also the mechanism for associating RFCs, incidents, problems, known errors and releases to CIs. Relations can be 1-to-1, 1-to-n and n-to-1.

Service Life-cycle State	Examples of Service Lifecycle Assets and CIs impacted	Service Strategy	Service Design	Service Transition	Service Operations	CSI
Service Strategy	Portfolios - service contract, customer Service Strategy requirements Service Lifecycle Model	A	C	C	R	C
Service Design	Service Package (including SLA) Service Design Package e.g. Service Model, Contract, Supplier's service management plan, Process interface definition, Customer Engagement plan Release Policy Release Package definition	I	A	C	R	C
Service Transition	Service Transition model Test plan Controlled environments Build/Installation plan Build specification Release plan Deployment plan CMS SKMS Release Package Release baseline Release documentation Test report	I	C	A	R	C
Service Operations	Service Operations model Service Support model Service Desk User assets User documentation Operations documentation Support documentation	I	C	C	A/R	R
Continual Service Improvement	CSI model Service improvement plan Service reporting process	A/C	A/C	A/C	R	A

Table 11.1   RACI table for configuration documentation in the lifecycle

CIs are classed by means of a **classification**, for instance: service, hardware, software documentation, personnel.

A **release unit** is the portion of the service or infrastructure, that is normally released together, in accordance with an organizations release policy. Releases are documented in the CMS for the support of the release and deployment process.

Releases can be classified into the following **release categories**:
- **major releases** - important deployment of new hardware and software with, in most cases, a considerable expansion of the functionality (V1.0, 2.0, etc.)
- **minor releases** - these usually contain a number of smaller improvements; some of these improvements were previously implemented as quick fixes but are now included integrally within a release (V1.1, V1.2, etc.)

- **emergency releases** - usually implemented as a temporary solution for a problem or known error (V1.1.1, V1.1.2, etc.)

3. Configuration control

Configuration control ensures that the CIs are adequately managed. No CIs can be added, modified, replaced or removed without following the agreed procedure. Establish guidelines and procedures for, among others:
- license management
- change management
- version management
- access control
- build control
- promotion
- deployment
- installation
- baseline configurations integrity management

4. Status accounting and reporting

The lifecycle of a component is classified into different stages and the stages that different types of CI go through must be properly documented. For instance, a release goes through the following stages: registered, accepted, installed, withdrawn.

Status reports give an insight into the current and historical data of each CI and the status changes that have occurred.

Different types of **service asset and configuration reports** are needed for configuration management. The reports may relate to individuals CIs, but also to a complete service. Such reports may consist of:
- a list of CIs and their baseline
- details on the current status and change history
- a list of unauthorized CIs detected
- reports on the unauthorized use of hardware and software

5. Verification and audit

SACM conducts audits to ensure that:
- there are no discrepancies between the documented baselines and the actual business environment to which they refer
- CIs physically exist in the organization or DML and spares stores, the functional and operational characteristics of CIs can be verified and checks can be made that records in the CM match the physical infrastructure
- release and configuration documentation is present before the release is rolled out

Document all exceptions that result from the audits and report them. Corrective actions (CIs that need to be added, changed or deleted) are handled via the change management process.

Audits are conducted at the following times:
- shortly after changes to the CMS
- before and after changes to IT services or infrastructure
- at random and planned intervals
- before a release to ensure the environment is as expected
- in response to the detection of unauthorized CIs
- following recovery from disasters

Audit tools can perform checks at regular intervals, for instance weekly. For example a desktop audit tool that compares the configuration of an individual's desktop against the "master" configuration that was installed.

Information management
Run backups of the CMS on a regular basis and save these in a secure place in a different location in case of any emergencies such as fire.

The CMS maintains information about backups of CIs, historical information on CIs, different versions of CIs and removed versions.

Interfaces
Updates to assets and CIs are **triggered** by RFCs, service requests and new assets and CIs.

SACM supports and has **interfaces** with all other service management processes. The most notable of these are:
- **change management** - for impact analyses
- **financial management** - for insight into costs, depreciations, maintenance and repairs
- **IT service continuity management** - to make the organization aware of the assets the business depends on, and for the control of key spares and software
- **incident and problem management** - for the diagnosis of problems and incidents
- **availability management** - for the detection of "points or failure"

SACM also has many **interactions** with release and deployment management. These processes benefit greatly from an integrated approach with SACM.

Metrics
The following **measures** are used to evaluate the performance of the SACM process:
- increased quality and accuracy of information about assets and CIs
- fewer errors as a result of outdated information
- shorter audits because the information is more accessible
- shorter diagnosis and resolution times for problems and incidents
- fewer discrepancies between the actual situation and that in the CMS

Implementation
Among others, the **challenges** in the SACM process are:
- convincing staff that they cannot circumvent the SACM process
- finding and justifying financial resources for SACM

- collecting too much data simply because it is available
- lack of management acceptance and support

Critical success factors of the SACM process are:
- determining the right level of detail and depth
- implementing a top-down approach for the configuration structure
- achieving the right level of accuracy
- using technology to automate the CMS and to enforce SACM guidelines

The following **risks** are acknowledged:
- too much technical focus as opposed to operational and service focus
- the CMS becomes outdated because, for instance, unauthorized personnel move hardware assets

11.4 Release and Deployment Management

Introduction
ITIL defines release and deployment management as follows:

> *Release and deployment management aims to build, test and deliver the capability to provide the services specified by service design and that will accomplish the stakeholders' requirements and deliver the intended objectives.*

The **goal** of release and deployment management is the deployment of releases into production, and the establishment of effective use of the service in order to deliver value to the customer and to be able to handover to service operations.

The **objective** of release and deployment management is to ensure that:
* release and deployment plans are in place
* release packages (compilation) are deployed successfully
* knowledge transfer to the customers takes place
* there is minimum disruption to the services

Scope
The processes, systems and functions for packaging, building, testing and deployment of a release into production and establishment of the service specified in the service design package before final handover to service operations.

Value for the business
Effective release and deployment management contributes to the business because:
* changes are realized faster, cheaper and with fewer risks, and the operational objectives are supported better
* the implementation approach is more consistent and the traceability requirements (e.g. audits, legislation etc.) are complied with more closely

Basic concepts

> *A **release** is a set of new or changed CIs that are tested and will be implemented into production together.*

A **release unit** is the portion of the service or infrastructure that is included in the release, in accordance with the organization's release guidelines.
It is important to determine the correct level of the release. For a business critical application it may make sense to include the complete application in the release unit, but for a website it may only have to be the HTML page that is changed.

In the **release design** different considerations apply in respect of the way in which the release is deployed. The most frequently occurring options for the rollout of releases are:
* **Big bang versus phased** - A big bang release deploys the new or changed service for all the users at the same time. A phased deployment deploys the release for part of the user base at a time.

- **Push and pull** - With a push approach the service component is deployment from the "center" to the target locations. With a pull approach the new release is made available to the users from a central location from which they download to their location at a time they choose.
- **Automated or manual** - Releases can, to a large extent, be automated; e.g. the use of installation software.

The release and deployment teams must have a good understanding of the relevant IT architecture involved in a release and deployment process. This understanding is essential to determine the sequence in which the activities are implemented and for mapping out all the interdependencies.

A **release package** is a single release unit or a structured set of release units. In the case of a new or a changed service all the elements of which the service consists - the infrastructure, hardware, software, applications, documentation, knowledge, etc. - must be taken into account. See Figure 11.8. For different types of packages, see 11.3 (SACM).

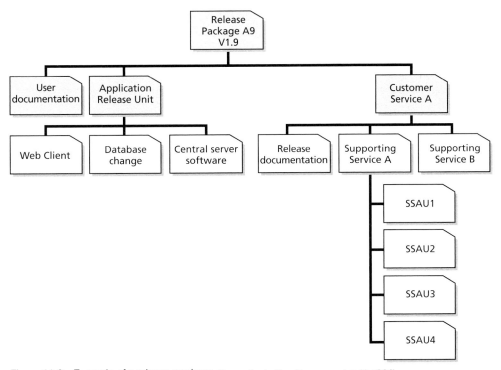

Figure 11.8   Example of a release package (Source: Service Transition was produced by OGC)

Activities, methods and techniques
The basic process activities of release and deployment management consist of:
1. planning
2. preparation for building, testing and deployment
3. building and testing

4. service testing and pilots
5. planning and preparing the deployment
6. transfer, deployment, and retirement
7. verify deployment
8. Early Life Support (ELS)
9. review and close

1. Planning

Prior to a deployment into production different plans are formulated. The type and number depends on the size and complexity of the environment and the changed or new service. Release and deployment plans form part of the overall Service Transition plan. Change management will approve or reject the plans. The plans will include the following:
• scope, content, risks, responsibilities and stakeholders in the release
• team responsible for the release
• approach for collaboration with all stakeholders

The following (sub) plans are relevant for release and deployment:
• **Pass/fail criteria** - Service Transition is responsible for the planning the pass/fail situations for every phase of the release and deployment.
• **Building and test plans** - Building and test plans are needed that describe the approach to the building, testing and maintenance of the pre-production environment; different environments are needed for each test type: for unit testing, service release testing and integration testing.

The V model is a convenient tool for mapping out the different configuration levels at which building and testing must take place. The left side of the V in this example starts with service specifications and ends with the detailed Service Design. The right side of the V reflects the test activities, by means of which the specifications on the left-hand side must be validated. In the middle we find the test and validation criteria (Figure 11.9).
• **Planning of pilots** - To test the new or changed service with part of the users first, a pilot can be planned; do not forget to include in the plans how the feedback from the users is to be collected and processed, and devise a rollout scenario.
• **Planning of release package (compilation) and build** - Formulate plans and procedures for:
  − pass/fail criteria
  − the management of changes and the communication with stakeholders
  − training of staff, knowledge transfer and readiness assessment of end users
  − the use of (service management) resources
  − the transfer of systems and users to the new service
• **Deployment planning** - With regard to deployment include the following considerations in the plan:
  − What is being deployed?
  − Who are the users?
  − What is the local situation?
  − Where are the users?
  − Who else needs to be notified?
  − Why is there a deployment?
  − What are the Critical Success Factors?

- **Logistical planning and delivery planning** - Once the deployment approach has been decided, logistical and delivery plans will be formulated with attention for the following points:
  - when and how will the service components be delivered
  - what should be done if there are delays
  - managing customs and other implications of international distributions
- **Financial and commercial planning** - Financial and commercial aspects must be checked before the deployment takes place.

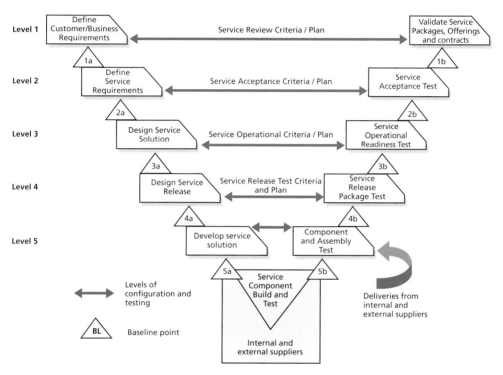

Figure 11.9 The service V model that reflects configuration and test levels (Source: Service Transition was produced by OGC)

2. Preparation for building (compilation), testing and deployment

Before approval can be given for the building and test phase, the service and release design is compared against the specifications of the new or changed service (validation). This comparison may highlight risks or issues relating to the service, the assets and CIs. These issues or risks are then prioritized and actions are undertaken to resolve them in good time. The service evaluation report documents the results of the validation.

3. Building and testing

The build and test phase of the release consists of the following activities:

- **Management of general (common) infrastructure and services** - Carefully manage the common services and infrastructure, as they may be of significant importance to the building and testing.

- **Use of release and building documentation** - The available documentation (procedures, templates, manuals) must be used throughout; this documentation supports the release team in acquiring and purchasing assets, CIs, services and products for the construction of an integrated release package; in this context also consider *proof of licenses* (it must be possible to produce the required licenses) of the various components.
- **Acquisition, purchasing and testing of CIs and components for the release** - CIs and components are acquired from projects, suppliers and partners; the purchasing activities include:
  - the recording or updating of the CIs in the CMS
  - ensuring that the licenses can be produced when necessary; also check the CIs and components for quality, legality and the requirements with respect to labeling and naming
- **Compilation of the release (release packaging)** - The key activities for building and compiling a release package are:
  - assembling and integrating the components
  - preparing the compilation and release documentation
  - installing and checking the release package
  - creating a baseline of the composition of the package
  - formulating a service message (that the release package is ready for use)
- **Structuring and controlling the test environments** - The test environments must be stable and able to be controlled.

4. Service testing and pilots

Test management is responsible for the coordination of the test activities and the planning and control of the implementation. Section 11.5 "Service validation and testing" comprehensively describes test management.

In this paragraph we limit ourselves to the tests that are conducted during the release and deployment process:
- **Service release test** - The service release test checks whether the service components work well together (integration), and that the release can be compiled, installed and tested in the target environment.
- **Service Operation "readiness testing"** - This test ensures that the service and the underlying applications and technical infrastructure can be transferred to the live environment in a controlled manner.
- **Pilots** - A pilot is intended to test whether there are elements of the service that do not meet specifications, or may pose a risk to the business.

5. Planning and preparing for deployment

These activities prepare the deployment group for deployment. The following need to be addressed:
- Are they ready for the implementation of the release package?
- Have they prepared the activity plan?
- Have the potential risks been mapped out?
- Is everyone sufficiently trained?
- Have there been any last-minute changes in the specifications?

In addition, the other aspects the team will be faced with are also assessed, such as financial aspects, the extent to which the organization is prepared, the infrastructure and other facilities and the available service management resources.

When planning a specific deployment, plans include: risk limitation, transfers, upgrades, logistical matters, knowledge transfer and communication. Finally, these plans have to be evaluated and an RFC must be created that is submitted to change management for approval. After this the service is ready for deployment.

6. Transfer, deployment, and retirement
The following activities are important during the deployment:
- **The transfer of financial assets** - This may be, for instance, the transfer of support and maintenance costs, license fees and contingency reserves (disaster recovery) to a third party.
- **Transfer and transition of business and organization** - When a service or service unit is transferred the organization itself will also have to be adapted; consider, for instance, new tasks, authorities and responsibilities.
- **Publication of documentation** - Distribute all documentation (guidelines, processes, procedures, manuals) that the users will need to take the new service into use.
- **Transfer of "service management capability"** - Transfer new or changed process information, systems and tools to the team that is responsible for the service management activities.
- **Transfer of the service** - Activities that are relevant in this process include:
  – analysis of service performance, issues and risks
  – configuration audits of service assets
  – updating of service catalogue
  – distribution of service notification
- **Deployment of the service** - All activities needed to distribute and install the service.
- **Cancellation of services** - Cancel redundant services.
- **Removal of redundant assets** - Remove assets that are redundant as a result of the new or changed service.

7. Verify deployment
When all the deployment activities have been completed it is important to verify that all the users, service operations, other staff and stakeholders are able to use the service as intended. This is also a good time to collect feedback on the deployment. Use this information for the improvement of future deployments.

8. Early life support
Early Life Support (ELS) is intended to offer extra support after the deployment of a new or changed service. ELS provides the means to resolve operational and support problems as quickly as possible, which means that users do not have to be confronted with service interruptions. These may be "teething problems" or improvements that can help to stabilize the service.

The deployment team also updates the documentation during the ELS phase and updates the knowledge bank with additional diagnostic information, known errors, workarounds and FAQs.

Service Transition will monitor the performance of the new or changed service during the ELS phase until all the exit criteria have been met, including:
- all users are able to use the service effectively and efficiently
- service and process owners are able to manage the service
- agreed service and performance levels are achieved

9. Review and close

In the review of a deployment, check whether:
- the knowledge transfer and training were adequate
- all user experiences have been documented
- all fixes and changes are complete and all problems, known errors and workarounds have been documented
- the quality criteria have been complied with
- the service is ready for transition from ELS into production

Also check whether there are issues that have to be passed on to CSI. The deployment is completed when the support is transferred to Operations. Finally, change management will conduct a Post Implementation Review (PIR).

To finalize the Service Transition as a whole a formal evaluation must be performed that is tailored to with the scale and scope of the change.

Information management

As CIs are deployed successfully the CMS is updated with information such as:
- new or changed CIs
- relationships between requirements and test cases
- installation and build plans
- logistics and delivery plans
- validation and test plans
- new or change locations and users
- status updates
- changes of ownership (of assets and CIs)
- licenses

Also, documented information for the service knowledge management system, such as information about the deployment, training and known errors, may be necessary.

Interfaces

The release process is triggered by an approved RFC.

Inputs for the release and deployment process are:
- approved RFC, service package, SLP, SDP, SAC, continuity plans
- release policies, design and model, construction model and plan
- technology, purchasing, service management and operation standards and plans
- exit and entry criteria for each phase of the release and deployment

Outputs from the release and deployment process are:

- release and deployment plans, completed RFC, service notifications, an updated service catalogue and service model
- new or changed service management documentation and service reports
- new tested service capability and environment
- SLA, OLAs and contracts
- Service Transition report and service capacity plan
- complete and accurate CI list with an audit trail for the CIs in the release package and also the new of changed service and infrastructure configurations

Metrics

Customer-related KPIs include:

- improvement of service performance
- reduction of the number of incidents
- improvement of customer and user satisfaction

Supplier-related KPIs include:

- lower costs for the diagnosis of incidents and problems
- reduction in the number of discrepancies in configuration audits compared with the real world

Implementation

Challenges in the release and deployment process include:

- the development of standard performance measurements and methods across projects and suppliers
- dependence on projects and suppliers
- understanding all the risks that may affect the Service Transition
- understanding the perspectives and starting points of the different stakeholders

Critical success factors in the release and deployment process include:

- new (or changed) service runs in the target environment and is tested against the Service Design
- new (or changed) service has proven itself in a pilot
- test models are re-usable for regression tests in future releases

Risks in the release and deployment process are:

- lack of clarity in the expectations and objectives of different stakeholders, ill-defined roles, tasks and responsibilities
- incompetent management, insufficient financial resources, lack of control, poor change management
- poor relationships with partners and service providers, insufficient support (commitment) from stakeholders
- risks relating to the technical infrastructure and applications

11.5 Service Validation and Testing

Introduction
Testing of services is an important contribution to the quality of IT service provision. Testing ensures that new (or changed) services are **fit for purpose** and **fit for use**.

Fit for purpose means that the service does what the client expects of it, so that the service supports the business. "Fit for use" addresses such aspects as availability, continuity, capacity and security of the service.

Insufficient attention to testing may result in: increase of incidents, issues and errors, extra service desk phone calls with questions regarding the functioning of the service, higher costs and a service that is improperly used.

The **goal** of service validation and testing is to provide a service that adds value to the customers and their business.

The **objective** of service validation and testing is to make sure that:
• the release delivers the expected outcomes and value for the customers within projected costs, capacity and constraints
• services are fit for purpose and fit for use
• specifications (requirements) by customer and other stakeholders are met

Scope
Service validation and testing is applied during the entire Service Lifecycle, and is aimed at testing the quality of service (units), and intended to verify whether the service provider has sufficient capacity and resources in order to provide a service or service release successfully.

Testing is also particularly supportive of the release and deployment processes. In addition, the evaluation process will be using test results.

Value for the business
Service interruptions may be damaging to business operations of service provider and clients who are recipients of the services. They may result in damage to reputation, financial loss and even (fatal) accidents. For example, the role of IT in hospitals, the automotive or aerospace industries can mean injury or death if service delivery fails.

Basic concepts
The **service model** describes the structure and dynamics of a service provided by Service Operation. The structure consists of core and supporting services and service assets needed. When a new (or changed) service is designed, developed and built, these service assets are tested in relation to design specifications and requirements. Activities, flow of resources, coordination, and interactions describe the dynamics (see Figure 11.10).

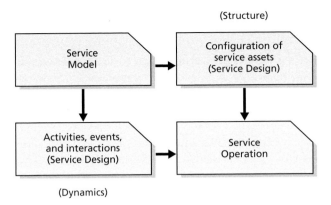

(Structure)

Figure 11.10   Service models describe the structure and dynamics of a service (Source: Service Transition was produced by OGC)

Policies for service validation and testing are:
- service quality policies
- risk policies
- reusability policies
- Service Transition policies
- release policies
- mandatory integral testing
- involving all stakeholders in testing
- change management policies

The **test strategy** defines the overall testing approach and the allocation of required resources. This strategy might be applicable to the entire organization, a collection of services or an individual service. All test strategies are developed in collaboration with the stakeholders. Attention is paid to objectives, scope, standards, test processes, test metrics, test approach, requirements of man and means and "deliverables".

A **test model** consists of a test plan, what is to be tested and test scripts which indicate the method by which each element must be tested. In order to ensure that the process can be repeated, test models must be structured in such a way that:
- the specification or design criteria being tested can be traced
- test activities, evaluation and reports can be audited
- test elements can be maintained and changed

Whether or not testing is effective will be determined, in part, by the degree to which the service meets requirements. These requirements, in turn, are based on the perspectives of those who use, provide, deploy or manage the service. The Service Design package therefore defines entry and exit criteria for all **test perspectives**.

By using **test models**, such as a **V model** (Figure 11.9) "validating and testing" becomes a part of the Service Lifecycle early in the process. The V model provides a useful framework for organizing the levels at which CIs must be managed. It also helps to determine which test activity should take place at which level. Tests can take place both within and between various levels.

There are very many different **test techniques** and **test approaches**. The technique and approach depends on the service type, risk profile, test goal and test level. Examples include: document review, modeling, simulation, scenario testing, role play and laboratory testing, live pilot.

Design considerations that are important for testing relate to finances (is the budget big enough?), documentation (is everything available, and in the correct format?), composition (build), testability (think of resources, time and facilities), traceability (traceable to specifications), when and where testing is to take place, and remediation (is there a backup plan?).

Also remember to take management and maintenance of test data into account in the design. This concerns the separation of test and live data, regulations with respect to data security, backing up of test data, and so on.

In addition to all kinds of functional and non-functional **test types**, role playing is also possible based on perspective (target group):
- **service requirements testing** "fit for purpose" (service provider, users and client) - does the service meet the specifications determined?
- **service level testing** (service level managers, operation managers and clients) - this concerns testing whether the new service meets the service levels determined
- **service assurance testing** "fit for use" (customer) - to verify availability, capacity, continuity and security
- **usability testing** (end users and maintainers) - to verify user-friendliness and usability for groups such as visually impaired users
- **contract and regulation testing** (service providers) - this could be for service providers who must (contractually) comply with ISO/IEC 20000 and industries that must comply with very specific regulations such as the (UK) Ministry of Defence and the pharmaceutical industry
- **service management testing** (service provider) - ISO/IEC 20000 could be used for this; ISO/IEC 20000 indicates the minimum requirements that processes must meet
- **operational testing** (system, services) - these could be stress tests, security and recoverability
- **regression testing** - being able to repeat earlier (successful) tests in order to compare new results with the previous ones

Activities, methods and techniques
Figure 11.11 schematically displays the testing process. The activities are not necessarily performed in this order; they might also take place parallel to each other. The following activities can be distinguished:
1. validation and test management
2. planning and design
3. verification test plan and design
4. prepare test environment
5. testing
6. evaluate exit criteria and report
7. clean up and closure

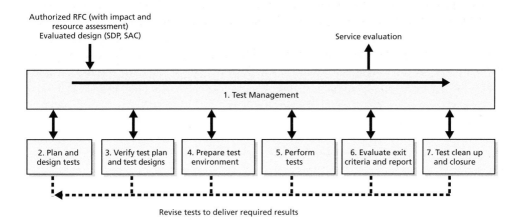

Figure 11.11   Schematic Display of the Test Process (Source: Service Transition was produced by OGC)

1. Validation and test management

Test management consists of planning and managing (control), and reporting on the activities taking place during all test phases of the Service Transition. This includes the following activities:

- planning of resources, and what is being tested at what time
- managing incidents, problems, errors, deviations, issues, risks (including during the discovery in the Transition phase)
- collecting test metrics; analyze, report and manage

2. Planning and design

Test planning and design activities take place early in the Service Lifecycle and relate to the following:

- resources such as hardware, network, number of staff members, capacity, ability and finances
- business/customer resources required
- supporting services
- schedule of milestones and delivery and acceptance

3. Verification of Test Plan and Design

Test plans and designs are verified to make sure that everything (including scripts) is complete, and that test models sufficiently take into account the risk profile of the service in question and all possible interfaces.

4. Preparation test environment

Prepare the test environment and make a baseline configuration of the test environment.

5. Testing

The tests are executed using manual or automated testing techniques and procedures. Testers register all results. If a test fails, the reason is documented. Proceed with the test as closely as possible according to test plans and scripts. Document the cause of the failure.

6. Evaluate exit criteria and report

The actual results are compared with projected results (exit criteria). Test results can be interpreted in terms of "pass/fail" (approval or not), any risks the tested object may contain for service provider or client, or in terms of costs required to reach the projected goal.

Collect the test results and recapitulate for the report. Examples of exit criteria are:
- the tested service complies with quality requirements
- the service and supporting IT infrastructure will enable the end user to perform all functions as defined
- configuration baselines are captured into the CMS

7. Clean up and closure

Make sure that the test environment is cleaned up. Review the test approach and identify improvements.

Information management

Testing benefits greatly by reuse, and for this reason it is advisable to create a library of relevant tests and ensure that it is up-to-date. Also record the way in which these tests should be executed and implemented.

No matter how well a test is designed, without good **test data**, the test is useless.
Therefore, take the upkeep of test data seriously. For this purpose, it is important that:
- test data is separated from live data
- data protection regulations are taken into account
- backup and recovery procedures are in place

Interfaces

Testing is **triggered** by the planned test activity in a release plan, test plan or plan for quality assurance.

Inputs to the test and validation processes are:
- the service package and Service Level Package (SLP)
- interface definitions by the service provider
- Service Design package
- release and deployment plans
- acceptance criteria and RFCs

Outputs of the test and validation process are:
- configuration baselines of the test environment
- testing carried out
- results from the tests
- analysis of results
- test incidents, problems, and error records
- improvement ideas (for CSI)
- updated data
- information and knowledge for the knowledge management system

Tests support all release and deployment steps in the Service Transition process. In addition, testing is **related** to Service Design, CSI, Service Operation and Service Strategy.

Metrics
The effectiveness of testing from a **client perspective** (external) can be measured by:
* reduction in the impact of incidents and errors in production that are attributable to a newly transitioned service
* more effective use of resources and involvement from the customer (e.g. user acceptance tests)
* a better understanding by all stakeholders of the roles and responsibilities that relate to the new or changed service

Service provider related (internal):
The test process must be executed as effectively and efficiently as possible. Potential measures to achieve this are:
* decreased effort and costs in setting up the test environment
* decrease in effort required to discover errors and decrease in the number of "repeated errors"
* reuse of test data
* decrease in the percentage of incidents related to errors discovered during testing
* number of known errors documented during prior test phases

Implementation
The greatest **challenge** still lies in the fact that testing is not taken seriously enough by many organizations. As a result, there is often a lack of funding.

Critical success factors are:
* issues are identified in an early stage of the lifecycle
* quality is built into every phase of the lifecycle, for example by using the V model
* reusable test models are designed, and testing provides the proof that all configurations have been built and implemented according to client requirements

Risks are:
* unclear expectations and objectives, lack of understanding that testing is a critical process in relation to quality of service provision
* lack of resources

11.6 Evaluation

Introduction
ITIL defines the evaluation process as:

> **Evaluation** *is a generic process that considers whether the performance of something is acceptable, value for money etc. - and whether it will be proceeded with, accepted into use, paid for etc.*

The **objective** of the ITIL evaluation process is to determine the performance of a service change. That performance is assessed on the basis of the predicted (intended) performance.

Scope
In this section, the scope is limited to the evaluation of new or changed services.

Value for the business
Evaluation delivers an important piece of input for CSI and the future improvement of service development and change management.

Policies, starting points and basic concepts
The following **policies** apply:
- Service designs or service changes are evaluated before the being transitioned
- all deviations between predicted and actual performance are managed by the customer (agent), e.g. acceptance yes/no
- the customer is involved in evaluation

The following **starting points** are important in the execution of the process:
- the unintended effects of a change (and its consequences) must be identified
- a service change is evaluated fairly, consistently, openly and objectively

Activities, methods and techniques
The evaluation process consists of the following activities:
1. planning the evaluation
2. evaluating the predicted performance
3. evaluating the actual performance

Figure 11.12 shows the evaluation process including input and output.

1. Planning the evaluation
When planning an evaluation, the intended and unintended effects of a change are analyzed. The intended effects must meet with the acceptance criteria; the unintended effects are often invisible for a long time and are difficult to predict.

2. Evaluating the predicted performance
Perform a risk assessment based on the customer's requirements (including the acceptance criteria), the predicted performance and the performance model. Send an interim assessment report to change management if the evaluation shows that the predicted performance represents

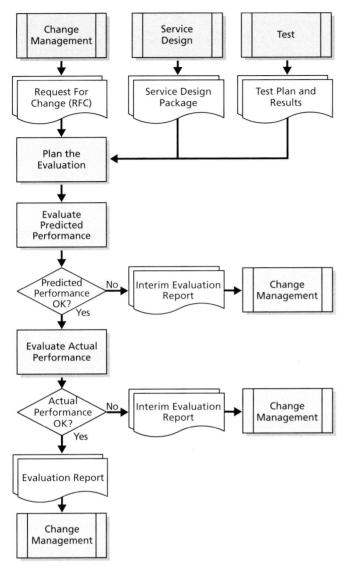

Figure 11.12   Evaluation process (Source: Service Transition was produced by OGC)

an unacceptable risk to the change or deviates from the acceptance criteria. Cease the evaluation activities while awaiting a decision from change management.

3. Evaluating the actual performance

After implementation of the service change, service operation reports on the actual performance of the service. Perform a second risk assessment, again based on the customer's requirements (including the acceptance criteria), the predicted performance and the performance model. Send a new interim assessment report to change management if the evaluation shows that the actual performance represents an unacceptable risk and cease the evaluation activities while awaiting a decision from change management.

Send an evaluation report to change management if the evaluation is approved. Such a report contains a risk profile, a deviations report, a qualification and validation statement (if necessary), and a recommendation (to accept or refuse the change).

Interfaces

Triggers for the evaluation process are:
- an evaluation request from the Service Transition manager or change management
- an evaluation activity in the project plan

Input for the evaluation process:
- the Service Design Package (SDP)
- Service Acceptance Criteria (SACs)
- test reports
- results

The evaluation report represents the **output**.

Metrics

Customer-related KPIs for evaluation are: differences in service performance (minimal and reducing) and the number of incidents (low and reducing).

Internal KPIs for evaluation are: the number of failed designs (zero) and evaluation time (low and reducing).

Implementation

Challenges include:
- delays in the evaluation schedule due to overdue delivery dates of projects and suppliers
- the development of standard performance measurement methods and creating a "risk management culture"
- considering risks from the various perspectives and building insight into the impact of risks on Service Transition

11.7 Knowledge Management

Introduction

The **goal** of knowledge management is to improve the quality of the (management's) decision-making process by ensuring that reliable and secure information is available during the Service Lifecycle.

The **objectives** of knowledge management are, among others:
- to support the service provider in order to improve the efficiency and quality of the services
- to ensure that the service provider's staff have adequate information available

Scope

Knowledge management is used throughout the entire lifecycle. In ITIL version 3 the book on Service Transition explains the basic principles of the process.

Value for the business

Knowledge management is particularly relevant during Service Transition, since relevant and appropriate knowledge is one of the key service elements being transitioned. Specific examples of the application of knowledge management during Service Transition are:
- training and knowledge transfer, intellectual property, compliance information and standards
- the documentation of errors, workarounds and test information

Basic concepts

Knowledge management is often visualized using the **DIKW** structure: **D**ata-**I**nformation-**K**nowledge-**W**isdom, see Figure 11.13.

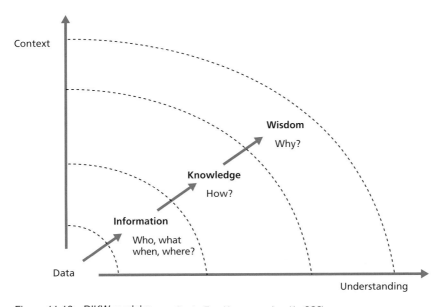

Figure 11.13   DIKW model (Source: Service Transition was produced by OGC)

The basis of the **Service Knowledge Management System (SKMS)** is formed by a considerable amount of data in a central database or configuration management system (CMS) and the CMDB: the CMDB feeds the CMS and the CMS provides input for the SKMS and so supports the decision-making process. However, the scope of the SKMS is broader: information is also stored that relates to matters such as:

* the experience and skills of staff
* information about peripheral matters such as the behavior of users and the performance of the organization
* requirements and expectations of service providers and partners

Activities, methods and techniques

Knowledge management consists of the following activities, methods and techniques:

1. knowledge management strategy
2. knowledge transfer
3. data and information management
4. the use of the SKMS

1. Knowledge management strategy

An organization needs an overall knowledge management strategy. If such a strategy is already in place, the service management knowledge strategy can link into it. Whether there is an existing strategy or not, the strategy must in any case cover the following elements:

* policies, procedures and methods for knowledge management
* the governance model, forthcoming organizational changes, the definition of roles and responsibilities and the financing
* the required technology and other resources
* performance measures
* establishing roles and responsibilities and ongoing funding

The knowledge management strategy also focuses specifically on documenting relevant knowledge, and on the data and information that support this knowledge.

2. Knowledge transfer

The transfer of knowledge is a challenging task, requiring, in the first place, an analysis to determine what the knowledge gap is between the department or person in possession of the knowledge and those in need of the knowledge. Based on the outcome of this analysis, a communication (improvement) plan is formulated to facilitate the knowledge transfer.

There are a number of knowledge transfer techniques, such as:

* **learning styles** - everyone has a different style of learning; the method must therefore be tailored to the target group in question
* **knowledge visualization** - this technique uses visual aids such as photos, diagrams, pictures and "storyboards" for knowledge transfer
* **driving behavior** - consider, for instance, service desk scripts and compulsory fields in software applications
* **seminars, "webinars", advertisements** - it is very effective to organize a special event for the launch of a new service

- **newsletter, newspaper** - regular communication channels such as newsletters or "e-alerts" lend themselves very well to the transfer of knowledge in small steps (incremental instead of "Big Bang")

3. Information management

Data and information management consists of the following activities:

- **establishing data and information requirements** - data and information are often collected without a clear idea of how the information will be used; this can be very expensive so it pays to determine the requirements first
- **definition of information architecture** - to effectively use data, an architecture needs to be created that corresponds with the requirements and the organization; an example of such an architecture can be seen in Figure 11.14
- **establishing data and information management procedures** - once the requirements and architecture are known the procedures for the control and support of the knowledge management can be formulated
- **evaluation and improvement** - as in all processes, evaluation is needed for the purpose of continual improvement

4. Use of the SKMS

Supplying services to customers in different time zones and regions and with different operating hours imposes strenuous requirements on the sharing of knowledge. For this reason the service provider must develop and maintain an SKMS system that is available to all stakeholders and suits all information requirements. An example of such a system can be seen in Figure 11.14.

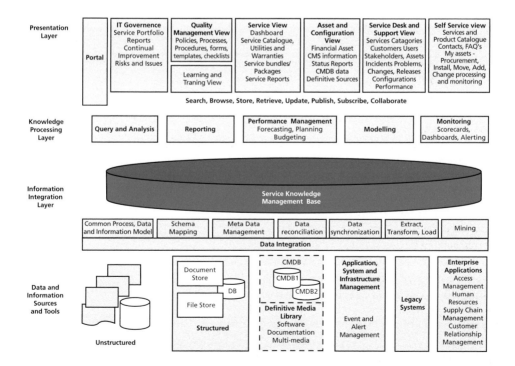

Figure 11.14   SKMS (Source: Service Transition was produced by OGC)

In addition to material for training and knowledge gathering it is useful to:
- incorporate (IT and business) terminology lists and their translation into the system
- document the operational processes and where they interface with IT
- include SLAs and other contracts that can change as a result of a Service Transition
- include known errors, workarounds and process diagrams

Interfaces

Errors discovered by the **service transition staff** are documented and analyzed. Service Transition makes information accessible to Service Operation regarding the consequences of these errors and any workarounds.

Service Transition staff collect information and data that is returned to Service Design via CSI, and feed back information to Service Design if a change in approach is needed.

Operations staff, such as incident management staff and first and second line staff, are the central "collection point" for information about the day-to-day routine of the managed services. It is essential that this information and knowledge is documented and transferred. Staff working in problem management are important users of this knowledge.

Metrics

Typical **indicators** for the contribution of the IT service provider are:
- successful implementation of new and changed services without few knowledge-related errors
- increased knowledge among target group
- higher number of answered questions
- reduced dependence on personnel for knowledge
- faster identification/location of diagnostic information about incidents and problems

The value of knowledge management to the organization is also determined, however difficult this may be.

Indicators relevant for the customer:
- shorter "early life support"
- shorter problem-solving times
- improved user experience
- fewer unnecessary error reports due to more targeted knowledge transfer

Metrics relevant for the service provider:
- the use of the knowledge base, extent of re-use of documentation
- errors reported by personnel or through an audit
- involvement of personnel in discussion and question/answer forums
- degree of reuse of material in documentation
- satisfaction with training courses, newsletters, web briefings etc.

Chapter 12

Functions and Processes in Service Operation

12.1 Event Management

Introduction
ITIL defines an event as follows:

> An **event** can be defined as any detectable or discernible occurrence that has significance for the management of the IT infrastructure or the delivery of IT service and evaluation of the impact a deviation may cause to the services.

Events are typically notifications created by an IT service, CI or monitoring tool. To ensure effective Service Operations, an organization must be aware of the status of its infrastructure and be able to detect deviations from the regular or expected operation. Good monitoring and control systems are required.

The **objective** of event management is to detect events, analyze them and determine the right management action. It provides the entry point for the execution of many Service Operation processes and activities.

Scope
Event management can be applied to any aspect of service management that requires control and can be automated. For example configuration items, security, software license monitoring and environmental conditions (e.g. detecting fire and smoke).

Value for the business
Event management generally has indirect value. Some examples of added value for the business:
- event management provides mechanisms for early detection of incidents
- event management makes it possible for some types of automated activity to be monitored by exception
- if event management is integrated into other service management processes, it may detect status changes or exceptions; this allows the right person or team to respond more quickly, thereby improving the process performance

• event management provides a basis for automated operations; this improves effectiveness and frees up costly human resources for more innovative work

Basic concepts

There are many different event types, such as:
• events that indicate a normal operation, such as a user logging on to use an application
• events that indicate an exception, such as a user who is trying to log on to an application with an incorrect password or a PC scan that reveals the installation of unauthorized software
• events that signify an unusual but not exceptional operation; it may provide an indication that the situation requires a little more supervision For example utilization of a server's memory reaches within five per cent of its highest acceptable level

Activities, methods and techniques

The diagram in Figure 12.1 reflects the flow of event management. It is a high level and generic representation and should be used as a reference point rather than an actual event management flowchart.

The main activities of the event management process are:
• **an event occurs** - events occur all the time, but they are not all detected or registered; it is therefore important for everyone who develops, designs, manages and supports IT services and IT infrastructure to understand what event types must be detected
• **event reporting** - most CIs are designed in such a way that they communicate specific information about themselves in one of the following ways:
  – a management tool probes a device and collects specific data; this is also called "polling"
  – the CI generates a report if certain conditions are met
• **event detection** - a management tool or agent detects an event report and reads and interprets it
• **event filtering** - decides whether or not the event is communicated to a management tool; if not, the device registers the event in a log file and refrains from taking any further action
• **the significance of events (event classification)** - an organization often uses its own classification to establish the importance of an event, but it is useful to use at least the following three broad categories:
  – *informative* - an event that does not require action and is not an exception, e.g. a user logging into an application; is generally stored in the system or service log files and saved for a certain period
  – *alert* - occurs when a service or device reaches a threshold; warns the specified person, process or tool to enable it to bring the situation under control and take the required action to prevent an exception; an example of an alert: memory capacity usage on a server is currently at 65% and increasing; if it reaches 75%, the response times are too long and it exceeds the OLA
  – *Exception* - means that a service or device is behaving abnormally and a failure to comply with an OLA or SLA; examples of exceptions are:
    ◆ a server is down
    ◆ the response time of a standard transaction over a network exceeds 15 seconds
    ◆ part of the network does not respond to routine queries

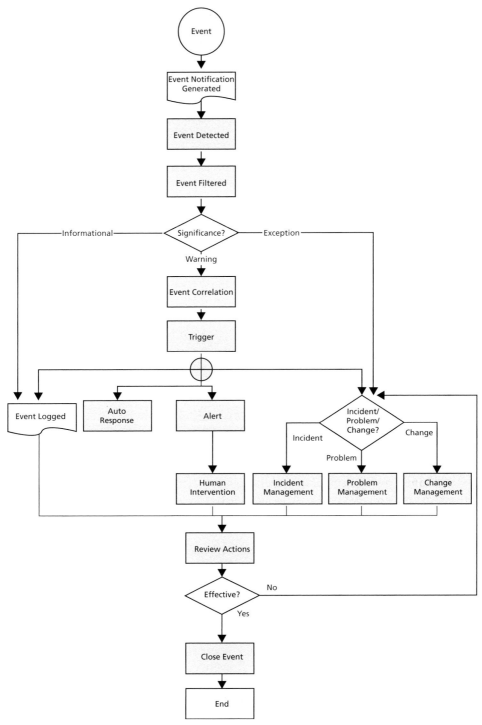

Figure 12.1   The event management process (Source: Service Operation was produced by OGC)

- **event correlation** - establishes the significance of an event and determines what actions should be taken
- **trigger** - if the event is recognized a response is required; the mechanism that initiates that response is called a *trigger*; there are different trigger types, including:
  - *incident triggers* generate a record in the incident management system, thereby starting up the incident management process
  - *scripts* execute specific actions, such as rebooting a device
  - *database triggers* deny a user access to specific records or fields, or create and delete entries in a database
- **response options** - the process provides a number of response options, a combination of which are allowed:
  - event logging
  - automatic response
  - alert and human intervention
  - submitting a *Request for Change (RFC)*
  - opening an incident record
  - open or link to a problem record
- **reviewing actions** - thousands of events are generated every day, which makes it impossible to assess each individual event formally; however, you should check all important events or exceptions to determine whether they have been treated correctly, or whether event types are counted; in many cases this can be done automatically
- **closing the event** - some events remain open until specific actions have been taken, e.g. an event linked to an open incident. However most events are not "opened" or "closed".

Interfaces

Any type of occurrence can **trigger** event management. The key is to determine what events are important and require action. Triggers include:

- exceptions at any level of CI performance defined in the design specifications, Operational Level Agreements or standard processing procedures
- an exception in a business process that is monitored by event management
- a status change in a device or database record
- completion of an automated task or job
- access of an application or database by a user

Event management can **interface** to any process that requires monitoring and control. The most important are incident, problem and change management. In addition, configuration management can use events to determine the current status of a CI in the infrastructure. Events represent a rich source of information for knowledge management systems.

Metrics

Metrics are required for every measuring period, to verify the effectiveness and efficiency of the event management process, e.g.

- number of events by category
- number of events by significance
- number and percentage of events requiring human intervention and whether this was performed

- the number and percentage of events that resulted in incidents or changes
- the number and percentage of each event type per platform or application

Implementation

The main **risks** are:
- being unable to realize sufficient funds
- establishing the right level of filtering
- being unable to maintain momentum during rollout of the required *monitoring agents*

Designing for event management

Event management is the basis for monitoring the performance and availability of a service. This is why availability and capacity management must specify and agree on the precise monitoring targets and mechanisms. Various instruments exist for this purpose:

- **instrumentation** - defines how best to monitor and manage the IT infrastructure and IT services, and creates an appropriate design.

  Determine:
  – what needs to be monitored
  – what monitoring type is required (active or passive, performance or output)
  – when the monitoring should generate an event
  – what type of information needs to be communicated
  – who is the audience

  Mechanisms that need to be designed include:
  – how will events be generated
  – does the CI already have event generation
  – what data will be used to populate the Event Record
  – are events generated automatically or does the CI have to be polled
  – where will events be logged and stored

- **error messages** - important for all components (hardware, software, networks, etc); design all software applications in such a way that they can support event management, e.g. by means of meaningful error messages or codes that clearly indicate what is going wrong, where and the likely causes

- **event detection and alert mechanisms** - for a good design, you need the following:
  – detailed knowledge of the Service Level Requirements of the service that is supported by every CI
  – information on who will support the CI
  – knowledge of the normal and abnormal state of affairs for the CI
  – information that can help determine problems with CIs

12.2 Incident Management

Introduction

The incident management process handles all incidents. These may be failures, questions or queries that are reported by users (generally via a call to the service desk) or technical staff, or that are automatically detected and reported by tools to monitor events.

ITIL defines an incident as:

> An **incident** is an unplanned interruption to an IT service or reduction in the quality of an IT service. Failure of a CI that has not yet affected service is also an incident.

The main **objective** of the incident management process is to resume the regular state of affairs as quickly as possible and minimize the impact on business processes.

Scope

Incident management covers every event that disrupts or might disrupt a service. This means that it includes events reported directly by users, either via the service desk or various tools.

Incidents can also be reported or logged by technical staff, which does not necessarily mean that every event is an incident.

While incidents and *service requests* are both reported to the service desk, they are not the same thing. *service requests* are not service disruptions but user requests for support, delivery, information, advice or documentation.

Value for the business

The value of incident management includes:
- the possibility to track and solve incidents results in reduced downtime for the business; as a result the service is available for longer
- the possibility to align IT operations with the business priorities; the reason is that incident management is able to identify business priorities and distribute resources dynamically
- the possibility to establish potential improvements for services

Incident management is clearly visible to the business, meaning that its value is easier to demonstrate than for other areas in Service Operations. For this reason, it is one of the first processes to be implemented in service management projects.

Basic concepts

The following elements should be taken into account in incident management:
- **Time limits** - Agree on time limits for all phases and use them as targets in Operational Level Agreements (OLAs) and Underpinning Contracts (UCs).
- **Incident models** - An incident model is a way to determine the steps that are necessary to execute a process correctly (in this case, the processing of certain incident types); it means that standard incidents will be handled correctly and within the agreed timeframes.

- **Major incidents** - A separate procedure is required for major incidents, with shorter timeframes and higher urgency; agree what a major incident is and map the entire incident priority system.

People sometimes confuse a major incident with a problem. However, an incident always remains an incident. Its impact or priority may increase, but it never becomes a problem. A problem is the underlying cause of one or more incidents and always remains a separate entity.

Activities, methods and techniques

The incident management process consists of the following steps (Figure 12.2):
1. identification
2. registration
3. classification
4. prioritization
5. diagnosis
6. escalation
7. investigation and diagnosis
8. resolution and recovery
9. closing

An incident is not handled until it is known to exist. This is called **incident identification**. From a business perspective, it is generally unacceptable to wait until a user experiences the impact of an incident and contacts the service desk. The organization must try to monitor all important components, so that failures or potential failures can be detected as early as possible and the incident management process can be initiated. In the perfect situation, incidents are solved before they have an impact on the users.

All incidents must be registered in full, including date and time: **incident registration**. This applies to incidents received via the service desk as well as those that are detected automatically via an event warning system. Register all relevant information relating to the nature of the incident to ensure a complete historical record. If the incident is transferred to other support groups, they will have all of the relevant information at their disposal. You should at least record:
- a unique reference number
- incident category
- incident urgency
- incident priority
- name/ID of the person and/or group who registered the incident
- description of symptoms
- activities undertaken to solve the incident

Use an appropriate **incident classification** coding for registration to record the precise call type. This is important at a later stage when incident types and frequencies are analyzed, to establish trends that can be used for problem management, provider management and other ITSM activities.

When registering an incident, it is possible that the available data are incomplete, misleading or incorrect. It is therefore important to check the classification of the incident and update it while

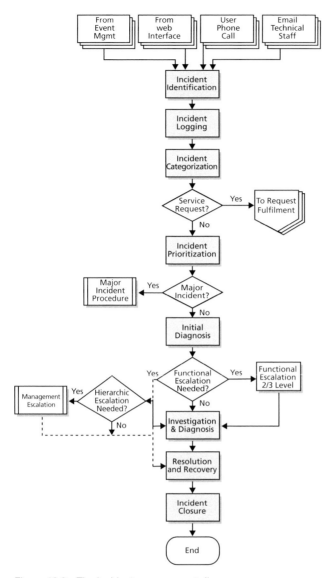

Figure 12.2   The incident management diagram (Source: Service Operation was produced by OGC)

concluding a call. An example of a categorized incident is: software, application, finance suite and purchase order system.

Another important aspect of registering every incident is to allocate the right **priority** code. Support agents and tools use this code to determine how they should handle the incident.
The priority of an incident can usually be determined by establishing its **urgency** (how fast does the business need a solution) and impact. The number of users touched by an incident is often an indication of its **impact**.

When a user reports an incident via the service desk, the service desk agent must try to record the greatest possible number of symptoms of the incident in terms of a first **diagnosis**. He also tries to establish what went wrong and how it should be corrected. Diagnostic scripts and *known error* information can be very useful in this context. If possible, the help desk agent solves the incident immediately and closes the incident.

If this is impossible, the incident is *escalated*.

This can be achieved in two ways:
- **Functional escalation** - If it is clear that the service desk cannot solve the incident (quickly enough), it must be escalated immediately for further support; if the organization has a second line support group and the service desk believes that they can solve the incident, it forwards the incident to the second line; if it is clear that more technical knowledge is required for the incident and the second line support is unable to solve the incident within the agreed timeframe, it must be escalated to the third line support group.
- **Hierarchical escalation** - The relevant IT managers must be warned in the event of more serious incidents (e.g. priority 1 incidents); hierarchical escalation is also used if there are inadequate resources to solve the incident; hierarchical escalation means that the organization calls upon the management higher up in the chain; senior managers are aware of the incident and can take the required steps, such as allocating additional resources or calling upon suppliers.

When handling an incident, each support group **investigates** what went wrong. It also makes a **diagnosis**. Document all these activities in the incident record to ensure that a complete overview of all activities is available.

In case of incidents where the user is only looking for information, the service desk must be able to provide the answer quickly and solve the *service request*.

If a possible solution has been determined, it must be implemented and tested: Solution and recovery. The following actions can then be taken:
- ask the user to perform specific operations on his desktop
- the service desk can execute the solution centrally or use remote software to take control of the user's computer and implement a solution
- ask a supplier to solve the error

The support group returns the incident to the service desk, which **closes the incident**. However, it first checks that the incident has been solved and that the users are satisfied with the solution. It must also close the classification, check that the user is satisfied, update the incident documentation, determine whether the incident could recur, and decide whether action should be taken to prevent this. The incident can then be formally closed.

Information management

Most information used by incident management is provided by incident management tools and incident records. Incident management also has access to the Configuration Management System (CMS). This makes it possible to identify the CIs touched by the incident. The impact of the incident can also be assessed.

Interfaces

Incidents can be **triggered** in many ways. The most common route is via a user who calls the service desk or completes an incident registration form via the internet. However, many incidents are registered more and more often by event management tools.

The processes below have **interfaces** with incident management:
- **Problem management** - Incidents are often caused by underlying problems that must be solved to prevent the incident from recurring. Incident management offers a place to report these problems.
- **Configuration management** - Configuration management provides the data used to identify and track incidents. The configuration management system (CMS) is used, among other things, to identify defective components and determine the impact of an incident. The CMS is also used to identify the users who are impacted by potential problems.
- **Change management** - If a change is necessary to implement a workaround or solution, it is registered as an RFC and executed by change management. Incident management is able to track and solve incidents resulting from inappropriate changes.
- **Capacity management** - Incident management triggers performance monitoring if a performance problem occurs. Capacity management can offer workarounds for incidents.
- **Availability management** - Availability management uses data from incident management to determine the availability of IT services, and establishes where the incident lifecycle can be improved.
- **Service Level Management (SLM)** - SLM monitors the agreements with customers concerning the support to be provided. Incident management reports to SLM. This process, for instance, can evaluate SLAs objectively and regularly. SLM establish acceptable service levels within which incident management must work.

Metrics

Metrics make it possible to assess the effectiveness, efficiency and operation of the incident management process. Examples of metrics are:
- the total number of incidents
- the number and percentage of major incidents
- the average cost per incident
- the number and percentage of incorrectly allocated incidents
- the percentage of incidents handled within the agreed timeframe

Implementation

Incident management has the following **challenges**:
- to detect incidents as quickly as possible
- to convince all staff (both technical teams and users) that all incidents must be registered and encourage them to use web-based options to solve incidents themselves
- the availability of information about problems and known errors, enabling incident management staff to learn from previous incidents and track the status of solutions
- integration with the configuration management system to determine the relationship between CIs and refer to the history of CIs when providing first line support

- integration with the service level management process; this helps incident management to determine the impact and priority of incidents correctly and to define and execute escalation procedures

The following **Critical Success Factors** (CSFs) are vital to successful incident management:
- a good service desk
- clearly defined SLA targets
- adequate support staff that is customer-oriented and technically qualified, and possesses the right competencies at all process levels
- integrated support tools to control and manage the process
- OLAs and UCs to influence and shape the behavior of all support personnel

Risks for successful incident management are:
- being overwhelmed by incidents that cannot be handled within an acceptable timeframe due to lack of well-trained resources
- incidents that make no progress because inadequate support tools fail to give warning or report progress
- lack of adequate information sources due to unsuitable tools or lack of integration
- no coinciding objectives or actions due to unaligned or nonexistent OLAs or UCs

12.3 Request Fulfilment

Introduction

ITIL uses the term service request as a general description for the varying requests that users submit to the IT department.

> A **service request** is a request from a user for information, advice, a standard change, or access to a service.

For example, a service request can be a request for a password change or the additional installation of a software application on a certain work station. Because these requests occur on a regular basis and involve little risk, it is better that they are handled in a separate process.

Request fulfilment (implementation of requests) processes service requests from the users. The **objectives** of the request fulfilment process are:
* to offer users a channel through which they can request and receive services; to this effect an agreed approval and qualification process must exist
* to provide users and customers with information about the availability of services and the procedure for obtaining these services
* to supply the components of standard services (for instance, licenses and software media)
* to assist with general information, complaints or comments

Scope

The process for handling requests depends on the nature of the request. In most cases the process can be divided into a series of activities that need to be completed. Some organizations treat the service requests as a special type of incident. However, there is an important difference between an incident and a service request. An incident is usually an unplanned event, whereas a service request tends to be something that can and must be planned.

Value for the business

The value of request fulfilment is the ability to offer fast and effective access to standard services that the business can use to improve the productivity or the quality of the business services and products.

Request fulfilment reduces the amount of "red tape" in requesting and receiving access to existing or new services. This reduces the cost for the supply of these services.

Basic concepts

Many service requests recur on a regular basis. This is why a process flow can be devised in advance, stipulating the phases needed to handle the requests, the individuals or support groups involved, time limits and escalation paths. The service request is usually handled as a standard change.

Activities, working methods and techniques

Request fulfilment consists of the following activities, methods and techniques:

- **menu selection** - by means of request fulfilment, users can submit their own service request via a link to service management tools; in the ideal situation the user will be offered a menu via a web interface, so that they can select and enter the details of a service request
- **financial approval** - most service requests have financial implications; the cost for handling a request must first be determined; it is possible to agree fixed prices for standard requests and give instant authorization for these requests; in all other cases the cost must first be estimated, after which the user must give permission
- **fulfillment** - the actual fulfillment activity depends on the nature of the service request; the service desk can handle simple requests, whereas others must be forwarded to specialist groups or suppliers
- **closure** - once the service request has been completed the service desk will close off the request

Interfaces

Most requests are **triggered** by a user who rings the service desk or a user who completes a request form on-screen. Many service requests come in via the service desks and can be handled through the incident management process. Some organizations choose to handle all requests via this route, others prefer a separate process.

There is also a strong **link** between request fulfillment, release management, asset management and configuration management, because some requests deal with the roll-out of new or improved components that can be implemented automatically.

Request fulfilment is dependent on information from the following **sources**:
- service requests
- Requests for Change
- service portfolio
- security policy

Metrics

The metrics required to evaluate the efficiency and effectiveness of request fulfilment are:
- the total number of service requests
- the breakdown of service requests by phase
- the size of the current backlog of outstanding service requests
- the average time for handling each type of service request
- the number and percentage of service requests that are handled within the agreed time
- the average cost per type of service request
- the level of customer satisfaction in respect of the handling of service requests

Implementation

Request fulfilment is faced with the following **challenges**:
- to clearly define and document the type of request that is being handled in the request fulfilment process, so that all parties know what the scope is

- to establish front-end options, so that users can make their own link to the request fulfilment process

Request fulfilment is dependent on the following **critical success factors**:
- there must be agreement about which services are standardized and who is authorized to request them; there must also be agreement about the cost of these services
- publication of these services for the benefit of the users, as part of the service catalogue
- there must be a definition of a standard fulfillment procedure for each service being requested
- there must be a <u>single</u> point of contact for requesting the service; this is often done via the service desk or via an internet request, but can also be made via an automated request directly in the request fulfilment procurement system
- self-service tools are needed to offer a front-end interface to users; it is important that this interface can communicate with the back-end fulfillment tools

Request fulfilment has the following **risks**:
- If the scope is ill-defined, people will not know exactly what the process is supposed to handle.
- Poorly designed or implemented user interfaces may make it difficult for users to submit requests.
- Poorly designed or realized back-end fulfillment processes may result in the system being unable to handle the number or type of requests being submitted.
- Insufficient monitoring capacity may result in no accurate metrics being collected.

12.4 Problem Management

Introduction
ITIL defines a problem as follows:

> *A **problem** is the cause of one or more incidents.*

Problem management is responsible for the control of the lifecycle of all problems. The primary **objective** of problem management is to prevent problems and incidents, eliminate repeating incidents and minimize the impact of incidents that cannot be prevented.

Scope
Problem management comprises all the activities needed to diagnose the underlying cause of incidents and to find a solution for these problems. It must also ensure that the solution is implemented via the correct control procedures, in other words through the use of change management and release management.

Value for the business
Problem management works together with incident management and change management to ensure improvements in the availability and quality of the IT service provision. When incidents are resolved the solution is registered. At a given moment this information is used to accelerate the incident handling and identify permanent solutions. This reduces the number of incidents and the handling time, resulting in shorter disruption times and fewer disruptions to the business critical systems.

Basic concepts
Many problems are unique and need to be handled separately. However, it is possible that some incidents may occur more than once as a result of underlying problems.

ITIL defines a known error as:

> *A **known error** is a problem that has a documented root cause and a workaround.*

ITIL defines a workaround as:

> ***Workaround**: reducing or eliminating the impact of an incident or problem for which a full resolution is not yet available.*

In addition to creating a Known Error Database (KEDB) for faster diagnoses, the creation of a **problem model** for the handling of future problems may be useful. Such a standard model supports with the steps that need to be taken, the responsibilities of people involved and the necessary timescales.

Activities, methods and techniques

Problem management consists of two important processes:
- **reactive problem management** - performed by Service Operation
- **proactive problem management** - initiated by Service Operation, but usually managed by CSI (Continual Service Improvement) (see also Chapter 13)

Reactive problem management consists of the following activities (Figure 12.3):
- identification
- registration
- classification
- prioritization
- investigation and diagnosis
- decide on workarounds
- identification of known errors
- resolution
- conclusion
- review
- correction of errors found

Identification of problems is carried out using the following methods:
- The service desk suspects or identifies an unknown cause of one or more incidents. This results in a problem registration. It may also be clear straightaway that an incident was caused by a major problem. In this case a problem registration takes place immediately.
- Analysis of an incident by the technical support group reveals that there is an underlying problem.
- There is automatic tracing of an infrastructural or application error, whereby event or alert tools automatically create an incident registration that highlights the need for a problem registration.
- The supplier reports a problem that needs to be resolved.
- Analysis of incidents takes place as part of corrective problem management. This results in a problem registration so that the underlying cause can be investigated further.

Analyze incident and problem data on a regular basis in order to identify trends. To this effect an efficient and detailed classification of incidents and problems is required, as well as regular reporting of patterns and problem areas.

Irrespective of the identification method, all details of the problem must be registered (**problem registration**), so that a comprehensive historic report is created. The information must be date and time stamped, so that proper control and escalation are possible.

Problems must be classified in the same way as incidents, so that the true nature of the problem can be established quickly and easily. **Problem classification** provides useful management information.

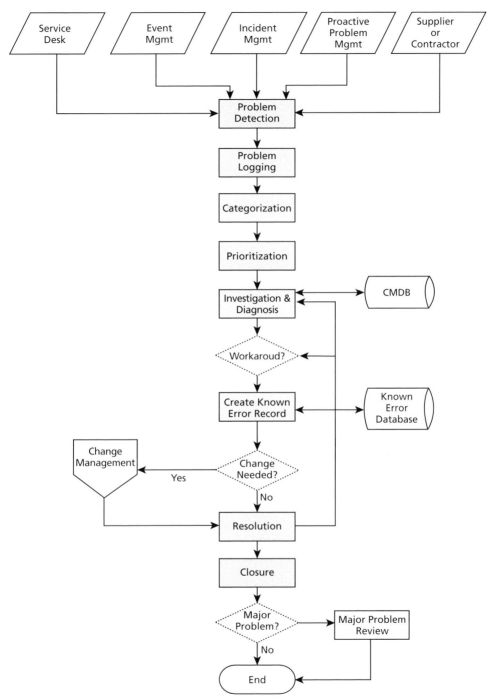

Figure 12.3   Problem management diagram (Based on OGC ITIL V3 material)

As is the case for incidents, problems must also be given a **priority** in the same manner and for the same reasons. In this context also take into account the frequency and impact of the related incidents and the seriousness of the problems. Examples of such considerations are:
• Can the system be repaired or does it need to be replaced?
• What are the costs?
• How many people, and with what expertise are needed to resolve the problem?
• How much time is needed to resolve the problem?
• How big is the problem?

In order to find the underlying cause of the problem and make a **diagnosis**, an **investigation** must be performed. The speed and nature of this investigation depend on the impact, seriousness and urgency of the problem. Use the proper level of resources and expertise to find a solution.

It is often useful to reproduce the problem, so that it becomes clear what went wrong. Next you can use different methods to determine what the best solution is. This is best done by using a test system that reflects production.

Many problem analysis, diagnosis and solution techniques are available, including:
• chronological analysis
• Pain Value Analysis
• Kepner-Tregoe
• brainstorming
• Ishikawa diagrams
• Pareto analysis

In some cases a temporary solution, a **workaround**, is possible for incidents that were caused by a problem. It is important, however, that the problem reporting remains open and that the details about the workaround are included in the problem reporting.

As soon as the diagnosis has been made, and especially if a workaround has been found, the **identified known errors** must be listed in a known error report and placed in the Known Error Database. Should other incidents and problems occur they can be identified and the service can be resumed more quickly.

As soon as a **solution** has been found it should, ideally, be applied to resolve the problem. In reality, there are preventative measures to make sure that the solution does not cause further problems. If a change in functionality is needed a *Request for Change* is required that must follow the steps of the change management process.

If the change has been completed and successfully evaluated and the solution has been applied, the problem report can formerly be **closed off**, as can the related incident reports that are still outstanding. Remember to check whether the report contains a full description of all the events.

After every **major problem** a **review** must be performed to learn lessons for the future. In particular the review must assess:

- what went well
- what went wrong
- what can be done better in future
- how the same problem can be prevented from recurring
- whether a third party is responsible and whether any follow-up actions are needed

It is very rare that new applications, systems or software releases do not contain **errors**. In most cases a priority system is used during testing that removes the most serious errors, but it is possible that minor errors are not corrected.

Information management

The *CMS* contains details on all the components of the IT infrastructure and on the relationship between these components. It is a valuable source for problem diagnosis and for the evaluation of the impact of problems.

The purpose of a **Known Error Database** (KEDB) is to store knowledge about incidents and problems and how they were remedied, so that a quicker diagnosis and solution can be found if further incidents and problems occur.

The known error registration must contain the exact details about the error and the symptoms that occurred, together with the exact details of a workaround or solution that can be implemented to resume the service or resolve the problem.

It may be that there is no business case for a permanent solution for certain problems. For instance, if the problem does not cause serious disruptions, a workaround already exists and the costs of resolving the problem exceed the advantages of a permanent solution, problem management may decide to tolerate the problem.

Like the configuration management system (CMS), the KEDB is part of a larger Service Knowledge Management System (SKMS) (Figure 12.4). The Section on "Service Transition" (Chapter 11) gives more information about the SKMS.

Interfaces

The majority of problem registrations are **triggered** as a response to one or more incidents, especially by service desk staff. Other problem registrations and corresponding known errors are triggered during testing, especially during so-called user acceptance tests that determine whether a release will proceed despite some known errors.

The following processes **interface** with problem management:

- **Service Transition**:
  - *change management* - problem management ensures that all solutions and workarounds for which change is necessary are implemented in a CI via an RFC; change management monitors the progress of these changes and keeps problem management informed

    – *configuration management* - problem management uses the CMS to identify wrong CIs and to determine the impact of problems and solutions

    – *release and deployment management* - is responsible for the rollout of problem fixes in a production environment

- **Service Design**:
  - *availability management* - helps determine how the disruption time can be minimized and how the production time (*uptime*) can be increased; a lot of the management information in problem management is passed on to availability management
  - *capacity management* - ensures the optimum use of resources and provides problem management with important information such as capacity registrations and performance matters; capacity management also supports the application of corrective measures
  - *IT Service Continuity Management (ITSCM)* - problem management acts as a starting point for ITSCM: a problem is not resolved if it does not have an important impact on the business

- **Continual Service Improvement**:
  - *service level management* - incidents and problems influence the quality of IT services provided by SLM; problem management contributes to improving service levels and the management information provided by it is used as the basis for some SLA review components

- **Service Strategy**:
  - *financial management* - problem management provides management information about the cost of resolving and preventing problems; in this way the information can be used as input for budgeting and accounting systems and Total Cost of Ownership calculations

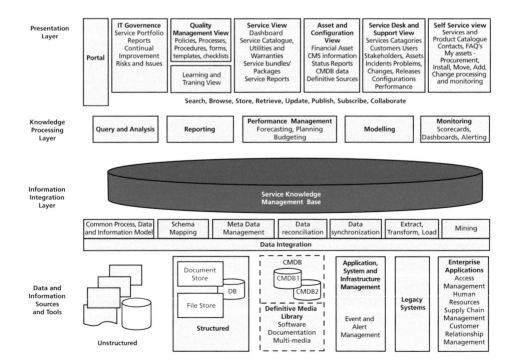

Figure 12.4   The Service Knowledge Management System (Based on OGC ITIL V3 material)

Metrics

The following metrics are used to evaluate the efficiency, effectiveness and implementation of the problem management process:
- the total number of problems that were registered in the period
- the percentage of problems that were resolved within SLA targets (and the percentage of problems that were not solved)
- the number and percentage of problems for which more time was needed to resolve them
- the backlog of outstanding problems and the trend (static, decreasing, increasing)
- the average costs for handling a problem
- the number of major problems (outstanding, closed and backlog)
- the percentage of successful major problem reviews
- the number of known errors added to the KEDB
- the accuracy percentage of the KEDB (from checks of the database)

Implementation

Problem management is highly dependent on the formulation of an effective incident management process and the use of the proper tools. These help to identify problems as quickly as possible.

12.5 Access Management

Introduction
Access management grants authorized users the right to use a service, but denies unauthorized users access. Some organizations also call it "rights management" or "identity management".

Scope
Access management ensures that users have access to a service, but it does not guarantee that access is always available at the agreed times. This is handled by availability management.

Access management can be initiated via a number of mechanisms, such as the service desk by means of a *service request*.

Value for the business
Access management has the following value:
• controlled access to services enables the organization to maintain confidentiality of its information more effectively
• staff have the right access level to do their jobs properly
• the risk of errors during data entry or the use of a vital service by an unqualified user is lower
• there is the option to withdraw access rights more easily when it is necessary access may be necessary for compliance (e.g. SOX, HIPAA, CobiT)

Basic concepts
Access management has the following basic concepts:
• **access** - refers to the level and scope of the functionality of a service or data that a user is allowed to use
• **identity** - refers to the information about the persons who the organization distinguish as individuals; establishes their status in the organization
• **rights** (also called privileges) - refers to the actual settings for a user; which service (group) they are allowed to use; typical rights include reading, writing, executing, editing and deleting
• **services or service groups** - most users have access to multiple services; it is therefore more effective to grant every user or group of users access to an entire series of services that they are allowed to use simultaneously
• **directory services** - refers to a specific type of tool used to manage access and rights

Activities, methods and techniques
Access (or limitation of access) can be requested via a number of mechanisms, such as:
• a standard request generated by the human resources department; this generally occurs when someone is hired, promoted or leaves the company
• a *Request for Change (RFC)*
• an RFC submitted via the request fulfilment process
• execution of an authorized script or option

Access management consists of the following activities:
• **Verification** - Access management must verify every access request for an IT service from two perspectives:

– Is the user requesting access truly the person he says he is?

– Does the user have a legitimate reason to use the service?

- **Granting rights** - Access management does not decide who gets access to what IT services; it only executes the policy and rules defined by Service Strategy and Service Design.

  The more groups and roles exist, the greater the chance of a role conflict occurring. In this context, role conflicts refer to a situation in which two specific roles or groups allocated to a user can cause trouble due to conflicting interests. One example is that one role requires access while the other forbids it.

- **Monitoring identity status** - User roles may vary over time, with an impact on their service needs; examples of what may change a role are: job changes, promotion, dismissal, retirement or death.

- **Registering and monitoring access** - Access management does not only respond to requests; it must also ensure that the rights it has granted are used correctly.

  This is why access monitoring and control must be included in the monitoring activities of all technical and application management functions as well as all Service Operation processes.

- **Revoking or limiting rights** - In addition to granting rights to use a service, access management is also responsible for withdrawing those rights; but it cannot make the actual decision.

Information management

The **identity** of a user is the information that distinguishes him as an individual and verifies his status in the organization. The following data may be used, for instance:

- name
- contact details such as phone number and (e-mail) address
- physical documentation, such as driver's license and passport
- numbers referring to a document or entry in a database, such as social security number and driver's license number
- biometric information, such as fingerprints, DNA and voice recognition patterns

While every **user** has a separate identity and every IT service can be considered an individual identity, it often makes sense to **group** them for easier management. Sometimes the terms user profile, user template or **user role** are used to describe this type of grouping.

Most organizations have a standard collection of services for all individual users regardless of their position or job. But some users have a special role. For instance, in addition to the standard services a user may also fulfill a marketing management role for which he needs access to several special marketing and financial modeling tools and data.

Interfaces

Access management is **triggered** by a user's request for access to a service (group). Such a request may originate with:

- an RFC
- a service request
- a request from the Human Resources (HR) department
- a request from a manager or department fulfilling an HR role or who has made a decision to use a service for the first time

Access management has **relationships** with various other processes. Since every access request for a service represents a change, change management plays an important part in controlling the access requests.

Service level management monitors the agreements concerning access to each service. This includes the criteria for who has access to a service, the costs and the access level granted to different types of users.

Access management also has a close relationship with configuration management. The CMS can be used for data storage and be studied to determine the current access details.

Metrics
Metrics used to measure the effectiveness and efficiency of access management are:
- the number of access requests (*service requests* and RFCs)
- the number of times access has been granted by a service, user or department
- the number of incidents required to reset access rights
- the number of incidents caused by incorrect access settings

Implementation
The **conditions** for successful access management include:
- the possibility to verify a user's identity
- the possibility to verify the identity of the person or entity granting permission
- the possibility to grant several access rights to an individual user
- a database of all users and the rights they have been granted

12.6 Monitoring and Control

Introduction

The measuring and control of services is based on a continuous cycle of monitoring, reporting and initiating action. We will discuss this cycle in detail because it is essential to the supply, support and improvement of services.

Basic concepts

Three terms play a leading role in monitoring and control:
- monitoring
- reporting
- control

Monitoring refers to the observation of a situation to discover changes that occur over time.

Reporting refers to the analysis, production and distribution of the output of the activity that is being monitored.

Control refers to the management of the usefulness or behavior of a device, system or service. There are three conditions for control:
1. the action must ensure that the behavior conforms to a defined standard or norm
2. the conditions leading to the action must be defined, understood and confirmed
3. the action must be defined, approved and suitable for these conditions

Activities, methods and techniques

The monitoring/control cycle

The best-known model for the description of control is the monitoring/control cycle. Although it is a simple model it has many complex applications in IT service management. In this section we describe the basic concepts of the model. Next we will show how important these concepts are for the service management lifecycle. Figure 12.5 reflects the basic principles of control.

This cycle measures an activity and its benefits by means of a pre-defined norm or standard to determine whether the results are within the target values for performance or quality. If this is not the case, action must be taken to improve the situation or resume the normal performance.

There are two types of monitoring/control cycles:
- **Open cycle systems** are designed for a specific activity, irrespective of the environmental conditions; making a backup, for instance, can be initiated at a specified moment and be completed regardless of other conditions.
- **Closed cycle systems** - Monitoring of an environment and responding to changes in this environment; if, in a network, the network transactions exceed a certain number, the control system will redirect the "traffic" via a backup circuit in order to regulate the network transactions.

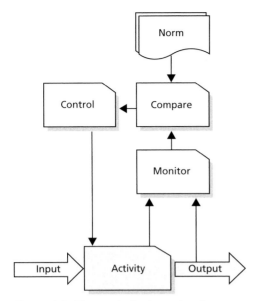

Figure 12.5   The monitoring/control cycle (Source: Service Operation was produced by OGC)

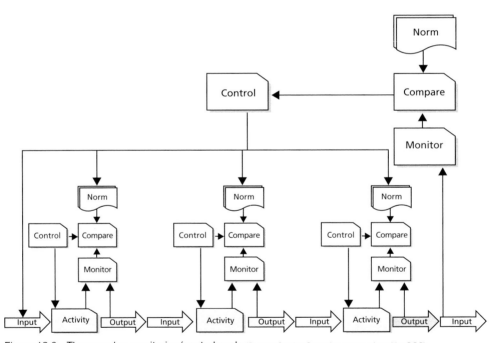

Figure 12.6   The complex monitoring/control cycle (Source: Service Operation was produced by OGC)

Figure 12.6 shows a **complex monitoring/control cycle**: a process that consists of three important activities. Each activity has an input and output and in turn this output is the input for the next activity. Every activity is controlled by its own monitoring/control cycle with the aid of a series of norms for that specific activity. A coordinating monitoring/control cycle monitors the entire process and ensures that all norms are suitable and are being complied with.

The monitoring/control cycle concept can be used to manage:
- the performance of activities in a process or procedure; in theory every activity and its related output can be measured to ensure that problems in the process are identified before the process is completed
- the effectiveness of the process or procedure as a whole
- the performance of a device or a series of devices

Answer the following questions to determine how the concept of monitoring/control cycles can be used in service management:
- How do we define what we need to monitor?
- How do we monitor (manually or automated)?
- What is a normal process?
- What do we depend on for a normal process?
- What happens before we receive the input?
- How often do we need to measure?

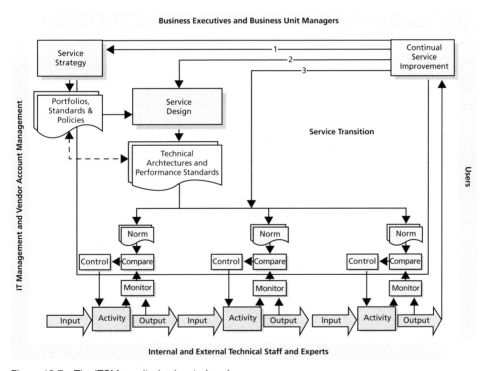

Figure 12.7   The ITSM monitoring/control cycle (Source: Service Operation was produced by OGC)

Figure 12.7 shows an **IT service management monitoring/control cycle** and shows how the control of a process or the components of that process can be used to provide a service.

There are two levels of monitoring:
- **internal monitoring and control** - focuses on activities and items that take place within a team or department, for instance a service desk manager who monitors the number of calls to determine how many members of staff are needed to answer the telephones
- **external monitoring and control** - the server management team monitors (on behalf of other groups) the CPU performance on important servers and keeps the workload under control; this allows essential applications to perform within the target values set by the application management

This distinction is important. If Service Operation focuses only on internal monitoring the infrastructure is well organized, but the organization has no idea what the quality of the services is or how they can improve this quality. If the organization focuses only on external monitoring it understands how bad the quality of the service is, but it does not know what causes this or how it can change this. In practice, most organizations use a combination of internal and external monitoring, but in many cases they are not linked.

Monitoring without control is irrelevant and ineffective. Monitoring must always be aimed at achieving the service and operational objectives. If, therefore, there is no clear reason for the monitoring of a system or service, there should be no monitoring.

In order for an organization to determine what it wants to monitor, therefore, it must first define the desired outcome: **monitoring and control objectives**. Ideally this process should start with the definition of *Service Level Requirements*. These will specify how the customers and users measure the quality of the service. In addition, these Service Level Requirements provide the input for the Service Design processes.
Availability management, for instance, will determine how the infrastructure must be configured to achieve the fewest possible disruptions.

An important part in determining what Service Operation will be monitoring and how it will get the processes under control is identifying the stakeholders of each service. A stakeholder can be defined as being anyone who has an interest in IT services being successfully supplied and received. Each stakeholder will consider, from his own perspective, what is necessary to provide or receive an IT service. Service Operation must know what these perspectives are in order to determine what needs to be monitored and what needs to be done with the output.

Tools
There are different types of monitoring tools, whereby the situation determines which **type of monitoring** is used:
- **Active versus passive monitoring**:
  - *Active monitoring* refers to the continuous "interrogation" of a device or system in order to determine its status.
  - *Passive monitoring* is more commonly known and refers to generating and passing on events to a device or monitoring agent.
- **Reactive versus proactive monitoring**:
  - *Reactive monitoring* is designed to request an action after a certain type of event or disruption.

- *Proactive monitoring* is used to trace patterns of events that indicate that a system or device may break down. Proactive monitoring is generally used in more mature environments, where these patterns can be detected earlier.
- **Continuous measuring versus exception-based measuring**:
  - *Continuous measuring* is aimed at the real-time monitoring of a system to ensure that it complies with a certain performance norm. As an example, an application server is available 99% of the agreed access time.
  - *Exception-based measuring* does not measure the current performance of a service or system, but discovers and reports exceptions. An example is the generation of an event if a transaction is not completed. It is used for less essential systems or for systems where costs are important.
- **Performance versus output** - There is an important distinction between reporting on the performance of components, teams or a department (*performance*) and reporting that shows that the service quality objectives (*output*) have been achieved. Service Operation carries out both types of monitoring, but ITIL focuses mainly on performance monitoring.

Metrics

It is important that organizations have robust measuring techniques and values that support their objectives. In this context, the following concepts are relevant:

- **Measuring** - Refers to all techniques that evaluate the scope, dimension or capacity of an item in relation to a standard or unit. Measuring is only useful when it is possible to measure the actual output of a system, function or process against a standard or desired level. For instance, a server must be capable of processing a minimum of 100 standard transactions per minute.
- **Metrics** - Concern the quantitative, periodic evaluation of a process, system or function, together with the procedures and tools that are used for this evaluation, and the procedures for interpreting them. This definition is important because it not only specifies what must be measured, but also how the measuring must be done, what the acceptable lower and upper performance limits are and what actions are necessary in the case of normal performance or an exception.
- **Key Performance Indicators (KPIs)** - Refer to a specific, agreed performance level to measure the effectiveness of an organization or process. KPIs are unique to each organization and are related to specific input, output and activities.

12.7 IT Operations

Introduction
To deliver the services as agreed with the customer, the service provider will first have to manage the technical infrastructure that is used to deliver the services. If no new customers are added and no new services have to be introduced, if no incidents occur in existing services, and if no changes have to be made in existing services - even then, the IT organization will be busy with a range of Service Operations. These activities focus on actually delivering the agreed service as agreed.

Operations bridge
The operations bridge is a central point of coordination that manages various events and routine operational activities, and reports on the status or performance of technological components.

An operations bridge brings together all vital observation points in the IT infrastructure so that they can be monitored and managed with minimum effort in a central location.

The operations bridge combines a great many activities, such as console management, event handling, first line network management and support outside office hours. In some organizations, the service desk is a part of the operations bridge.

Activities, methods and techniques

Job scheduling
IT operations executes standard routines, queries or reports that technical and application management teams have handed over as part of the service or of routine daily maintenance tasks.

Backup and restore
Essentially, backup and restore is a component of good continuity planning. Service Design must therefore ensure that there are good backup strategies for every service. Service Transition must ensure that they are tested in the right way.

Furthermore, some organizations - such as financial service providers and listed companies - must implement and monitor a formal backup and restore strategy as required by the law and regulations. The precise requirements vary per country and industry.

An organization must protect its data, which includes **backup** and storage of data in reserved locations where it is protected and, if necessary, accessible.

A complete backup strategy must be agreed with the business, which must cover the following elements:
- what data should the backup include, and how often must it be made?
- how many generations of data must be retained?
- the backup type and the checkpoints that are used
- the locations used for storage and the rotation schedule
- transport methods

- required tests
- planned recovery point; the point to which data must be recovered after an IT service resumes
- planned recovery time; the maximum allowed time to resume an IT service after an interruption
- how will it be checked that the backups are functional when they need to be restored?

In all cases, the IT operations staff must be qualified in backup and restore procedures. These procedures must be documented properly in the procedure manual of IT operations. Where necessary, you should include specific requirements or targets in OLAs or UCs, and specify user or customer obligations and activities in the relevant SLA.

A **restore** can be initiated from several sources, varying from an event indicating data corruption to a *service request* from a user or customer. A restore may be necessary in case of:
- corrupt data
- lost data
- a calamity plan / IT service continuity situation
- historical data required for forensic investigation

Print and output

Many services provide their information in **print** or electronic form (**output**). The service provider must ensure that the information ends up in the right places, correctly and in the right form. Information security often plays a part in this respect.

The customer should notify the service provider in time of a temporarily increased need for print and output.

Laws and regulations may play an important part in print and output. Archiving important or sensitive data is particularly important.

Service providers are generally deemed to be responsible for maintaining the infrastructure to make the print and output available to the customer (printers, storage). In this case, that task must be laid down in the SLA.

12.8 Service Desk

A service desk is a **functional unit** with associates involved in differing service events. These service events come in by phone, internet or infrastructure, events which are reported automatically.

The service desk is a very important element of the IT department of an organization. It must be the only contact point for IT users and it deals with all incidents and service requests. The associates often use software tools to record and manage all events.

Justification and role of a service desk

Many organizations consider a service desk the best means for a first line support in case of IT problems. A service desk offers the following benefits:

- improved customer service, better perception of the service on the part of the client and greater client satisfaction
- greater access through one single contact, communication and information point
- client and user requests are resolved better and quicker
- improved cooperation and communication
- less negative impact on business
- better managed and controlled infrastructure
- better use of resources through IT support and increased productivity of company associates
- more meaningful management information for decisions concerning support

Service desk objectives

The primary purpose of the service desk is to resume "normal service" to the user as soon as possible. This may be resolving a technical error, but also filling a service request or answering a question.

Organizational structure of a service desk

There are many ways to organize a service desk. The solution will be different for each organization. The most important options are:

- local service desk
- centralized service desk
- virtual service desk
- 24-hour service
- specialized service desk groups

These options are elaborated further below. In practice, an organization will implement a structure that combines a number of these options in order to satisfy the needs of the business.

The **local service desk** is located at or physically close to the users it is supporting. Because of this, communications are often much smoother and the visible presence is attractive for some users. However, a local service desk is expensive and may be inefficient if the amount of service events does not really justify a service desk.

There may be a few sound reasons for maintaining a local service desk:

- linguistic, cultural and political differences
- different time zones

- specialized groups of users
- existence of adjusted or special services for which specialized knowledge is required
- status of the users

The number of service desks can be reduced by installing them at one single location (or by reducing the number of local service desks). In that case, the associates are assigned to one or more **centralized service desk** structures. This may be less expensive and more efficient, because fewer associates can deal with the service events (calls), while the level of knowledge of the service desk is bound to increase.

By using technology, specifically the internet, and the use of support tools, it is possible to create the impression of a centralized service desk, whereas the associates are in fact spread out over a number of geographic or structural locations: this is the **virtual service desk**.

Some international organizations like to combine two or more geographically spread out service desks in order to offer a **24/7 service**. In this way, a service desk in Asia, for example, can deal with incoming service events during standard office hours, whereby at the end of that period, a service desk in Europe takes care of any outstanding events. That desk deals with those service events together with its own events and at the end of the day, responsibility is transferred to a service desk in America, which then returns responsibility to the Asian service desk, thus completing the cycle.

It may be attractive for some organizations to create specialized **service desk groups**, so that incidents relating to a specific IT service are routed straight to the specialized group. In this way, incidents can be resolved more promptly.

The **environment** of the service desk must be carefully selected, preferably a location where workstations have adequate space with natural light. A quiet environment with good acoustics is equally important, because the associates should not be bothered by each other's telephone conversations. Ergonomic office furniture is also important.

Service desk personnel

Care should be taken that a sufficient **number of associates** are available, so that the service desk can meet the business demand at any time. The number of service events can, of course, strongly fluctuate from day-to-day and hour to hour. An organization will take peak hours and quiet periods into account.

A decision should be made as to which skill levels are necessary for the service desk personnel. To determine the required **skill level**, weigh the arranged resolution times against the complexity of the **supported systems**, and "the outlay the business is willing to pay". The optimal and most efficient approach is generally a first line support via the service desk, which records the service event and transmits escalations promptly to more expert second-level and third-level support groups.

If the skill levels have been established, the service desk must be directed in a way that the associates receive and maintain the necessary skills. During all work hours, there has to be a good mix of skills present.

It is essential that all service desk associates receive sufficient **training**. All new associates must follow a formal introduction program. The precise content of it will vary with each new associate, subject to the existing expertise and experience.

In order to keep the service desk associates up-to-date, a program is necessary so that they can be kept informed of new developments, services and techniques. The timing of these type of activities is essential, because they should not impact the normal tasks. Many service desks organize short training sessions during quiet periods when the associates are handling fewer service events.

It is very important that all IT associates realize the importance of the service desk and the people working there. A considerable attrition of associates has a disturbing effect and can lead to an incoherent service. Thus the managers have to engage in efforts **to retain the associates**.

Many organizations find it meaningful to appoint a number of so-called **super users** in the user community. They function as contact persons with the IT organization in general and the service desk in particular.

Organizations can provide the super users extra training and use them as communication channel. They can be asked to filter requests and certain problems on behalf of the user community. If an important service or component is down, causing an extra burden for many users, this may lead to many reactions coming in.

Super users do not provide support for the entire IT. In many cases, the super user will offer support only for a specific application, module or business unit. As a business user a super user often has thorough knowledge of important company processes and knows how services are working in practice. It is very useful to share this with the service desk, so that it can offer better quality services in the future.

Metrics

In order to evaluate the performance of the service desk at regular time intervals, **metrics** must be established. In this way, the maturity, efficiency, effectiveness and potentials can be established and the service desk actions improved.

Metrics for the performance of a service desk must be selected carefully and realistically. It is common to select those metrics which are readily available and which point to a possible indicator for the performance. However, this can be misleading. The total number of service events that a service desk has received, for example, is not an indicator by itself of a good or bad performance, and can, in fact, be caused by events which do not impact on the service desk.

In order to determine this, further analysis and more detailed metrics are necessary which are researched for a certain period of time. Besides the statistics mentioned earlier regarding the handling of service events, the metrics consist, among others, of:

- first line handling time; the percentage of service events, which are resolved by the first level, without the necessity to escalate to other support groups
- average time to resolve an incident (or other type of service call) (if it is resolved by the first level)
- average time to escalate an incident (if a first line solution is not possible)
- average handling costs of an incident
- percentage of client and user updates which are executed within the target values, as set forth in the SLA objectives
- average time to evaluate and close out a resolved incident

Besides following "hard" metrics in the performance of the service desk, it is also important to use "soft" metrics: **the client and user Satisfaction Surveys** (e.g. Do clients and users find that their phone calls are properly answered? Was the service desk associate friendly and professional?). User or client can best complete this type of metrics, but specific questions about the service desk itself may also be asked.

Outsourcing the service desk

The decision to contract out or outsource is a strategic subject for Senior Managers and is discussed in detail in Chapter 3 and 4 (Service Strategy and Service Design).

Regardless of the reasons for outsourcing or the size of the outsource contract, it is important that the organization remains responsible for the activities and services rendered by the service desk. The organization is ultimately responsible for the outcome of the decision and must therefore decide which service is going to be offered.

If the service desk is being outsourced, the **tools** must be consistent with the tools being used by the organizations client. Outsourcing is frequently seen as a chance to replace obsolescent or inadequate tools; however, serious integration problems often arise between the new and existing tools and processes.

Ideally, the service desk being outsourced must use the same **tools and processes** to enable a smooth process stream between the service desk and the second and third level support groups.

The **SLA targets** for incident handling and handling times must be arranged with the clients and between all teams and departments; OLA and underlying contract objectives must be coordinated and in tune with separate support groups, so that they support the SLA targets.

Chapter 13

Functions and Processes in Continual Service Improvement

13.1 CSI Improvement Process

Introduction
The **CSI improvement process** or **7-step improvement process** describes how to measure and report. Improvement takes place according to the P-D-C-A Cycle. The CSI plan phase results in a **Service Improvement Plan (SIP)**. The next section will explain how an organization can set up such a plan.

Activities, methods and techniques
If service level management discovers that something could improve, they will pass this on to CSI. CSI can think up activities to accomplish these improvements. CSI will create a SIP for execution purposes. This will turn "improvement" into an IT process with input, activities, output, roles and reports.

CSI will measure and process these measurements in a continual improvement process (Figure 13.1). This will take place in **seven steps from measurement to improvement**:
1. **What *should* you measure?** - What would be the ideal situation? This must follow from the vision (Phase I of the CSI model) and precede the assessment of the current situation (Phase II of the CSI model).
2. **What *can* you measure?** - This step follows from Phase III of the CSI model: where do we want to be? By researching what the organization can measure, it will discover new business requirements and new IT options. By using a *gap analysis* CSI can find areas for improvement and plan these (Phase IV of the CSI model).
3. **Gather data (measure)** - In order to verify whether the organization has reached its goal (Phase V of the CSI model), it must perform measurements. The measurements must follow from its vision, mission, goals and objectives.
4. **Process data** - The processing of data is also necessary for monitoring purposes. This must happen according to CSFs and KPIs determined.
5. **Analyze data** - Discrepancies, trends and possible explanations are prepared for presentation to the business. This is also an important part of Phase V of the CSI model.

6. **Present and use information** - This is where the stakeholder is informed whether his goals have been achieved (still Phase V).
7. **Implement corrective action** - Create improvements, establish a new baseline and start the cycle from the top.

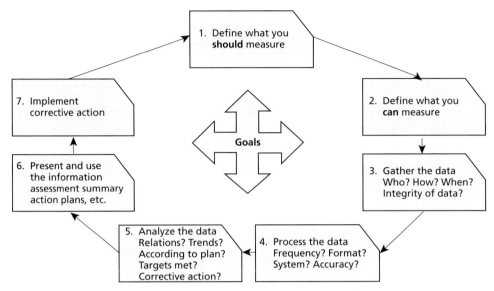

Figure 13.1   The CSI Improvement Process (7-step improvement process) (Source: Continual Service Improvement was produced by OGC)

The cycle is preceded and closed by **identification of vision and goals** *(identify)*. This is where the vision, strategy, tactical and operational goals are charted. This step returns in Phase I of the CSI model: determine the vision. Figure 13.2 shows how the CSI model and the CSI improvement process mesh together.

Steps 1 and 2 should be the direct result of the strategic, tactical and operational goals of the organization. They are iterative: in every step you should question whether you are measuring what you should be measuring and whether the measured values are reliable and useful. Answer these questions together with the business in order to be sure that you will be able to provide it with useful information in Step 6.

If no **baseline** has yet been determined, that measurement must take place first. The first measuring results will be the baseline. Every level should be charted in this process: strategic goals and objectives, tactical process maturity and operational **metrics** and KPIs. In this way, a knowledge spiral develops: the information from Step 6 in the operational level is input for Step 3 (gather data) of the tactical level, and information from the tactical level will provide data to the strategic level (Figure 13.3).

If there is little data available, you must first determine a basic measurement system. Start collecting consistent data, for example by having IT staff record data in the same way. You can also measure the process maturity of current processes to discover those processes that deviate

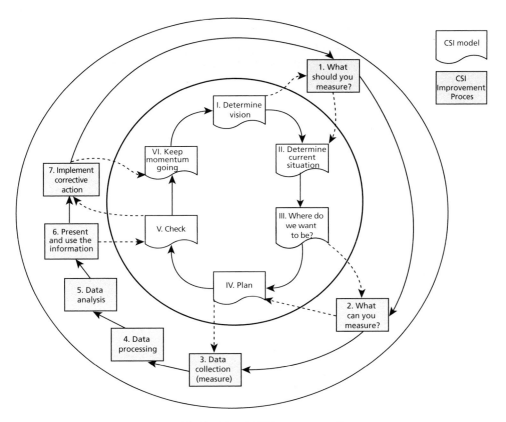

Figure 13.2   Connection between CSI Model and CSI Improvement Process

most from *best practice*. However, this will only show a lack of data, you will not be collecting any new information in this way.

Never allow "measuring" to become a goal unto itself. Before a manager decides what he will be measuring and for how long, he should contemplate why he should measure and how he will put the results to use. This depends on the goal of the manager. The four most common reasons to measure are:
• **validate** - to test prior decisions
• **direct** - set direction to activities in order to reach goals
• **justify** - support for the necessity of a certain action
• **intervene** - determine a point at which corrective actions or changes in the process are required

It is always important to keep sight of these reasons, including while measuring is taking place. After every report, the manager should wonder: "do we (still) need this?" The questions "what am I really measuring?" and "how will I retrieve that information?" are also very important, they should return at every step.

The responsibility for this lies with the owner of every dashboard, they must create useful reports and make sure that the (customer) organization actually uses them.

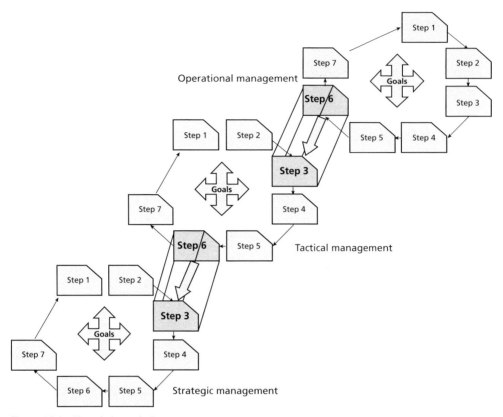

Figure 13.3   Knowledge spiral (Based on OGC ITIL V3 material)

If you follow the seven steps of the improvement process, these questions will appear by themselves. More details about these steps follow below.

Step 1 - What should you measure?

In a perfect world, the **service owners** determine what they should measure. For this reason, they will chart the activities that are needed for the service management processes, or to provide services. Then they plan which measurements will show whether the services actually provide what was agreed with the business, and the way in which they can measure whether processes are proceeding smoothly.

The final list should reflect the visions, missions, goals and objectives of the business and IT, synchronized to each other. This should result in a number of CSFs, as well as *Service Level Targets*. The job descriptions of IT staff should also be related to this.

Have discussions with the business and the service providers for this purpose, and use the service catalogue and *Service Level Requirements* (SLRs) as starting points. Determine priorities based on the business priorities. In this, also remember internal and external service providers: what of theirs should you be measuring in order to determine whether you can provide your service?

Input for Step 1:
- service level requirements and goals
- service catalogue
- vision, mission, goals and objectives of the organization as a whole, and of the various units
- legal requirements
- governance requirements
- budget
- balanced scorecard

The **output** of Step 1 is a list of what you should be measuring, including:
- CSFs
- KPIs
- metrics
- measurements

Step 2 - What can you measure?

There may be a discrepancy between your "ideal list" from Step 1 and actual options. Based on existing tools, organizational culture and process maturity, determine what you can measure.

Chart what has been measured, which reports and databases the organization is generating and whether these are kept up-to-date. Also determine the risk if you decide not to measure something: how does that compare to the costs of the measurement? If you are unable to measure something, it should not be included in the SLA.

Finally, determine the differences between the "ideal list" and the list with possible measurements. It is possible that existing tools must be adjusted, or that new tools are required in order to move closer to the ideal list.

More information about CSFs and KPIs can be found under "Basic concepts" in the Section about CSI in Chapter 7 ("Metrics and KPIs"). Step 4 in the CSI process, process data, also provides additional information.

Input for Step 2:
- list including what to measure from Step 1, including CSFs, KPIs and metrics
- process flows
- procedures
- work instructions
- technical and user manuals for existing tools
- existing reports

Output of Step 2:
- list of what can be measured, including CSFs, KPIs and metrics
- list of required adjustments to tools
- list of required new tools

Step 3 - Gather data (measuring)

Steps 1 and 2 will indicate which data is required and measurable. Define measurements according to SMART. In order to collect data, you must **monitor**. This can be done using tools, but also manually. Monitoring should be focused on a service, process, tool, organization or CI. This does not always have to relate to infrastructure. It might also focus on discovering the degree to which staff are complying to a process.

CSI stresses discovery of areas for improvement. These are often exceptions to the rule, such as unsolved incidents. Both tools, as well as people, can provide warnings regarding exceptions.

If an organization consistently meets an SLA's requirement, CSI can also see if they can reach the same level for lower costs or whether they might be able to provide a higher level of service.

The design of a new service or adjustment to an existing service is the perfect occasion to include the monitoring requirements in the service requirements.

Business requirements for monitoring will change over time. This is why Service Operation and CSI must design a process that will help business and IT reach an agreement about what should be monitored and why.

If staff are collecting data **manually**, they must agree to the following:
- Who is responsible for monitoring and collecting data?
- How will data be collected?
- When and how often will data be collected?
- Which criteria guarantee the correctness and reliability of data?

Data gathering consists of the following **activities**:
- based on the SIP, goals, objectives and business requirements, specify which process activities you must monitor:
  - specify monitoring requirements
  - define requirements for data collection
  - record results
  - apply for approval from the internal IT department
- determine how and how often you want to collect data
- determine which tools are required, develop or buy these, or customize existing tools
- test and install the tool
- write monitoring procedures and work instructions
- create a monitoring plan and discuss it; ask for approval from internal and external IT service providers
- realize availability and capacity planning
- start monitoring and gathering data
- organize the data in a logical fashion in a report
- evaluate data in order to be sure that it is correct and useful

Input for Step 3:
- list stating what you should measure
- list stating what you can measure
- list stating what you will be measuring
- existing SLAs
- new business requirements
- existing monitoring and data gathering options
- availability and capacity planning
- SIPs
- prior trend analyses
- gap analysis report
- customer satisfaction studies

Output for Step 3:
- current availability and capacity planning
- monitoring plan
- monitoring procedures
- selected tools
- data concerning the ability of IT to meet business expectations
- data collection
- agreement on the reliability and applicability of data

If it turns out that data collected cannot be used or is unreliable, at least put it to use analyzing which data will be needed. For this purpose, repeat steps one and two.

Step 4 - Process data

Here you will process the raw data from Step 3 into the required format for the target audience. Follow the path from metric via KPI to CSF, right back to the vision if necessary (Figure 13.4).

Translate the data into a depiction of the service performance from a business perspective. The business is not interested in knowing that a server was available 99.99% of the time if it had no access to it. Collect data logically so that data analysis (Step 5) becomes easier. Tools can generate reports for this. At this point, data becomes *information*, according to the DIKW model (see Chapter 11).

Data processing consists of the following **activities**:
- define the requirements of the processed data based on strategy, goals and SLAs
- determine how data is being processed; for new services or processes, it is preferable to select shorter intervals; is this by hour, day, week or month?
- determine the data grouping based on the method of analysis and target group; formulate the requirements for tools; develop or buy them; test and install them
- develop procedures to process data, and train people in the procedures
- create a monitoring plan and discuss it; ask for approval from internal and external IT service providers
- update availability and capacity planning
- start data processing

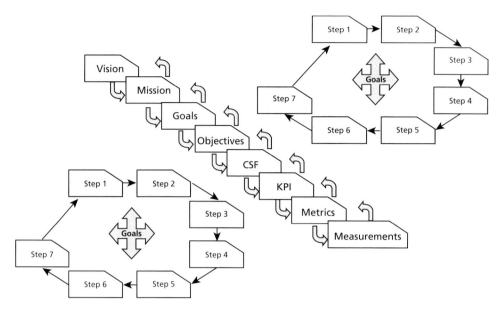

Figure 13.4   From vision to measurements and back (Based on OGC ITIL V3 material)

* group the data in a logical fashion
* evaluate data accuracy

Input for Step 4:
* data gathered by monitoring
* reporting requirements
* SLAs and OLAs (Operational Level Agreements)
* service catalogue
* list with metrics, KPIs, CSF, objectives and goals
* reporting frequency
* reporting templates

Output for Step 4:
* current availability and capacity planning
* reports
* processed, logically grouped data ready for analysis

Step 5 - Analyze data

Without analysis, data is "only" information. It does not provide understanding of areas for improvement. Analysis evaluates whether IT services support the goals and objectives determined. The data will be applied to answer questions such as:
* Can clear trends be observed?
  - Are they positive or negative?
  - Are they in line with the goals?
  - Did we expect these trends?
  - What are potential explanations?

- Are changes necessary?
- Will we meet planning and goals?
- Are there structural, underlying problems?

Discuss the answers to these questions internally with the IT department first, in order to discover improvement options in collaboration. For example, think of training, testing and documentation. A logical start is to discover the "weakest link": the least efficient process activity. This is often the place where the most profit can be gained.

Because of prior discussions about improvement options, IT will make the first move in the dialogue with the business that follows analysis. A good analysis of the information is also to the business' advantage. This will allow a more accurate determination of whether improvement is required on the basis of strategic, tactical and operational goals. At this point, information becomes *knowledge*, according to the DIKW model.

Step 6 - Present and use information (service reporting)

Step six, **service reporting** (see also Section 13.2 "Service reporting" for a more detailed description) must translate knowledge into *wisdom* which is required to make strategic, tactical and operational decisions. Convincingly support with facts any added value IT will have for the business. For this purpose, present information to various stakeholders, at all levels of the organization. Include the use of marketing and communication techniques. Adjust the message and method to **your target group and its requirements**. Normally, there are three possible target groups: the business, senior (IT) management, and the internal IT organization.

Staff members in different organizational levels have different requirements. Therefore, distinguish these by **staff members and their requirements**, such as strategic thinkers, directors, managers and supervisors, team leaders and staff.

In order to provide useful reports to a customer, these reports should be set up from a **business perspective**, which is to say, from an **end-to-end perspective** - a customer is not interested in details about the functioning of the technical infrastructure through which services are provided, but only in the service itself.

Take the time to set up a **reporting framework** together with the business and Service Design: a policy that is formulated according to the rules by which you report. Determine this per business unit, so that you can distinguish between, for example, production and sales departments. Once this has been determined, data can easily be translated into meaningful reports, sometimes even fully automated.

Step 7 - Implement corrective action

An organization will not be able to implement all of the determined improvement options immediately. For this reason, options should be assigned a **priority** based on the organizational goals and external regulations determined in the Service Strategy. After this, the Service Design can develop the improvements, after which Service Transition will roll them out in the live environment and Service Operation will incorporate them in daily operation. During the entire cycle, continue to measure, analyze and report in order to see whether SLAs and KPIs still meet requirements. In addition, continue to pay attention to communication, training and documentation.

In retrospect, measure whether desired improvements have produced the effect you expected in terms of profits, ROI and VOI. As a result, study whether additional improvement is necessary, and start over with Step 1.

13.2 Service Reporting

Introduction

The **service reporting process** is the process which is responsible for the generation and supply of reports about the results achieved and the developments in service levels. It should agree with the business on the lay-out, contents and frequency of the reports.

Figure 13.5 shows how the service reporting process converts knowledge into the *wisdom* which is needed to make strategic, tactical and operational decisions.

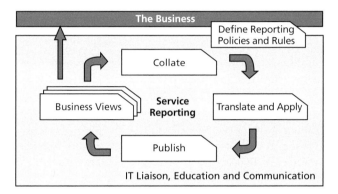

Figure 13.5   Service reporting process (Source: Continual Service Improvement was produced by OGC)

Activities, methods and techniques

The service reporting process distinguishes the following activities:
- gather data
- process the data into information and apply this to the organization publish the information
- fine-tune the reporting to the business

Support the process with a set of reporting guidelines.

Gather data

IT departments frequently gather large amounts of data, which are not all equally interesting to the business. Start, therefore, by determining the goal and target group of the report and consider how the report is going to be used. Is management going to read it, can managers and department heads consult it online or are you going to present the results at a meeting? And what will be done with it next?

Process and apply data
The business likes to see a hierarchical overview of the performance over the past period. But it is particularly interested in events from the past that may impact, today or in the future, the performance of the business and how the IT department is going to combat those threats.

Present data with cross references to contracted and chargeable service elements. Process these into the language the business understands. Report not only on whether the IT department achieves the SLA arrangements, but indicate also what incidents have occurred and what IT has done to resolve them and to avoid repetition, and what IT is doing to elevate positive exceptions to standard items.

Do not only concentrate on the past but also on the future. This is an excellent marketing opportunity for the IT department in order to clarify the added value to the business. If possible, connect this value directly to the positive or negative experiences of the business.

Publish information
Publish information for the different stakeholders at all levels of the organization and use marketing and communication techniques. Fine-tune the message and method to your target group and its needs from a business perspective. As a rule there are three possible target groups:
- **The business** - wants to know if the IT service provider has delivered the promised services, in SLA terms, and which measures are being taken by the service provider if this is not the case.
- **Senior IT Management** - wants to know if the CSFs and KPIs are attained. It looks at which strategic and tactical improvements are necessary. It needs frequent presentations in the form of a IT Balanced Scorecard.
- **IT Internal** - is interested in KPIs and *metrics,* in order to locate, plan and coordinate improvement potential.

Tune the reporting to the business
Consider by data group if it is valuable for the target group. For example, the business often wants to know *how long* a service was unavailable, since an availability percentage does not provide much insight into its opportunities to use the service. Whether or not the mainframe or the service was available the entire time, is not useful information for the business, but more so the fact that it could not reach the service. Look at this from an *end-to-end* perspective.

Figure 13.6 gives a picture of four different organizational levels and their interests:
1. **strategic thinkers** - want short reports, with lots of attention to the risks, organization image, profitability and cost savings
2. **directors** - want more detailed reports which summarize the development measured in time, indicating how processes support the company goals, and warning of risks
3. **managers and supervisors** - deal with observing the goals, team and process performance, distribution of resources and improvement initiatives. Measurements and reports must indicate how the process results are contributing to this
4. **team leaders and staff** - will look to emphasize the individual contribution to the company result; focus should be to fix individual metrics, acknowledge their skills and consider which training potential is available in order to involve them in the processes

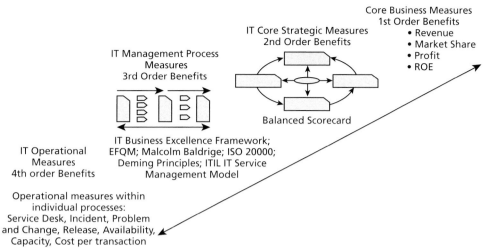

Figure 13.6   Different organizational levels and their needs (Source: Continual Service Improvement was produced by OGC)

Consider the business goals when preparing the presentations. It is only then that IT can answer the question regarding its added value. Besides the negative exceptions, also list the (anticipated) positive results in the presentation.

Use a practical approach: indicate what has happened and what IT has done to resolve it. And in order to prevent a repeat, what IT is doing to elevate positive exceptions to standard practice. A table showing what has been achieved and what has not is not necessarily complicated, see Table 13.1.

Period => Target	January	February	March	April	May	June	July	August
A								░
B			░					
C								░
D				░	░			░
E								
F								░
Legend:								
Goal achieved:								
Goal not achieved:	░							
Goal threatened:								

Table 13.1   Overview of the Service Level Achievements accomplished

Take the time, together with the business and using the service draft, to make up a business-focused reporting framework: a policy that formulates the rules according to which you will be reporting. This should at least contain:
• target groups and their view of the services delivered
• agreement as to what should be measured and what to report

- defining all terms and upper and lower limits
- basis for all calculations
- report planning
- access to reports and media used
- meetings to discuss the reports

Establish this by business Unit. In this way, you can distinguish between the production and sales departments, for example. All reporting, however, must form part of the same reporting framework. Once this has been established, the data can simply be converted into meaningful reports, sometimes even fully automated.

In it, provide clear answers to the core questions, state where the threats and pitfalls lie, where the number of threats has diminished, and what has been improved. Also fine tune the media to the target group: paper reports, online or oral presentation.

Careful and effective automatic reporting is crucial for a successful and continual reporting system that creates value for the business. Evaluate continually whether the existing reporting provides clear and unambiguous information about the performance of the IT department and adjust your reporting, if this is no longer the case.

References

Application Management. (2002). OGC. London: TSO.

Bon, J. van, M. Pieper, & A. van der Veen (Eds.) (2006). *Foundations of IT Service Management, based on ITIL.* Zaltbommel: Van Haren Publishing for itSMF.

Business Perspective Volume 1. (2004). OGC. London: TSO.

Business Perspective Volume 2. (2006). OGC. London: TSO.

Cambridge Advanced Learner's Dictionary, http://dictionary.cambridge.org/

ICT Infrastructure Management. (2002). OGC. London: TSO.

ITIL. Continual Service Improvement (2007). OGC. London: TSO.

ITIL. Service Design (2007). OGC. London: TSO.

ITIL. Service Operation (2007). OGC. London: TSO.

ITIL. Service Strategy (2007). OGC. London: TSO.

ITIL. Service Transition (2007). OGC. London: TSO.

Kaplan, R., & D. Norton (1992, January-February). The Balanced Scorecard - measures that drive performance. *Harvard Business Review*, Vol. 70, No. 1, p. 71-79.

Kaplan, R., & D. Norton (1993, September-October). Putting the Balanced Scorecard to work. *Harvard Business Review*, Vol. 71, No. 5, p. 134-142.

Kotter, J.P. (1996). *Leading Change.* Cambridge (MA): Harvard Business School Press.

Mintzberg, H. (1994). *The Rise and Fall of Strategic Planning: reconceiving roles for planning, plans, planners.* New York: The Free Press.

Nolan, R. (1973). Managing the computer resource: a stage hypothesis. *Communications of the ACM*, Vol. 16, Issue 7, July, p. 399 - 405.

Planning to Implement Service Management. (2002). OGC. London: TSO.

Rummler, G. A., & A.P. Brache (1995, 2nd edition). *Improving Performance: How to Manage the White Space in the Organization Chart.* San Francisco: Jossey-Bass.

Security Management. (1999). OGC. London: TSO.

Service Delivery. (2001). OGC. London: TSO.

Service Support. (2000). Office of Government Commerce (OGC). London: TSO.

Software Asset Management. (2003). OGC. London: TSO.

Zeithaml, V.A., A. Parasuraman, & L. Berry (1990). *Delivering Quality Service.* New York: The Free Press. (SERVQUAL model)

Van Grembergen W., De Haes S., Guldentops E. (2003). *Structures, Processes and relational mechanisms for Information Technology Governance: Theories and practices, Strategies for Information Technology Governance*, book edited by Van Grembergen W., Idea Group Publishing.

Glossary

Where a term is relevant to a particular phase in the Lifecycle of an IT Service, or to one of the Core ITIL publications, this is indicated at the beginning of the definition. This glossary is based on the "ITIL V3 Glossary v3.1.24" of 11 May 2007.

Acceptance	Formal agreement that an IT Service, Process, Plan, or other Deliverable is complete, accurate, Reliable and meets its specified Requirements. Acceptance is usually preceded by Evaluation or Testing and is often required before proceeding to the next stage of a Project or Process. See Service Acceptance Criteria.
Access Management	(Service Operation) The Process responsible for allowing Users to make use of IT Services, data, or other Assets. Access Management helps to protect the Confidentiality, Integrity and Availability of Assets by ensuring that only authorized Users are able to access or modify the Assets. Access Management is sometimes referred to as Rights Management or Identity Management.
Account Manager	(Service Strategy) A Role that is very similar to Business Relationship Manager, but includes more commercial aspects. Most commonly used when dealing with External Customers.
Accounting	(Service Strategy) The Process responsible for identifying actual Costs of delivering IT Services, comparing these with budgeted costs, and managing variance from the Budget.
Accredited	Officially authorized to carry out a Role; for example, an Accredited body may be authorized to provide training or to conduct Audits.
Active Monitoring	(Service Operation) Monitoring of a Configuration Item or an IT Service that uses automated regular checks to discover the current status. See Passive Monitoring.
Activity	A set of actions designed to achieve a particular result. Activities are usually defined as part of Processes or Plans, and are documented in Procedures.
Agreed Service Time	(Service Design) A synonym for Service Hours, commonly used in formal calculations of Availability. See Downtime.
Agreement	A Document that describes a formal understanding between two or more parties. An Agreement is not legally binding, unless it forms part of a Contract. See Service Level Agreement, Operational Level Agreement.
Alert	(Service Operation) A warning that a threshold has been reached, something has changed, or a Failure has occurred. Alerts are often created and managed by System Management tools and are managed by the Event Management Process.
Analytical Modelling	(Service Strategy) (Service Design) (Continual Service Improvement) A technique that uses mathematical Models to predict the behaviour of a Configuration Item or IT Service. Analytical Models are commonly used in Capacity Management and Availability Management. See Modelling.
Application	Software that provides Functions that are required by an IT Service. Each Application may be part of more than one IT Service. An Application runs on one or more Servers or Clients. See Application Management, Application Portfolio.
Application Management	(Service Design) (Service Operation) The Function responsible for managing Applications throughout their Lifecycle.
Application Portfolio	(Service Design) A database or structured Document used to manage Applications throughout their Lifecycle. The Application Portfolio contains key Attributes of all Applications. The Application Portfolio is sometimes implemented as part of the Service Portfolio, or as part of the Configuration Management System.
Application Service Provider (ASP)	(Service Design) An External Service Provider that provides IT Services using Applications running at the Service Provider's premises. Users access the Applications by network connections to the Service Provider.

Application Sizing	(Service Design) The Activity responsible for understanding the Resource Requirements needed to support a new Application, or a major Change to an existing Application. Application Sizing helps to ensure that the IT Service can meet its agreed Service Level Targets for Capacity and Performance.
Architecture	(Service Design) The structure of a System or IT Service, including the Relationships of Components to each other and to the environment they are in. Architecture also includes the Standards and Guidelines which guide the design and evolution of the System.
Assembly	(Service Transition) A Configuration Item that is made up from a number of other CIs; for example, a Server CI may contain CIs for CPUs, Disks, Memory etc.; an IT Service CI may contain Hardware, Software and other CIs. See Component CI, Build.
Assessment	Inspection and analysis to check whether a Standard or set of Guidelines is being followed, that Records are accurate, or that Efficiency and Effectiveness targets are being met. See Audit.
Asset	(Service Strategy) Any Resource or Capability. Assets of a Service Provider include anything that could contribute to the delivery of a Service. Assets can be one of the following types: Management, Organization, Process, Knowledge, People, Information, Applications, Infrastructure and Financial Capital.
Asset Management	(Service Transition) Asset Management is the Process responsible for tracking and reporting the value and ownership of financial Assets throughout their Lifecycle. Asset Management is part of an overall Service Asset and Configuration Management Process. See Asset Register.
Asset Register	(Service Transition) A list of Assets, which includes their ownership and value. The Asset Register is maintained by Asset Management.
Attribute	(Service Transition) A piece of information about a Configuration Item. Examples are name, location, Version number and Cost. Attributes of CIs are recorded in the Configuration Management Database (CMDB). See Relationship.
Audit	Formal inspection and verification to check whether a Standard or set of Guidelines is being followed, that Records are accurate, or that Efficiency and Effectiveness targets are being met. An Audit may be carried out by internal or external groups. See Certification, Assessment.
Authority Matrix	Synonym for RACI.
Automatic Call Distribution (ACD)	(Service Operation) Use of Information Technology to direct an incoming telephone call to the most appropriate person in the shortest possible time. ACD is sometimes called Automated Call Distribution.
Availability	(Service Design) Ability of a Configuration Item or IT Service to perform its agreed Function when required. Availability is determined by Reliability, Maintainability, Serviceability, Performance and Security. Availability is usually calculated as a percentage. This calculation is often based on Agreed Service Time and Downtime. It is Best Practice to calculate Availability using measurements of the Business output of the IT Service.
Availability Management	(Service Design) The Process responsible for defining, analysing, Planning, measuring and improving all aspects of the Availability of IT Services. Availability Management is responsible for ensuring that all IT Infrastructure, Processes, Tools, Roles, etc. are appropriate for the agreed Service Level Targets for Availability.
Availability Management Information System (AMIS)	(Service Design) A virtual repository of all Availability Management data, usually stored in multiple physical locations. See Service Knowledge Management System.
Availability Plan	(Service Design) A Plan to ensure that existing and future Availability Requirements for IT Services can be provided Cost Effectively.
Back-out	Synonym for Remediation.
Backup	(Service Design) (Service Operation) Copying data to protect against loss of Integrity or Availability of the original.

Balanced Scorecard	(Continual Service Improvement) A management tool developed by Drs. Robert Kaplan (Harvard Business School) and David Norton. A Balanced Scorecard enables a Strategy to be broken down into Key Performance Indicators. Performance against the KPIs is used to demonstrate how well the Strategy is being achieved. A Balanced Scorecard has 4 major areas, each of which has a small number of KPIs. The same 4 areas are considered at different levels of detail throughout the Organization.
Baseline	(Continual Service Improvement) A Benchmark used as a reference point; for example:
• An ITSM Baseline can be used as a starting point to measure the effect of a Service Improvement Plan.
• A Performance Baseline can be used to measure changes in Performance over the lifetime of an IT Service.
• A Configuration Management Baseline can be used to enable the IT Infrastructure to be restored to a known Configuration if a Change or Release fails.
Benchmark	(Continual Service Improvement) The recorded state of something at a specific point in time. A Benchmark can be created for a Configuration, a Process, or any other set of data; for example, a benchmark can be used in:
• Continual Service Improvement, to establish the current state for managing improvements
• Capacity Management, to document Performance characteristics during normal operations
• See Benchmarking, Baseline.
Benchmarking	(Continual Service Improvement) Comparing a Benchmark with a Baseline or with Best Practice. The term Benchmarking is also used to mean creating a series of Benchmarks over time, and comparing the results to measure progress or improvement.
Best Practice	Proven Activities or Processes that have been successfully used by multiple Organizations. ITIL is an example of Best Practice.
Brainstorming	(Service Design) A technique that helps a team to generate ideas. Ideas are not reviewed during the Brainstorming session, but at a later stage. Brainstorming is often used by Problem Management to identify possible causes.
British Standards Institution (BSI)	The UK National Standards body, responsible for creating and maintaining British Standards. See http://www.bsi-global.com for more information.
See ISO.
Budget	A list of all the money an Organization or Business Unit plans to receive, and plans to pay out, over a specified period of time.
See Budgeting, Planning.
Budgeting	The Activity of predicting and controlling the spending of money. Consists of a periodic negotiation cycle to set future Budgets (usually annual) and the day-to-day monitoring and adjusting of current Budgets.
Build	(Service Transition) The Activity of assembling a number of Configuration Items to create part of an IT Service. The term Build is also used to refer to a Release that is authorized for distribution; for example, Server Build or laptop Build.
See Configuration Baseline.
Build Environment	(Service Transition) A controlled Environment where Applications, IT Services and other Builds are assembled prior to being moved into a Test or Live Environment.
Business	(Service Strategy) An overall corporate entity or Organization formed of a number of Business Units. In the context of ITSM, the term Business includes public sector and not-for-profit organizations, as well as companies. An IT Service Provider provides IT Services to a Customer within a Business. The IT Service Provider may be part of the same Business as their Customer (Internal Service Provider), or part of another Business (External Service Provider).
Business Capacity Management (BCM)	(Service Design) In the context of ITSM, Business Capacity Management is the Activity responsible for understanding future Business Requirements for use in the Capacity Plan.
See Service Capacity Management.

Business Case	(Service Strategy) Justification for a significant item of expenditure. Includes information about Costs, benefits, options, issues, Risks, and possible problems. See Cost Benefit Analysis.
Business Continuity Management (BCM)	(Service Design) The Business Process responsible for managing Risks that could seriously impact the Business. BCM safeguards the interests of key stakeholders, reputation, brand and value creating activities. The BCM Process involves reducing Risks to an acceptable level and planning for the recovery of Business Processes should a disruption to the Business occur. BCM sets the Objectives, Scope and Requirements for IT Service Continuity Management.
Business Continuity Plan (BCP)	(Service Design) A Plan defining the steps required to Restore Business Processes following a disruption. The Plan will also identify the triggers for Invocation, people to be involved, communications, etc. IT Service Continuity Plans form a significant part of Business Continuity Plans.
Business Customer	(Service Strategy) A recipient of a product or a Service from the Business; for example, if the Business is a car manufacturer then the Business Customer is someone who buys a car.
Business Impact Analysis (BIA)	(Service Strategy) BIA is the Activity in Business Continuity Management that identifies Vital Business Functions and their dependencies. These dependencies may include Suppliers, people, other Business Processes, IT Services, etc. BIA defines the recovery requirements for IT Services. These requirements include Recovery Time Objectives, Recovery Point Objectives and minimum Service Level Targets for each IT Service.
Business Objective	(Service Strategy) The Objective of a Business Process, or of the Business as a whole. Business Objectives support the Business Vision, provide guidance for the IT Strategy, and are often supported by IT Services.
Business Operations	(Service Strategy) The day-to-day execution, monitoring and management of Business Processes.
Business Perspective	(Continual Service Improvement) An understanding of the Service Provider and IT Services from the point of view of the Business, and an understanding of the Business from the point of view of the Service Provider.
Business Process	A Process that is owned and carried out by the Business. A Business Process contributes to the delivery of a product or Service to a Business Customer; for example, a retailer may have a purchasing Process which helps to deliver Services to their Business Customers. Many Business Processes rely on IT Services.
Business Relationship Management	(Service Strategy) The Process or Function responsible for maintaining a Relationship with the Business. BRM usually includes: • managing personal Relationships with Business managers • providing input to Service Portfolio Management • ensuring that the IT Service Provider is satisfying the Business needs of the Customers
Business Relationship Manager (BRM)	(Service Strategy) A Role responsible for maintaining the Relationship with one or more Customers. This Role is often combined with the Service Level Manager Role. See Account Manager.
Business Service	An IT Service that directly supports a Business Process, as opposed to an Infrastructure Service which is used internally by the IT Service Provider and is not usually visible to the Business. The term Business Service is also used to mean a Service that is delivered to Business Customers by Business Units; for example, delivery of financial services to Customers of a bank, or goods to the Customers of a retail store. Successful delivery of Business Services often depends on one or more IT Services.
Business Service Management (BSM)	(Service Strategy) (Service Design) An approach to the management of IT Services that considers the Business Processes supported and the Business value provided. This term also means the management of Business Services delivered to Business Customers.
Business Unit	(Service Strategy) A segment of the Business which has its own Plans, Metrics, income and Costs. Each Business Unit owns Assets and uses these to create value for Customers in the form of goods and Services.

Call	(Service Operation) A telephone call to the Service Desk from a User. A Call could result in an Incident or a Service Request being logged.
Call Centre	(Service Operation) An Organization or Business Unit which handles large numbers of incoming and outgoing telephone calls. See Service Desk.
Call Type	(Service Operation) A Category that is used to distinguish incoming requests to a Service Desk. Common Call Types are Incident, Service Request and Complaint.
Capability	(Service Strategy) The ability of an Organization, person, Process, Application, Configuration Item or IT Service to carry out an Activity. Capabilities are intangible Assets of an Organization. See Resource.
Capability Maturity Model (CMM)	(Continual Service Improvement) The Capability Maturity Model for Software (also known as the CMM and SW-CMM) is a model used to identify Best Practices to help increase Process Maturity. CMM was developed at the Software Engineering Institute (SEI) of Carnegie Mellon University. In 2000, the SW-CMM was upgraded to CMMI® (Capability Maturity Model Integration). The SEI no longer maintains the SW-CMM model, its associated appraisal methods, or training materials.
Capability Maturity Model (CMMI)	(Continual Service Improvement) Capability Maturity Model® Integration (CMMI) is a process improvement approach developed by the Software Engineering Institute (SEI) of Carnegie Mellon University. CMMI provides organizations with the essential elements of effective processes. It can be used to guide process improvement across a project, a division, or an entire organization. CMMI helps integrate traditionally separate organizational functions, set process improvement goals and priorities, provide guidance for quality processes, and provide a point of reference for appraising current processes. See http://www.sei.cmu.edu/cmmi/ for more information. See CMM, Continuous Improvement, Maturity.
Capacity	(Service Design) The maximum Throughput that a Configuration Item or IT Service can deliver whilst meeting agreed Service Level Targets. For some types of CI, Capacity may be the size or volume; for example, a disk drive.
Capacity Management	(Service Design) The Process responsible for ensuring that the Capacity of IT Services and the IT Infrastructure is able to deliver agreed Service Level Targets in a Cost Effective and timely manner. Capacity Management considers all Resources required to deliver the IT Service, and plans for short, medium and long-term Business Requirements.
Capacity Management Information System (CMIS)	(Service Design) A virtual repository of all Capacity Management data, usually stored in multiple physical locations. See Service Knowledge Management System.
Capacity Plan	(Service Design) A Capacity Plan is used to manage the Resources required to deliver IT Services. The Plan contains scenarios for different predictions of Business demand, and costed options to deliver the agreed Service Level Targets.
Capacity Planning	(Service Design) The Activity within Capacity Management responsible for creating a Capacity Plan.
Capital Expenditure (CAPEX)	(Service Strategy) The Cost of purchasing something that will become a financial Asset; for example, computer equipment and buildings. The value of the Asset is Depreciated over multiple accounting periods.
Capital Item	(Service Strategy) An Asset that is of interest to Financial Management because it is above an agreed financial value.
Capitalization	(Service Strategy) Identifying major Cost as capital, even though no Asset is purchased. This is done to spread the impact of the Cost over multiple accounting periods. The most common example of this is software development, or purchase of a software license.
Category	A named group of things that have something in common. Categories are used to group similar things together; for example, Cost Types are used to group similar types of Cost; Incident Categories are used to group similar types of Incident; CI Types are used to group similar types of Configuration Item.

Certification	Issuing a certificate to confirm Compliance to a Standard. Certification includes a formal Audit by an independent and Accredited body. The term Certification is also used to mean awarding a certificate to verify that a person has achieved a qualification.
Change	(Service Transition) The addition, modification or removal of anything that could have an effect on IT Services. The Scope should include all IT Services, Configuration Items, Processes, Documentation, etc.
Change Advisory Board (CAB)	(Service Transition) A group of people that advises the Change Manager in the Assessment, prioritisation and scheduling of Changes. This board is usually made up of representatives from all areas within the IT Service Provider, the Business, and Third Parties such as Suppliers.
Change Case	(Service Operation) A technique used to predict the impact of proposed Changes. Change Cases use specific scenarios to clarify the scope of proposed Changes and to help with Cost Benefit Analysis. See Use Case.
Change History	(Service Transition) Information about all changes made to a Configuration Item during its life. Change History consists of all those Change Records that apply to the CI.
Change Management	(Service Transition) The Process responsible for controlling the Lifecycle of all Changes. The primary objective of Change Management is to enable beneficial Changes to be made, with minimum disruption to IT Services.
Change Model	(Service Transition) A repeatable way of dealing with a particular Category of Change. A Change Model defines specific pre-defined steps that will be followed for a Change of this Category. Change Models may be very simple, with no requirement for approval (e.g. Password Reset) or may be very complex with many steps that require approval (e.g. major software Release). See Standard Change, Change Advisory Board.
Change Record	(Service Transition) A Record containing the details of a Change. Each Change Record documents the Lifecycle of a single Change. A Change Record is created for every Request for Change that is received, even those that are subsequently rejected. Change Records should reference the Configuration Items that are affected by the Change. Change Records are stored in the Configuration Management System.
Change Request	Synonym for Request for Change.
Change Schedule	(Service Transition) A Document that lists all approved Changes and their planned implementation dates. A Change Schedule is sometimes called a Forward Schedule of Change, even though it also contains information about Changes that have already been implemented.
Change Window	(Service Transition) A regular, agreed time when Changes or Releases may be implemented with minimal impact on Services. Change Windows are usually documented in SLAs.
Charging	(Service Strategy) Requiring payment for IT Services. Charging for IT Services is optional, and many Organizations choose to treat their IT Service Provider as a Cost Centre.
Chronological Analysis	(Service Operation) A technique used to help identify possible causes of Problems. All available data about the Problem is collected and sorted by date and time to provide a detailed timeline. This can make it possible to identify which Events may have been triggered by others.
CI Type	(Service Transition) A Category that is used to Classify CIs. The CI Type identifies the required Attributes and Relationships for a Configuration Record. Common CI Types include: hardware, Document, User, etc.
Classification	The act of assigning a Category to something. Classification is used to ensure consistent management and reporting. CIs, Incidents, Problems, Changes, etc. are usually classified.
Client	A generic term that means a Customer, the Business or a Business Customer; for example, Client Manager may be used as a synonym for Account Manager. The term client is also used to mean: • a computer that is used directly by a User; for example, a PC, Handheld Computer, or Workstation • the part of a Client-Server Application that the User directly interfaces with, for example, an email Client
Closed	(Service Operation) The final Status in the Lifecycle of an Incident, Problem, Change etc. When the Status is Closed, no further action is taken.
Closure	(Service Operation) The act of changing the Status of an Incident, Problem, Change, etc. to Closed.

COBIT	(Continual Service Improvement) Control Objectives for Information and related Technology (COBIT) provides guidance and Best Practice for the management of IT Processes. COBIT is published by the IT Governance Institute. See http://www.isaca.org/ for more information.
Code of Practice	A Guideline published by a public body or a Standards Organization, such as ISO or BSI. Many Standards consist of a Code of Practice and a Specification. The Code of Practice describes recommended Best Practice.
Cold Standby	Synonym for Gradual Recovery.
Commercial off the Shelf (COTS)	(Service Design) Application software or Middleware that can be purchased from a Third Party.
Compliance	Ensuring that a Standard or set of Guidelines is followed, or that proper, consistent accounting or other practices are being employed.
Component	A general term that is used to mean one part of something more complex; for example, a computer System may be a component of an IT Service, an Application may be a Component of a Release Unit. Components that need to be managed should be Configuration Items.
Component Capacity Management (CCM)	(Service Design) (Continual Service Improvement) The Process responsible for understanding the Capacity, Utilization, and Performance of Configuration Items. Data is collected, recorded and analysed for use in the Capacity Plan. See Service Capacity Management.
Component CI	(Service Transition) A Configuration Item that is part of an Assembly; for example, a CPU or Memory CI may be part of a Server CI.
Component Failure Impact Analysis (CFIA)	(Service Design) A technique that helps to identify the impact of CI failure on IT Services. A matrix is created with IT Services on one edge and CIs on the other. This enables the identification of critical CIs (that could cause the failure of multiple IT Services) and of fragile IT Services (that have multiple Single Points of Failure).
Computer Telephony Integration (CTI)	(Service Operation) CTI is a general term covering any kind of integration between computers and telephone Systems. It is most commonly used to refer to Systems where an Application displays detailed screens relating to incoming or outgoing telephone calls. See Automatic Call Distribution, Interactive Voice Response.
Concurrency	A measure of the number of Users engaged in the same Operation at the same time.
Confidentiality	(Service Design) A security principle that requires that data should only be accessed by authorized people.
Configuration	(Service Transition) A generic term, used to describe a group of Configuration Items that work together to deliver an IT Service, or a recognizable part of an IT Service. Configuration is also used to describe the parameter settings for one or more CIs.
Configuration Baseline	(Service Transition) A Baseline of a Configuration that has been formally agreed and is managed through the Change Management process. A Configuration Baseline is used as a basis for future Builds, Releases and Changes.
Configuration Control	(Service Transition) The Activity responsible for ensuring that adding, modifying or removing a CI is properly managed; for example, by submitting a Request for Change or Service Request.
Configuration Identification	(Service Transition) The Activity responsible for collecting information about Configuration Items and their Relationships, and loading this information into the CMDB. Configuration Identification is also responsible for labelling the CIs themselves, so that the corresponding Configuration Records can be found.
Configuration Item (CI)	(Service Transition) Any Component that needs to be managed in order to deliver an IT Service. Information about each CI is recorded in a Configuration Record within the Configuration Management System and is maintained throughout its Lifecycle by Configuration Management. CIs are under the control of Change Management. CIs typically include IT Services, hardware, software, buildings, people, and formal documentation such as Process documentation and SLAs.
Configuration Management	(Service Transition) The Process responsible for maintaining information about Configuration Items required to deliver an IT Service, including their Relationships. This information is managed throughout the Lifecycle of the CI. Configuration Management is part of an overall Service Asset and Configuration Management Process.

Configuration Management Database (CMDB)	(Service Transition) A database used to store Configuration Records throughout their Lifecycle. The Configuration Management System maintains one or more CMDBs, and each CMDB stores Attributes of CIs, and Relationships with other CIs.
Configuration Management System (CMS)	(Service Transition) A set of tools and databases that are used to manage an IT Service Provider's Configuration data. The CMS also includes information about Incidents, Problems, Known Errors, Changes and Releases; and may contain data about employees, Suppliers, locations, Business Units, Customers and Users. The CMS includes tools for collecting, storing, managing, updating and presenting data about all Configuration Items and their Relationships. The CMS is maintained by Configuration Management and is used by all IT Service Management Processes. See Configuration Management Database, Service Knowledge Management System.
Configuration Record	(Service Transition) A Record containing the details of a Configuration Item. Each Configuration Record documents the Lifecycle of a single CI. Configuration Records are stored in a Configuration Management Database.
Configuration Structure	(Service Transition) The hierarchy and other Relationships between all the Configuration Items that comprise a Configuration.
Continual Service Improvement (CSI)	(Continual Service Improvement) A stage in the Lifecycle of an IT Service and the title of one of the Core ITIL publications. Continual Service Improvement is responsible for managing improvements to IT Service Management Processes and IT Services. The Performance of the IT Service Provider is continually measured and improvements are made to Processes, IT Services and IT Infrastructure in order to increase Efficiency, Effectiveness, and Cost Effectiveness. See Plan-Do-Check-Act (P-D-C-A Cycle).
Continuous Availability	(Service Design) An approach or design to achieve 100% Availability. A Continuously Available IT Service has no planned or unplanned Downtime.
Continuous Operation	(Service Design) An approach or design to eliminate planned Downtime of an IT Service. Note that individual Configuration Items may be down even though the IT Service is Available.
Contract	A legally binding Agreement between two or more parties.
Contract Portfolio	(Service Strategy) A database or structured Document used to manage Service Contracts or Agreements between an IT Service Provider and their Customers. Each IT Service delivered to a Customer should have a Contract or other Agreement which is listed in the Contract Portfolio. See Service Portfolio, Service Catalogue.
Control	A means of managing a Risk, ensuring that a Business Objective is achieved, or ensuring that a Process is followed. Example Controls include Policies, Procedures, Roles, RAID, door-locks, etc. A control is sometimes called a Countermeasure or safeguard. Control also means to manage the utilization or behavior of a Configuration Item, System or IT Service.
Control Objectives for Information and related Technology (COBIT)	See COBIT.
Control perspective	(Service Strategy) An approach to the management of IT Services, Processes, Functions, Assets, etc. There can be several different Control Perspectives on the same IT Service, Process, etc., allowing different individuals or teams to focus on what is important and relevant to their specific Role. Example Control Perspectives include Reactive and Proactive management within IT Operations, or a Lifecycle view for an Application Project team.
Control Processes	The ISO/IEC 20000 Process group that includes Change Management and Configuration Management.
Core Service	(Service Strategy) An IT Service that delivers basic Outcomes desired by one or more Customers. See Supporting Service, Core Service Package.

Core Service Package (CSP)	(Service Strategy) A detailed description of a Core Service that may be shared by two or more Service Level Packages. See Service Package.
Cost	The amount of money spent on a specific Activity, IT Service, or Business Unit. Costs consist of real cost (money), notional cost such as people's time, and Depreciation.
Cost Benefit Analysis	An Activity that analyses and compares the Costs and the benefits involved in one or more alternative courses of action. See Business Case, Net Present Value, Internal Rate of Return, Return on Investment, Value on Investment.
Cost Centre	(Service Strategy) A Business Unit or Project to which Costs are assigned. A Cost Centre does not charge for Services provided. An IT Service Provider can be run as a Cost Centre or a Profit Centre.
Cost Effectiveness	A measure of the balance between the Effectiveness and Cost of a Service, Process or activity, A Cost Effective Process is one which achieves its Objectives at minimum Cost. See KPI, Return on Investment, Value for Money.
Cost Element	(Service Strategy) The middle level of category to which Costs are assigned in Budgeting and Accounting. The highest level category is Cost Type; for example, a Cost Type of 'people' could have cost elements of payroll, staff benefits, expenses, training, overtime, etc. Cost Elements can be further broken down to give Cost Units; for example, the Cost Element 'expenses' could include Cost Units of Hotels, Transport, Meals, etc.
Cost Management	(Service Strategy) A general term that is used to refer to Budgeting and Accounting, sometimes used as a synonym for Financial Management.
Cost Type	(Service Strategy) The highest level of category to which Costs are assigned in Budgeting and Accounting; for example, hardware, software, people, accommodation, external and Transfer. See Cost Element, Cost Type.
Cost Unit	(Service Strategy) The lowest level of category to which Costs are assigned, Cost Units are usually things that can be easily counted (e.g. staff numbers, software licenses) or things easily measured (e.g. CPU usage, Electricity consumed). Cost Units are included within Cost Elements; for example, a Cost Element of 'expenses' could include Cost Units of Hotels, Transport, Meals, etc. See Cost Type.
Countermeasure	Can be used to refer to any type of Control. The term Countermeasure is most often used when referring to measures that increase Resilience, Fault Tolerance or Reliability of an IT Service.
Course Corrections	Changes made to a Plan or Activity that has already started, to ensure that it will meet its Objectives. Course corrections are made as a result of Monitoring progress.
CRAMM	A methodology and tool for analyzing and managing Risks. CRAMM was developed by the UK Government, but is now privately owned. Further information is available from http://www.cramm.com/
Crisis Management	The Process responsible for managing the wider implications of Business Continuity. A Crisis Management team is responsible for Strategic issues such as managing media relations and shareholder confidence, and decides when to invoke Business Continuity Plans.
Critical Success Factor (CSF)	Something that must happen if a Process, Project, Plan, or IT Service is to succeed. KPIs are used to measure the achievement of each CSF; for example, a CSF of 'protect IT Services when making Changes' could be measured by KPIs such as 'percentage reduction of unsuccessful Changes', 'percentage reduction in Changes causing Incidents', etc.
Culture	A set of values that is shared by a group of people, including expectations about how people should behave, ideas, beliefs and practices. See Vision.
Customer	Someone who buys goods or Services. The Customer of an IT Service Provider is the person or group who defines and agrees the Service Level Targets. The term Customers is also sometimes informally used to mean Users, for example, 'this is a Customer focused Organization'.
Customer Portfolio	(Service Strategy) A database or structured Document used to record all Customers of the IT Service Provider. The Customer Portfolio is the Business Relationship Manager's view of the Customers who receive Services from the IT Service Provider. See Contract Portfolio, Service Portfolio.

Dashboard	(Service Operation) A graphical representation of overall IT Service Performance and Availability. Dashboard images may be updated in real-time, and can also be included in management reports and web pages. Dashboards can be used to support Service Level Management, Event Management or Incident Diagnosis.
Data-to-Information-to-Knowledge-to-Wisdom (DIKW)	A way of understanding the relationships between data, information, knowledge and wisdom. DIKW shows how each of these builds on the others.
Definitive Media Library (DML)	(Service Transition) One or more locations in which the definitive and approved versions of all software Configuration Items are securely stored. The DML may also contain associated CIs such as licenses and documentation. The DML is a single logical storage area even if there are multiple locations. All software in the DML is under the control of Change and Release Management and is recorded in the Configuration Management System. Only software from the DML is acceptable for use in a Release.
Deliverable	Something that must be provided to meet a commitment in a Service Level Agreement or a Contract. Deliverable is also used in a more informal way to mean a planned output of any Process.
Demand Management	Activities that understand and influence Customer demand for Services and the provision of Capacity to meet these demands. At a Strategic level Demand Management can involve analysis of Patterns of Business Activity and User Profiles. At a Tactical level it can involve use of Differential Charging to encourage Customers to use IT Services at less busy times. See Capacity Management.
Deming Cycle	Synonym for Plan-Do-Check-Act (PDCA) Cycle.
Dependency	The direct or indirect reliance of one Process or Activity upon another.
Deployment	(Service Transition) The Activity responsible for movement of new or changed hardware, software, documentation, Process, etc., to the Live Environment. Deployment is part of the Release and Deployment Management Process. See Rollout.
Depreciation	(Service Strategy) A measure of the reduction in value of an Asset over its life. This is based on wearing out, consumption or other reduction in the useful economic value.
Design	(Service Design) An Activity or Process that identifies Requirements and then defines a solution that is able to meet these Requirements. See Service Design.
Detection	(Service Operation) A stage in the Incident Lifecycle. Detection results in the Incident becoming known to the Service Provider. Detection can be automatic, or can be the result of a User logging an Incident.
Development	(Service Design) The Process responsible for creating or modifying an IT Service or Application. Also used to mean the Role or group that carries out Development work.
Development Environment	(Service Design) An Environment used to create or modify IT Services or Applications. Development Environments are not typically subjected to the same degree of control as Test Environments or Live Environments. See Development.
Diagnosis	(Service Operation) A stage in the Incident and Problem Lifecycles. The purpose of Diagnosis is to identify a Workaround for an Incident or the Root Cause of a Problem.
Diagnostic Script	(Service Operation) A structured set of questions used by Service Desk staff to ensure they ask the correct questions, and to help them Classify, Resolve and assign Incidents. Diagnostic Scripts may also be made available to Users to help them diagnose and resolve their own Incidents.
Differential Charging	A technique used to support Demand Management by charging different amounts for the same IT Service Function at different times.
Direct Cost	(Service Strategy) A cost of providing an IT Service which can be allocated in full to a specific Customer, Cost Centre, Project, etc., for example, cost of providing non-shared servers or software licenses. See Indirect Cost.

Directory Service	(Service Operation) An Application that manages information about IT Infrastructure available on a network, and corresponding User access Rights.
Do Nothing	(Service Design) A Recovery Option. The Service Provider formally agrees with the Customer that Recovery of this IT Service will not be performed.
Document	Information in readable form. A Document may be paper or electronic. For example, a Policy statement, Service Level Agreement, Incident Record, diagram of computer room layout. See Record.
Downtime	(Service Design) (Service Operation) The time when a Configuration Item or IT Service is not Available during its Agreed Service Time. The Availability of an IT Service is often calculated from Agreed Service Time and Downtime.
Driver	Something that influences Strategy, Objectives or Requirements. For example new legislation or the actions of competitors.
Early Life Support	(Service Transition) Support provided for a new or Changed IT Service for a period of time after it is Released. During Early Life Support the IT Service Provider may review the KPIs, Service Levels and Monitoring Thresholds, and provide additional Resources for Incident and Problem Management.
Economies of scale	(Service Strategy) The reduction in average Cost that is possible from increasing the usage of an IT Service or Asset. See Economies of Scope.
Economies of scope	(Service Strategy) The reduction in Cost that is allocated to an IT Service by using an existing Asset for an additional purpose. For example delivering a new IT Service from existing IT Infrastructure. See Economies of Scale.
Effectiveness	(Continual Service Improvement) A measure of whether the Objectives of a Process, Service or Activity have been achieved. An Effective Process or Activity is one that achieves its agreed Objectives. See KPI.
Efficiency	(Continual Service Improvement) A measure of whether the right amount of resources have been used to deliver a Process, Service or Activity. An Efficient Process achieves its Objectives with the minimum amount of time, money, people or other resources. See KPI.
Emergency Change	(Service Transition) A Change that must be introduced as soon as possible. For example, to resolve a Major Incident or implement a Security patch. The Change Management Process will normally have a specific Procedure for handling Emergency Changes. See Emergency Change Advisory Board (ECAB).
Emergency Change Advisory Board (ECAB)	(Service Transition) A sub-set of the Change Advisory Board who make decisions about high impact Emergency Changes. Membership of the ECAB may be decided at the time a meeting is called, and depends on the nature of the Emergency Change.
Environment	(Service Transition) A subset of the IT Infrastructure that is used for a particular purpose. For Example: Live Environment, Test Environment, Build Environment. It is possible for multiple Environments to share a Configuration Item, for example, Test and Live Environments may use different partitions on a single mainframe computer. Also used in the term Physical Environment to mean the accommodation, air conditioning, power system, etc. Environment is also used as a generic term to mean the external conditions that influence or affect something.
Error	(Service Operation) A design flaw or malfunction that causes a Failure of one or more Configuration Items or IT Services. A mistake made by a person or a faulty Process that impacts a CI or IT Service is also an Error.
Escalation	(Service Operation) An Activity that obtains additional Resources when these are needed to meet Service Level Targets or Customer expectations. Escalation may be needed within any IT Service Management Process, but is most commonly associated with Incident Management, Problem Management and the management of Customer complaints. There are two types of Escalation, Functional Escalation and Hierarchic Escalation.

eSourcing Capability Model for Client Organizations (eSCM-CL)	(Service Strategy) A framework to help Organizations guide their analysis and decisions on Service Sourcing Models and Strategies. eSCM-CL was developed by Carnegie Mellon University. See eSCM-SP.
eSourcing Capability Model for Service Providers (eSCM-SP)	(Service Strategy) A framework to help IT Service Providers develop their IT Service Management Capabilities from a Service Sourcing perspective. eSCM-SP was developed by Carnegie Mellon University. See eSCM-CL.
Estimation	The use of experience to provide an approximate value for a Metric or Cost. Estimation is also used in Capacity and Availability Management as the cheapest and least accurate Modeling method.
Evaluation	(Service Transition) The Process responsible for assessing a new or Changed IT Service to ensure that Risks have been managed and to help determine whether to proceed with the Change. Evaluation is also used to mean comparing an actual Outcome with the intended Outcome, or comparing one alternative with another.
Event	(Service Operation) A change of state which has significance for the management of a Configuration Item or IT Service. The term Event is also used to mean an Alert or notification created by any IT Service, Configuration Item or Monitoring tool. Events typically require IT Operations personnel to take actions, and often lead to Incidents being logged.
Event Management	(Service Operation) The Process responsible for managing Events throughout their Lifecycle. Event Management is one of the main Activities of IT Operations.
Exception Report	A Document containing details of one or more KPIs or other important targets that have exceeded defined Thresholds. Examples include SLA targets being missed or about to be missed, and a Performance Metric indicating a potential Capacity problem.
Expanded Incident Lifecycle	(Availability Management) Detailed stages in the Lifecycle of an Incident. The stages are Detection, Diagnosis, Repair, Recovery, Restoration. The Expanded Incident Lifecycle is used to help understand all contributions to the Impact of Incidents and to Plan how these could be controlled or reduced.
External Customer	A Customer who works for a different Business to the IT Service Provider. See External Service Provider, Internal Customer.
External Metric	A Metric that is used to measure the delivery of IT Service to a Customer. External Metrics are usually defined in SLAs and reported to Customers. See Internal Metric.
External Service Provider	(Service Strategy) An IT Service Provider which is part of a different Organization to their Customer. An IT Service Provider may have both Internal Customers and External Customers. See Type III Service Provider.
External Sourcing	Synonym for Outsourcing.
Facilities Management	(Service Operation) The Function responsible for managing the physical Environment where the IT Infrastructure is located. Facilities Management includes all aspects of managing the physical Environment, for example, power and cooling, building Access Management and environmental Monitoring.
Failure	(Service Operation) Loss of ability to Operate to Specification, or to deliver the required output. The term Failure may be used when referring to IT Services, Processes, Activities, Configuration Items, etc. A Failure often causes an Incident.
Failure Modes and Effects Analysis (FMEA)	An approach to assessing the potential Impact of Failures. FMEA involves analysing what would happen after Failure of each Configuration Item, all the way up to the effect on the Business. FMEA is often used in Information Security Management and in IT Service Continuity Planning.

Fast Recovery	(Service Design) A Recovery Option which is also known as Hot Standby. Provision is made to Recover the IT Service in a short period of time, typically less than 24 hours. Fast Recovery typically uses a dedicated Fixed Facility with computer Systems, and software configured ready to run the IT Services. Immediate Recovery may take up to 24 hours if there is a need to Restore data from Backups.
Fault	Synonym for Error.
Fault Tolerance	(Service Design) The ability of an IT Service or Configuration Item to continue to Operate correctly after Failure of a Component part.
	See Resilience, Countermeasure.
Fault Tree Analysis (FTA)	(Service Design) (Continual Service Improvement) A technique that can be used to determine the chain of Events that leads to a Problem. Fault Tree Analysis represents a chain of Events using Boolean notation in a diagram.
Financial Management	(Service Strategy) The Function and Processes responsible for managing an IT Service Provider's Budgeting, Accounting and Charging Requirements.
First-line Support	(Service Operation) The first level in a hierarchy of Support Groups involved in the resolution of Incidents. Each level contains more specialist skills, or has more time or other Resources. See Escalation.
Fishbone Diagram	Synonym for Ishikawa Diagram.
Fit for Purpose	An informal term used to describe a Process, Configuration Item, IT Service, etc., that is capable of meeting its Objectives or Service Levels. Being 'Fit for Purpose' requires suitable Design, implementation, Control and maintenance.
Fixed Cost	(Service Strategy) A Cost that does not vary with IT Service usage, for example, the cost of Server hardware.
	See Variable Cost.
Fixed Facility	(Service Design) A permanent building, available for use when needed by an IT Service Continuity Plan.
	See Recovery Option, Portable Facility.
Follow the Sun	(Service Operation) A methodology for using Service Desks and Support Groups around the world to provide seamless 24 * 7 Service. Calls, Incidents, Problems and Service Requests are passed between groups in different time zones.
Fulfilment	Performing Activities to meet a need or Requirement; for example, by providing a new IT Service, or meeting a Service Request.
Function	A team or group of people and the tools they use to carry out one or more Processes or Activities; for example, the Service Desk.
	The term Function also has two other meanings:
	• an intended purpose of a Configuration Item, Person, Team, Process, or IT Service; for example, one Function of an Email Service may be to store and forward outgoing mails, one Function of a Business Process may be to dispatch goods to Customers
	• to perform the intended purpose correctly, 'The computer is Functioning'
Functional Escalation	(Service Operation) Transferring an Incident, Problem or Change to a technical team with a higher level of expertise to assist in an Escalation.
Gap Analysis	(Continual Service Improvement) An Activity which compares two sets of data and identifies the differences. Gap Analysis is commonly used to compare a set of Requirements with actual delivery.
	See Benchmarking.
Governance	Ensuring that Policies and Strategy are actually implemented, and that required Processes are correctly followed. Governance includes defining Roles and responsibilities, measuring and reporting, and taking actions to resolve any issues identified.
Gradual Recovery	(Service Design) A Recovery Option which is also known as Cold Standby. Provision is made to Recover the IT Service in a period of time greater than 72 hours. Gradual Recovery typically uses a Portable or Fixed Facility that has environmental support and network cabling, but no computer Systems. The hardware and software are installed as part of the IT Service Continuity Plan.

Guideline	A Document describing Best Practice that recommends what should be done. Compliance to a guideline is not normally enforced. See Standard.
Help Desk	(Service Operation) A point of contact for Users to log Incidents. A Help Desk is usually more technically focused than a Service Desk and does not provide a Single Point of Contact for all interaction. The term Help Desk is often used as a synonym for Service Desk.
Hierarchic Escalation	(Service Operation) Informing or involving more senior levels of management to assist in an Escalation.
High Availability	(Service Design) An approach or Design that minimizes or hides the effects of Configuration Item Failure on the Users of an IT Service. High Availability solutions are Designed to achieve an agreed level of Availability and make use of techniques such as Fault Tolerance, Resilience and fast Recovery to reduce the number of Incidents, and the Impact of Incidents.
Hot Standby	Synonym for Fast Recovery or Immediate Recovery.
Identity	(Service Operation) A unique name that is used to identify a User, person or Role. The Identity is used to grant Rights to that User, person, or Role. Example identities might be the username SmithJ or the Role 'Change manager'.
Immediate Recovery	(Service Design) A Recovery Option which is also known as Hot Standby. Provision is made to Recover the IT Service with no loss of Service. Immediate Recovery typically uses mirroring, load balancing and split site technologies.
Impact	(Service Operation) (Service Transition) A measure of the effect of an Incident, Problem or Change on Business Processes. Impact is often based on how Service Levels will be affected. Impact and Urgency are used to assign Priority.
Incident	(Service Operation) An unplanned interruption to an IT Service or a reduction in the Quality of an IT Service. Failure of a Configuration Item that has not yet impacted Service is also an Incident; for example Failure of one disk from a mirror set.
Incident Management	(Service Operation) The Process responsible for managing the Lifecycle of all Incidents. The primary Objective of Incident Management is to return the IT Service to Users as quickly as possible.
Incident Record	(Service Operation) A Record containing the details of an Incident. Each Incident record documents the Lifecycle of a single Incident.
Indirect Cost	(Service Strategy) A Cost of providing an IT Service which cannot be allocated in full to a specific Customer; for example, Cost of providing shared Servers or software licenses. Also known as Overhead. See Direct Cost.
Information Security Management (ISM)	(Service Design) The Process that ensures the Confidentiality, Integrity and Availability of an Organization's Assets, information, data and IT Services. Information Security Management usually forms part of an Organizational approach to Security Management which has a wider scope than the IT Service Provider, and includes handling of paper, building access, phone calls etc., for the entire Organization.
Information Security Management System (ISMS)	(Service Design) The framework of Policy, Processes, Standards, Guidelines and tools that ensures an Organization can achieve its Information Security Management Objectives.
Information Security Policy	(Service Design) The Policy that governs the Organization's approach to Information Security Management.
Information Technology (IT)	The use of technology for the storage, communication or processing of information. The technology typically includes computers, telecommunications, Applications and other software. The information may include Business data, voice, images, video, etc. Information Technology is often used to support Business Processes through IT Services.
Infrastructure Service	An IT Service that is not directly used by the Business, but is required by the IT Service Provider, so they can provide other IT Services; for example, Directory Services, naming services, or communication services.
Insourcing	Synonym for Internal Sourcing.

Integrity	(Service Design) A security principle that ensures data and Configuration Items are only modified by authorized personnel and Activities. Integrity considers all possible causes of modification, including software and hardware Failure, environmental Events and human intervention.
Interactive Voice Response (IVR)	(Service Operation) A form of Automatic Call Distribution that accepts User input, such as key presses and spoken commands, to identify the correct destination for incoming Calls.
Intermediate Recovery	(Service Design) A Recovery Option which is also known as Warm Standby. Provision is made to Recover the IT Service in a period of time between 24 and 72 hours. Intermediate Recovery typically uses a shared Portable or Fixed Facility that has computer Systems and network Components. The hardware and software will need to be configured, and data will need to be restored, as part of the IT Service Continuity Plan.
Internal Customer	A Customer who works for the same Business as the IT Service Provider. See Internal Service Provider, External Customer.
Internal Metric	A Metric that is used within the IT Service Provider to Monitor the Efficiency, Effectiveness or Cost Effectiveness of the IT Service Provider's internal Processes. Internal Metrics are not normally reported to the Customer of the IT Service. See External Metric.
Internal Rate of Return (IRR)	(Service Strategy) A technique used to help make decisions about Capital Expenditure. IRR calculates a figure that allows two or more alternative investments to be compared. A larger IRR indicates a better investment. See Net Present Value, Return on Investment.
Internal Service Provider	(Service Strategy) An IT Service Provider which is part of the same Organization as their Customer. An IT Service Provider may have both Internal Customers and External Customers. See Type I Service Provider, Type II Service Provider, Insource.
Internal Sourcing	(Service Strategy) Using an Internal Service Provider to manage IT Services. See Service Sourcing, Type I Service Provider, Type II Service Provider.
International Organization for Standardization (ISO)	The International Organization for Standardization (ISO) is the world's largest developer of Standards. ISO is a non-governmental organization which is a network of the national standards institutes of 156 countries. Further information about ISO is available from http://www.iso.org/
International Standards Organization	See International Organization for Standardization (ISO).
Internet Service Provider (ISP)	An External Service Provider that provides access to the Internet. Most ISPs also provide other IT Services such as web hosting.
Invocation	(Service Design) Initiation of the steps defined in a plan; for example initiating the IT Service Continuity Plan for one or more IT Services.
Ishikawa Diagram	(Service Operation) (Continual Service Improvement) A technique that helps a team to identify all the possible causes of a Problem. Originally devised by Kaoru Ishikawa, the output of this technique is a diagram that looks like a fishbone.
ISO 9000	A generic term that refers to a number of international Standards and Guidelines for Quality Management Systems. See http://www.iso.org/ for more information. See ISO.
ISO 9001	An international Standard for Quality Management Systems. See ISO 9000, Standard.
ISO/IEC 17799	(Continual Service Improvement) ISO Code of Practice for Information Security Management. See Standard.
ISO/IEC 20000	ISO Specification and Code of Practice for IT Service Management. ISO/IEC 20000 is aligned with ITIL Best Practice.
ISO/IEC 27001	(Service Design) (Continual Service Improvement) ISO Specification for Information Security Management. The corresponding Code of Practice is ISO/IEC 17799. See Standard.

IT Directorate	(Continual Service Improvement) Senior Management within a Service Provider, charged with developing and delivering IT services. Most commonly used in UK Government departments.
IT Infrastructure	All of the hardware, software, networks, facilities, etc., that are required to Develop, Test, deliver, Monitor, Control or support IT Services. The term IT Infrastructure includes all of the Information Technology, but not the associated people, Processes and documentation.
IT Operations	(Service Operation) Activities carried out by IT Operations Control, including Console Management, Job Scheduling, Backup and Restore, and Print and Output Management.
	IT Operations is also used as a synonym for Service Operation.
IT Operations Control	(Service Operation) The Function responsible for Monitoring and Control of the IT Services and IT Infrastructure.
	See Operations Bridge.
IT Operations Management	(Service Operation) The Function within an IT Service Provider which performs the daily Activities needed to manage IT Services and the supporting IT Infrastructure. IT Operations Management includes IT Operations Control and Facilities Management.
IT Service	A Service provided to one or more Customers by an IT Service Provider. An IT Service is based on the use of Information Technology and supports the Customer's Business Processes. An IT Service is made up from a combination of people, Processes and technology and should be defined in a Service Level Agreement.
IT Service Continuity Management (ITSCM)	(Service Design) The Process responsible for managing Risks that could seriously impact IT Services. ITSCM ensures that the IT Service Provider can always provide minimum agreed Service Levels, by reducing the Risk to an acceptable level and Planning for the Recovery of IT Services. ITSCM should be designed to support Business Continuity Management.
IT Service Continuity Plan	(Service Design) A Plan defining the steps required to Recover one or more IT Services. The Plan will also identify the triggers for Invocation, people to be involved, communications, etc. The IT Service Continuity Plan should be part of a Business Continuity Plan.
IT Service Management (ITSM)	The implementation and management of Quality IT Services that meet the needs of the Business. IT Service Management is performed by IT Service Providers through an appropriate mix of people, Process and Information Technology.
	See Service Management.
IT Service Management Forum (itSMF)	The IT Service Management Forum is an independent Organization dedicated to promoting a professional approach to IT Service Management. The itSMF is a not-for-profit membership Organization with representation in many countries around the world (itSMF chapters). The itSMF and its membership contribute to the development of ITIL and associated IT Service Management Standards. See http://www.itsmf.com/ for more information.
IT Service Provider	(Service Strategy) A Service Provider that provides IT Services to Internal Customers or External Customers.
IT Steering Group (ISG)	A formal group that is responsible for ensuring that Business and IT Service Provider Strategies and Plans are closely aligned. An IT Steering Group includes senior representatives from the Business and the IT Service Provider.
ITIL	A set of Best Practice guidance for IT Service Management. ITIL is owned by the OGC and consists of a series of publications giving guidance on the provision of Quality IT Services, and on the Processes and facilities needed to support them. See http://www.itil.co.uk/ for more information.
Job Description	A Document which defines the Roles, responsibilities, skills and knowledge required by a particular person. One Job Description can include multiple Roles, for example the Roles of Configuration Manager and Change Manager may be carried out by one person.
Job Scheduling	(Service Operation) Planning and managing the execution of software tasks that are required as part of an IT Service. Job Scheduling is carried out by IT Operations Management, and is often automated using software tools that run batch or online tasks at specific times of the day, week, month or year.
Kano Model	(Service Strategy) A Model developed by Noriaki Kano that is used to help understand Customer preferences. The Kano Model considers Attributes of an IT Service grouped into areas such as Basic Factors, Excitement Factors, Performance Factors, etc.

Kepner & Tregoe Analysis	(Service Operation) (Continual Service Improvement) A structured approach to Problem solving. The Problem is analyzed in terms of what, where, when and extent. Possible causes are identified. The most probable cause is tested. The true cause is verified.
Key Performance Indicator (KPI)	(Continual Service Improvement) A Metric that is used to help manage a Process, IT Service or Activity. Many Metrics may be measured, but only the most important of these are defined as KPIs and used to actively manage and report on the Process, IT Service or Activity. KPIs should be selected to ensure that Efficiency, Effectiveness, and Cost Effectiveness are all managed. See Critical Success Factor.
Knowledge Base	(Service Transition) A logical database containing the data used by the Service Knowledge Management System.
Knowledge Management	(Service Transition) The Process responsible for gathering, analyzing, storing and sharing knowledge and information within an Organization. The primary purpose of Knowledge Management is to improve Efficiency by reducing the need to rediscover knowledge. See Data-to-Information-to-Knowledge-to-Wisdom, Service Knowledge Management System.
Known Error	(Service Operation) A Problem that has a documented Root Cause and a Workaround. Known Errors are created and managed throughout their Lifecycle by Problem Management. Known Errors may also be identified by Development or Suppliers.
Known Error Database (KEDB)	(Service Operation) A database containing all Known Error Records. This database is created by Problem Management and used by Incident and Problem Management. The Known Error Database is part of the Service Knowledge Management System.
Known Error Record	(Service Operation) A Record containing the details of a Known Error. Each Known Error Record documents the Lifecycle of a Known Error, including the Status, Root Cause and Workaround. In some implementations a Known Error is documented using additional fields in a Problem Record.
Lifecycle	The various stages in the life of an IT Service, Configuration Item, Incident, Problem, Change, etc. The Lifecycle defines the Categories for Status and the Status transitions that are permitted. For example: • The Lifecycle of an Application includes Requirements, Design, Build, Deploy, Operate, Optimise. • The Expanded Incident Lifecycle includes Detect, Respond, Diagnose, Repair, Recover, Restore. • The lifecycle of a Server may include: Ordered, Received, In Test, Live, Disposed, etc.
Line of Service (LOS)	(Service Strategy) A Core Service or Supporting Service that has multiple Service Level Packages. A line of Service is managed by a Product Manager and each Service Level Package is designed to support a particular market segment.
Live	(Service Transition) Refers to an IT Service or Configuration Item that is being used to deliver Service to a Customer.
Live Environment	(Service Transition) A controlled Environment containing Live Configuration Items used to deliver IT Services to Customers.
Maintainability	(Service Design) A measure of how quickly and Effectively a Configuration Item or IT Service can be restored to normal working after a Failure. Maintainability is often measured and reported as MTRS. Maintainability is also used in the context of Software or IT Service Development to mean ability to be Changed or Repaired easily.
Major Incident	(Service Operation) The highest Category of Impact for an Incident. A Major Incident results in significant disruption to the Business.
Managed Services	(Service Strategy) A perspective on IT Services which emphasizes the fact that they are managed. The term Managed Services is also used as a synonym for Outsourced IT Services.
Management Information	Information that is used to support decision-making by managers. Management Information is often generated automatically by tools supporting the various IT Service Management Processes. Management Information often includes the values of KPIs such as 'Percentage of Changes leading to Incidents', or 'first time fix rate'.
Management of Risk (M_o_R)	The OGC methodology for managing Risks. M_o_R includes all the Activities required to identify and Control the exposure to Risk which may have an impact on the achievement of an Organization's Business Objectives. See http://www.m-o-r.org/ for more details.

Management System	The framework of Policy, Processes and Functions that ensures an Organization can achieve its Objectives.
Manual Workaround	A Workaround that requires manual intervention. Manual Workaround is also used as the name of a Recovery Option in which The Business Process Operates without the use of IT Services. This is a temporary measure and is usually combined with another Recovery Option.
Marginal Cost	(Service Strategy) The Cost of continuing to provide the IT Service. Marginal Cost does not include investment already made; for example the cost of developing new software and delivering training.
Market Space	(Service Strategy) All opportunities that an IT Service Provider could exploit to meet business needs of Customers. The Market Space identifies the possible IT Services that an IT Service Provider may wish to consider delivering.
Maturity	(Continual Service Improvement) A measure of the Reliability, Efficiency and Effectiveness of a Process, Function, Organization, etc. The most mature Processes and Functions are formally aligned to Business Objectives and Strategy, and are supported by a framework for continual improvement.
Maturity Level	A named level in a Maturity model such as the Carnegie Mellon Capability Maturity Model Integration.
Mean Time Between Failures (MTBF)	(Service Design) A Metric for measuring and reporting Reliability. MTBF is the average time that a Configuration Item or IT Service can perform its agreed Function without interruption. This is measured from when the CI or IT Service starts working, until it next fails.
Mean Time Between Service Incidents (MTBSI)	(Service Design) A Metric used for measuring and reporting Reliability. MTBSI is the mean time from when a System or IT Service fails, until it next fails. MTBSI is equal to MTBF + MTRS.
Mean Time To Repair (MTTR)	The average time taken to repair a Configuration Item or IT Service after a Failure. MTTR is measured from when the CI or IT Service fails until it is Repaired. MTTR does not include the time required to Recover or Restore. MTTR is sometimes incorrectly used to mean Mean Time to Restore Service.
Mean Time to Restore Service (MTRS)	The average time taken to Restore a Configuration Item or IT Service after a Failure. MTRS is measured from when the CI or IT Service fails until it is fully Restored and delivering its normal functionality. See Maintainability, Mean Time to Repair.
Metric	(Continual Service Improvement) Something that is measured and reported to help manage a Process, IT Service or Activity. See KPI.
Middleware	(Service Design) Software that connects two or more software Components or Applications. Middleware is usually purchased from a Supplier, rather than developed within the IT Service Provider. See Off the Shelf.
Mission Statement	The Mission Statement of an Organization is a short but complete description of the overall purpose and intentions of that Organization. It states what is to be achieved, but not how this should be done.
Model	A representation of a System, Process, IT Service, Configuration Item, etc., that is used to help understand or predict future behaviour.
Modelling	A technique that is used to predict the future behavior of a System, Process, IT Service, Configuration Item, etc. Modelling is commonly used in Financial Management, Capacity Management and Availability Management.
Monitor Control Loop	(Service Operation) Monitoring the output of a Task, Process, IT Service or Configuration Item; comparing this output to a predefined norm; and taking appropriate action based on this comparison.
Monitoring	(Service Operation) Repeated observation of a Configuration Item, IT Service or Process to detect Events and to ensure that the current status is known.
Near-Shore	(Service Strategy) Provision of Services from a country near the country where the Customer is based. This can be the provision of an IT Service, or of supporting Functions such as Service Desk. See On-shore, Off-shore.

Net Present Value (NPV)	(Service Strategy) A technique used to help make decisions about Capital Expenditure. NPV compares cash inflows to cash outflows. Positive NPV indicates that an investment is worthwhile. See Internal Rate of Return, Return on Investment.
Notional Charging	(Service Strategy) An approach to Charging for IT Services. Charges to Customers are calculated and Customers are informed of the charge, but no money is actually transferred. Notional Charging is sometimes introduced to ensure that Customers are aware of the Costs they incur or as a stage during the introduction of real Charging.
Objective	The defined purpose or aim of a Process, an Activity or an Organization as a whole. Objectives are usually expressed as measurable targets. The term Objective is also informally used to mean a Requirement. See Outcome.
Off the Shelf	Synonym for Commercial Off the Shelf.
Office of Government Commerce (OGC)	OGC owns the ITIL brand (copyright and trademark). OGC is a UK Government department that supports the delivery of the government's procurement agenda through its work in collaborative procurement and in raising levels of procurement skills and capability with departments. It also provides support for complex public sector projects.
Office of Public Sector Information (OPSI)	OPSI license the Crown Copyright material used in the ITIL publications. They are a UK Government department who provide online access to UK legislation, license the re-use of Crown copyright material, manage the Information Fair Trader Scheme, maintain the Government's Information Asset Register and provide advice and guidance on official publishing and Crown copyright.
Off-shore	(Service Strategy) Provision of Services from a location outside the country where the Customer is based, often in a different continent. This can be the provision of an IT Service, or of supporting Functions such as Service Desk. See On-shore, Near-shore.
On-shore	(Service Strategy) Provision of Services from a location within the country where the Customer is based. See Off-shore, Near-shore.
Operate	To perform as expected. A Process or Configuration Item is said to Operate if it is delivering the Required outputs. Operate also means to perform one or more Operations; for example, to Operate a computer is to do the day-to-day Operations needed for it to perform as expected.
Operation	(Service Operation) Day-to-day management of an IT Service, System, or other Configuration Item. Operation is also used to mean any pre-defined Activity or Transaction; for example loading a magnetic tape, accepting money at a point of sale, or reading data from a disk drive.
Operational	The lowest of three levels of Planning and delivery (Strategic, Tactical, Operational). Operational Activities include the day-to-day or short term Planning or delivery of a Business Process or IT Service Management Process. The term Operational is also a synonym for Live.
Operational Cost	Cost resulting from running the IT Services. Often repeating payments; for example staff costs, hardware maintenance and electricity (also known as 'current expenditure' or 'revenue expenditure'). See Capital Expenditure.
Operational Expenditure (OPEX)	Synonym for Operational Cost.
Operational Level Agreement (OLA)	(Service Design) (Continual Service Improvement) An Agreement between an IT Service Provider and another part of the same Organization. An OLA supports the IT Service Provider's delivery of IT Services to Customers. The OLA defines the goods or Services to be provided and the responsibilities of both parties; for example there could be an OLA: • between the IT Service Provider and a procurement department to obtain hardware in agreed times • between the Service Desk and a Support Group to provide Incident Resolution in agreed times See Service Level Agreement.

Operations Bridge	(Service Operation) A physical location where IT Services and IT Infrastructure are monitored and managed.
Operations Control	Synonym for IT Operations Control.
Operations Management	Synonym for IT Operations Management.
Opportunity Cost	(Service Strategy) A Cost that is used in deciding between investment choices. Opportunity Cost represents the revenue that would have been generated by using the Resources in a different way; for example the Opportunity Cost of purchasing a new Server may include not carrying out a Service Improvement activity that the money could have been spent on. Opportunity cost analysis is used as part of a decision-making processes, but is not treated as an actual Cost in any financial statement.
Optimize	Review, Plan and request Changes, in order to obtain the maximum Efficiency and Effectiveness from a Process, Configuration Item, Application, etc.
Organization	A company, legal entity or other institution. Examples of Organizations that are not companies include International Standards Organization or itSMF. The term Organization is sometimes used to refer to any entity which has People, Resources and Budgets; for example a Project or Business Unit.
Outcome	The result of carrying out an Activity; following a Process; delivering an IT Service; etc. The term Outcome is used to refer to intended results, as well as to actual results. See Objective.
Outsourcing	(Service Strategy) Using an External Service Provider to manage IT Services. See Service Sourcing, Type III Service Provider.
Overhead	Synonym for Indirect cost.
Pain Value Analysis	(Service Operation) A technique used to help identify the Business Impact of one or more Problems. A formula is used to calculate Pain Value based on the number of Users affected, the duration of the Downtime, the Impact on each User, and the cost to the Business (if known).
Pareto Principle	(Service Operation) A technique used to prioritise Activities. The Pareto Principle says that 80% of the value of any Activity is created with 20% of the effort. Pareto Analysis is also used in Problem Management to prioritise possible Problem causes for investigation.
Partnership	A relationship between two Organizations which involves working closely together for common goals or mutual benefit. The IT Service Provider should have a Partnership with the Business, and with Third Parties who are critical to the delivery of IT Services. See Value Network.
Passive Monitoring	(Service Operation) Monitoring of a Configuration Item, an IT Service or a Process that relies on an Alert or notification to discover the current status. See Active Monitoring.
Pattern of Business Activity (PBA)	(Service Strategy) A Workload profile of one or more Business Activities. Patterns of Business Activity are used to help the IT Service Provider understand and plan for different levels of Business Activity. See User Profile.
Percentage utilization	(Service Design) The amount of time that a Component is busy over a given period of time; for example, if a CPU is busy for 1800 seconds in a one hour period, its utilization is 50%.
Performance	A measure of what is achieved or delivered by a System, person, team, Process or IT Service.
Performance Anatomy	(Service Strategy) An approach to Organizational Culture that integrates, and actively manages, leadership and strategy, people development, technology enablement, performance management and innovation.
Performance Management	(Continual Service Improvement) The Process responsible for day-to-day Capacity Management Activities. These include Monitoring, Threshold detection, Performance analysis and Tuning, and implementing Changes related to Performance and Capacity.
Pilot	(Service Transition) A limited Deployment of an IT Service, a Release or a Process to the Live Environment. A Pilot is used to reduce Risk and to gain User feedback and Acceptance. See Test, Evaluation.

Plan	A detailed proposal which describes the Activities and Resources needed to achieve an Objective; for example, a Plan to implement a new IT Service or Process. ISO/IEC 20000 requires a Plan for the management of each IT Service Management Process.
Plan-Do-Check-Act (PDCA)	(Continual Service Improvement) A four stage cycle for Process management, attributed to Dr W Edwards Deming. Plan-Do-Check-Act is also called the Deming Cycle.
	PLAN: Design or revise Processes that support the IT Services
	DO: Implement the Plan and manage the Processes
	CHECK: Measure the Processes and IT Services, compare with Objectives and produce reports
	ACT: Plan and implement Changes to improve the Processes
Planned Downtime	(Service Design) Agreed time when an IT Service will not be available. Planned Downtime is often used for maintenance, upgrades and testing.
	See Change Window, Downtime.
Planning	An Activity responsible for creating one or more Plans; for example, Capacity Planning.
PMBoK	A Project management Standard maintained and published by the Project Management Institute. PMBoK stands for Project Management Body of Knowledge. See http://www.pmi.org/ for more information.
	See PRINCE2.
Policy	Formally documented management expectations and intentions. Policies are used to direct decisions, and to ensure consistent and appropriate development and implementation of Processes, Standards, Roles, Activities, IT Infrastructure, etc.
Portable Facility	(Service Design) A prefabricated building, or a large vehicle, provided by a Third Party and moved to a site when needed by an IT Service Continuity Plan.
	See Recovery Option, Fixed Facility.
Post Implementation Review (PIR)	A Review that takes place after a Change or a Project has been implemented. A PIR determines if the Change or Project was successful, and identifies opportunities for improvement.
Practice	A way of working, or a way in which work must be done. Practices can include Activities, Processes, Functions, Standards and Guidelines.
	See Best Practice.
Prerequisite for Success (PFS)	An Activity that needs to be completed, or a condition that needs to be met, to enable successful implementation of a Plan or Process. A PFS is often an output from one Process that is a required input to another Process.
Pricing	(Service Strategy) The Activity for establishing how much Customers will be Charged.
PRINCE2	The standard UK government methodology for Project management. See http://www.ogc.gov.uk/prince2/ for more information.
	See PMBoK.
Priority	(Service Transition) (Service Operation) A Category used to identify the relative importance of an Incident, Problem or Change. Priority is based on Impact and Urgency, and is used to identify required times for actions to be taken; for example, the SLA may state that Priority2 Incidents must be resolved within 12 hours.
Proactive Monitoring	(Service Operation) Monitoring that looks for patterns of Events to predict possible future Failures. See Reactive Monitoring.
Proactive Problem Management	(Service Operation) Part of the Problem Management Process. The Objective of Proactive Problem Management is to identify Problems that might otherwise be missed. Proactive Problem Management analyses Incident Records, and uses data collected by other IT Service Management Processes to identify trends or significant Problems.
Problem	(Service Operation) A cause of one or more Incidents. The cause is not usually known at the time a Problem Record is created, and the Problem Management Process is responsible for further investigation.
Problem Management	(Service Operation) The Process responsible for managing the Lifecycle of all Problems. The primary Objectives of Problem Management are to prevent Incidents from happening, and to minimize the Impact of Incidents that cannot be prevented.

Problem Record	(Service Operation) A Record containing the details of a Problem. Each Problem Record documents the Lifecycle of a single Problem.
Procedure	A Document containing steps that specify how to achieve an Activity. Procedures are defined as part of Processes. See Work Instruction.
Process	A structured set of Activities designed to accomplish a specific Objective. A Process takes one or more defined inputs and turns them into defined outputs. A Process may include any of the Roles, responsibilities, tools and management Controls required to reliably deliver the outputs. A Process may define Policies, Standards, Guidelines, Activities, and Work Instructions if they are needed.
Process Control	The Activity of planning and regulating a Process, with the Objective of performing the Process in an Effective, Efficient, and consistent manner.
Process Manager	A Role responsible for Operational management of a Process. The Process Manager's responsibilities include Planning and coordination of all Activities required to carry out, monitor and report on the Process. There may be several Process Managers for one Process; for example, regional Change Managers or IT Service Continuity Managers for each data centre. The Process Manager Role is often assigned to the person who carries out the Process Owner Role, but the two Roles may be separate in larger Organizations.
Process Owner	A Role responsible for ensuring that a Process is 'Fit for Purpose'. The Process Owner's responsibilities include sponsorship, Design, Change Management and continual improvement of the Process and its Metrics. This Role is often assigned to the same person who carries out the Process Manager Role, but the two Roles may be separate in larger Organizations.
Production Environment	Synonym for Live Environment.
Profit Centre	(Service Strategy) A Business Unit which charges for Services provided. A Profit Centre can be created with the objective of making a profit, recovering Costs, or running at a loss. An IT Service Provider can be run as a Cost Centre or a Profit Centre.
Pro-forma	A template, or example Document, containing example data that will be replaced with the real values when these are available.
Program/ Programme	A number of Projects and Activities that are planned and managed together to achieve an overall set of related Objectives and other Outcomes.
Project	A temporary Organization, with people and other Assets required to achieve an Objective or other Outcome. Each Project has a Lifecycle that typically includes initiation, Planning, execution, Closure, etc. Projects are usually managed using a formal methodology such as PRINCE2.
Projected Service Outage (PSO)	(Service Transition) A Document that identifies the effect of planned Changes, maintenance Activities and Test Plans on agreed Service Levels.
PRojects IN Controlled Environments (PRINCE2)	See PRINCE2
Qualification	(Service Transition) An Activity that ensures that IT Infrastructure is appropriate, and correctly configured, to support an Application or IT Service. See Validation.
Quality	The ability of a product, Service, or Process to provide the intended value. For example, a hardware Component can be considered to be of high Quality if it performs as expected and delivers the required Reliability. Process Quality also requires an ability to monitor Effectiveness and Efficiency, and to improve them if necessary. See Quality Management System.
Quality Assurance (QA)	(Service Transition) The Process responsible for ensuring that the Quality of a product, Service or Process will provide its intended Value.
Quality Management System (QMS)	(Continual Service Improvement) The set of Processes responsible for ensuring that all work carried out by an Organization is of a suitable Quality to reliably meet Business Objectives or Service Levels. See ISO 9000.

Quick Win	(Continual Service Improvement) An improvement Activity which is expected to provide a Return on Investment in a short period of time with relatively small Cost and effort. See Pareto Principle.
RACI	(Service Design) (Continual Service Improvement) A Model used to help define Roles and Responsibilities. RACI stands for Responsible, Accountable, Consulted and Informed. See Stakeholder.
Reactive Monitoring	(Service Operation) Monitoring that takes action in response to an Event. For example submitting a batch job when the previous job completes, or logging an Incident when an Error occurs. See Proactive Monitoring.
Reciprocal Arrangement	(Service Design) A Recovery Option. An agreement between two Organizations to share resources in an emergency; for example, Computer Room space or use of a mainframe.
Record	A Document containing the results or other output from a Process or Activity. Records are evidence of the fact that an Activity took place and may be paper or electronic; for example, an Audit report, an Incident Record, or the minutes of a meeting.
Recovery	(Service Design) (Service Operation) Returning a Configuration Item or an IT Service to a working state. Recovery of an IT Service often includes recovering data to a known consistent state. After Recovery, further steps may be needed before the IT Service can be made available to the Users (Restoration).
Recovery Option	(Service Design) A Strategy for responding to an interruption to Service. Commonly used Strategies are Do Nothing, Manual Workaround, Reciprocal Arrangement, Gradual Recovery, Intermediate Recovery, Fast Recovery, Immediate Recovery. Recovery Options may make use of dedicated facilities, or Third Party facilities shared by multiple Businesses.
Recovery Point Objective (RPO)	(Service Operation) The maximum amount of data that may be lost when Service is Restored after an interruption. Recovery Point Objective is expressed as a length of time before the Failure; for example, a Recovery Point Objective of one day may be supported by daily Backups, and up to 24 hours of data may be lost. Recovery Point Objectives for each IT Service should be negotiated, agreed and documented, and used as Requirements for Service Design and IT Service Continuity Plans.
Recovery Time Objective (RTO)	(Service Operation) The maximum time allowed for recovery of an IT Service following an interruption. The Service Level to be provided may be less than normal Service Level Targets. Recovery Time Objectives for each IT Service should be negotiated, agreed and documented. See Business Impact Analysis.
Redundancy	Synonym for Fault Tolerance. The term Redundant also has a generic meaning of obsolete, or no longer needed.
Relationship	A connection or interaction between two people or things. In Business Relationship Management it is the interaction between the IT Service Provider and the Business. In Configuration Management it is a link between two Configuration Items that identifies a dependency or connection between them; for example, Applications may be linked to the Servers they run on, IT Services have many links to all the CIs that contribute to them.
Relationship Processes	The ISO/IEC 20000 Process group that includes Business Relationship Management and Supplier Management.
Release	(Service Transition) A collection of hardware, software, documentation, Processes or other Components required to implement one or more approved Changes to IT Services. The contents of each Release are managed, Tested, and Deployed as a single entity.
Release and Deployment Management	(Service Transition) The Process responsible for both Release Management and Deployment.
Release Identification	(Service Transition) A naming convention used to uniquely identify a Release. The Release Identification typically includes a reference to the Configuration Item and a version number; for example Microsoft Office 2003 SR2.

Release Management	(Service Transition) The Process responsible for Planning, scheduling and controlling the movement of Releases to Test and Live Environments. The primary Objective of Release Management is to ensure that the integrity of the Live Environment is protected and that the correct Components are released. Release Management is part of the Release and Deployment Management Process.
Release Process	The name used by ISO/IEC 20000 for the Process group that includes Release Management. This group does not include any other Processes. Release Process is also used as a synonym for Release Management Process.
Release Record	(Service Transition) A Record in the CMDB that defines the content of a Release. A Release Record has Relationships with all Configuration Items that are affected by the Release.
Release Unit	(Service Transition) Components of an IT Service that are normally Released together. A Release Unit typically includes sufficient Components to perform a useful Function; for example one Release Unit could be a Desktop PC, including Hardware, Software, Licenses, Documentation, etc.; a different Release Unit may be the complete Payroll Application, including IT Operations Procedures and User training.
Release Window	Synonym for Change Window.
Reliability	(Service Design) (Continual Service Improvement) A measure of how long a Configuration Item or IT Service can perform its agreed Function without interruption. Usually measured as MTBF or MTBSI. The term Reliability can also be used to state how likely it is that a Process, Function, etc. will deliver its required outputs. See Availability.
Remediation	(Service Transition) Recovery to a known state after a failed Change or Release.
Repair	(Service Operation) The replacement or correction of a failed Configuration Item.
Request for Change (RFC)	(Service Transition) A formal proposal for a Change to be made. An RFC includes details of the proposed Change, and may be recorded on paper or electronically. The term RFC is often misused to mean a Change Record, or the Change itself.
Request Fulfillment	(Service Operation) The Process responsible for managing the Lifecycle of all Service Requests.
Requirement	(Service Design) A formal statement of what is needed; for example, a Service Level Requirement, a Project Requirement or the required Deliverables for a Process. See Statement of Requirements.
Resilience	(Service Design) The ability of a Configuration Item or IT Service to resist Failure or to Recover quickly following a Failure; for example, an armoured cable will resist failure when put under stress. See Fault Tolerance.
Resolution	(Service Operation) Action taken to repair the Root Cause of an Incident or Problem, or to implement a Workaround. In ISO/IEC 20000, Resolution Processes is the Process group that includes Incident and Problem Management.
Resolution Processes	The ISO/IEC 20000 Process group that includes Incident Management and Problem Management.
Resource	(Service Strategy) A generic term that includes IT Infrastructure, people, money or anything else that might help to deliver an IT Service. Resources are considered to be Assets of an Organization. See Capability, Service Asset.
Response Time	A measure of the time taken to complete an Operation or Transaction. Used in Capacity Management as a measure of IT Infrastructure Performance, and in Incident Management as a measure of the time taken to answer the phone, or to start Diagnosis.
Responsiveness	A measurement of the time taken to respond to something. This could be Response Time of a Transaction, or the speed with which an IT Service Provider responds to an Incident or Request for Change, etc.
Restoration of Service	See Restore.
Restore	(Service Operation) Taking action to return an IT Service to the Users after Repair and Recovery from an Incident. This is the primary Objective of Incident Management.

Retire	(Service Transition) Permanent removal of an IT Service, or other Configuration Item, from the Live Environment. Retired is a stage in the Lifecycle of many Configuration Items.
Return on Investment (ROI)	(Service Strategy) (Continual Service Improvement) A measurement of the expected benefit of an investment. In the simplest sense it is the net profit of an investment divided by the net worth of the assets invested.
	See Net Present Value, Value on Investment.
Return to Normal	(Service Design) The phase of an IT Service Continuity Plan during which full normal operations are resumed; for example, if an alternate data centre has been in use, then this phase will bring the primary data centre back into operation, and restore the ability to invoke IT Service Continuity Plans again.
Review	An evaluation of a Change, Problem, Process, Project, etc. Reviews are typically carried out at predefined points in the Lifecycle, and especially after Closure. The purpose of a Review is to ensure that all Deliverables have been provided, and to identify opportunities for improvement.
	See Post Implementation Review.
Rights	(Service Operation) Entitlements, or permissions, granted to a User or Role; for example the Right to modify particular data, or to authorize a Change.
Risk	A possible Event that could cause harm or loss, or affect the ability to achieve Objectives. A Risk is measured by the probability of a Threat, the Vulnerability of the Asset to that Threat, and the Impact it would have if it occurred.
Risk Assessment	The initial steps of Risk Management. Analysing the value of Assets to the business, identifying Threats to those Assets, and evaluating how Vulnerable each Asset is to those Threats. Risk Assessment can be quantitative (based on numerical data) or qualitative.
Risk Management	The Process responsible for identifying, assessing and controlling Risks.
	See Risk Assessment.
Role	A set of responsibilities, Activities and authorities granted to a person or team. A Role is defined in a Process. One person or team may have multiple Roles; for example, the Roles of Configuration Manager and Change Manager may be carried out by a single person.
Rollout	(Service Transition) Synonym for Deployment. Most often used to refer to complex or phased Deployments or Deployments to multiple locations.
Root Cause	(Service Operation) The underlying or original cause of an Incident or Problem.
Root Cause Analysis (RCA)	(Service Operation) An Activity that identifies the Root Cause of an Incident or Problem. RCA typically concentrates on IT Infrastructure failures.
	See Service Failure Analysis.
Running Costs	Synonym for Operational Costs.
Scalability	The ability of an IT Service, Process, Configuration Item, etc. to perform its agreed Function when the Workload or Scope changes.
Scope	The boundary, or extent, to which a Process, Procedure, Certification, Contract, etc. applies; for example, the Scope of Change Management may include all Live IT Services and related Configuration Items; the Scope of an ISO/IEC 20000 Certificate may include all IT Services delivered out of a named data centre.
Second-line Support	(Service Operation) The second level in a hierarchy of Support Groups involved in the resolution of Incidents and investigation of Problems. Each level contains more specialist skills, or has more time or other Resources.
Security	See Information Security Management.
Security Management	Synonym for Information Security Management.
Security Policy	Synonym for Information Security Policy.
Separation of Concerns (SoC)	(Service Strategy) An approach to Designing a solution or IT Service that divides the problem into pieces that can be solved independently. This approach separates 'what' is to be done from 'how' it is to be done.
Server	(Service Operation) A computer that is connected to a network and provides software Functions that are used by other computers.

Service	A means of delivering value to Customers by facilitating Outcomes Customers want to achieve without the ownership of specific Costs and Risks.
Service Acceptance Criteria (SAC)	(Service Transition) A set of criteria used to ensure that an IT Service meets its functionality and Quality Requirements and that the IT Service Provider is ready to Operate the new IT Service when it has been Deployed. See Acceptance.
Service Analytics	(Service Strategy) A technique used in the Assessment of the Business Impact of Incidents. Service Analytics Models the dependencies between Configuration Items, and the dependencies of IT Services on Configuration Items.
Service Asset	Any Capability or Resource of a Service Provider. See Asset.
Service Asset and Configuration Management (SACM)	(Service Transition) The Process responsible for both Configuration Management and Asset Management.
Service Capacity Management (SCM)	(Service Design) (Continual Service Improvement) The Activity responsible for understanding the Performance and Capacity of IT Services. The Resources used by each IT Service and the pattern of usage over time are collected, recorded, and analyzed for use in the Capacity Plan. See Business Capacity Management, Component Capacity Management.
Service Catalogue	(Service Design) A database or structured Document with information about all Live IT Services, including those available for Deployment. The Service Catalogue is the only part of the Service Portfolio published to Customers, and is used to support the sale and delivery of IT Services. The Service Catalogue includes information about deliverables, prices, contact points, ordering and request Processes. See Contract Portfolio.
Service Continuity Management	Synonym for IT Service Continuity Management.
Service Contract	(Service Strategy) A Contract to deliver one or more IT Services. The term Service Contract is also used to mean any Agreement to deliver IT Services, whether this is a legal Contract or an SLA. See Contract Portfolio.
Service Culture	A Customer oriented Culture. The major Objectives of a Service Culture are Customer satisfaction and helping the Customer to achieve their Business Objectives.
Service Design	(Service Design) A stage in the Lifecycle of an IT Service. Service Design includes a number of Processes and Functions and is the title of one of the Core ITIL publications. See Design.
Service Design Package	(Service Design) Document(s) defining all aspects of an IT Service and its Requirements through each stage of its Lifecycle. A Service Design Package is produced for each new IT Service, major Change, or IT Service Retirement.
Service Desk	(Service Operation) The Single Point of Contact between the Service Provider and the Users. A typical Service Desk manages Incidents and Service Requests, and also handles communication with the Users.
Service Failure Analysis (SFA)	(Service Design) An Activity that identifies underlying causes of one or more IT Service interruptions. SFA identifies opportunities to improve the IT Service Provider's Processes and tools, and not just the IT Infrastructure. SFA is a time constrained, project-like activity, rather than an ongoing process of analysis. See Root Cause Analysis.
Service Hours	(Service Design) (Continual Service Improvement) An agreed time period when a particular IT Service should be Available; for example, 'Monday-Friday 08:00 to 17:00 except public holidays'. Service Hours should be defined in a Service Level Agreement.
Service Improvement Plan (SIP)	(Continual Service Improvement) A formal Plan to implement improvements to a Process or IT Service.

Service Knowledge Management System (SKMS)	(Service Transition) A set of tools and databases that are used to manage knowledge and information. The SKMS includes the Configuration Management System, as well as other tools and databases. The SKMS stores, manages, updates, and presents all information that an IT Service Provider needs to manage the full Lifecycle of IT Services.
Service Level	Measured and reported achievement against one or more Service Level Targets. The term Service Level is sometimes used informally to mean Service Level Target.
Service Level Agreement (SLA)	(Service Design) (Continual Service Improvement) An Agreement between an IT Service Provider and a Customer. The SLA describes the IT Service, documents Service Level Targets, and specifies the responsibilities of the IT Service Provider and the Customer. A single SLA may cover multiple IT Services or multiple Customers. See Operational Level Agreement.
Service Level Management (SLM)	(Service Design) (Continual Service Improvement) The Process responsible for negotiating Service Level Agreements, and ensuring that these are met. SLM is responsible for ensuring that all IT Service Management Processes, Operational Level Agreements, and Underpinning Contracts, are appropriate for the agreed Service Level Targets. SLM monitors and reports on Service Levels, and holds regular Customer reviews.
Service Level Package (SLP)	(Service Strategy) A defined level of Utility and Warranty for a particular Service Package. Each SLP is designed to meet the needs of a particular Pattern of Business Activity. See Line of Service.
Service Level Requirement (SLR)	(Service Design) (Continual Service Improvement) A Customer Requirement for an aspect of an IT Service. SLRs are based on Business Objectives and are used to negotiate agreed Service Level Targets.
Service Level Target	(Service Design) (Continual Service Improvement) A commitment that is documented in a Service Level Agreement. Service Level Targets are based on Service Level Requirements, and are needed to ensure that the IT Service Design is 'Fit for Purpose'. Service Level Targets should be SMART, and are usually based on KPIs.
Service Maintenance Objective	(Service Operation) The expected time that a Configuration Item will be unavailable due to planned maintenance Activity.
Service Management	Service Management is a set of specialized organizational capabilities for providing value to customers in the form of services.
Service Management Lifecycle	An approach to IT Service Management that emphasizes the importance of coordination and Control across the various Functions, Processes, and Systems necessary to manage the full Lifecycle of IT Services. The Service Management Lifecycle approach considers the Strategy, Design, Transition, Operation and Continuous Improvement of IT Services.
Service Manager	A manager who is responsible for managing the end-to-end Lifecycle of one or more IT Services. The term Service Manager is also used to mean any manager within the IT Service Provider. Most commonly used to refer to a Business Relationship Manager, a Process Manager, an Account Manager or a senior manager with responsibility for IT Services overall.
Service Operation	(Service Operation) A stage in the Lifecycle of an IT Service. Service Operation includes a number of Processes and Functions and is the title of one of the Core ITIL publications. See Operation.
Service Owner	(Continual Service Improvement) A Role which is accountable for the delivery of a specific IT Service.
Service Package	(Service Strategy) A detailed description of an IT Service that is available to be delivered to Customers. A Service Package includes a Service Level Package and one or more Core Services and Supporting Services.
Service Pipeline	(Service Strategy) A database or structured Document listing all IT Services that are under consideration or Development, but are not yet available to Customers. The Service Pipeline provides a Business view of possible future IT Services and is part of the Service Portfolio which is not normally published to Customers.

Service Portfolio	(Service Strategy) The complete set of Services that are managed by a Service Provider. The Service Portfolio is used to manage the entire Lifecycle of all Services, and includes three Categories: Service Pipeline (proposed or in Development); Service Catalogue (Live or available for Deployment); and Retired Services.
	See Service Portfolio Management, Contract Portfolio.
Service Portfolio Management (SPM)	(Service Strategy) The Process responsible for managing the Service Portfolio. Service Portfolio Management considers Services in terms of the Business value that they provide.
Service Potential	(Service Strategy) The total possible value of the overall Capabilities and Resources of the IT Service Provider.
Service Provider	(Service Strategy) An Organization supplying Services to one or more Internal Customers or External Customers. Service Provider is often used as an abbreviation for IT Service Provider.
	See Type I Service Provider, Type II Service Provider, Type III Service Provider.
Service Provider Interface (SPI)	(Service Strategy) An interface between the IT Service Provider and a User, Customer, Business Process, or a Supplier. Analysis of Service Provider Interfaces helps to co-ordinate end-to-end management of IT Services.
Service Provisioning Optimisation (SPO)	(Service Strategy) Analysing the finances and constraints of an IT Service to decide if alternative approaches to Service delivery might reduce Costs or improve Quality.
Service Reporting	(Continual Service Improvement) The Process responsible for producing and delivering reports of achievement and trends against Service Levels. Service Reporting should agree the format, content and frequency of reports with Customers.
Service Request	(Service Operation) A request from a User for information, or advice, or for a Standard Change or for Access to an IT Service; for example, to reset a password, or to provide standard IT Services for a new User. Service Requests are usually handled by a Service Desk, and do not require an RFC to be submitted.
	See Request Fulfilment.
Service Sourcing	(Service Strategy) The Strategy and approach for deciding whether to provide a Service internally or to Outsource it to an External Service Provider. Service Sourcing also means the execution of this Strategy.
	Service Sourcing includes:
	• Internal Sourcing - Internal or Shared Services using Type I or Type II Service Providers
	• Traditional Sourcing - Full Service Outsourcing using a Type III Service Provider
	• Multi-vendor Sourcing - Prime, Consortium or Selective Outsourcing using Type III Service Providers
Service Strategy	(Service Strategy) The title of one of the Core ITIL publications. Service Strategy establishes an overall Strategy for IT Services and for IT Service Management.
Service Transition	(Service Transition) A stage in the Lifecycle of an IT Service. Service Transition includes a number of Processes and Functions and is the title of one of the Core ITIL publications.
	See Transition.
Service Utility	(Service Strategy) The Functionality of an IT Service from the Customer's perspective. The Business value of an IT Service is created by the combination of Service Utility (what the Service does) and Service Warranty (how well it does it).
	See Utility.
Service Validation and Testing	(Service Transition) The Process responsible for Validation and Testing of a new or Changed IT Service. Service Validation and Testing ensures that the IT Service matches its Design Specification and will meet the needs of the Business.
Service Valuation	(Service Strategy) A measurement of the total Cost of delivering an IT Service, and the total value to the Business of that IT Service. Service Valuation is used to help the Business and the IT Service Provider agree on the value of the IT Service.

Service Warranty	(Service Strategy) Assurance that an IT Service will meet agreed Requirements. This may be a formal Agreement such as a Service Level Agreement or Contract, or may be a marketing message or brand image. The Business value of an IT Service is created by the combination of Service Utility (what the Service does) and Service Warranty (how well it does it). See Warranty.
Serviceability	(Service Design) (Continual Service Improvement) The ability of a Third Party Supplier to meet the terms of their Contract. This Contract will include agreed levels of Reliability, Maintainability or Availability for a Configuration Item.
Shift	(Service Operation) A group or team of people who carry out a specific Role for a fixed period of time; for example, there could be four shifts of IT Operations Control personnel to support an IT Service that is used 24 hours a day.
Simulation modelling	(Service Design) (Continual Service Improvement) A technique that creates a detailed Model to predict the behaviour of a Configuration Item or IT Service. Simulation Models can be very accurate but are expensive and time consuming to create. A Simulation Model is often created by using the actual Configuration Items that are being modelled, with artificial Workloads or Transactions. They are used in Capacity Management when accurate results are important. A simulation model is sometimes called a Performance Benchmark.
Single Point of Contact	(Service Operation) Providing a single consistent way to communicate with an Organization or Business Unit; for example, a Single Point of Contact for an IT Service Provider is usually called a Service Desk.
Single Point of Failure (SPOF)	(Service Design) Any Configuration Item that can cause an Incident when it fails, and for which a Countermeasure has not been implemented. A SPOF may be a person, or a step in a Process or Activity, as well as a Component of the IT Infrastructure. See Failure.
SLAM Chart	(Continual Service Improvement) A Service Level Agreement Monitoring Chart is used to help monitor and report achievements against Service Level Targets. A SLAM Chart is typically color coded to show whether each agreed Service Level Target has been met, missed, or nearly missed during each of the previous 12 months.
SMART	(Service Design) (Continual Service Improvement) An acronym for helping to remember that targets in Service Level Agreements and Project Plans should be Specific, Measurable, Achievable, Relevant and Timely.
Snapshot	(Service Transition) The current state of a Configuration as captured by a discovery tool. Also used as a synonym for Benchmark. See Baseline.
Source	See Service Sourcing.
Specification	A formal definition of Requirements. A Specification may be used to define technical or Operational Requirements, and may be internal or external. Many public Standards consist of a Code of Practice and a Specification. The Specification defines the Standard against which an Organization can be Audited.
Stakeholder	All people who have an interest in an Organization, Project, IT Service, etc. Stakeholders may be interested in the Activities, targets, Resources, or Deliverables. Stakeholders may include Customers, Partners, employees, shareholders, owners, etc. See RACI.
Standard	A mandatory Requirement. Examples include ISO/IEC 20000 (an international Standard), an internal security Standard for Unix configuration, or a national government Standard for how financial Records should be maintained. The term Standard is also used to refer to a Code of Practice or Specification published by a Standards Organization such as ISO or BSI. See Guideline.
Standard Change	(Service Transition) A pre-approved Change that is low Risk, relatively common and follows a Procedure or Work Instruction; for example, password reset or provision of standard equipment to a new employee. RFCs are not required to implement a Standard Change, and they are logged and tracked using a different mechanism, such as a Service Request. See Change Model.

Standard Operating Procedures (SOP)	(Service Operation) Procedures used by IT Operations Management.
Standby	(Service Design) Used to refer to Resources that are not required to deliver the Live IT Services, but are available to support IT Service Continuity Plans; for example, a Standby data centre may be maintained to support Hot Standby, Warm Standby or Cold Standby arrangements.
Statement of requirements (SOR)	(Service Design) A Document containing all Requirements for a product purchase, or a new or changed IT Service. See Terms of Reference.
Status	The name of a required field in many types of Record. It shows the current stage in the Lifecycle of the associated Configuration Item, Incident, Problem, etc.
Status Accounting	(Service Transition) The Activity responsible for recording and reporting the Lifecycle of each Configuration Item.
Storage Management	(Service Operation) The Process responsible for managing the storage and maintenance of data throughout its Lifecycle.
Strategic	(Service Strategy) The highest of three levels of Planning and delivery (Strategic, Tactical, Operational). Strategic Activities include Objective setting and long-term Planning to achieve the overall Vision.
Strategy	(Service Strategy) A Strategic Plan designed to achieve defined Objectives.
Super User	(Service Operation) A User who helps other Users, and assists in communication with the Service Desk or other parts of the IT Service Provider. Super Users typically provide support for minor Incidents and training.
Supplier	(Service Strategy) (Service Design) A Third Party responsible for supplying goods or Services that are required to deliver IT services. Examples of suppliers include commodity hardware and software vendors, network and telecom providers, and Outsourcing Organizations. See Underpinning Contract, Supply Chain.
Supplier and Contract Database (SCD)	(Service Design) A database or structured Document used to manage Supplier Contracts throughout their Lifecycle. The SCD contains key Attributes of all Contracts with Suppliers, and should be part of the Service Knowledge Management System.
Supplier Management	(Service Design) The Process responsible for ensuring that all Contracts with Suppliers support the needs of the Business, and that all Suppliers meet their contractual commitments.
Supply Chain	(Service Strategy) The Activities in a Value Chain carried out by Suppliers. A Supply Chain typically involves multiple Suppliers, each adding value to the product or Service. See Value Network.
Support Group	(Service Operation) A group of people with technical skills. Support Groups provide the Technical Support needed by all of the IT Service Management Processes. See Technical Management.
Support Hours	(Service Design) (Service Operation) The times or hours when support is available to the Users. Typically these are the hours when the Service Desk is available. Support Hours should be defined in a Service Level Agreement, and may be different from Service Hours; for example, Service Hours may be 24 hours a day, but the Support Hours may be 07:00 to 19:00.
Supporting Service	(Service Strategy) A Service that enables or enhances a Core Service; for example, a Directory Service or a Backup Service. See Service Package.
SWOT Analysis	(Continual Service Improvement) A technique that reviews and analyses the internal strengths and weaknesses of an Organization and the external opportunities and threats which it faces SWOT stands for Strengths, Weaknesses, Opportunities and Threats.
System	A number of related things that work together to achieve an overall Objective; for example: • a computer System including hardware, software and Applications • a management System, including multiple Processes that are planned and managed together; for example a Quality Management System • a Database Management System or Operating System that includes many software modules that are designed to perform a set of related Functions

System Management	The part of IT Service Management that focuses on the management of IT Infrastructure rather than Process.
Tactical	The middle of three levels of Planning and delivery (Strategic, Tactical, Operational). Tactical Activities include the medium term Plans required to achieve specific Objectives, typically over a period of weeks to months.
Tag	(Service Strategy) A short code used to identify a Category; for example, tags EC1, EC2, EC3, etc. might be used to identify different Customer outcomes when analyzing and comparing Strategies. The term Tag is also used to refer to the Activity of assigning Tags to things.
Technical Management	(Service Operation) The Function responsible for providing technical skills in support of IT Services and management of the IT Infrastructure. Technical Management defines the Roles of Support Groups, as well as the tools, Processes and Procedures required.
Technical Observation (TO)	(Continual Service Improvement) A technique used in Service Improvement, Problem investigation and Availability Management. Technical support staff meet to monitor the behaviour and Performance of an IT Service and make recommendations for improvement.
Technical Service	Synonym for Infrastructure Service.
Technical Support	Synonym for Technical Management.
Tension Metrics	(Continual Service Improvement) A set of related Metrics, in which improvements to one Metric have a negative effect on another. Tension Metrics are designed to ensure that an appropriate balance is achieved.
Terms of Reference (TOR)	(Service Design) A Document specifying the Requirements, Scope, Deliverables, Resources and schedule for a Project or Activity.
Test	(Service Transition) An Activity that verifies that a Configuration Item, IT Service, Process, etc., meets its Specification or agreed Requirements. See Service Validation and Testing, Acceptance.
Test Environment	(Service Transition) A controlled Environment used to Test Configuration Items, Builds, IT Services, Processes, etc.
Third Party	A person, group, or Business who is not part of the Service Level Agreement for an IT Service, but is required to ensure successful delivery of that IT Service; for example a software Supplier, a hardware maintenance company, or a facilities department. Requirements for Third Parties are typically specified in Underpinning Contracts or Operational Level Agreements.
Third-line Support	(Service Operation) The third level in a hierarchy of Support Groups involved in the resolution of Incidents and investigation of Problems. Each level contains more specialist skills, or has more time or other Resources.
Threat	Anything that might exploit a Vulnerability. Any potential cause of an Incident can be considered to be a Threat; for example, a fire is a Threat that could exploit the Vulnerability of flammable floor coverings. This term is commonly used in Information Security Management and IT Service Continuity Management, but also applies to other areas such as Problem and Availability Management.
Threshold	The value of a Metric which should cause an Alert to be generated, or management action to be taken; for example, 'Priority1 Incident not solved within 4 hours', 'more than 5 soft disk errors in an hour', or 'more than 10 failed changes in a month'.
Throughput	(Service Design) A measure of the number of Transactions, or other Operations, performed in a fixed time; for example, 5,000 emails sent per hour, or 200 disk I/Os per second.
Total Cost of Ownership (TCO)	(Service Strategy) A methodology used to help make investment decisions. TCO assesses the full Lifecycle Cost of owning a Configuration Item, not just the initial Cost or purchase price. See Total Cost of Utilization.
Total Cost of Utilization (TCU)	(Service Strategy) A methodology used to help make investment and Service Sourcing decisions. TCU assesses the full Lifecycle Cost to the Customer of using an IT Service. See Total Cost of Ownership.

Total Quality Management (TQM)	(Continual Service Improvement) A methodology for managing continual Improvement by using a Quality Management System. TQM establishes a Culture involving all people in the Organization in a Process of continual monitoring and improvement.
Transaction	A discrete Function performed by an IT Service; for example, transferring money from one bank account to another. A single Transaction may involve numerous additions, deletions and modifications of data. Either all of these complete successfully or none of them is carried out.
Transition	(Service Transition) A change in state, corresponding to a movement of an IT Service or other Configuration Item from one Lifecycle status to the next.
Transition Planning and Support	(Service Transition) The Process responsible for Planning all Service Transition Processes and co-ordinating the resources that they require. These Service Transition Processes are Change Management, Service Asset and Configuration Management, Release and Deployment Management, Service Validation and Testing, Evaluation, and Knowledge Management.
Trend Analysis	(Continual Service Improvement) Analysis of data to identify time related patterns. Trend Analysis is used in Problem Management to identify common Failures or fragile Configuration Items, and in Capacity Management as a Modelling tool to predict future behaviour. It is also used as a management tool for identifying deficiencies in IT Service Management Processes.
Tuning	The Activity responsible for Planning Changes to make the most efficient use of Resources. Tuning is part of Performance Management, which also includes Performance Monitoring and implementation of the required Changes.
Type I Service Provider	(Service Strategy) An Internal Service Provider that is embedded within a Business Unit. There may be several Type I Service Providers within an Organization.
Type II Service Provider	(Service Strategy) An Internal Service Provider that provides shared IT Services to more than one Business Unit.
Type III Service Provider	(Service Strategy) A Service Provider that provides IT Services to External Customers.
Underpinning Contract (UC)	(Service Design) A Contract between an IT Service Provider and a Third Party. The Third Party provides goods or Services that support delivery of an IT Service to a Customer. The Underpinning Contract defines targets and responsibilities that are required to meet agreed Service Level Targets in an SLA.
Unit Cost	(Service Strategy) The Cost to the IT Service Provider of providing a single Component of an IT Service; for example, the Cost of a single desktop PC, or of a single Transaction.
Urgency	(Service Transition) (Service Design) A measure of how long it will be until an Incident, Problem or Change has a significant Impact on the Business; for example, a high Impact Incident may have low Urgency, if the Impact will not affect the Business until the end of the financial year. Impact and Urgency are used to assign Priority.
Usability	(Service Design) The ease with which an Application, product, or IT Service can be used. Usability Requirements are often included in a Statement of Requirements.
Use Case	(Service Design) A technique used to define required functionality and Objectives, and to Design Tests. Use Cases define realistic scenarios that describe interactions between Users and an IT Service or other System. See Change Case.
User	A person who uses the IT Service on a day-to-day basis. Users are distinct from Customers, as some Customers do not use the IT Service directly.
User Profile (UP)	(Service Strategy) A pattern of User demand for IT Services. Each User Profile includes one or more Patterns of Business Activity.
Utility	(Service Strategy) Functionality offered by a Product or Service to meet a particular need. Utility is often summarized as 'what it does'. See Service Utility.
Validation	(Service Transition) An Activity that ensures a new or changed IT Service, Process, Plan, or other Deliverable meets the needs of the Business. Validation ensures that Business Requirements are met even though these may have changed since the original Design. See Verification, Acceptance, Qualification, Service Validation and Testing.

Value Chain	(Service Strategy) A sequence of Processes that creates a product or Service that is of value to a Customer. Each step of the sequence builds on the previous steps and contributes to the overall product or Service. See Value Network.
Value for Money	An informal measure of Cost Effectiveness. Value for Money is often based on a comparison with the Cost of alternatives. See Cost Benefit Analysis.
Value Network	(Service Strategy) A complex set of Relationships between two or more groups or organizations. Value is generated through exchange of knowledge, information, goods or Services. See Value Chain, Partnership.
Value on Investment (VOI)	(Continual Service Improvement) A measurement of the expected benefit of an investment. VOI considers both financial and intangible benefits. See Return on Investment (ROI).
Variable Cost	(Service Strategy) A Cost that depends on how much the IT Service is used, how many products are produced, the number and type of Users, or something else that cannot be fixed in advance. See Variable Cost Dynamics.
Variable Cost Dynamics	(Service Strategy) A technique used to understand how overall Costs are impacted by the many complex variable elements that contribute to the provision of IT Services.
Variance	The difference between a planned value and the actual measured value. Commonly used in Financial Management, Capacity Management and Service Level Management, but could apply in any area where Plans are in place.
Verification	(Service Transition) An Activity that ensures a new or changed IT Service, Process, Plan, or other Deliverable is complete, accurate, Reliable and matches its Design Specification. See Validation, Acceptance, Service Validation and Testing.
Verification and Audit	(Service Transition) The Activities responsible for ensuring that information in the CMDB is accurate and that all Configuration Items have been identified and recorded in the CMDB. Verification includes routine checks that are part of other Processes; for example, verifying the serial number of a desktop PC when a User logs an Incident. Audit is a periodic, formal check.
Version	(Service Transition) A Version is used to identify a specific Baseline of a Configuration Item. Versions typically use a naming convention that enables the sequence or date of each Baseline to be identified; for example, Payroll Application Version 3 contains updated functionality from Version 2.
Vision	A description of what the Organization intends to become in the future. A Vision is created by senior management and is used to help influence Culture and Strategic Planning.
Vital Business Function (VBF)	(Service Design) A Function of a Business Process which is critical to the success of the Business. Vital Business Functions are an important consideration of Business Continuity Management, IT Service Continuity Management and Availability Management.
Vulnerability	A weakness that could be exploited by a Threat; for example, an open firewall port, a password that is never changed, or a flammable carpet. A missing Control is also considered to be a Vulnerability.
Warm Standby	Synonym for Intermediate Recovery.
Warranty	(Service Strategy) A promise or guarantee that a product or Service will meet its agreed Requirements. See Service Validation and Testing, Service Warranty.
Work in Progress (WIP)	A Status that means Activities have started, but are not yet complete. It is commonly used as a Status for Incidents, Problems, Changes, etc.
Work Instruction	A Document containing detailed instructions that specify exactly what steps to follow to carry out an Activity. A Work Instruction contains much more detail than a Procedure and is only created if very detailed instructions are needed.
Workaround	(Service Operation) Reducing or eliminating the Impact of an Incident or Problem for which a full Resolution is not yet available; for example, by restarting a failed Configuration Item. Workarounds for Problems are documented in Known Error Records. Workarounds for Incidents that do not have associated Problem Records are documented in the Incident Record.

Workload   The Resources required to deliver an identifiable part of an IT Service. Workloads may be
                  Categorized by Users, groups of Users, or Functions within the IT Service. This is used to assist in
                  analyzing and managing the Capacity, Performance and Utilization of Configuration Items and IT
                  Services. The term Workload is sometimes used as a synonym for Throughput.

Index

A

Access management 116, 294
Accounting 42
Active redundancy 211
Actual performance 267
Added value 161, 320
Advanced Service Management Professional
  Diploma 10
Agency principle 16
Analysis 316
Analytical modeling 53
Analyze data 166
Application analyst 131
Application manager 131
APM Group (APMG) 4
Application 83
Application architecture 72
Application management 83
Application management departments
  organization 130
Application service provision 75
Architecture design 72
Assessment 152
Attributes 247
Automated or manual 253
Availability 25
Availability management 78, 166, 207
Availability Management Information System
  (AMIS) 212
Availability manager 86

B

Backup and restore 117, 302
Balanced Scorecard (BSC) 156
Baseline 146, 310
Benchmark 154
Best practices 9
Big bang versus phased 252
Build 255
Building and test environment management
  102
Business capacity management 202
Business case, 54

Business continuity management 217
Business Impact Analysis (BIA) 89, 194, 216
Business perspective 317
Business Process Outsourcing (BPO) 75
Business service catalogue 194
Business Service Management (BSM) 74, 80

C

Capabilities 26, 56
Capability Maturity Model Integration
  (CMMI) 11
Capability trap 53
Capacity 25
Capacity management 78, 201
Capacity Management Information System
  (CMIS) 205
Categorizing 237
Centralization 44
Centralized service desk 305
Certification scheme 10
Change 97, 233
Change Advisory Board (CAB) 102, 235
Change authority 102
Change management 97, 163, 233
Change manager 102
Classification 248
Closed cycle systems 297
Closed loop systems 116
CMS management team 102
CMS manager 102
Co-sourcing 75
Communication 176
Complementary portfolio 19
Complex monitoring/control cycle 298
Component capacity management 203
Component Failure Impact Analysis (CFIA)
  166
Computer Assisted/Aided Software
  Engineering tools (CASE) 84
Configuration baseline 245
Configuration documentation 247
Configuration identification 246
Configuration Item (CI) 243

Configuration Management Database (CMDB) 244, 270
Configuration management plan 246
Configuration Management System (CMS) 244
Configuration manager 101, 102
Configuration structure 246
Continual Service Improvement (CSI) 139
Continuity 25
Continuous representation 11
Control 173
Core library 19
Core Service Package (CSP) 192
Core services 43
Corrective measures 223
Cost items 184
Cost types 184
Critical Success Factors (CSFs) 144
CSI improvement process 147, 309
CSI manager 151, 162
CSI model 146, 309
CSI policies 145
Culture 177
Customer-based SLA 198
Customer-focused 171

D
Data 145
Data, Information, Knowledge and Wisdom (DIKW) 145, 269
Database administration 118
Data layer 244
Decentralization 44
Definitive Media Library (DML) 245
Definitive spares 245
Demand Management (DM) 43, 168, 190
Demand modeling 183
Deming cycle 141
Department 110, 175
Deployment manager 102
Design aspects 70
Desktopsupport 119
Detective measures 222
Diagnosis 281
DIKW 145, 269
Directory services 119

Division 110, 175

E
Early Life Support (ELS) 102, 257
Effective, 173
Efficient, 173
Emergency change 235
Emergency Change Advisory Board (ECAB) 235
Emergency release 230, 249
Empowerment 141
Encapsulation 16
End-to-end perspective 317
End values 48
Environment architecture 72
Evaluation 99
Event 114, 273
Event management 114, 273
Examination Institute for Information Science (EXIN) 4
Exams 10
Expanded Incident Lifecycle 166
External business view 110
External focus 171
External monitoring and control 116, 300

F
Facility and data center management 119
Fallback situation 236
Fault Tree Analysis (FTA) 166
Federated CMDB 245
Feedback and learning 16
Financial management 42
Fire-fighter trap 53
First-line support 122
Foundation Certificate 10
Foundation Level 10
Four Ps 22, 221
Function 17, 47, 110, 175
Functional escalation 281
Functional requirements 80
Functional silos 17

G
Gap analysis 309
Good practice 15

Governance 145
Greenfield 105
Group 175

H
Heterogeneous redundancy 211
Hierarchical escalation 281
Homogeneous redundancy 211
Hybrid organization structures 134

I
Identification of problems 288
Identity management 294
Impact 237
Implementation review 152
Implement corrective actions 168
Improvements 160
In-sourcing 75
Incident 278
Incident classification 279
Incident identification 279
Incident management 114, 278
Incident manager 132
Incident registration 279
Incremental approach 76
Information 145
Information architecture 72
Information integration layer 244
Information security management
   79, 220
Information Security Management System
   (ISMS) 79, 221
Information Systems Examination Board
   ISEB) 4
Input 172
Instrumental values 48
Intermediate Level 10
Internal focus 171
Internal IT view 110
Internal monitoring and control 116, 300
Internet/web management 119
Iterative approach 76
ITIL 9
ITIL Diploma 10
IT governance 10
IT infrastructure architecture 72

IT Service Continuity Management
   (ITSCM) 79, 215
IT Service Management Forum (itSMF) 3
IT service management monitoring/
   control cycle 299

J
Job scheduling 117

K
Key Performance Indicator (KPI) 144
Knowledge 145
Knowledge management 99, 168
Knowledge processing layer 244
knowledge process outsourcing 75
Knowledge spiral 310
Known Error Database (KEDB) 287, 291

L
Labels 247
Library 19
Line management 46
Line of Service (LOS) 192
Local service desk 304

M
Mainframes 117
Major release 230, 248
Management- and operational requirements
   80
Manager Certificate 10
Matrix structure 46
Maturity 11, 12
Mean Time Between Failures (MTBF) 61,
   211
Mean Time Between Service Incidents
   (MTBSI) 211
Mean Time To Repair (MTTR) 211
Mean Time to Restore Service (MTRS) 61,
   210
Measure 147, 309
Measuring and control 297
Metric 144
Middleware 119
Middleware management 119
Minor release 230, 248

Monitor 314
Monitor and gather data 164
Monitoring and control 116
Monitoring and control cycle 116
MoSCoW 81
Multi-level SLA 198
Multi-sourcing 75

N
Naming conventions 246
Network management 118

O
Office of Government Commerce (OGC) 2
Open cycle systems 297
Open loop systems 116
Operational health 112
Operational Level Agreement (OLA) 197
Operations 302
Operations bridge 302
Organizational change 140
Organizational change management 103
Organizational culture 48
Outcome 172
Output 172
Outsourcing 49, 75

P
Passive redundancy 211
Pattern 23
Performance indicators 173
Permanent production roles 148
Perspective 22
Phases 18
Pilots 254, 256
Plan 23
Planning and control 173
Policies and standards 173
Portfolio 178
Position 175
Post-program ROI 55
Post Implementation Review (PIR) 163,
    239, 258
Practitioner Certificate 10
Pre-program ROI 54
Predicted performance 266

Present and use 167
Presentation layer 244
Preventive measures 222
Priority 280
Proactive organization 112
Proactive problem management 115, 288
Problem 287
Problem management 115, 287
Problem manager 133
Problem model 287
Procedure 173
Process 17, 73, 172, 178
Process data 165
Process model 171
Process owner 148, 152
Process ownership 46
Program 178
Project 17, 73, 172, 178
Proprietary knowledge 15
Provisioning value 182
Push and pull 253

R
RACI 85
RACI table 247
Rapid Application Development (RAD) 76
Reactive organization 112
Reactive problem management 115, 288
Reductive measures 222
Release 252
Release and deployment management 98,
    252
Release package 253
Release packaging and build manager 102
Release unit 248, 252
Remediation planning 236
Report 147, 309
Reporting framework 317, 321
Repressive measures 223
Request for Change (RFC) 235
Request fulfilment 115, 284
Resources 26
Response 111
Retired services 37
Return on Investment (ROI) 160
Rights management 294

Risk 65
Risk-evaluation manager 102
Risk analysis 65
Risk categorization 237
Risk category 237
Risk management 66
Role 110, 175

S
Secure library 245
Secure store 245
Security 25
Security manager 86
Service 15
Service-based SLA 198
Service Asset and Configuration Management
    (SACM) 97, 242
Service asset manager 101
Service assets 59
Service capacity management 203
Service catalogue 35, 193, 194
Service Catalogue Management (SCM) 78,
    193
Service catalogue manager 86
Service design manager 86
Service Design Package (SDP) 230
Service desk 122, 304
Service desk analysts 131
Service desk groups 305
Service desk manager 131
Service desk supervisor 131
Service Failure Analysis (SFA) 166
Service gap model 156
Service Improvement Plan (SIP) 147, 309
Service Improvement Program (SIP) 89
Service Investment Analysis 183
Service Knowledge Management System
    (SKMS) 270, 291
Service knowledge manager 102
Service Level Agreement (SLA) 78, 197
Service Level Management (SLM) 78, 163,
    197
Service level manager 86, 150
Service Level Package (SLP) 192
Service Lifecycle 17
Service management 15

Service management lifecycle 110
Service manager 148, 150
Service Operation 109, 110
Service operation functions 121
Service owner 148, 151, 312
Service package 43, 191
Service pipeline 36
Service portfolio 34, 60, 71, 187, 193
Service Portfolio Management (SPM) 44,
    187
Service Provider Interfaces (SPI) 49
Service reporting 317, 319
Service request 278, 284
Services architecture 72
Service strategies 57
Service Strategy 21
Service Transition 93
Service transition manager 100
Service transition plan 231
Service validation and testing 98, 260
Service valuation 42
Service value potential 182
Seven step improvement process 147, 309
Simulation 53
Snapshot 245
SOC principle 48
Specialization & coordination 16
Stability 111
Staged representation 12
Stakeholder analysis 105
Stakeholder management 104
Stakeholder map 104
Standard change 235
standard routines 302
Storage and archiving 118
Super users 131, 306
Supplier and Contract Database (SCD) 225
Supplier management 79, 225
Swim-lane diagram 157
SWOT-analysis 156
System 16
System dynamics 53

T
Team 110, 175
Technical Observation Post (TOP) 166

Technical service catalogue 194
Test support 102
Throughput 172
Tools 176
Tool trap 53
Total Cost of Utilization (TCU) 63
Transition planning and support 96, 229
Type I internal service provider 28
Type II Shared Services Unit 28, 29
Type III external service provider 28, 30

U

Underpinning Contract (UC) 278
Unified Process and the Dynamic Systems
   Development Method (DSDM) 76
Usability requirements 80
Utility 24

V

Value 15
Value concepts 182
Value network 26
Value on Investment (VOI) 160
Variable Cost Dynamics (VCD) 42, 184
Virtual service desk 305
Vision 141, 146
V model 254

W

Warranty 24
Wisdom 145, 319
Work instructions 173

ISO/IEC 20000

ISO/IEC 20000: An Introduction
Promoting awareness of the certification for organizations within the IT Service Management environment.

ISBN 978 90 8753 081 5 (english edition)

English
€49.95
excl tax

Implementing ISO/IEC 20000 Certification: The Roadmap
Practical advice, to assist readers through the requirements of the standard, the scoping, the project approach, the certification procedure and management of the certification.

ISBN 978 90 8753 082 2 (english edition)

English
€39.95
excl tax

ISO/IEC 20000: A Pocket Guide
A quick and accessible guide to the fundamental requirements for corporate certification.

ISBN 978 90 77212 79 0 (english edition)

English
€15.95
excl tax